Japanese Labour and Management in Transition

Japanese management techniques and industrial relations are a continued source of great interest and even wonder. Policy makers and businesses in other countries have paid great attention to Japanese practices and often sought to emulate them.

Japanese Labour and Management in Transition brings together an array of Japanese academic researchers, from different disciplines, who have tackled a complex subject in a comprehensive fashion. The book is divided into two parts, the first covering recent trends in Japanese labour markets, labour law and corporate strategy before turning to analysis of changes in supply and demand within different categories of worker. The second looks at the interaction between the state, management and labour at the national level, followed by an examination of management and labour in recently privatised sectors, changes in enterprise unionism and industrial relations in small firms.

Japanese Labour and Management in Transition is the most comprehensive overview of Japanese industrial relations available. It provides essential reading to students, researchers and business people wishing to understand the current changes in Japanese business and employment relations.

Mari Sako is Reader in Industrial Relations at the London School of Economics and Political Science. **Hiroki Sato** is a Professor at the University of Tokyo.

Books published under the joint imprint of LSE/Routledge are works of high academic merit approved by the Publications Committee of the London School of Economics and Political Science. These publications are drawn from the wide range of academic studies in the social sciences for which the LSE has an international reputation.

Japanese Labour and Management in Transition

Diversity, flexibility and participation

Edited by Mari Sako and Hiroki Sato

London and New York

First published 1997
by Routledge
11 New Fetter Lane, London EC4P 4EE

Transferred to Digital Printing 2004

Simultaneously published in the USA and Canada
by Routledge
29 West 35th Street, New York, NY 10001

Typeset in Times by
Florencetype Ltd, Stoodleigh, Devon

British Library Cataloguing in Publication Data
A catalogue record for this book is available from the British Library

Library of Congress Cataloging in Publication Data
Japanese Labour and Management in Transition / edited by Mari Sako and
Hiroki Sato
  p.   cm.
  Includes bibliographical references and index
  1. Industrial relations – Japan. 2. Labor – Japan. 3. Management – Japan.
  4. Labor market – Japan. 5. Trade-unions – Japan.
  I. Sako, Mari. II. Sato, Hiroki.
  HD8726.5.J384 1997
  331'.0952–dc20 96-26286 CIP

ISBN 0–415–11434–9
ISBN 0–415–11435–7 (pbk)

Contents

Part II

Figures

viii *List of figures*

Tables

Contributors

Hiroyuki Fujimura, Associate Professor of Industrial Relations, Department of Economics, Shiga University.

Yoshio Higuchi, Professor of Labour Economics, Department of Commerce, Keio University.

Koichiro Imano, Professor of Human Resources Management, Department of Economics, Gakushuin University.

Takashi Kawakita, Professor of Industrial Sociology, Department of Business Administration, Hosei University.

Keisuke Nakamura, Associate Professor of Industrial Relations, Institute of Social Science, Tokyo University.

Michio Nitta, Professor of Industrial Relations, Institute of Social Science, Tokyo University.

Naoto Ohmi, Central Executive Standing Committee Member, Zensen (The Japanese Federation of Textile, Garment, Chemical, Food and Allied Industries Workers' Unions).

Mari Sako, Reader in Industrial Relations, Department of Industrial Relations, London School of Economics and Political Science.

Hiroki Sato, Professor of the Information Centre for Social Science Research on Japan, Institute of Social Science, Tokyo University.

Atsushi Seike, Professor of Labour Economics, Department of Commerce, Keio University.

Toru Shinoda, Associate Professor of Politics, Department of Social Science, Waseda University.

Kazuo Sugeno, Professor of Labour Law, Department of Law, Tokyo University.

Yasuo Suwa, Professor of Labour Law, Department of Sociology, Hosei University.

Akira Wakisaka, Professor of Labour Economics, Department of Economics and Management Studies, Okayama University.

Foreword

This book represents our attempt at a multi-faceted analysis of industrial relations in Japan, mainly covering the period from the 1980s until the early 1990s. It uses an interdisciplinary approach embodying the perspectives of labour economics, industrial sociology, business science, education and labour law.

Over the last two decades, the environmental conditions surrounding the Japanese economy have changed substantially, making a significant impact both on the country's industrial relations and its labour market. On the demand side for labour, inexorable changes took place in Japan's industrial and job structures, as technologies advanced rapidly, particularly in mechanical and electronic fields, and the economy further strengthened its information and service orientation. On the supply side, however, Japan's labour force continued its rapid ageing trend, while experiencing an increasing job shift to white-collar work and a rise in the number of workers with higher educational qualifications. The number of working women, particularly housewives in part-time jobs, continued to rise sharply, while the number of young workers declined and the inflow of foreign labour increased markedly. Meanwhile, the value system related to work and leisure gradually changed, and employment practices became more diversified, such as by the use of temporary employment services.

After successfully coping with the second oil crisis in 1979 and the recessionary pressure in the mid-1980s caused by the yen's appreciation, Japan enjoyed sustained economic prosperity for a while. The 'bubble' burst in the 1990s, however, plunging the economy into a protracted period of severe recession. Employment continued to decline until unemployment reached 3.4 per cent in the autumn of 1995, the worst record ever for the country. In the same year, scandals and mismanagement at some major financial institutions were exposed – an unthinkable event in the past.

The political environment in Japan has also experienced a fundamental change. The collapse of socialism in the Soviet Union and East Europe helped dissipate ideological differences and conflict in Japan's political arena as well as in its labour movement. The framework of political stability, the so-called '1955 system', maintained for many years under the rule of successive Liberal Democratic administrations, crumbled. The splintering of the Liberal Democratic Party and the resulting birth of the Shinshin Party (or the New Frontier Party), the formation of the coalition government between the Liberal Democrats and the Japan Socialists and the transformation of the Japan Socialist Party into the Social Democratic Party of Japan (whose dissolution is expected shortly) all indicate the current degree of political instability in Japan and make it difficult to form any reliable prediction of the future shape of the country's political environment.

In spite of all the shake-ups and breakdowns in the nation's political and economic system during the 15 years surveyed by this book, Japan's economy – from a macro perspective – generally managed to outperform those of other Western countries. Japanese industries showed their superior competitiveness in the expanded international markets and under globalised economic conditions. In fact, their success led to serious trade conflict abroad, even giving rise to 'Japan bashing' in some countries.

While the nation experienced such trouble, labour–management relations in Japan continued to adapt to the variety of environmental and structural changes that were taking place. Workers' employment and working conditions steadily improved: wage levels rose to match those enjoyed by the top ranks in the industrialised world and working hours continued to go down to the levels prevalent in United Kingdom and the United States. Japan managed to achieve these improvements without the period of lengthy inflation or long-term mass unemployment that some Western economies suffered. Meanwhile, the tripartite relations among trade unions, employers' organisations and government continued to improve, as better communication between them began to replace the ideological conflict and adversarial relations that often characterised their relationship in the past. Such developments helped the number of cases of collective labour disputes to continue to decline. More recently, however, during the protracted recession in the 1990s, many corporations made 'restructuring efforts', causing public concern and leading commentators to argue that the so-called 'Japanese-style employment system and practices' were now crumbling. Nevertheless, it appears from all the indicators that the foundation of stable labour-management relations in Japan remains unshaken and intact. We have not seen anything reminiscent of the large-scale reductions in workforce and the protracted labour campaigns raged against such a management policy that characterised industrial relations in Japan in the 1950s and 1960s.

Two trends seem to have evolved from these developments. On the one hand in Japan, as in other industrialised nations, 'labour–management relations' no longer seem to command the attention they did before, either as a subject of academic interest or as an issue of management practice. If anything, indifference to or a light regard of labour–management relations seems to have gradually spread. The term 'labour–management relations' has been replaced by the terms 'human resources management' or 'human resources development' which appear to attract attention as issues of topical interest.

On the other hand, there has been a sharp increase in international interest in Japan's industrial relations and the mechanisms which underlie the operation of the Japanese labour market. Not only has there been an increase in both the quantity and quality of studies by foreign scholars, but international exchanges – at both the academic and practitioner levels – have increased. This has been accompanied by the diffusion of knowledge concerning the labour–management relations at Japanese companies operating outside of Japan. Since most of them were generally regarded as success stories, the question of their 'universal applicability and value' and 'exportability' became subjects for serious discussion among managers as well as students of management sciences. At the same time, 'the unique peculiarities' and 'cultural peculiarities' reflected in Japan's labour-management relations system came under critical scrutiny, and in particular were set against the fundamental principles and standards of Western industrial democracy. In the view of many critics who doubted the universality of the Japanese system, the system was still immature and retained various weaknesses.

Is the apparent industrial peace, which arguably contributed to the decline in interest in labour–management relations, indeed something permanent and structural? Which of the two international evaluations of the Japanese system is true and correct? Or, are both of them in error? Or, are both partially right and partially wrong?

The key to solving such questions lies in ascertaining the following: What are the structural characteristics of Japanese industrial relations? How were they formulated? How well do they respond to environmental changes, newly emerging situations and a new set of problems?

This book represents an attempt to provide answers to these questions. The contributors are all leading researchers in their respective fields in Japan. They address issues that either have not been seriously discussed in previous publications or have not been adequately dealt with: the employment of workers by small businesses; white-collar workers; working women; whether there should exist a system of labour–management consultation or worker participation that supplements or replaces collective bargaining; the type of personnel administration system that adequately responds to new situations; and labour laws pertaining to individual workers in a high mobility labour market.

It is my hope that this book will help contribute towards comprehensive understanding of the latest developments in industrial relations in Japan.

March 1996
Taishiro Shirai
Professor Emeritus, Hosei University
Adviser, Japan Institute of Labour

Acknowledgements

This book project originated, as many books do, in a casual observation over dinner by the two editors in 1993. It was that British researchers' appetite for understanding recent changes in industrial relations in Japan far outstripped the availability of English language materials addressing these issues. We decided at the time that there were enough Japanese researchers whose work was not well known abroad, and that a compilation of their recent work would contribute to filling this information gap.

Contributors to this volume were identified through the editors' personal network. Most of them met at Hosei University in April 1993 to discuss the contents of each chapter. Subsequent to the meeting, contributors met at various research workshops and conferences in and out of Japan, but not specifically to discuss this book project. This book therefore free-rides on the goodwill and the diligence of an existing network of researchers, and because of this, we would like to thank all the contributors for finding time to write their chapters. We are also grateful to the Institute of Social Science, University of Tokyo, for granting permission to reproduce parts of the Institute's Occasional Paper No. 10 for Chapter 11.

Support for the book was provided by Rodo Mondai Research Senta (Japanese Labour Research Centre) and later also by the Centre for Economic Performance (CEP) at the London School of Economics. The preparation of the manuscript was much aided by the editorial assistance of Jacquie Gauntlett and Maria Paisley who skilfully rendered non-native speakers' English into comprehensible prose. We also appreciate the good work of David Winn, Sandra Bayne, David Cairncross, Martine Hulman, Leslie Mason and Fumiaki Moriya who provided typing, administrative, translating, and editing assistance at various stages of preparing this book.

Last but not least, thanks to Victoria Smith, the Routledge editor, for patience and for making this book possible.

Introduction
Forces for homogeneity and diversity in the Japanese industrial relations system

Mari Sako

The study of industrial relations in post-war Japan seems to have completed a full circle in fifty years. The culturalist interpretation which treated the Japanese situation as unique had at one time given way to a functionalist convergence perspective. But more recently, the latter seems to have been superseded by a perspective which allows for persistent diversity due to national institutions. As part of this trend, the debate concerning Japan has shifted from one which regarded Japanese patterns of industrial relations as backward and in need of modernisation (for which the Anglo-American model was dominant) towards one which puts forward the Japanese model as a viable alternative to the Anglo-American or the German models of industrial relations. This shift is a welcome one, and calls for a renewed look at the Japanese industrial relations system as a holistic model with interrelated and mutually reinforcing elements.

Observers of industrial relations in Japan have been plagued with the question of culturalist versus economically rational explanations of why Japanese patterns differ from patterns seen in other advanced industrialised countries (see Shimada 1983 for a good survey). In the 1950s, the culturalist interpretation of the Japanese employment system predominated (e.g. Abbeglen (1958) who attributed it to feudalistic practices). Japanese academics, not least the Marxists among them, highlighted the backward and peculiarly Japanese nature of industrial development. In the 1960s, however, much influenced by the functionalist perspective of Dunlop's (1958) and Clark Kerr *et al.*'s (1960) work, research was conducted to show that Japanese workers were behaving in an economically rational manner given the constraints they faced (e.g. Marsh and Mannari 1976). In the 1970s and 1980s, culturalist explanations of the Japanese economic miracle persisted, particularly in popular writings. In reaction, economists (e.g. Aoki 1988, Koike 1988) theorised about the behaviour of Japanese firms and workers using generalisable propositions. Explicitly comparative case studies (Dore 1973) and surveys (e.g. Lincoln and Kalleberg 1990) also contributed to broadening the arena of universal explanations. However, while documenting cross-national differences, for example in collective bargaining structures or workers' attitudes, may be relatively straightforward, providing explanations of identified differences proved more difficult. In fact, the search for universal explanations eventually led to the realisation that we need to examine domains of activity outside industrial relations. In other words, since a country's industrial relations behaviour is embedded in broader social and cultural structures, comparative industrial relations must involve, not comparing one dimension like trade union density at a time, but comparing the whole national system of industrial relations. And the more we go down this route of examining the whole system which has interlocking and mutually reinforcing elements, the more it seems impossible to transfer some elements to another national setting in a piecemeal fashion.

This book has been compiled with a view to highlighting how such interlocking and mutually reinforcing elements of the Japanese industrial relations system have been operating in the last two decades or so. In effect, the book explores the ways in which the Japanese system has been responding to the socio-economic changes that accompanied Japan's rise to 'economic superpower' status in the 1980s and 1990s in the wake of its successful response to the oil crises of the 1970s. It is hoped that when all the chapters are put together, a holistic view of the Japanese system, from the national level down to the workplace level, will emerge. The disadvantage of this approach, of course, is that except in a few cases, it is left up to the reader to draw comparative lessons. But the advantage of this approach is that more details can be provided than is allowed in a comparative volume which tries to deal with a country's entire industrial relations situation in one chapter (e.g. Bamber and Lansbury 1993, Locke *et al.* 1995). Such single chapter treatment of industrial relations in Japan has had to put a constraint on the coverage of topics, and therefore either reinforced the stereotypical notion of lifetime employment in large firms or left the readers frustrated by lack of details in such areas as small firms and peripheral workers. There is a clear demand for understanding Japanese management and labour, which goes beyond the stereotype. There is also a need to analyse how much diversity exists and is permitted in a system which upholds homogeneity as an abiding principle.

Often posed, yet insufficiently answered, questions abound. For example, is the difference between the privileged core workers and the rest the same as that found in Western societies? And is this gap widening? Even for the core workers, is the Japanese employment system finally coming to an end? Or is this yet another alarmist cry which will die down once the economy recovers? If Japanese trade unions are declining as elsewhere, are there alternative voice mechanisms which effectively represent worker interests? This book provides plenty of research evidence on the recent Japanese industrial relations system so that these questions can be addressed in a theoretically rigorous manner.

The book consists of contributions from fourteen authors, who are either economists, lawyers, political scientists or sociologists. Fortunately, diversity in disciplinary approaches is valued in Japanese academic institutions, and it proved not too difficult to identify appropriate authors who are conducting leading primary research on the assigned topics. Many of the authors have participated in internationally collaborative research projects, and therefore share theoretical perspectives which are common across the English-speaking global academic community. While attempts were made to make the coverage of topics in the book as comprehensive as possible, there are obvious gaps as well as some biases in focus, which are explained below. This introduction also summarises the main findings of the book, not chapter by chapter, but by identifying common themes which are relevant to the study of comparative industrial relations.

The book is structured into two parts. Part I outlines recent trends in Japanese labour markets, labour law and corporate strategy, before turning to the analysis of changes in the demand and supply of specific categories of workers, namely white-collar workers, women, older workers, and foreign workers. Part II looks at the interaction between the state, management and labour at the national level, changing industrial relations in the privatised industries, the annual Spring Offensive as a medium for examining industry-level coordination, worker participation, changes in enterprise unionism, and industrial relations in small firms, the majority of which do not have unions. Most chapters focus on developments since the mid-1970s to the present day with an emphasis on secular trends rather than short-term adjustments. There are good English language books (for example Shirai 1983) which cover the development of industrial relations in Japan until the first oil shock in 1973. Therefore, this book presumes a certain level of understanding of the Japanese industrial relations system in the 1970s on the part of the reader.

Having said that, what are the emerging differences between the Japanese industrial relations system in the 1970s and the 1990s? Are the essential elements of the system being preserved, or is the system being transformed into a fundamentally different domain? Interestingly, every economic recession in the post-war period led to speculations about the end of the Japanese employment system. With the benefit of hindsight, such speculations appear like crying wolf, although painful adjustments had to be made to preserve the system. For the first time in its post-war history the Japanese economy suffered a recession in 1974 (the year of a negative real GNP (gross natural product) growth rate of –0.2 per cent). Subsequently, every time recessionary pressures were felt, after the 1979 second oil shock, and the 1985 yen appreciation, businesses raised an alarm, but the crisis mentality of all three actors – the government, labour and management – led to pooling together of resources to overcome problems. Some argue that the 1990s recession is yet another such episode, while others argue that there is something fundamentally different about the 1990s circumstances which may indeed transform the Japanese industrial relations system.

In order to shed light on this debate, we will proceed as follows. First, an ideal typical model of industrial relations in Japan, based mainly on the perception of enterprise-level industrial relations in the 1970s, will be presented. Then we will examine the realities by focusing on changes from the 1970s to the 1990s.

THE CLASSICAL JAPANESE MODEL[1]

Lifetime employment, seniority-plus-merit (*nenko*) pay, and enterprise unionism were enshrined as the three pillars of industrial relations in Japan (OECD 1973). The first two are normative principles, while the third is a structural characteristic. A later OECD report concluded that Japan was unique not so much in these three pillars but in a fourth pillar, namely the social norms within the enterprise, such as a strong identification of employees with the firm (OECD 1977). For the purpose of identifying mutually reinforcing elements of the Japanese model, a useful starting point is the conceptualisation of the firm as a community (Dore 1987). The antithesis of the Japanese model in the elaboration below is the Anglo-American model.

The firm as community

The firm is not a mere property of shareholders but a community in which regular workers are treated as full members. Managers are senior employees who have been internally promoted, not appointed agents who act on behalf of shareholders. Consequently, managers identify more with junior employees than with shareholders. A sense of community is reinforced by a relative absence of status distinction and differences in terms and conditions of employment between managers and workers, and between white-collar and blue-collar workers. Management and workers have a shared goal to make the firm prosper in the long run.

For a community to be viable, there has to be a two-way process between management and workers. In particular, not only should the firm offer employment security and a career to its employees, the employees must also expect employment security and identify with the firm. The boundary of the firm as community, and hence the criterion for full membership in the community, are defined by the matching in mutual expectations between the firm and its employees. If employees wish to stay on in the firm but the firm is unwilling to offer employment security, no community would emerge. Conversely, if the firm offers employment security but employees do not want it, then no community would emerge either.

The stability of employment which derives from the so-called lifetime employment principle is a necessary, but not a sufficient, condition for the creation and the maintenance of the firm as community. In this sense, the firm as community is not just a nexus of bilateral psychological contracts between the employer and individual employees. The community consists of members – usually male regular workers – with common interest, as indicated by the lack of 'them and us' feelings between management and labour. This feeling of common interest is reinforced by the corporate governance structure which restricts shareholders' control, the internal promotion and reward system which is specific to the firm, and the enterprise-based union structure.

Common interest, however, does not fully capture the essence of the firm as community; perhaps 'community consciousness' would be a better term to bring out the aspect of social identity which workers as members entertain towards the firm. This social identity derives from the relative homogeneity of the quality of labour within the firm, both by attribute (i.e. gender) and by ability and educational achievements. It is reinforced by 'welfare corporatism' (Dore 1973), the provision of welfare benefits by the firm on the understanding that it is the firm's responsibility to guarantee the livelihood of the employees. Employment security is an important issue because of this managerial ideology, and the firm's holistic concern for individual employees, including family circumstances and life outside work, is a natural extension of this ideology. From the worker's viewpoint, enterprise community consciousness may manifest itself as a psychological commitment to the firm not just as a place of work but also as a focal point in life outside work. In this sense, membership in the firm as community is often linked to status in society.

The above emphasis on community consciousness rather than on common interest enables us to move away from blindly applying the unitarist frame of reference to the Japanese firm. The firm as community is not a commune but a hierarchical organisation in which there are junior and senior members whose interests do not match perfectly. Hence, negotiations and give-and-take compromises are common in Japanese firms.

Worker commitment and flexibility in return for employment security

As pointed out above, management does its utmost to guarantee the livelihood of workers in the firm. This amounts to management offering security of income by way of stable employment. 'Lifetime employment' in this sense is offered, however, in return for workers agreeing to commit to the firm. Where unions exist, the promise of no layoffs is negotiated in return for flexible job reassignments whenever restructuring of the firm becomes necessary. 'Lifetime employment', or employment security until a mandatory retirement age, is a principle which both workers and management value most, and which may be offered by management as a *quid pro quo* for wage restraint or corporate rationalisation as long as the moral contract is deemed unbroken. The firm's objective to remain competitive by controlling costs is not achieved by treating workers as disposable resources to be hired and fired, but by other means (such as investment in equipment and training, and just-in-time stock management).

The practice of recruiting workers straight from school or university for employment until retirement necessitates taking a long-term view in human resource management. Management invests substantial resources into the business of recruiting the 'best' workers. It emphasises not only initial training, returns for which can always be recouped later, but also continuous further training so that the skills of older workers whom they must retain do not atrophy. Thus, enterprise-based training in a broad range of knowledge and skills is a feature of the Japanese model.

Employees do not work for a job but for a career in a company. White-collar graduate employees tend to be treated as generalists whose job assignments may be unrelated to the subject of study at university or college. Blue-collar workers are also willing to experience a broad range of tasks, to engage in problem-solving and quality improvements, and to work in teams. These features of work organisation are in contrast to the job demarcation and functional specialisation found in many Anglo-American workplaces, and contribute to the efficiency and flexibility of production in Japanese factories. Employment security underlined by the lifetime employment principle may explain workers' willingness to be flexible. But it is not in itself a sufficient condition for workers to become motivated to learn new skills.

Seniority-plus-merit (*nenko*) principle in pay and promotion

Workers' incentive to better themselves and to be flexible is further underpinned by a system of pay and internal promotion based on the *nenko* principle. *Nenko* is not just about seniority (*nen*) but also about merit(*ko*). This is evident with respect to promotion. Regular employees are promoted on seniority initially so that those in the same cohort experience promotion at equal pace. It is not until after 10 to 15 years of service, that some employees are promoted faster than others, on merit. This late timing of decisive selection gives management a long period to screen for more capable employees. The initial prolonged period of promotion on seniority also provides greater motivation for all workers to develop and improve their capability than if they were selected from the start into a 'fast track' and a slower stream.

Promotion typically concerns moves up dual hierarchies in organisations. One is the ordinary line hierarchy with such job positions as team leader, section manager and departmental manager. The other, known as *shokuno shikaku tokyu*, is a kind of qualification system in which employees are placed along the hierarchy of grades (*tokyu*) according to skill qualifications (*shokuno shikaku*), as determined by their level of knowledge, proficiency, experience, skill, general capabilities and seniority. Promotion of both types results from performance evaluation or appraisals. It is quite common for promotion in the qualification grade system *not* to lead also to promotion in the line hierarchy at the same time, since, for instance, there is a range of qualification grades which are considered appropriate to correspond to the position of a departmental manager. Clearly delineating these two types of promotion forces management to separate the evaluation of an employee's performance of specific job responsibilities from the evaluation of his or her underlying capability. Merit (*ko*) refers loosely to excelling in both performance on the job and underlying capability. Even after the initial 10 or 15 years, however, seniority as a criterion for promotion creeps in via an implicit understanding that with seniority comes experience and accumulated wisdom, which tends to lead to promotion up the qualification grade hierarchy.

Pay is not a 'rate for the job'. The total reward package consists of basic pay, bonus and welfare benefits. A component of basic pay is directly linked to seniority, measured by the length of service within the firm. Pay is also linked to merit via a pay component which depends on the qualification grade and another component which relates to job responsibilities. But as mentioned above, these components also provide an indirect link to seniority. Other person-related criteria, such as an employee's educational level, gender and the number of dependents, are also used to determine pay.

Enterprise unionism

The basic unit for organising workers is the enterprise. Although there are no legal restrictions on having more than one union at a workplace, the predominant mode is one union per enterprise. Blue-collar and white-collar workers belong to the same union. Since craft unions are rare, as are competing unions within an enterprise, Japanese unions do not concern themselves with job demarcation. The enterprise structure of unions reinforces the principle of the firm as community, since the union does not constitute an alternative dimension to the firm which may compete for workers' loyalty and identification.

Because of this, however, enterprise unions are seen to be in a weaker bargaining position *vis-à-vis* management than industrial unions. In the eyes of those with the Anglo-American model in mind, the union's fortunes are too closely tied to the fortunes of the enterprise. However, instead of questioning whether enterprise unions are *bona fide* unions or not, the Japanese model asserts that the enterprise structure of unions fundamentally alters the implicit definition of what the union is for. Unions do not merely fight with management over the relative shares of capital and labour; it is assumed that managers also seek to keep payments to capital providers to the minimum possible. Disputes between management and the union reflect, instead, the difference between the interests of the lower ranks of the community hierarchy (for example more wages now rather than investment which may deliver more wages later) and the concerns of the management who are more 'responsibly' preoccupied with the firm's long-term future. The viability of the enterprise union depends on the viability of the firm as community which in turn depends on the defence of the 'lifetime employment' principle. In this sense, both manage-ment and the enterprise union representing the lower ranks in the community have an incentive to broaden the scope of discussion, through collective bargaining and joint consultation, in order to preserve the 'life-time employment' principle. The union's access to sensitive managerial information in the process of such discussion constitutes a significant source of power for enterprise unions.

The Japanese model with the above features is often admired for its outcomes, one of which is the low incidence of industrial conflict, which may be attributed most to the understanding between management and labour that workers' cooperation over productivity and quality improve-ments would last in so far as management promises employment security. The resulting stability in employment relationships, flexible work prac-tices and enterprise-based training lead to high productivity growth. Another desirable outcome of the Japanese model is low unemployment, since the rationalisation or the restructuring efforts of corporations is made without treating labour as disposable resources.

WHAT HAS CHANGED IN THE LAST TWO DECADES?

The Japanese model spelt out above is intentionally highly stylised, and the ideal typical skeleton is in need of filling out with empirical meat. This section therefore provides an account of how each element of the model looked in reality in the 1970s and in what way it has been transformed by the 1990s.

Boundaries of the firm as community are expanding

As mentioned earlier, members of the firm as community are the recipi-ents of stable employment opportunities within the firm, who themselves expect and want stable employment within the firm. But 'lifetime employ-ment' was a misnomer even in the early 1970s when the mandatory retirement age was typically 55 in large firms. Many remained economi-cally active, often self-employed, beyond that age. Moreover, the core workers coexisted with other workers, often women and those working for smaller firms, some of whom might have wanted employment secu-rity but were the first ones to go in industrial adjustment (Dore 1986).

What has changed in the 1990s? Has the definition of the membership of the community changed? And more drastically, is the principle of the firm as community breaking down? 'Yes' and 'no' appear to be the short answers to these questions. First, in so far as core workers are concerned, they are benefiting from a greater stability of employment. In particular, the average length of service of regular workers aged 45–49 in manufacturing establishments with over 1,000 employees grew from 23 years in 1973 to 27 years in 1993 for high school graduate employees and from 21 years to 23 years for university graduate employees (see Sato, Chapter 4). As Higuchi (in Chapter 1) points out in his international comparisons of job tenure, there is no significant difference between Japan and other countries with respect to white-collar and female workers. What is most remarkable about Japan is the long length of service among male blue-collar workers (many of whom are high school graduates). It is for these workers that the length of service has grown most in the last two decades. (One contributory factor to the lengthening of job tenure is the raising of the mandatory retirement age beyond 55. In the 1990s, the majority of large firms have a retirement age of 60, and are planning to extend it to 65 in the year 2000 (see Seike, Chapter 6).)

However, the major focus of rationalisation in the 1990s is not blue-collar workers but white-collar workers. The 1970s saw much rationalisation on the shop-floor which led to the creation of 'lean production' workplaces. In 1990s, the shop-floor remains lean, while slower corporate growth is aggravating the problem of excess white-collar workers as fewer opportunities arise for internal promotion. In order to defend the principle of lifetime employment, large firms are increasingly resorting to seconding and transferring their core employees to their affiliates and subsidiaries. Thus, the practice of continuous employment within a single enterprise is slowly giving way to the practice of continuous employment within a group of enterprises (Sato, Chapter 4, Inagami 1995). This shift may be regarded either as externalising the problem by throwing core workers into the periphery, or extending the boundary of the firm as community to include enterprise groups. Which is it? A full answer requires an examination of the peripheral sector.

The core-periphery model of labour markets is a useful analytical tool. In one version, the core is defined as the labour force which benefits from stable employment and functional flexibility, while the periphery consists of numerically flexible workers who provide a buffer for the core (Atkinson and Meager 1986). Has the core contracted and the periphery expanded in the Japanese labour markets in the last two decades? At a superficial level, a growing rate of labour force participation by women and the presence of foreign workers in the 1990s seem to point to an affirmative answer to this question. In fact, between 1982 and 1992, the proportion of non-regular workers (including temporary and dispatched workers) increased from 8 per cent to 10 per cent of the male employee workforce and from 31 per cent to 38 per cent of the female employee workforce (Japan Productivity Centre 1994, p. 102). However, on deeper examination, it becomes evident that the boundary between the core and the periphery cannot be simply drawn on the basis of workers' attributes such as gender or nationality. In particular, Wakisaka shows in Chapter 5 that part-time workers, the majority of whom are women, are on the increase in Japan as elsewhere, but that the average job tenure of part-timers in Japan has increased over time. Thus, an increase in the proportion of part-timers in the labour force cannot be interpreted simply as a rise in numerical flexibility. Some part-time workers in Japan are clearly treated as quasi-members of the firm as community, although the majority of women remain outside the community, either because neither the firm nor the individual employee calls for membership, or because there is a mismatch between the expectations of the firm and those of the female employee.

Similarly, Imano shows in Chapter 7 that foreign workers are not all recruited in the open external market for hiring and firing according to business fluctuations. Foreign workers were hardly an issue in 1970s Japan. They became topical in the mid-1980s when the yen appreciation combined with the domestic labour shortage led to an inflow of foreign workers and an increase in Japanese foreign direct investment. The law governing the area of Japanese companies accepting foreign workers as trainees was formulated so as to fulfil the dual objective of technical assistance to developing countries and promotion of foreign direct investment. In particular, subsidies were given to Japanese companies which brought workers at their overseas subsidiaries, their suppliers or customers to Japan for training. Although these trainees are not permitted to stay for more than 2 years in Japan, their expected return to the original overseas subsidiaries or related companies mirrors the employment practice for Japanese workers.

Nitta (Chapter 11) examines the core-periphery model from the angle of business strategy. Specifically, he poses the question: Does the employment system have to become more diversified as businesses in mature sectors adopt a product diversification strategy? Diversification was very much a topical business strategy of the 1980s see Kawakita, Chapter 3), and Nitta's study constitutes a detailed examination of a more general pattern spelt out by Kawakita on the link between corporate strategy and human resource strategy. Interestingly, the lifetime employment principle which may at first sight be a centrifugal force externalising non-homogeneous elements of the labour force is actually a centripetal force binding diversified subsidiaries and affiliates to be part of the same community. In the case of the chemical textiles industry in the 1980s, Nitta shows that rather than bringing in expertise from outside, newly created affiliated companies in such areas as chemicals and plastics were mostly manned by transferred workers from within each corporation. Moreover, working conditions, including wages, did not diverge much among the old and newly created operations in diverse sectors partly because of tighter corporate group-wide coordination among enterprise unions (see Sako (Chapter 10) also for a similar trend in the automobile industry).

The boundary of the enterprise group as community is not necessarily just among firms with shareholding links; sometimes, suppliers with no shareholding links to their customer company are included in the community of such an extensive enterprise group. As suppliers, they benefit from relational contracting and are not treated as mere buffers (Aoki 1988, Asanuma 1989, Sako 1992). Thus, not all small firms are in the periphery, and only because these firms have a stable trading relationship with the core firm can the latter second and transfer employees to them. Older employees who are transferred to affiliates and suppliers may suffer a decline in status or esteem, but do not feel betrayed in so far as the employer's guarantee of their livelihood – which comes with full membership of the community – is concerned. The moment relocated employees feel they are expunged from the membership list, as happened in a few recent cases, the lifetime employment principle would be severely jeopardised. That is why the way in which redundancies are handled, rather than whether redundancies are made or not, matters so much in maintaining the moral contract of worker cooperation in return for employment security. The 1990s recession in fact has led to an average of 300,000 redundancies per annum, out of a total employee workforce of just over 50 million (Ministry of Labour 1995a).

There is sufficient evidence that in the 1990s, the majority of managers and workers think it desirable and feasible to maintain the Japanese employment system, albeit with modifications (see Sugeno and Suwa, Chapter 2, for survey evidence). The most significant modification is a shift from continuous employment within a single enterprise to that within an extended enterprise grouping. The principle of lifetime employment continues to be upheld by management because without it, the motivational basis of workers' and unions' cooperation would falter. For this reason, even in the case of privatisation of the railways and the telecommunications companies, employment reductions were achieved without compulsory redundancies (see Ohmi, Chapter 9). But in order to maintain the lifetime employment principle, pressures are placed elsewhere in the system.

Seniority-plus-merit principle gives way?

One pressure point is the pay and promotion dimension. In Chapter 2, Sugeno and Suwa cite survey evidence in the 1990s that the majority of both managers and unions want to see ability and other criteria besides seniority introduced in pay and promotion. Kawakita (in Chapter 3) also shows that in a 1995 survey of managers, the introduction of an ability-based human resource policy was one of the most important objectives for two-thirds of the respondents. Several contributors to this volume agree with this prognosis. For example, in Chapter 1 Higuchi shows that employment adjustment is slower in Japan than in other countries, while wages are not as flexible as often thought. Given the added pressure to make wages more flexible, Higuchi argues in favour of an ability-based wage system. But none of the contributors spell out precisely what such a wage system should look like, and this is a gap in this book. A major reason for this is that no one is prepared to completely abandon the seniority-based principle for Japanese firms. It is unclear at what point the motivational basis for the seniority principle would start to break down if the ability-based principle were to be gradually fortified. It is also unclear in what ways the ability-based principle (*noryoku shugi*) should be implemented.

Just like the speculation about the end of lifetime employment, the end of seniority-based pay and promotion has been mooted for a few decades. In fact, the dilution of the seniority principle started in the 1960s, when job responsibility pay (*shokumu kyu*) was introduced with the adoption of job evaluation in certain industries such as steel (Ishizuka 1996). The 1970s and the 1980s saw the introduction and the diffusion of ability-based pay (*shokuno kyu*), although as pointed out in the previous section, an element of seniority tended to creep into this pay component via promotion in the qualification rank. Recessionary pressures and the need for restructuring give businesses an incentive to link pay to performance so as to increase the overall efficiency of their operations. So what is different about the debate in the 1990s from that in the 1970s?

First, the conditions which were present in the 1970s are present in a more intense manner in the 1990s. For example, the prolonged slow corporate growth in the 1990s is putting pressure on the seniority-followed-by-merit principle which was applied to the promotion of white-collar university graduate employees in large firms in the 1970s (see Sato, Chapter 4). According to Sato, the following conditions must hold in order to retain the delayed timing of decisive selection in internal promotion: (a) a reasonably high rate of, and opportunity for, promotion to senior posts; (b) a small dispersion in the skill levels within a cohort of recruits before decisive selection occurs; and (c) employees' shared aspiration to rise up the rank of management. Condition (a) has been jeopardised by slow corporate growth, and condition (b) by the growth in the proportion of those graduating from universities. One possible modification which some companies have adopted is to start decisive differentiation among members of a recruitment cohort earlier in their career. However, this has the disadvantage of undermining condition (c), thus demotivating employees at an early stage of their career. An alternative, preferred, modification is to change the rules of promotion, from having a single managerial ladder to having multiple progression routes with functional specialisations (called the 'multi-track career system').

However, it is unclear to what extent firms can disperse employees' aspiration for promotion, and make specialist career tracks as prestigious as the core management track.

Another quantitative intensification of the pressure to modify the seniority-plus-merit principle is the ageing of the population. Seike (in Chapter 6) notes that in order to make older workers more attractive to employers, the seniority-based wage system should be revised. In his view, companies must adopt a flatter wage profile if they are to be persuaded to extend their retirement age from 60 to 65 in accordance with the recent change in pension provisions. In fact, the rate at which pay increases with age, with a peak at 52 or 53, continued to increase in the 1970s but has been declining since the 1980s (Japan Productivity Centre 1994, pp. 107–8). In other words, the element of seniority in pay, defined in this way, has been declining in the last decade or so. But how likely is a further erosion of seniority in the future? Seike goes all the way in arguing for a wage which reflects workers' contributions and abilities in the short run. But there is no consensus in Japan on whether this principle should be applied just to older workers or to all employees.

Perhaps the most striking difference for the 1990s is that workers themselves (and particularly young competent employees) are interested in a more immediate recognition of their capabilities. Thus, Rengo-affiliated unions are advocating 'a fair wage differential' according to ability or performance so as to motivate and reward workers. There is even survey evidence that both employees and management regard a fair wage differential within a firm, controlling for age, to be 30 per cent above and 20 per cent below average (Ministry of Labour 1995b). The same survey shows that the firms desire a larger wage dispersion for older workers, while in contrast, employees want a larger wage dispersion by ability the younger they are.

From the unions' point of view, it may perhaps be easier to apply this thinking to white-collar than to blue-collar workers, and white-collar workers are becoming a larger proportion of their membership. But even in the few public-sector organisations where unions had previously resisted the idea, they conceded to the adoption of performance-related pay in the post-privatised JRs and NTT (see Ohmi, Chapter 9). In reality, however, information sharing and coordination on both sides of the industry during the Shunto process of wage bargaining put a brake on varying the wage system too much between companies (see Sako, Chapter 10).

To summarise, feasible alternatives to the seniority-plus-merit principle are difficult to come by, because of the fragile balance in reconciling competing motivational forces, one relying on treating workers homogeneously, and the other relying on differential treatment. The latter is increasingly gaining support, and has been promoted by the introduction of ability and performance-related pay. Moreover, from the 1970s to the 1990s, there has been a shift in focus in determining pay and promotion, away from a long-term assessment of employees' underlying capability during their lifetime employed career towards a short-term evaluation of performance demonstrated on the job. However, the homogeneous treatment of workers is unlikely to be abandoned as long as the principle of the firm as community is retained. For this gives the firm the obligation to support the livelihood of workers, and pay is therefore not merely a reward for work done. In this respect, there is likely to be reluctance to vary pay by performance or ability too much, lest below-average performers suffer from a loss of their livelihood.

Are enterprise unions viable?

In 1970 unions organised 11.6 million workers; in 1993 they organised 12.7 million workers. Despite this increase in the absolute number of members, the union density declined from 35.4 per cent to 24.2 per cent. Fujimura (in Chapter 13) surveys research which explains why such a decline has occurred. In Japan, structural factors (such as industry sectoral composition) explain at most 30 per cent of the decline. The existing studies point to the failure to organise newly created establishments as a significant factor in Japan as elsewhere. The reason behind this failure, however, is due more to the lack of interest on the part of employees to organise unions than to employers' opposition. There is evidence that employees are not attracted to unions because they look to unions for instrumental ends, namely a union mark-up on wages which is quite small in Japan. This is partly because there is much spill-over of wage increases from the union to the non-union sector during the Shunto wage bargaining process (see Sako, Chapter 10). Moreover, other non-union employee representative bodies, particularly in small firms, appear to be operating as an alternative effective mechanism for employee voice (see Sato, Chapter 14).

If one assumes that enterprise unions have the same purpose as industrial or craft unions of protecting workers against a management with functionally different objectives, then the enterprise structure of unions has several disadvantages. One is their susceptibility to managerial interference and pressure. This may manifest itself in a lack of bargaining power by unions. Enterprise unions may become too closely linked to the fortunes of the enterprise, with a resulting wage restraint in the recent Spring Offensive (Shunto) rounds (see Sako, Chapter 10). Despite various attempts at creating a functional equivalent of industrial unions by strengthening coordination at higher levels, unions have ended up consolidating more along the lines of corporate groupings (see Sako, Chapter 10, and Nitta, Chapter 11). For example, enterprise unions at Toyota and its suppliers have formed a federation (*roren*), which in turn affiliates to the industry-level body, the Confederation of Japan Automobile Workers' Unions. Inagami's (1995) survey shows that around a third of unions formed such corporate group-based union federations before 1973, and another third between 1973 and the time of the survey in 1992/3. Thus, one change from the 1970s to the 1990s is the proliferation of union organisation along the lines of corporate groupings, which parallels the extension of the boundary of the firm as community.

If enterprise unions are so closely tied to the fortunes of the enterprise or the enterprise group, do they lack the independence and the voice to protect their members' interests? The degree of independence and the strength of union voice differ from union to union, and by no means are all enterprise unions like company unions. In this respect, Inagami (1995) develops a typology of enterprise unions in Japan, with 'active' unions prevalent in manufacturing, and less 'active' unions more common in banks and trading companies. Here, an active union is defined as one which has significant voice in management, and whose leaders are entrusted with confidential information by management. Nakamura also points out, in Chapter 12, that judging from unions' voice in functional matters such as job transfers, 20–30 per cent of Japanese unions are actively involved in influencing managerial decisions, while 40 per cent are passive and are informed of the decisions after the event. Thus, there is variety among enterprise unions in their degree of voice and influence. Such diversity has probably always existed since the 1970s, although it might have increased with the UI (Union Identity) movement which is geared towards rejuvenating union activities in innovative ways (see Fujimura, Chapter 13).

The Union Identity movement took off in the late 1970s as a response by leading enterprise unions to put a stop to union decline. Both membership decline and the difficulty in recruiting union officers led individual unions to look for ways of increasing the attractiveness of unions to their members. The movement very much took the enterprise structure of the unions as given, and addressed first the issue of union democracy, i.e. better communication between union leaders and members, and second the issue of union participation in managerial decision making. They were meant to transform the image of unions in the eyes of their members. However, as noted below, achieving the latter objective may have had the detrimental effect of undermining the first objective.

As Fujimura (Chapter 13) explains, there are four major types of UI programmes. The first is symbolic, and involves such things as new logos and slogans for enterprise unions. The second programme, called the 'total welfare policy', is akin to the credit card unionism which spread in the Anglo-American world, and offers legal and other services to members with diverse needs. The third programme is the organisation of non-regular employees such as part-time workers. The last programme is the active participation of unions in managerial decision making.

Of the UI programmes, perhaps the most difficult to evaluate is the last one, concerning union participation in management. This is due to both conceptual and empirical reasons. Conceptually, the Anglo-American model would regard union participation in management as susceptible to co-optation, particularly for Japanese unions because of their enterprise structure. The career development of union leaders, many of whom return to the firm as top managers, is often cited as evidence of management's incorporation of labour. In this framework, the source of union power is workers' threat to exit and resources outside the firm. In an alternative framework of the Japanese model, in which unions are enterprise-based and in which workers do not exercise the threat to exit the firm, unions are also judged by their strength in influencing managerial decision making on behalf of their members. But enterprise unions' main power resource is their access to confidential management information, not their ability to mobilise resources outside the firm. Here lies the empirical difficulty in verifying how much useful information union leaders actually have due to confidentiality. Moreover, it is not transparent to outsiders whether such information is put to use to influence management decisions in ways which are different from those which might have been taken in the absence of union participation.

Despite these difficulties, at least union leaders themselves feel that their effectiveness in participating in strategic managerial decision making has increased from the 1970s to the 1990s (Inagami 1995). Part of this increase in worker participation is due to the greater need for employment adjustment since 1973. Since the cost of exit is high for both workers and the firm, management has been willing to allow employees to exercise voice so as to avoid layoffs. Another reason for the perceived effectiveness of worker participation at the strategic level is that it has spread as part of a system of participation at all levels down to the workshop level in the form of quality control circles (see Nakamura, Chapter 12). However, while greater union participation in managerial decisions is good for furthering industrial democracy in so far as union leaders are concerned, these leaders may face a rift from rank-and-file who do not see the process of negotiation between top management and union leaders over confidential managerial matters. This situation poses another threat to union decline.

In short, enterprise unions have both problems which are common to industrial or craft unions (namely density decline) and problems which are different. Viewed through the Anglo-American lens, all enterprise unions suffer structurally from weak bargaining power, managerial interference, and the inability to organise peripheral and retired workers. However, conceptually and in reality, enterprise unions have both weaknesses and strengths (e.g. access to managerial information) when compared to industrial or craft unions. The Union Identity movement takes the enterprise structure of unions as given partly because union leaders see the advantage in retaining the structure. Also, the neo-corporatist arrangement of Shunto combined with Rengo's policy of participation has overcome some of the limitations of enterprise unionism (see the following section, Japanese-style neo-corporatism?). However, at the enterprise level, the challenge for unions remains how to cope with diverse membership when they have been used to homogeneous regular worker membership, and how to redefine their role at the workplace in such a way which is transparent to the members.

Japanese-style neo-corporatism?

In the 1970s, forces were already under way to unify the labour movement at the national level (see Shinoda, Chapter 8). However, outside observers continued to focus on industrial relations at the enterprise level, in part because the classical Japanese model ignored the higher levels, and in part because what was happening at the higher levels in the 1970s was nothing worth emulating. The 1970s was still a decade of fragmented unions, with varying degrees of radical anti-establishment ideologies aligning themselves with equally fragmented opposition parties. Some political scientists who did study the national-level system in Japan came to the conclusion that labour was largely excluded from the policy-making process, hence the label 'corporatism without labour' (Pempel and Tsunekawa 1979).

In the 1990s, and particularly after the formation of Rengo as the largest National Centre in 1989, no one would apply the same label. As Shinoda (Chapter 8) shows, Rengo holds regular policy consultations with each government ministry, and produces an annual document which spells out Rengo's demands in all aspects of government policy. These corporatist activities are a culmination of labour's aspiration to overcome the limits of enterprise unionism. Their limitations were brought home when the post-1973 inflation undermined workers' real living standards; unions realised that real wages could not be defended sufficiently through enterprise-level bargaining only. Moreover, wages were not everything for workers' living standards; and national policy-making channels were considered better than enterprise channels to realise 'quality-oriented' or 'lifestyle-oriented' demands in such matters as housing, work hours and childcare.

Whether the 1990s arrangement is best characterised as corporatist is a moot point. As Shinoda (in Chapter 8) and Inagami *et al.* (1994) point out, macro- and meso-corporatist arrangements in Japan are grounded in the decentralised micro-corporatist relationships at the enterprise level. Moreover, policy demands made by the labour movement include neo-liberal elements, such as privatisation and deregulation. Also, the government bureaucracy, rather than political parties in government, plays a role in intermediating the interests of labour and management. In these respects, Japanese-style neo-corporatism is different from the Social Democratic corporatist model of Sweden and Germany.

Lastly, as a problem common to all types of corporatism, Rengo faces the dilemma of reconciling the ideal of an encompassing organisation with the reality of internal divisions. Rengo, as the culmination of the labour unification movement, intends to be all-encompassing, and therefore professes to be the defender of the needs of all working people, including those beyond its immediate membership. But as a result, Rengo's ideology is vague and its constituency is not clear to all. The inter-sectoral clashes, between the public sector and private sector unions, between the export-oriented sector and the protected domestic sector, and between large and small firms, were what the formation of Rengo intended to eliminate. Yet, conflict of interest continues to exist both within and outside Rengo's organisational boundary (see Shinoda, Chapter 8 for details). One clear evidence of the failure of Rengo to be all-encompassing is that it captured only 62.3 per cent of union membership in 1993, while 28 per cent remained unaffiliated to any of the national centres (including the pro-communist Zenroren (with 7.2 per cent) and the left-wing socialist Zenrokyo (capturing 2.5 per cent)).

What do all these changes in the last two decades add up to? It is not a simple matter of increased numerical flexibility in the ever larger periphery, the externalisation of labour markets, greater wage flexibility, weaker unions and so on. The basic principle of the firm as community continues to be valued by both sides of the industry. Consequently, employment security is defended by extending the domain of community from a single firm to an enterprise grouping. While the supply side in the Japanese labour markets points to the need to diversify employment prac-tices, Japanese companies are able to only marginally move away from the homogeneous treatment of employees as members based on the seniority-plus-merit principle. Japanese unions are responding by acqui-escing to the need for diversity in treatment of individual employees, but they themselves are structurally swayed by the forces for homegenisation particularly within firms and corporate groupings.

OTHER UNIVERSAL THEMES

It is evident from the discussion above that the classical Japanese model is in need of modification for the 1990s. This section focuses on a number of theoretical and policy issues which are common in Japan and other industrialised countries.

A corporate governance framework

The often ignored connection between managers' relation with owners and industrial relations has been brought into focus by the fashionable concern – starting in the Anglo-American economies – with corporate governance. Corporate governance in the Anglo-American model is about how management as agents can be made to act properly on behalf of their principal, the shareholders. However, in the recent industrial relations literature (for example, Locke *et al.* 1995), 'corporate governance' has come to mean more broadly how the workplace is governed, and thus involves the identification of the mechanisms – such as bargaining and consultation – through which various stakeholders interact. This slippage in the use of the concept 'corporate governance' appears to be in part due to an attempt to accommodate alternative conceptions of the firm other than the Anglo-American one, in Japan and in social democratic countries.

In this book also, the corporate governance dimension is discussed both through the Anglo-American lens and through adopting the broader stakeholder definition. As an example of the former, Nakamura (in Chapter 12) argues that the feebleness of shareholders explains why top management in Japanese companies allow workers to participate in strategic decision making. In particular, shareholders tend not to be vocal in governing Japanese corporations, which are in effect run by managers who are senior employees rather than agents working on behalf of shareholders. Workers and management therefore tend to have similar objectives. As an example of the latter, Fujimura (Chapter 13) raises the question: if management is not accountable to the shareholders, then are there any other actors who check management behaviour? A well-researched alternative actor is the 'main bank' (Aoki and Patrick 1994). However, Fujimura (in Chapter 13) argues that employees and their representative organisations have exercised checks on management in such a way as to defend the long-term viability of the firm. In this way, the Japanese reality contributes to the awareness that taking other actors besides labour and management into the analysis of industrial relations is useful for furthering understanding of industrial relations and for policy formulation.

Decentralisation and the enterprise focus

Decentralisation and deregulation have been a dominant policy theme in the 1980s. In industrial relations, decentralisation in collective bargaining structures occurred partly due to managerial offensive against unions but also due to the importance of enterprise-level qualitative issues for maintaining industrial competitiveness (Katz 1993). Japan has always had an enterprise focus. But as Chapters 8 (Shinoda) and 10 (Sako) show, there has always been higher-level coordination on both sides of the industry. And there is no tendency towards decentralisation in Japan. For example, enterprise groupings, rather than individual enterprises, are becoming a unit for the internal labour market. Unions are also consolidating their organisation along these lines. Industry-level and inter-sectoral coordination during the Spring Offensive was strengthened on both sides of the industry since the mid-1970s. At the national level, Rengo was inaugurated in 1989 to unify the labour movement and to engage in neo-corporatist activities. Moreover, although Japanese employers have greater bargaining power *vis-à-vis* unions in the 1990s than in the 1970s, they show no sign of abating coordination with each other. Thus, the Japanese reality indicates that while the enterprise focus accounts for much of the smooth functioning of the Japanese industrial relations system, the existence of informal as well as formal higher-level coordination by both employers and unions should not be underestimated.

Diversity of employment relations

Individual contracts, to suit the needs and requirements of diverse individuals, are becoming popular in both private and public sectors in Britain. Despite the persistent trend towards the homogeneous treatment of employees in Japanese firms, there are supply-side pressures for enhancing the diversity in the treatment of women, older workers and professionals. Sugeno and Suwa, in Chapter 2, discuss the need for labour law to accommodate this increasing diversity in work style, and to change the goal of the law from the protection of workers as collectivity to the regulation of workers as diverse individuals. Japanese companies are themselves innovating to accommodate diversity, for example by devising a multi-track career system for white-collar graduate workers (see Sato, Chapter 4), so that specialists (such as R&D researchers) do not all have to become general managers if they wish to rise to the top. Some changes in company policy are in response to legal changes, as in the case of the Equal Employment Opportunity Law. Women are now admitted to either of the two career tracks, one leading to general management and the other a limited clerical route. Wakisaka (Chapter 5) expresses scepticism about the success of this system because of the evidence that not all women stick to their initial career intentions. Given the limits to facilitating the diversity of employment contracts if left to the inititatives of individual companies, the legal agenda spelt out by Sugeno and Suwa in Chapter 2 is quite ambitious. They see the new goal of labour law as smoothing the functioning not only of external labour markets (e.g. by enhancing the usefulness of public employment placement agencies) but also of internal labour markets (by regulating the individual grievance procedure which lies outside the union channel).

Employee voice: union and their alternatives

Due to a widespread decline in union density, there is a growing interest in alternative forms of employee representation (see, for example Kaufman and Kleiner 1993). A similar concern exists in Japan also, although there, the debate over legal changes is focused around the small firm sector.

The Ministry of Labour's surveys on labour–management communication show that labour–management consultation systems (including joint consultative committees (JCCs)) have spread from 72.4 per cent in 1977 to 84.1 per cent in 1989 of unionised establishments, and from 37.5 per cent in 1977 to 44.2 per cent in 1989 of non-union establishments (Ministry of Labour 1989). Unlike German works councils, these JCCs are not legally mandated. But over time, JCCs spread with relatively little legal backing, in part due to management's lifetime employment strategy which predisposes both management and labour to talk through problems in order to safeguard their top priority objective of employment security.

Even at small and medium-sized enterprises (SMEs), effective alternative voice mechanisms to trade unions exist in the form of employee organisations and joint consultation committees (see Sato, Chapter 14). In Japan, SMEs employ roughly 70 per cent of all workers. At these establishments, around a third have unions. But if employee organisations with voice (defined as those which discuss working conditions such as wages and hours) and joint consultation committees are taken into account, just over half of SMEs have some form of employee representation. Sato (Chapter 14) asks the question: are such effective voice mechanisms contributing to the perception of a reduced need to set up unions? Hisamoto (1993) provides evidence from a non-union employee survey by Rengo Soken that voice-type employee organisations and trade unions may be substitutes; that is, those with voice-type employee organisations perceived less need for a union than those without.

More generally, there is much recent evidence in Japan of a 'representation gap', namely a level of worker representation in non-union settings below that which workers desire. First, the 1989 Survey on Labour–Management Communication found that of the 36.6 per cent of individual respondents who did not have a union at their workplace, 11.8 per cent said 'unions are definitely necessary' and 38 per cent that 'it would be better to have a union' (Ministry of Labour 1989, p. 85). Thus, exactly half of non-union employees were suffering from a 'representation gap'. Next, the aforementioned Rengo Soken survey asked the question 'Do you think that trade unions are necessary?' to which 21.3 per cent of non-union employees said 'definitely necessary' and a further 43.5 per cent that 'it would be better to have a union' (Tachibanaki and Rengo Soken 1993).

In this context, Sugeno and Suwa (in Chapter 2) draw our attention to the current, yet little heard of, debate in Japan over legalising JCCs so as to compensate for weak unions or the absence of unions. However, they assert that legalising JCCs would not satisfactorily address the issue of the social role of unions at industrial, regional and national levels. Moreover, given the enterprise structure of unions, legal regulation over the jurisdiction of unions and works councils would be rather difficult.

In conclusion, the above themes of flexibility, diversity and participation evidently apply to industrial relations systems of various countries. For example, in the US, the Dunlop Commission (1994) strongly recommended promoting employee representation as a way of coping with union decline. In Britain also, the breakdown of national and industry-level collective bargaining and the decline in union density have led the Trades Union Congress to consider ways of introducing European Works Councils without undermining the union as the main channel of representation (TUC 1995). In Germany, a concern for flexibility and competitiveness has led to the unions acquiescing to a greater dispersion of actual wages from those agreed at the industry-level. However, as is evident in Japan, the inter-play among industrial relations actors – or stakeholders – is such that flexibility is always balanced against rigidities (in the form of seniority-based stable employment), diversity against forces for homogeneity (at least within the firm or the enterprise group), and participation against management's right to manage. It is this fine balancing act in which the Japanese industrial relations system appears to excel, and which may account for the continued viability of the basic principles underlying the system.

Lastly, the study of Japanese industrial relations has contributed much to theory building in various disciplines, and it is hoped that this book contributes to this continued effort. The Appendix guide on how to identify relevant data and information on industrial relations in Japan is provided so as to assist readers in conducting their own investigation. Many researchers to date have asked the question: Do Western theories apply in Japan? A common finding has tended to be 'yes to some extent, but not fully'. But why? Social scientists have been struggling with two potentially fruitful routes of enquiry. One is to focus on the possibility that Western theories are not general enough to capture the Japanese situation (Aoki 1988). Another is to focus on the unique 'path dependent' history of Japanese labour and management. This book contains examples of both in analysing such concepts as corporatism and decentralisation.

NOTE

1   This label derives from Inagami and Kawakita (forthcoming).

REFERENCES

Abbeglen, J.C. (1958) *The Japanese Factory: Aspects of its Social Organisation*, Glencoe: The Free Press.
Aoki, Masahiko (1988) *Information, Incentives and Bargaining in the Japanese Economy*, New York: Cambridge University Press.
Aoki, Masahiko and Patrick, Hugh (1994) *The Japanese Main Bank System*, Oxford: Clarendon Press.

Asanuma, Banri (1989) 'Manufacturer-supplier relationships in Japan and the concept of relation-specific skill', *Journal of the Japanese and International Economies*, vol. 3, pp. 1–30.
Atkinson, John and Meager, Nigel (1986) *Changing Work Patterns*, London: National Economic Development Office.
Bamber, Greg and Lansbury, Russell (1993) *International and Comparative Industrial Relations* (2nd edn), London and New York: Routledge.
Dore, Ronald (1973) *British Factory – Japanese Factory*, Berkeley: University of California Press.
—— (1986) *Flexible Rigidities*, London: Athlone Press.
—— (1987) *Taking Japan Seriously*, London: Athlone Press.
Dunlop Commission on Future of Worker–Management Relations (1994) *Report and Recommendations*, Washington DC: Departments of Labour and Commerce.
Dunlop, John T. (1958) *Industrial Relations System*, New York: Holt.
Hisamoto, Norio (1993) 'Kumiai hitsuyokan to sono yoin' ('The perception of the necessity for unions and its causes'), in T. Tachibanaki and Rengo Soken (eds).
Inagami, Takeshi (ed.) (1995) *Seijuku Shakai no Naka no Kigyobetsu Kumiai (Enterprise Unions in a Mature Society)*, Tokyo: Japan Institute of Labour.
Inagami, T. and Kawakita, T. (forthcoming) *Rodo (Labour)*, Koza Shakaigaku Series 6, Tokyo: University of Tokyo Press.
Inagami, Takeshi, Whittaker, H., Ohmi, N., Shinoda, T., Shianodaira, Y. and Tsujinaka, Y. (1994) *Neo-koporatizumu no Kokusai Hikaku (International Comparative Research on Neo-corporatism)*, Tokyo: Japan Institute of Labour.
Ishizuka, Takuo (1996) 'Tekko sogo kakusha no jinji chingin seido kaitei' ('Reform of the personnel management and wage systems at the steel companies'), *Nihon Rodo Kenkyu Zasshi*, vol. 430, pp. 51–60.
Japan Productivity Centre (1994) *1994 Nenban Roshi Kankei Hakusho: Nihonteki Koyokanko to Aratana Jinzai Katsuyo Senryaku (1994 White Paper on Industrial Relations: Japanese-style Employment Practices and a New Human Resource Utilisation Strategy)*, Tokyo: Japan Productivity Centre for Socio-Economic Development.
Katz, Harry C. (1993) 'The decentralisation of collective bargaining: a literature review and comparative analysis', *Industrial and Labor Relations Review*, 47(1), pp. 3–22.
Kaufman, Bruce E. and Kleiner, Morris M. (eds) (1993) *Employee Representation: Alternative and Future Directions*, Madison: IRRA.
Kerr, Clark, Dunlop, John T., Harbison, Frederick and Meyers, Charles (1960) *Industrialism and Industrial Man*, Cambridge, MA: Harvard University Press.
Koike, Kazuo (1988) *Understanding Industrial Relations in Modern Japan*, London: Macmillan.
Lincoln, James and Kalleberg, A. (1990) *Culture, Commitment and Control*, Cambridge: Cambridge University Press.
Locke, Richard, Kochan, T. and Piore, M. (1995) *Employment Relations in a Changing World Economy*, Cambridge, MA: MIT Press.
Marsh, Robert and Mannari, Hiroshi (1976) *Modernisation and the Japanese Factory*, Princeton, NJ: Princeton University Press.
Ministry of Labour (1989) *Roshi Communication Chosa (Survey on Labour–Management Communication)*, Tokyo: Ministry of Labour.
—— (1995a) *Rodo Hakusho (White Paper on Labour)*, Tokyo: Japan Institute of Labour.
—— (1995b) *Nihonteki Koyo Seido Ankeeto Chosa Hokokusho (Report on the Survey of Japanese-style Employment System)*, Tokyo: Nihonteki Koyo Seido Kenkyukai (led by Takeshi Inagami).

OECD (Organisation for Economic Cooperation and Development) (1973) *Manpower Policy in Japan*, Paris: OECD.

— (1977) *The Development of Industrial Relations Systems: Some Implications of Japanese Experience*, Paris: OECD.

Pempel, T.J. and Tsunekawa, K. (1979) 'Corporatism without labour? The Japanese anomaly', in P.C. Schmitter and G. Lehmbruch (eds) *Trends Toward Corporatist Intermediation*, London: Sage.

Sako, Mari (1992) *Prices, Quality and Trust: Inter-firm Relations in Britain and Japan*, Cambridge: Cambridge University Press.

Shimada, Haruo (1983) 'Japanese industrial relations – a new general model? A survey of the English-language literature', in T. Shirai (ed.).

Shirai, Taishiro (ed.) (1983) *Contemporary Industrial Relations in Japan*, Madison, WI: University of Wisconsin Press.

Tachibanaki, Toshiaki and Rengo Soken (eds) (1993) *Rodo Kumiai no Keizaigaku* (*Economics of Trade Unions*), Tokyo: Toyo Keizai Shinposha.

Trades Union Congress (TUC) (1995) *Your Voice at Work: TUC Proposal for Rights to Representation at Work*, London: TUC.

Part I

1 Trends in Japanese labour markets

Yoshio Higuchi

INTRODUCTION

It is usually said that labour practice in Japan has two characteristic features: 'long-term employment' and the 'seniority-wage system'. Firms go on raising wages as their employees acquire more skills with longer service. The workers, on the other hand, expect higher wages for longer tenure within single firms which in turn increases the job retention rate (Hashimoto and Raisian 1985, Mincer and Higuchi 1988).

The long-term employment system helps the firms in training personnel, sharing information among employees and developing interest in the performance of the firm. At the same time, such a system gives workers the benefit of job security, which is considered an attractive employment condition for risk-averse workers. Moreover, with increased labour productivity, resulting from both a relationship of trust between workers and management and long-term competition for promotion among the workers under this system, it has the merit of contributing to the growth of the economy as a whole through stronger competition.

While the long-term employment system has these merits, a number of disadvantages also emerge. As firms must maintain job security of employees even during recession, labour cost is liable to be inflexible. Moreover, as employees get older an increase in personnel costs becomes unavoidable under the seniority-wage system. Even if the workers are dissatisfied with a firm, they patiently stay with it for a long time without moving to other firms because of higher job-turnover cost.

In addition, problems for the economy as a whole may also arise as a result of the effective utilisation of the labour market. With the progress of the international division of labour, where the industrial structure changes greatly, some industries might have surplus labour while certain others might face labour shortages. In a flexible labour market this problem can be rather smoothly solved through the reallocation of labour by way of job turnover, but in a labour market with a dominant long-term employment system it is difficult to solve this problem quickly.

The Japanese economy is now faced with a new situation. The older population is growing, while the high economic growth experienced in the past can no longer be expected. Moreover, the international division of labour and the Japanese Government's policy of deregulation are imposing great changes on the industrial structure itself. How are Japanese firms trying to solve the problems, which arise in this situation, while making the best use of the merits of long-term employment? This chapter examines this question, and reviews such problems through international comparison and time-series analysis.

PRESENT STATUS OF THE JAPANESE LONG-TERM EMPLOYMENT SYSTEM: AN INTERNATIONAL COMPARISON

How does the Japanese employment system compare with other countries? Figure 1.1 shows the average job tenure by sex and age in Japan, the USA and Germany, as presented in the OECD Employment Outlook (OECD 1993). This figure confirms the following three points.

1. As pointed out earlier, for Japanese males of less than 50 years of age average job tenure is very long and job retention is high. The difference in job tenure between Japan and the USA is quite large, but not so large when compared to Germany.
2. In the case of Japanese males of over 55 years of age, the average job tenure decreases rapidly and becomes less than that of Germany and the USA. The mandatory retirement age is set at a remarkably low age in Japanese firms and most of the employees leave firms to go to other firms or by taking early retirement.[1] Retired employees do not leave the labour market either, instead, they work for other firms.[2]
3. The average job tenure for Japanese females is longer than that for females in the USA but there is only a slight difference between Japan and Germany for females of a younger age. The job tenure of German females aged 40 and over is, however, longer than in Japan. In contrast to other advanced countries, the Japanese female labour force shows 'M-type' characteristics even today in terms of age, reflecting the fact that many women leave the firms for marriage or child care and return to work once their children have grown up.

Table 1.1 shows the levels for average job tenure and long-term employment in various countries including France and Spain. It can be observed from the table that, except for the USA, there is no big difference in the ratio of long-term employees and that job retention rate is high. It is also clear that the latter rate is higher for those who are above 40 years of age. If examined according to sex, the average job tenure of Japanese males is the longest among the five countries. Female workers in Japan rank fourth, followed only by the USA. The difference between

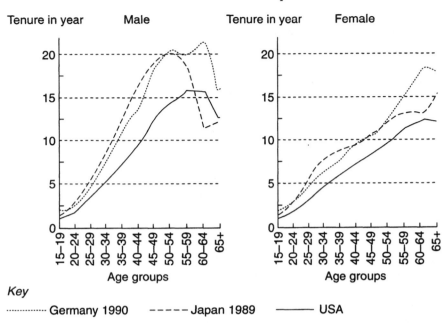

Figure 1.1 Average tenure profiles by age and sex in Japan, the USA and Germany

Source: OECD (1993)

Table 1.1 Index of long-term employment in Japan, former West Germany, France, Spain and the USA

	Japan	*Former West Germany*	*France*	*Spain*	*USA*
The retention rate of male employees in their early forties with job tenure of 10–14 years after working 5 years in the same company (per cent)	80.2	72.5	85.5	86.7	55.4
Ratio of persons working in the same company for over 20 years to the total employed workers (per cent)	19.6	16.7	15.8	18.4	8.8
Average job tenure of male workers (in years)	12.5	12.1	10.6	10.6	7.5
Average job tenure of female workers (in years)	7.3	8.0	9.1	8.2	5.9

Source: OECD (1993)

the average job tenure of males and females is the largest in Japan at 5.2 years. There the long-term employment system is limited to the top stratum of males in large firms. When women or workers in small firms are included, the difference between Japan and Germany or France is not so large as generally emphasized.

Next, let us look at the characteristics of the Japanese wage profile for tenured workers. Table 1.2 compares the wage profile of regular male workers in Japan and the UK. Wage increases are similar in both countries for job tenure of up to 10 years. But a difference appears for a tenure of 10 years or more. In the UK, the size of wage increases, particularly for the production workers, decreases greatly, while that in Japan continues to rise. Compared to the wage of the production worker, the wage for office and administrative personnel continues to grow greatly even in the UK, but the increase is quite small when compared to Japan. As a result, the average wage of workers working for over 10 years in Japan and the UK differs greatly. A similar tendency can also be observed in Table 1.3 where age is used to compare the wage profile for Japan and other EU countries.

The basic data for the wage index was calculated from the production workers' wage before tax (i.e. before the deduction of social security/tax) and included various allowances and overtime pay for these workers in the EU. For office administration and technical workers, the monthly salary, including allowances was used. This does not include the bonus due as a result of increases in company profits. In Japan, the wage is the

Table 1.2   Wage of regular male employees by job tenure in Japan and the UK

			Job tenure				
			Less than 1 year	1–2 years	3–4 years	5–9 years	10 years or more
Production workers	Total workforce	UK	100	108.9	115.6	121.1	126.3
		Japan	100	108.0	114.8	128.3	160.0
	30–39 years old	UK	100	103.7	105.5	105.6	106.3
		Japan	100	104.7	106.9	114.4	128.5
Office and administrative workers	Total work force	UK	100	113.9	122.5	133.6	152.4
		Japan	100	110.3	119.4	132.7	183.7
	30–39 years old	UK	100	107.5	107.6	110.6	114.2
		Japan	100	106.0	108.0	111.3	126.1

Sources: UK: Department of Employment (1979). Japan: Ministry of Labour (1980)

Note: UK: Hourly wage for production workers; weekly wage for office, administrative and technical workers.   Japan: Calculated from stipulated monthly income; regular employees in case of both Japan and the UK.

Table 1.3 Wage index of various countries by age group for male production workers and male office and administrative workers

	Less than 18 years old	18–20 years old	21–29 years old	30–44 years old	45–54 years old	More than 55 years old
Production workers						
Japan	84.4	100	135.0	176.7	183.5	144.7
Germany	67.4	100	117.3	122.3	118.4	110.9
France	80.9	100	119.8	130.1	127.1	120.0
Italy	79.5	100	118.5	126.6	124.9	121.8
Luxembourg	50.9	100	115.0	123.4	121.7	115.8
Belgium	67.0	100	121.0	127.3	125.1	117.6
The Netherlands	65.6	100	156.0	169.1	167.7	160.2

	Less than 21 years old	21–24 years old	25–29 years old	30–44 years old	45–54 years old	More than 55 years old
Office, administrative and technical workers						
Japan	79.9	100	128.4	185.7	227.5	178.0
Germany	72.4	100	130.0	152.6	149.8	143.3
France	71.7	100	133.3	175.0	185.7	175.0
Italy	80.6	100	126.8	172.5	195.3	203.9
Luxembourg	77.7	100	128.4	160.6	167.1	180.7
Belgium	72.6	100	128.2	164.9	170.3	156.3
The Netherlands	61.1	100	135.4	182.0	199.4	184.9

Sources: Japan: Ministry of Labour (1976). Other countries: Statistical Office of the European Communities (1972)

Note: The wage index is based on the wage of the 18–20-year-old production worker taken as 100 and also that of 21–24-year-old office, administrative and technical workers as 100.

monthly amount set within a prescribed limit which includes various allowances for production, office, administrative and technical workers. The wage is on a before-tax basis and includes the charge for workers' social security payments. While in the case of Japanese production workers wage can be converted into an hourly rate, wage by job tenure cannot. Therefore, to enable a comparison to be drawn, the monthly wage has been used. The age groups selected for production workers are 18–19 years of age instead of 18–20 years of age, 20–29 years of age instead of 21–29 years of age and for office workers, less than 20 years of age instead of 21 years of age, and 20–24 years of age instead of 21–24 years of age. Other groupings remain the same.

Compared to office and administrative workers, the growth of wage increases for production workers is less in all countries. This trend can also be seen in Japan, but the growth is larger than that for production workers in other countries. While the difference between the wages of office and administrative workers in their early forties in Japan and other countries is small, the gap widens for those in their late forties, arising from the wage increases which continue to occur for this age band in Japan.

Nevertheless, when a worker exceeds the age of 55, the wage in Japan declines sharply, though it is maintained at its earlier level in other countries. This sharp drop in wage results from the earlier mandatory retirement age in Japan after which lower wages are paid to those rejoining work. The characteristic steep rise in wage levels is seen only for middle-aged males.

BUSINESS CYCLE, EMPLOYMENT ADJUSTMENT AND WAGE ADJUSTMENT

It would be useful here to have an overview of the recent moves made by the Japanese firms to see how they have adapted the long-term employment system to cope with changes in business conditions. Figure 1.2 shows the percentage of the manufacturing industries which have introduced employment controls since 1987. After the G7 Plaza Accord in 1985, the Japanese economy suffered from a recession accompanied by a high appreciation of the yen which continued up to 1987. During this period, even manufacturers suffered from a sharp drop in demand and substantial cuts in output.

After the latter half of 1987, the so-called "bubble economy business" started, and there was a broad recovery in demand at the end of 1991. However, the sudden drop in stock prices and the rapid increase in unrecoverable credits (bad debts) dragged the Japanese economy into recession again. Let us see how the firms controlled employment to overcome the effects of recession.

As shown in Figure 1.2, one step taken was the curtailment of overtime work. In the first quarter of 1992, when the recession started, there were already many firms that had curtailed overtime work. In the fourth quarter of 1993, when the recession was at its peak, nearly 40 per cent of firms were restricting overtime work. The next measure introduced was the relocation or transfer of personnel elsewhere within the firm as well as to subsidiaries within the same business group. As the recession continued, management of workforce levels was achieved by firms stopping the hiring of new workers and the renewal of contracts with part-timers, and then the introduction of layoffs. However, firms still retained the idea of maintaining security of employment for regular employees.

The curtailment of overtime work was particularly strong in large firms. In 1989, when business was good, annual overtime was 246 hours per person in large companies with more than 500 workers, compared with 1993, when overtime was 153 hours, a drop of 93 hours. On the other hand, during the same period overtime in small companies with 30 to 99 workers was cut from 162 hours to 121 hours, a reduction of 41 hours.

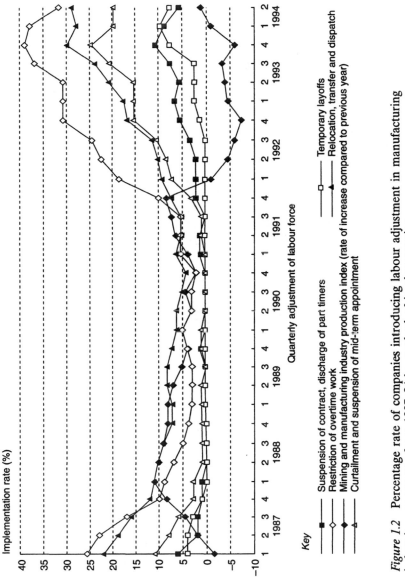

Implementation rate (%)

Quarterly adjustment of labour force

Key

Suspension of contract, discharge of part timers
Restriction of overtime work
Mining and manufacturing industry production index (rate of increase compared to previous year)
Curtailment and suspension of mid-term appointment

Temporary layoffs
Relocation, transfer and dispatch

Figure 1.2 Percentage rate of companies introducing labour adjustment in manufacturing industries per quarter from 1987–94 by method of implementation

Source: Ministry of Labour (various years) *Rodo Kezai Doko Chosa (Survey on Labour Economic Trends)*

Large companies tended to use the labour time as a buffer to regulate employment levels.

Figure 1.3 shows the long-term transition of separation and job accession rates by sex in the firms. It is to be noticed in this figure that both rates decreased after the oil crisis compared with the high-growth period of 1960s. A decline in job changers also occurred. Job changers included those who quit voluntarily for personal reasons as well as those who were laid off due to management policy. In Japan, those who quit voluntarily normally accounted for a higher ratio of the separation rate. However, because of the reduced job opportunities during the time of recession, the overall separation rate was reduced. In Figure 1.3, the shaded portion represents the period when the employees decreased as the accession rate fell below the separation rate. In this period, it was not a case of the workforce being reduced by a management decision to increase layoffs but, rather, a case of this being achieved by further suppression of the accession rate, despite the lower separation rate.

This kind of labour adjustment is likely to lead to massive cuts in female employees. As can be seen from the scale of the vertical axis in Figure 1.3, women account for higher job accession and separation rates than men. During a recession, in order to raise the separation rate, employers use a system of encouraging early retirement, but this measure has its limitations. As long as employment security is guaranteed, the workforce must be lowered by reducing recruitment.

As a result, this reduction in new employment opportunities presents more difficulties for female workers seeking jobs, as they already have higher accession and separation rates than their male counterparts. Moreover, in Japan, there is no established seniority rule for the period of layoff, as there is for American production workers. Thus middle-aged and older workers with higher wages are likely to be the objects of employment adjustment.

When labour adjustment in the manufacturing industries in the USA, Japan and the UK is analysed using the quarterly OECD Main Economic Indicators data for 1970–91, it can be seen that the greatest change in employment with respect to output took place in the USA, followed by the UK, while the speed at which this adjustment took place was also the fastest in the USA (Higuchi 1996). Here, adjustment to an optimum level was completed in about one year, while Japan needed 1.6 years and the UK 2.4 years.

When expressed in terms of total man-hours instead of the number of workers, the scale of employment adjustment in all countries shows an increase in both the speed as well as the amount of adjustment required to respond to the change in production volume. Japan has the highest rate of increase. Even if the adjustment is small during the process of change, the personnel cost cannot be called inflexible when the wage adjustment is massive.

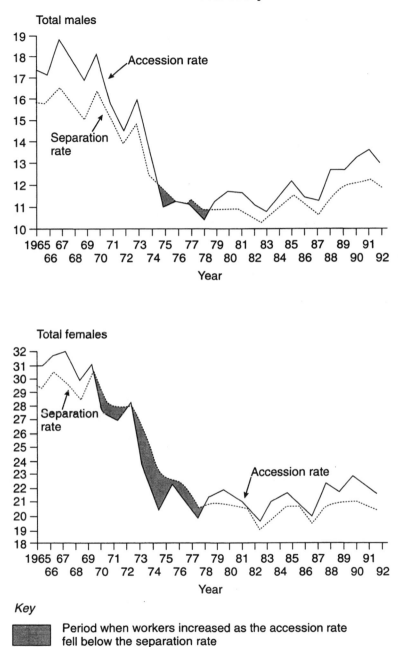

Figure 1.3 Time-series transition of job accession and separation rates of regular workers

Source: Ministry of Labour (various years) *Koyo Doko Chosa* (*Survey on Employment Trends*)

Was the wage adjustment really as large as expected? Figure 1.4 shows the rate of change in the total wage earned per regular worker and the rate of bonus and overtime allowance received. In this figure, the total gross wage greatly reflects the business situation. The rate of wage increase was high during the 1988–90 period when business was better, but this rate dropped in 1985–87 and 1992–93 when business was in recession.

The breakdown of the change in total gross wage shows that the rate of increase of the prescribed basic wage is relatively stable, and the change in the total wage earned is brought about mainly by the changes in bonus and overtime allowances. Overtime allowance is naturally changed according to the length of overtime worked and it is reduced during a period of recession when overtime is curtailed. On the other hand, the bonus reflects the performance of the firm and the assessment of each individual's achievement.

When discussing wage flexibility, the conclusion will differ depending on whether the per capita wage or the hourly wage is considered. As the per capita wage includes the change in overtime allowance and bonus, it varies greatly. On the other hand, with the hourly wage rate, the effect of changes in overtime allowance is offset and the rate of change in the wage is reduced. Table 1.4 shows the standard deviation and mean value of the rate of change in wage compared to the previous year in the manufacturing industry in Japan, the USA and the UK for 1970–91. During this period, working hours were increasing in the USA and, compared to the total per capita wage, the average rate of increase in the hourly wage was small. By contrast, the average increase in the hourly wage rate was higher than the increase in per capita wage in Japan and the UK because

Table 1.4   A comparison of the rates of change in wage increases compared to previous year in Japan, the USA and the UK manufacturing industry (1970–91)

	Japan % (SD)	USA % (SD)	UK % (SD)
Per capita nominal wage	8.37 (6.89)	6.04 (2.87)	12.23 (4.92)
Nominal hourly wage	8.86 (8.16)	5.94 (2.77)	12.38 (5.59)
Per capita real wage (deflator = producer price index)	5.03 (5.21)	0.46 (4.49)	2.18 (3.99)
Per capita real wage (deflator = consumer price index)	2.72 (3.30)	–0.10 (2.95)	2.10 (2.91)
Real hourly wage rate (deflator = producer price index)	5.46 (5.75)	0.33 (3.83)	2.28 (3.95)
Real hourly wage rate (deflator = consumer price index)	3.13 (3.93)	–0.22 (2.01)	2.22 (3.08)

Source: OECD (1970–91)

Note: SD = Standard Deviation.

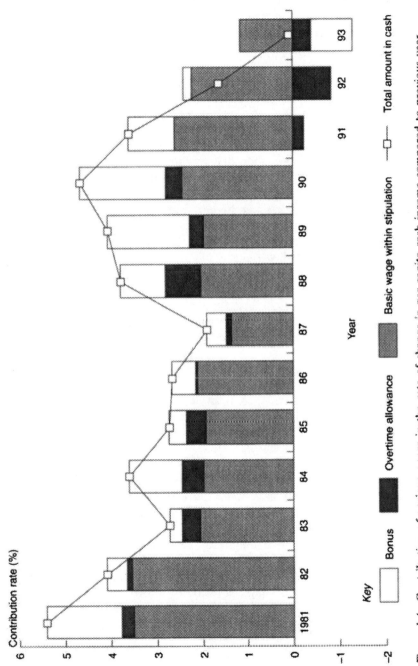

Figure 1.4 Contribution of various wages in the rate of change in per capita cash income compared to previous year

Source: Ministry of Labour (various years) *Maigetsu Kinro Tokei Chosa (Monthly Labour Survey)*

of the shortening of working hours. When we observe the standard deviation, we find that compared to the USA and the UK, the standard deviation of the change in the hourly wage rate is much higher in Japan.

In comparing wage flexibility, another important point that has to be taken into consideration is whether this discussion should be based on the nominal or real wage. In basing the discussion on the real wage, the selection of a price deflator also becomes important. Of the three countries under consideration, the rise in the nominal wage is the highest in the UK where the inflation rate is also high. So the rate of increase in the real wage in the UK is lower than that in Japan. In the USA, hardly any rise in the real wage can be observed over the past 20 years.

In all three countries (Japan, the USA and the UK) the increase in the consumer price index is much higher than the producer price index. This is why, when compared to the increase in real wage deflated by consumer price, the increase in real wage deflated by producer price is high. The difference between them is particularly great in Japan, where the consumer price is much higher than the producer price.

From the workers' perspective, an increase in real wage deflated by the consumer price means a rise in their standard of living. On the other hand, viewed from the perspective of employers in the manufacturing industries, a rise in real wages deflated by the producer price means a relative increase in the personnel cost relative to the producer price. The fact that the latter is far greater than the former means that the firms feel they are under great pressure with regard to personnel costs, while the workers do not find any improvement in their lifestyle.

The difference between the consumer price and the producer price is generated by the distribution margin and service fee involved. This means that the distribution margin increased greatly in Japan, that is, the producer price was low as a result of international competition, while the rate of price increase of the domestic industry, protected by government regulation, was high. This is a major reason why it was necessary for manufacturing industries to ask for relaxation of government control (deregulation).

The above description is a long-term view of the way wage change occurs. Let us now look at what differences might exist between these countries in terms of variances in wage caused by short-term fluctuations in business. An analysis of wage adjustment shows that, in Japan, the USA and the UK, the effect of the output level on the nominal hourly wage rate is the largest in Japan, and a statistically significant result is observed in the USA and the UK.[3] On the other hand, the speed of adjustment is different for the three countries depending on the types of variables used, but no distinct difference is confirmed.

Employment adjustment and wage adjustment in these countries greatly influence the change in labour's relative share of total added value. In the countries with a speedy adjustment, business becomes depressed and when output is reduced, employment is also reduced, with wage increases being restricted. So the labour share in total income is changed little. On the other hand, delayed adjustment will maintain the previous wage and employment despite the reduction in output. The labour income share is thus raised during a depressed business period. In America, labour income share is stable regardless of business conditions, while in Japan it reflects the delay in the employment adjustment and is much raised in a period of business recession.

EMPLOYMENT ADJUSTMENT IN THE SPINNING INDUSTRY

Employment adjustment to short-term shocks in the business cycle was slow in Japan, but let us see how it was working to cope with the long-term structural changes in the industrial environment. The exchange rate of the US dollar was 250 yen in 1985, but it came down to less than 100 yen in 1994. The higher yen value lowered the competitive power of Japanese products, and exports were hampered while imports increased. Furthermore, higher productivity in the Asian countries threatened the superiority of Japanese products, and greatly affected the activities of Japanese firms.

Under such a business environment, industrial output declined, while employment in the service industries, domestic industries (such as those industries handling imported products or raw materials), was expanding. As a result, even when supply and demand were balanced in the labour market of the country as a whole, great changes were seen in the industrial structure and personnel policy of each firm. A closer examination of the influence of the higher value of the yen on production in Japanese industries follows. This section examines the Japanese spinning industry, a telling example of Japanese employment adjustment mechanisms at work in the face of declining product demand in the long term, due to a rise in international competition. While the Japanese spinning industry prospered in the early 1960s to a degree that threatened American industry, it entered a period of rapid decline in demand in the 1970s (see Dore 1986). This was due largely to its peculiar labour management philosophy, referred to as *shizengen* (natural wastage) which opposes layoffs and waits for workers to initiate separation, thus avoiding labour disputes.

According to Werner International Managing Consultants (Japanese Spinners' Association 1993b), the hourly wage rate in the Japanese Spinning Industry as of 1993 (including the total direct cost, various allowances and expenses, converted at the applicable exchange rate) is 67 times higher than that of China, the largest exporter to Japan; 56 times higher than Indonesia, 53 times higher than Pakistan, 42 times higher than India and 6.5 times higher than Korea. Japanese labour costs are

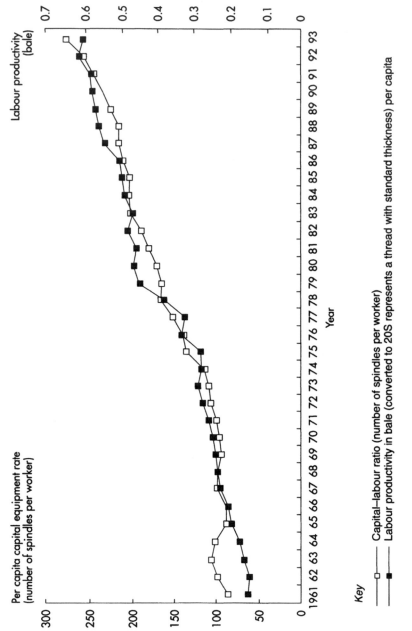

Figure 1.5 Transition of labour productivity and per capita capital equipment rate in the spinning industry

Source: Japanese Spinners' Association (various years) *Boseki Jijo Sankosho (Statistics on the Japanese Spinning Industry)*

2.3 times higher than that of the UK, 2.0 times higher than the USA and 1.4 times higher than France, all of which are industrialised countries. Naturally there are differences in the quality of products and labour-productivity among the countries – hence the difference in hourly wage rate does not directly lead to a difference in production costs. However, the higher labour cost in Japan is clearly a big threat to the international competitive power of Japanese products.

By improving labour productivity through equipment investment or shutdown of less efficient plants, the Japanese spinning industry has been making efforts for many years to reduce the difference in labour costs. Figure 1.5 shows the transition of labour productivity and per capita capital equipment rate in the spinning industry. In the 1961–93 period, the capital equipment rate increased 3.2 times, and labour productivity went up 4.1 times, but even then, Japanese spinning products were losing their superiority.

Figure 1.6 shows the transition in domestic demand for both imported and exported cotton products. Domestic demand increased with the growth of the economy, but it did not lead to an increase in the demand for domestic products. Rather it led to an increase in imported products. Against the increase in demand, domestic output decreased substantially,

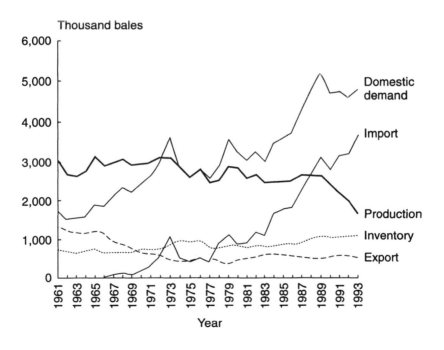

Figure 1.6 Transition of supply and demand of cotton products

Note: 1 bale = 181.436 kilograms.

whereas the number of secondary products imported increased in a massive way. Up to 1966, exports were higher than imports, but by 1993 imports exceeded exports by 55.51 billion yen when 75.8 per cent of the domestic demand for cotton products was met by imported goods (Japanese Spinners' Association, 1993a).

On the other hand, Japanese industries were confronted by a stronger yen, and the ratio of local production to direct investment was higher. As to the overseas ventures of industries related to spinning, synthetic textiles and dyeing, 19 Japanese plants started operations overseas between 1965 and 1969. That number continues to increase. In the 1990–94 period 51 plants were established outside Japan. This move is clearly related to the rising yen, for within this period of the yen's continued steep rise the number of businesses that started production abroad increased sharply. Japanese spinning manufacturers based in Asia marketed 56.1 per cent of the products domestically and exported about 14.2 per cent to Japan. As these figures show, the amounts of reverse exports from Japanese manufacturers in Asian countries to Japan are increasing very rapidly.

As output has decreased and wages increase, labour demand in the spinning industry has dropped. Figure 1.7 shows the trend in the number of member plants and their employees of the Japanese Spinners' Association. There were 227 spinning plants in 1961, and these decreased to 88 plants as of June 1994. The number of industrial spinning workers decreased from 110,000 to 16,000 persons.

Let us now see what methods were adopted to reduce the workforce. The first was to stop supplementary appointments to replace retired workers. In the case of the spinning industry, there were many female workers and their retention rate was not high. As to male employees, high school graduates in 1989 accounted for a retention rate of 55.8 per cent after three years in all the industries. In the spinning industry, the rate was 57.5 per cent, a little higher than the ratio for all the industries (Ministry of Labour 1995, Japanese Spinners' Association 1993b). The total retention rate for females and males was 52.9 per cent after three years for all the industries, while in the spinning industry it was 42.7 per cent.[4] If the number of employees who quit is added to those retiring at the mandatory age limit, the separation rate shows a yearly increase.

Newly appointed employees decreased from about 20,000 in 1975 to 6,000 in 1993. Total employees decreased from 110,000 in 1975 to 36,000 in 1994. Female workers, who had the higher quitting rate, decreased particularly sharply, while the percentage of females in the total workforce decreased from 65 per cent to 50 per cent during this period. There was also a substantial increase in temporary workers, from 8.1 per cent of the entire workforce in 1975 to 17.4 per cent in 1994.

When the closure of a plant became unavoidable and the decrease by 'natural wastage' (*shizengen*) was no longer sufficient, employees were

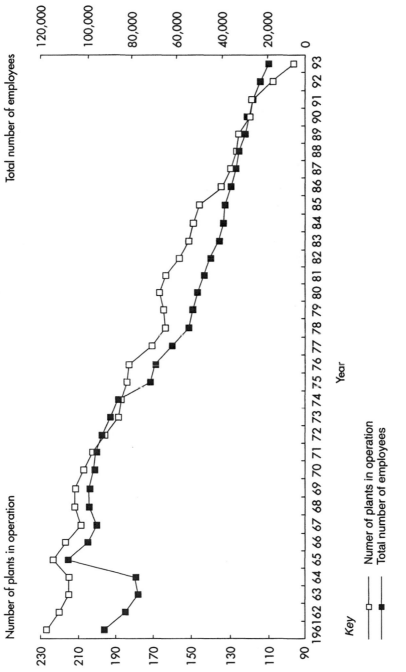

Figure 1.7 Number of operational plants and production workers in the Japanese spinning industry

Source: Japanese Spinners' Association (various years) *Boseki Jijo Sankosho (Statistics on the Japanese Spinning Industry)*

asked to consider reallocation to other workplaces. The spinning industry advanced into new areas once the spinning business began to decline. In March 1994, ten leading spinning companies had an average of 30 per cent of their sales in non-textile products. The industries tried to secure the employment of the workers by reallocating them to other or new sections. For those who did not wish to be transferred elsewhere, special measures were taken to place them in jobs in other industries or to pay higher retirement allowances to those who were retiring.

In the event of an unavoidable closure of a plant, the textile industry's union, Zensen, demanded in 1970 that a rationalisation plan be set out in a manual based on three principles. These were:

1. The establishment of a consultation process;
2. The prevention of a drop in working conditions; and
3. Security of job and training opportunities.

Firms have been making efforts to respond to these demands. Major labour disputes have so far been avoided, with the exception of strikes at Hokuyou Textile and the Sawing Machine Inspection Association in 1971 (Zensen 1975).

However, Japanese firms have begun to consider the dilemma of excess labour in the recent recession more seriously than they had done during the oil crises in the 1970s for the following reasons.

1. Inability to find growing industries, including tertiary industries, which will absorb their surplus workers.
2. Expectations of a natural decrease have been dashed because the number of female workers, who have a high quit rate, is already limited in the long process of employment adjustment.
3. An increase in the number of older workers who are less capable of adjusting their skills to a new occupation.

CHANGES IN THE FIRM ENVIRONMENT AND THE LABOUR MARKETS

The period of high economic growth in Japan ended with the first oil crisis in 1973, after which the growth rate fell remarkably. The real GNP grew at an annual rate of 9 per cent during 1960–65 and at 11 per cent during 1965–70. However, the growth rate declined to 4.5 per cent in the period 1970–75 which was repeated in the period 1975–80, 3.8 per cent in 1980–85 and 3.5 per cent in 1985–93. This stagnation in economic growth also greatly affected labour practices within Japanese firms. While the 1970s employment adjustment was mainly for blue-collar workers in manufacturing industries, the 1990s adjustment has been for white-collar workers, including management-level employees and those in tertiary industries (see Ministry of Labour 1995).

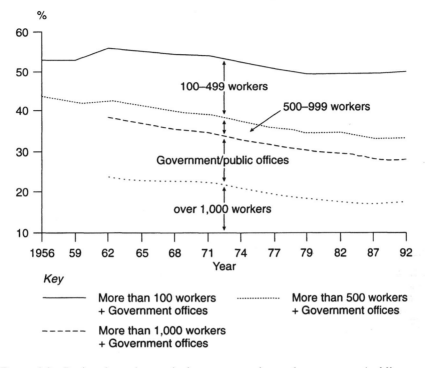

Figure 1.8 Ratio of employees in large companies and government/public agencies

Source: Management and Coordination Agency (various years) *Shugyo Kozo Kihon Chosa (Employment Status Survey)*

The decline in economic growth rate resulted in reduced job opportunity. Figure 1.8, which shows the number of employees according to the scale of the firm, clearly indicates that the rate of employment in large firms is reduced. According to Koshiro (1995), the number of employees working in the firms listed in the first section of the Tokyo stock market fell from 11 per cent in 1970 to 7 per cent in 1993.

Such a decrease in job opportunities resulted in a lower separation rate for the regular workers compared to the period before the oil crises, as seen in Figure 1.3. Despite an increase in the rate of young workers aspiring to change jobs, the 'preferred' job openings were scarce. Thus, the rate of actual job changers decreased because the rise in the job change rate of young workers was overtaken by the large decline in that of middle-aged and older workers.

The determination of Japanese firms to continue to maintain security of employment for regular workers once they have entered the firm was strong even after the growth rate declined. Large firms transferred their

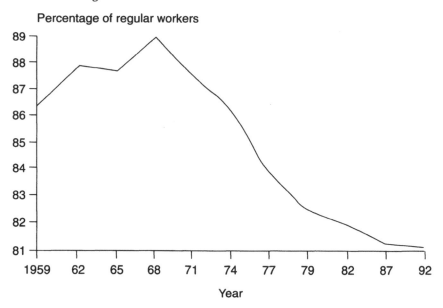

Figure 1.9   The percentage of regular employees in the total workforce

Source: Management and Coordination Agency (various years) *Shugyo Kozo Kihon Chosa* (*Employment Status Survey*)

surplus workers to affiliated firms, and thereby maintained job security within the group of firms. On the other hand, with regard to hiring, firms restricted the appointment of regular workers to avoid inflexibility of personnel cost. To cope with increased demands caused by business recovery, temporary workers were hired for whom the question of long-term employment did not arise. This temporary workforce included blue-collar workers, part-timers and employees contracted to work for limited periods.[5]

Figure 1.9 shows that the proportion of regular workers in the total workforce began to decrease recently. To avoid inflexibility of personnel cost, firms are moving away from trying to produce internally the products which can be subcontracted to outsiders and towards getting them produced outside Japan.

In the period from 1977 to 1992, the total number of employees in all the industries increased only 1.23 times, whereas workers serving subcontractors increased 2.60 times (Management and Coordination Agency 1977, 1992). Such a move is also visible in Figure 1.8, which shows a lower ratio of employees in large firms.

Japanese firms wish both to maintain their international competitive power even though the yen exchange rate is high, and to maintain secu-

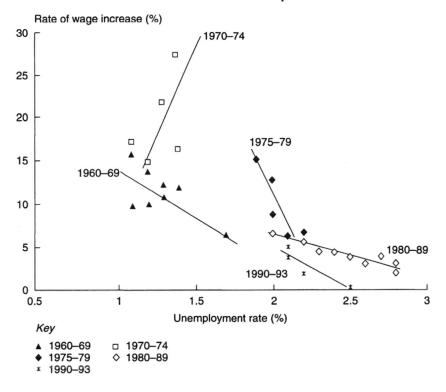

Figure 1.10 The Philips Curve in Japan

Source: Unemployment: Statistics Bureau, Management and Coordination Agency (various years) *Rodoryoku Chosa (Labour Force Survey)*. Wages: Ministry of Labour (various years) *Maigetsu Kinro Tokei Chosa (Monthly Labour Survey)*

rity of employment for their workers, and each aim is reflected in the wage level. Figure 1.10 shows the Philips Curve in Japan. The curve has shifted downwards in recent years, and it indicates a reduced rate of wage increase for the same rate of unemployment.

The business trend in Japan turned substantially brighter from 1987 until 1991, and the labour market was characterised by continuous labour shortage. However, at the spring labour offensive of recent years, management emphasis was placed on the higher wage in Japan compared to other countries when evaluated in terms of the existing exchange rate. Following the reasoning that a higher wage would weaken the international competitiveness of Japanese firms and would affect job security, a compromise was reached by setting a lower rate of wage increase.

In recent years, it has been noticed that decisions on wage levels are greatly influenced not only by the supply and demand situation in domestic labour markets but also by competition from foreign countries. As a result, the Philips Curve has moved downward recently.

In the changing environment of Japanese firms, another factor that influences a firm's employment policy is the ageing population. Under the seniority wage system, the increase in the number of old people means a higher wage on average. If the wage is decided by the annual performance of each worker, the increase of old people would not add to the problem of the firms. However, as shown by Lazear (1979) and Chuma and Higuchi (1995), if the delayed payment wage system were to be adopted, further increases in personnel costs would occur with the growth in the number of older people due to the need for training and higher monitoring costs. This is because they are being paid a higher wage than they would have been paid if based on their individual current productivity, even though an overall wage matching their performance would be paid over their working life.

In this situation, firms have several options. Of these, Japanese firms most commonly suppress personnel costs either by reducing the number of older employees by encouraging voluntary early retirement, or reducing the wage of older employees by relaxing the slope of the age–wage profile. Figure 1.11 shows the wage profile by age in 1977 and 1992. It indicates that, in particular, university graduates were given less pay increases as they became older in 1992 than in 1977.

CONCLUSION

The speed of employment adjustment to short-term changes in the business cycle by Japanese firms is slow because of the emphasis placed on employees' job security. The speed of wage adjustment is not high either. The wage rate is increased even in a period of business recession.

Firms had adopted a policy of not laying off their regular workforce by setting age limits for retirement or by getting employees to leave voluntarily during prolonged periods of stagnation in demand resulting from structural changes in industries. In the labour market as a whole, the separation rate of both males and females in Japan was not as low as in Germany. Moreover, as the age limit was set at a lower level, there was a natural decrease in the number of personnel employed. When this was not sufficient, efforts were made to transfer jobs smoothly through discussions held in advance between the labour force and management. As long as the economy grew, there were some industries that had enough scope to absorb the surplus personnel of other industries. In this case, with the cooperation of the firms, smooth job transfers were possible.

At present, the major problems in Japan are the lower growth rate, the higher yen value and the increasing age of the population. These issues also affect the employment policy of Japanese firms. With lower economic growth, the main regular employees can expect to continue to enjoy the long-term employment relations that had always occurred in the past,

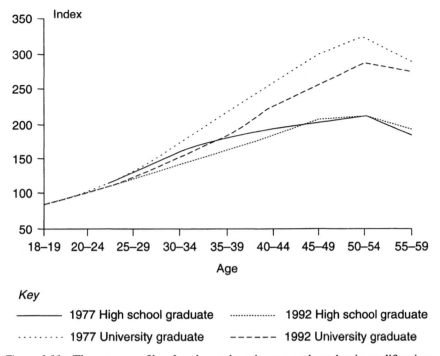

Figure 1.11 The wage profile of male workers by age and academic qualification

Source: Ministry of Labour (various years) *Chingin Kozo Kihon Chosa* (*Basic Survey of Wage Structure*)

Note: Salary for 20–24-year-old is indexed at 100

while the workers preferring short-term employment are being increased, with outside workers or subcontractors being utilised more and more to tackle the situation. As a result, the inside labour market shows greater long-term job tenure than before, but, on the other hand, the number of workers in such a labour market is decreasing. The higher yen value is also putting a brake on wage rises as are the increase in the older population and the reduction in the wage profile slope.

Following the recent drop in the birth rate in Japan, it is estimated that the younger population will dramatically decrease from now onwards, resulting in an anticipated reduction in labour supply. According to the Employment Policy Division of the Ministry of Labour statistics, the working population of 63.84 million will increase to 66.97 million by the year 2000, reflecting a reduced rate of growth. Such a decline in the growth of the working population will have an enormous impact on the employment practices of Japanese firms.

Many females and older people have so far been regarded as supplementary workers, and have not been considered as suitable candidates for long-term employment. A further decrease in the working population will bring about a serious problem for firms as to how to take on people from these groups regardless of sex or age. In the 1987–91 period of booming business, the decrease in the working population was a great concern. Many firms had established childcare programmes in order to attract or retain talented women employees.

Childcare programmes were legalised in 1991, due to an increased social demand for a higher birth rate. For the elderly, the retirement age had been raised. Many firms had introduced long-term or extended employment programmes and programmes of re-employment for those past retirement age. It was at that point that business entered into a recession and the move to employ surplus workers changed. The predicted decline in the future labour supply has been forgotten by firms and even now, the younger population can be seen to be decreasing steadily.

In the late 1990s, labour demand may decrease in Japanese firms because of tough international competition and an increase in foreign investment relative to domestic investment. In the early twenty-first century, however, since labour supply is predicted to decline because of a reduction in the number of young people and an increase in the number of elderly people, Japanese firms are likely to face a labour shortage. The need for capable and creative employees will rise, in order for Japanese firms to maintain competitiveness. It will be more important for Japanese firms not only to maintain work incentives for current employees, but also to enlarge the skills of employees who have not been considered core workers up to now. Japanese firms must maintain their current system of job security, for dissolution of this system will mean the elimination of worker motivation. However, Japanese firms must adjust their wage structures so as to make the most of workers' abilities. In short, Japanese firms are likely to find it necessary to change to a system of wage based on merit if they are to counter the difficulties brought on by an ageing society. In conclusion, the continuation of the incentive structure provided by job security must be supplemented by additional worker incentives in the form of merit pay.

NOTES

1 According to the 1993 Survey on Employment Management by the Ministry of Labour, the retirement age limit is set at less than 59 years of age in 20 per cent of the firms with over 30 employees, at 60 years in 74 per cent of the firms, and at over 61 years in 6 per cent of the firms. The firms with a retirement age younger than 55 years was 52 per cent in 1974 which dropped to 9.7 per cent in 1993. The initiatives to delay retirement age to 60 years of age have increased over the last 20 years. But, on the other hand, the number of companies which introduced early retirement programme was increasing, in particular during recession.

2 According to the 1993 Yearbook of Labour Statistics published by the International Labour Organisation, the labour force participation rate for Japanese males of 60–64 years of age is 75.0 per cent compared with more

than 18.0 per cent in France, 35.0 per cent in Germany, 54.2 per cent in the UK and 55.1 per cent in the USA.
3 The wage adjustment function used for statistics can be expressed by the following formula with W as the wage, X as the output, and P as the price index.

$$W_t = a1 + a2X + a3P + (1 - \lambda) W_{t-1}$$

Where, 'λ' represents adjustments in speed.
The estimated values of λ when using the data of nominal wages per worker (the quarterly OECD Main Economic Indicators data for 1970–91) are 0.429 in Japan, 0.776 in the USA and 0.498 in the UK. Those using the data of the nomical hourly wage rates are 0.332, 0.534 and 0.501 respectively (Higuchi 1996).
4 Among the female workers employed in the spinning industries after graduation from middle and high school, there are also many workers living in dormitories, who are studying in high schools and junior colleges. Many such workers use their educational achievements to obtain employment in other industries. This results in a higher separation rate for the spinning industry than found in other industries, and is one of the reasons why the rate is so high in this particular sector.
5 In Japan, the definition of a part-time worker differs depending on statistics. Part-time workers might be defined as workers who work for less than 35 hours per week, they may be workers designated as "so-called" part-time workers by their firms, or they may be all the workers excluding the regular employees. Their working hours therefore could be the same as those of regular workers. There may be many part-time workers employed without a specified contract period. In Japan, an employment contract of over one year is not legally recognised and the period of such contract is restricted to less than one year. Accordingly, many part-time workers are included among the regular employees in Figure 1.9 without their period of work being clearly defined. See Chapter 5 for more details on part-time workers.

REFERENCES

Chuma, H. and Higuchi, Y. (1995) 'Keizai kankyo no henka to choki koyo shisutemu' ('Changes in the economic environment and Japanese employment system'), in T. Inoki and Y. Higuchi (eds) *Nihon no Koyo Shisutemu to Rodo Shijo* (*The Japanese Employment System and Labour Market*), Tokyo: Nihon Keizai Shinbunsha.
Department of Employment (1979) *New Earnings Survey*, London: Department of Employment.
Dore, R. (1986) *Flexible Rigidities: Industrial Policy and Structural Adjustment in the Japanese Economy 1970–80*, Stanford: Stanford University Press.
Hashimoto, M. and Raisian, J. (1985) 'Employment, tenure and earnings profiles in Japan and the United States', *American Economic Review*, 75(4), pp. 721–35.
Higuchi, Y. (1996) *Rodo Keizaigaku* (Labour Economics), Tokyo: Toyo Keizai Shinposha.
Japanese Spinners' Association (1993a) *Boseki Jijo Sankosho* (*Statistics on the Japanese Spinning Industry*), Osaka: Japanese Spinners' Association.
—— (1993b) *Monthly Report of the Japanese Spinning Industry* (July), Osaka: Japanese Spinners' Association.
Koshiro, K. (1995) *Roshi Kankei Hakusho* (*White Paper on Industrial Relations*), Ch. 1, Tokyo: Japan Productivity Center for Socio-Economic Development.
Lazear, E.P. (1979) 'Why is there mandatory retirement?' *Journal of Political Economy*, 87(6), pp. 1261–84.

Management and Coordination Agency (1956–1992) *Shugyo Kozo Kihon Chosa (Employment Status Survey)*, Tokyo: Management and Coordination Agency.
Mincer, J. and Higuchi, Y. (1988) 'Wage structure and labour turnover in the United States and Japan', *Journal of Japanese and International Economies*, 2(2), pp. 97–133.
Ministry of Labour (1976/80) *Chingin Kozo Kihon Chosa (Basic Survey of Wage Structure)*, Tokyo: MOL.
—— (1980) *Chingin Kozo Kihon Chosa (Basic Survey of Wage Structure)*, Tokyo: MOL.
—— (1995) *Rodo Hakusho (Labour White Paper)*, Tokyo: MOL
—— (various years) *Rodo Keizai Doko Chosa (Survey on Labour Economic Trends)*, Tokyo: MOL.
—— (various years) *Koyo Doko Chosa (Survey on Employment Trends)*, Tokyo: MOL.
—— (various years) *Maigetsu Kinro Tokei Chosa (Monthly Labour Survey)*, Tokyo: MOL.
Organisation for Economic Cooperation and Development (1970–1991) *Main Economic Indicators*, Paris: OECD.
—— (1993) *Employment Outlook*, Chart 4.6, Paris: OECD.
Statistical Office of the European Communities (1972) *Structure of Earnings in Industry*, Brussels: Office for Official Publications of the European Communities.
Zensen (1975) *Zensen Domeishi (History of Zensen)*, Vol. 6, Tokyo: Zensen.

2 Labour law issues in a changing labour market

In search of a new support system

Kazuo Sugeno and Yasuo Suwa

A PROFILE OF JAPANESE LABOUR LAW AND THE MOVEMENT FOR ITS REFORM

Labour law systems of industrialised countries developed in response to the challenges presented by a new socio-economic environment that resulted from two shifts: one from an agricultural to an industrial society, and the other from small-scale factories to large-scale machinery-operated manufacturing plants. Japan received and developed such systems before and after World War II.

Before the war, learning mainly from British factory legislation, Japan enacted the Factory Law in 1911 to protect minors and women from excessive labour and to establish some of the essential labour standards such as compensation for industrial accidents and occupational diseases. The state labour inspection system was established to enforce these standards. The government also ratified the ILO (International Labour Organisation) Convention No. 2, and the Employment Exchange Law of 1920 established public employment offices while banning private labour placement businesses.

After the war, as a means of full-scale democratisation of Japanese society under the American Occupation, post-war labour legislation was passed which laid the foundation for the contemporary labour law systems in Japan. The first measure to emerge was the Trade Union Law of 1945, which spelled out the legal exemption of trade unions and their members from criminal and civil liabilities as expressed in the British trade union legislation, set forth the legal effects of collective agreements as defined in the German collective agreement law, and established the Labour Relations Commission composed of neutral, labour and management members. The Commission was endowed the jurisdiction to mediate over labour disputes by the Labour Relations Adjustment Law of 1946 and to adjudicate on employers' unfair labour practices by the 1949 amendment of the Trade Union Law in line with the American Wagner Act of 1935. As regards the standards of employment relations, the Labour Standards Law of 1947, with its comprehensive coverage, established basic rules for employment contracts and statutory standards for working conditions, utilising the pre-war experiences and taking the ILO standards into full consideration. With regard to the employment exchange, the Employment

Security Law of 1947 re-established a network of public employment offices and reinforced the regulation of private employment placement services to prevent worker exploitation in the process of labour exchanges. The Labour Ministry was established by the 1946 law to promote labour administration in the country.

The half century of development in labour law in post-war Japan was structured by the above mentioned legislation. This development can be divided by the 1973 oil shock which had a profound impact on Japanese economic systems. Development before the oil crisis is characterised by an improvement in labour standards resulting from the enactment of the Minimum Wage Law of 1959 and the Occupational Safety and Hygiene Law of 1972, together with the frequent revisions of the Workers' Accident Insurance Law of 1947. Along with such statutory development, the court created a body of case law which established significant rules for union–management relations which gave rise to many difficult legal issues in the process of its maturation. The court in particular clarified the conditions for legal strikes, picketing and lock-outs and contributed to the stabilisation of industrial relations. Case law also cultivated the rules for protecting workers from abusive use of personnel management prerogatives exercised in dismissals, disciplinary actions, transfers and changes in working conditions.

The post-oil crisis development is portrayed, on the other hand, by legislation embodying the government's active employment policy to assist firms to carry out reorganisation and restructuring with the least threat to employment. The most notable measure was the enactment of the Employment Insurance Law of 1974 which set up the system to provide subsidies from the employment insurance fund. Using the employment insurance fund as a major resource, many statutes followed to assist structurally depressed industries and regions with programmes aimed at the preservation and creation of employment. This period is also marked by the legislation to cope with the new worker demands in the labour market, such as the Equal Employment Opportunity Law of 1985 to enhance the status of the rapidly increasing number of female workers and to meet the pressure of international feminism; the Employment Stability Law for Older Workers of 1986 to promote employment of older workers who continue to participate but are disadvantaged in the labour market; and the 1987 amendment of the Labour Standards Law to promote the reduction of the internationally criticised long working hours found in Japanese enterprises.

The above is a historical profile of Japanese labour law. As can be seen, it maintains the conventional systems and ideas common to industrialised countries despite its newly added original features. However, this conventional labour law is challenged in the context of socio-economic transformations commonly taking place in post-industrial societies. Awareness of such trends has spread among academics and industrial relations (specialists) in Japan, as demonstrated by the fact that the reform of various aspects of labour law is discussed by the major advisory councils and study groups in the government (for example, the Central Employment Security Council, the Central Labour Standards Council, the Women and Minors Council and the Labour Standards Study Group) as well as at academic conferences (such as the recent semi-annual conferences of the Japan Labour Law Association). Yet the guiding, fundamental principles that should lead to the formation of new labour law have not been genuinely investigated. As a part of the legal system which supports the market economy, labour law contributes to the structuring of the market economy framework by engineering the labour market systems. With this fundamental understanding, this chapter aims at re-evaluating the functions of conventional labour law and seeks to comprehend the concepts and principles of labour law to be instituted in the next decade of Japanese society.

CHANGES IN THE JAPANESE EMPLOYMENT SYSTEM

Changes in the environment

The core mechanisms of the Japanese labour market are: (1) an employment relationship from the time of hire at a young age, ending at retirement at the in-firm retirement age with mutual commitment to continuous employment throughout the period; (2) a system which involves the long-term and systematic cultivation and deployment of human resources under an encompassing management right to personnel deployment; (3) a system which uses length of service and age as crucial standards for wages and other employee treatment; and (4) enterprise unionism, in which long-term employees of the single enterprise combine themselves with their common fate and promote the cooperative relationship with management for the prosperity of the enterprise.

This 'Japanese employment system' evolved through the deliberate efforts of the industrial relations groups who sought to establish a system most suited to the social and economic environment in which Japan was situated after the War. The system has worked well in these socio-economic conditions. At present, however, amidst the trends of socio-economic changes that are underway, it has become apparent that the employment system needs reforms to suit its new environment (e.g. the White Paper on Labour 1993, pp. 97; the White Paper on Labour 1994, pp. 100; the White Paper on Economy 1994, pp. 322).

This new environment can be summarised in the following ways:

(1) Japanese industries had long enjoyed a position in the global marketplace of a late-developer, where they could easily expand exports by taking advantage of lower personnel costs and utilising technologies already developed. However, this 'catching up' position has now ceased

as a result of the maturation of industry, and the intensification of global competition caused both by the rapid industrialisation of the Asian countries and resurgence of American industries. Japanese export industries have become 'front-runner' in the expansive global market and are required to exert creativity and originality in technology and product development. Their position, as a consequence, has become vulnerable to fluctuations in the international economy such as the appreciation of the yen and a world-wide recession.

(2) The labour force which has kept expanding for half a century is now evolving towards a structural reduction due to a radical decline in fertility. A significant decrease and shortage of younger workers in particular is anticipated, while there is a growing proportion of older workers in the labour market resulting from the rapid ageing of the population. On the other hand, the structure and the nature of industries have been changing and are expected to change more rapidly to accommodate the globalised and service oriented economy. Instead of relying on quantity of labour for massive, uniform production and services, enterprises are increasingly required to depend on quality of labour and the ability to use information for presenting high added value and diverse products and services in the market. Table 2.1 shows the trends of workforce population.

Changes in the labour market

In response to the new economic surroundings mentioned above, the labour market is expected to undergo the several changes. The most significant foreseeable change is the diminution and dilution of long-term employment and an increase in labour mobility. Both labour and management maintain a deep attachment to the long-term employment system with its merits in stable employment and efficient human resource development. The system will therefore remain intact for quite a while with its strong inertia although it is likely to undergo significant modification.[1] However, multinational enterprises are likely to seek more

Table 2.1 Trends in the working population (millions)

	1990	*2000*	*2010*
Total workforce population (15 years or older)	63.84	67.79	66.03
Younger workforce (15–29 years old)	14.75	15.56	11.90
	(23.1%)	(23.0%)	(18.0%)
Middle-aged workforce (30–54 years old)	36.17	36.64	36.25
	(56.9%)	(54.0%)	(54.9%)
Older workforce (55 years or older)	12.92	15.59	17.88
	(20.2%)	(23.0%)	(27.1%)

Source: Projection made by the Ministry of Labour 1994 (official but unpublished)

internationally viable employment and human resource systems to attract talented professionals and enhance productivity. Furthermore, as a macro-environmental factor, elements that will stimulate evolution of the employment system, such as inevitable alterations in industrial structure, structural decrease in the labour force (particularly young workers), and individualistic trends in worker attitudes, will increase in influence.

In the medium to long term, workers at the core of enterprise management will relatively decrease in number, and the labour turnover rate will rise with the increase in job changes and mid-career hirings. In the future, management will have greater discretion in discarding redundant workers; talented workers will enjoy a greater freedom of choice. Yet one of the dilemmas management will face in decreased mutual attachment will be the disincentive for investment in education and training for the cultivation of human resources. Many firms will therefore try to maintain a long-term commitment for core employees in their real sense in order to secure quality personnel in key positions.

Another significant trend already taking place is the shift from seniority-based to merit-based treatment. The Japanese seniority system, based on long-term employment, has always dealt with similar workers in more or less the same way with respect to job assignment, remuneration and promotion, and has treated workers (particularly men with families) in accordance with their life cycles. This system of treatment is now under-going even greater change than that affecting the long-term relationship itself.[2] Already in many enterprises, individual workers are treated, to a significant extent, in accordance with their volition and ability as reflected in the short term. The remuneration and career systems are increasingly incorporated with job responsibilities and performance evaluation, partic-ularly for managerial and professional employees.

For such an ability-based system to function effectively, a more indi-vidualised form of management and a subsequent strengthening of the concept and function of the individual contract is necessary. The system also requires the liberalisation of working time management since the traditional yardstick of the quantity of working time has been replaced by new performance and achievement criteria. Mechanisms to assure fair-ness in performance evaluation and equality of opportunity will be required, while the smooth processing of grievances arising in such eval-uation schemes will become imperative. Furthermore, skill development will be more individually initiated than the conventional dependence on company oriented education and training.

The obvious change that is also occurring is diversification in working styles. The generalist male full-time worker is no longer the only prevailing working form. Increasingly various employment forms coexist with flex-ible working patterns among women, and younger and older workers. Such a trend is increasing the number of workers in disadvantageous positions although it has the merit of expanding their employment opportunities. Enterprises will further enhance diversity in working styles to effectively utilise new sources of labour, that is, younger, female or older workers. To manage the increasingly diversified types of workers, the conventional collective and uniform employment contract will also have to be diversified and individualised.

The fourth major change is the reorganisation of the enterprise structure from a pyramid society type to a horizontal networking type. The growing importance of information as well as the development of information systems, computerisation of offices and plants, and increasingly high levels of education among the labour force are inducing the enterprise organisation to shift from the traditional pyramid structure with multi-layered middle management towards a network-type structure in which workers in professional functions cooperate in a flexible way with upper echelons of management. Firms are thereby reducing the time and cost involved in management decisions and creating an institutional structure that can respond quickly to environmental changes. Running parallel to this organisational change is the increasing emphasis on professional employees with cross-firm expertise rather than the generalist type of managerial employees with firm-confined skills. The conventional career and wage system which orientated every employee to climb up the managerial ladder needs to be more diversified and specialised in order to motivate talented professionals.

THE LABOUR MARKET AND THE LAW

The market and the law

Legal structures provide a framework for socio-economic systems and establish procedural and substantial rules for their operation. If the socio-economic systems which provide the basis for legal structures undergo changes, it is inevitable that the legal structures will evolve accordingly.

The market economy entrusts the supply and demand forces to facilitate business interaction, and allows them to determine the value of commodities or services. It is based upon the idea that such mechanisms for determining market value are more efficient and reliable than manipulative methods of price determination. The market economy brings its attributes into full play when it enables individuals through their ingenuity to engage in free exchanges in the marketplace. However, when unjust means such as fraud or violence are utilised, market mechanisms are disrupted. When black market economics or rule violations run rampant, not only is the market impeded from functioning properly, but also private citizens are adversely affected. The market economy should not only be an unrestricted arena for interaction or a means of attaining short-term goals. For it to be effective and to produce beneficial results in the long run, it needs the appropriate infrastructure for its fine-tuning.

As in other democratic market economies, the law in Japan systematises the political and social premises of the market mechanism through guaranteeing individual freedom and rights, instituting a democratic political structure, and maintaining the systems for peace and order. It also establishes market rules through the civil code, commercial law, corporate law, anti-trust law and intellectual property law, enabling the market mechanisms to manifest their merits while suppressing the demerits. In this light, the history of contemporary law has been the accumulation of various intertwined regulations to assure that the framework of the core marketplace would be preserved and its implementation undisrupted. This is particularly so with regard to those 'market failures' that could not be remedied if left to the market alone – public policies have been pursued to provide supplementary systems. Important aspects of education, medical care, the environment, and social welfare have been dealt with through such public policies.

The conventional labour market and labour law: the protection of workers as a collectivity

Labour law in industrialised countries originated in the latter half of the nineteenth and the beginning of the twentieth century and has developed into an important supplementary system to the market economy. It was social regulation which prevented 'the subordinate worker in market exchanges' from being sacrificed through the market mechanism. Traditional labour law regulated both the external labour market where the supply and demand forces make cross firm adjustments and the internal labour market where those forces operate within the firm.

In the external labour market, the major task of labour law was to set up public training institutions and to assist in-firm training programmes in order to enhance vocational skills (in Japan, the Vocational Ability Development Law of 1985), to offer public employment-exchange services to help workers obtain jobs while strictly regulating private intermediary businesses (the Employment Security Law of 1947), and to provide benefits to workers who have lost their jobs to mitigate hardship during their unemployment (the Employment Insurance Law of 1974).

Moreover, in the contractual dealings of terms and conditions of employment, workers were greatly disadvantaged by a labour surplus which has been a dominant feature of the labour market. Thus, in order to safeguard worker positions in labour market transactions, standards for terms and conditions of employment were established through legislation while the collective bargaining power of workers was ensured. In the former, the significant issues falling under regulation were wages, working time, dismissal, safety and health, and compensation for work-related injuries and diseases (the Labour Standards Law of 1947, the Minimum Wage Law of 1959, the Occupational Safety and Hygiene Law of 1972, the Workers' Accident Compensation Insurance Law of 1947, etc.). In the latter, the law guaranteed workers the right to organise and act collectively and set up the mechanism for resolving disputes involving workers' collective demands and actions. The law in many countries went further to institutionalise the process of collective bargaining or to give collective agreements a binding effect (in Japan, the Trade Union Law of 1949 and the Labour Dispute Adjustment Law of 1947).

There are of course significant cross-country variations in the regulation of the external labour market. One of the most conspicuous differences arises in the attitude towards the regulation of atypical employment. Japan does not restrict management's recourse to fixed term contracts as is done in France or Germany. The regulation of worker leasing businesses (temporary employment services) is also distinctive in the way that the law limits the use of leased workers for the enumerated special jobs as discussed later (the Worker Leasing Business Law of 1985).

As for the internal labour market, legal regulations also establish standards and rules to protect workers in various aspects of employee treatment such as hiring, job assignment, transfers, retirement and dismissals. A distinct characteristic of Japanese labour law in this area is that much of the regulation laid down by the labour legislation in Western Europe is attained by the practice of employment and industrial relations as well as case law reflecting such practice. For example, there is no statute in Japan requiring valid reasons for dismissals. But it is very difficult for management involved in long-term employment relations to resort to dismissals, either disciplinary or economic, and the court formulated strict requirements for dismissals in the form of case law. The government developed subsidy programmes to reinforce efforts to maintain jobs under such an employment system (the Employment Insurance Law of 1974, etc.). On the other hand, the court recognises ample management prerogatives to develop and deploy human resources in the internal labour market, while at the same time restricting their use being abused.

Furthermore, information sharing and joint consultation is developed for managerial decisions affecting employees in the internal labour market, however it is not institutionalised by law as in many European countries, but is administered by custom and practice. Joint consultation is not undertaken by the works councils organised separately from industrial unions but by enterprise unions that perform both collective bargaining and employee representation functions. Another feature of Japanese labour law is the gradual application of legal regulation to promote gender equality in the labour market as compared to the strong and comprehensive regulation in the USA or the European Community. The Equal Employment Opportunity Law of 1985 narrowly defines illegal discriminatory practices with no notion of indirect discrimination, and entrusts much of the regulation to the competent authority's administrative guidance.

Despite these characteristics, Japanese labour law shares basic ideas with Western labour law: the conceptualisation of labour relations as contractual relationships; recognition of workers' subordinate nature in those relations; imposition of legal rules and standards on contractual relationships; the organisation of the workers' collective voice in those relations.

Furthermore, in the field of social security, measures to secure the well-being of workers and other citizens were taken by the development of state pensions and other social insurance systems as well as national assistance and other welfare systems. In particular, the social insurance systems for workers were different from other welfare systems in the involvement of employers as joint or sole contributors. Even here, the protection of the weaker party was consistently implemented.

In this way, labour law implements social policy to compensate for market deficiencies. It also plays a significant role in the formation of economic policy through its influence upon the economy by the imposition of a framework on market functions. Such characteristics of labour law in the nineteenth to twentieth centuries led to its being referred to as 'social law'. In responding to market failures and protecting the weaker party, social law introduced public law regulation into the originally private labour relationship. In contrast to social law, private law had in mind relationships of equal standing among citizens when establishing a framework for private transactions. Labour law clearly manifested its public law character despite its fundamentally private law base when it instituted direct state intervention for the socio-economic policy of protecting the subordinate.

Environmental changes of labour law: the emergence of individual workers

Throughout the twentieth century, the role of labour law in improving workers' socio-economic status has been significant in industrialised nations. Shaped by social systems and socio-economic developments, the reality of the labour market mechanism has changed greatly in Japan as in many other developed economies. Workers' economic lives have improved due to economic development and income redistribution, and a more stable lifestyle has been attained through social security in times of unemployment, sickness, or old age. Diffusion of education and vocational training systems have improved workers' skills and abilities. Workers searching for employment are increasingly relying on job advertisements and private employment agencies rather than on public employment exchange services. Uneducated subordinate labourers who have no choice but to go along with their employers' exploitative domination have become fewer. In many countries, the notion of employment security has evolved resulting in greater restrictions in dismissals, and there have been remarkable improvements in wages, working time, health and safety, and other working conditions. Workers now have a strong voice in industrial relations and national politics at various levels through their organisations.

The changes described above in the socio-economic environment also appear as changes in the concept of work and worker image. The young male worker working on-site can no longer be said to be typical. Not only is there a decrease in manual workers and an increase in white-collar workers, but also the distinction of blue- and white-collar workers is blurred by the technological innovations and the expansion of service activities; workers engaging in professional, managerial and artistic activities are becoming more conspicuous. The economy is increasingly becoming 'soft', that is service-, information- and knowledge-oriented; individualised labour that relies upon creativity and originality is growing in importance. Such trends have created an era of higher levels of education and lifelong learning. Moreover, new working styles such as the various types of part-time and temporary work have spread, and further diversified the workforce. The prototype of employment relationships tackled by the original labour legislation has in many respects become obsolete.[3]

In the labour law perspective, a fundamental change to be focused upon is that workers who were regarded in the past as 'the absolutely weaker party' in the labour market have decreased in number, and those who are the 'relatively weaker party' or who 'should no longer be regarded as the weaker party' have become more conspicuous. In other words, as a result of socio-economic maturation, workers regulated by labour law have shifted from those who are suited to statutory, uniform and collective protection, the 'workers collectivity', to 'individual workers', who have individual talent and initiative and to whom voluntary regulation is suited. The appearance of 'individual workers' in the labour arena alters the basic premise of past labour law regulations.

Such an individualistic trend is more apparent in workers' attitudes towards unions and collective labour relations, which have been formed on the basis of the understanding that regulation of labour relations through worker coalition is the most desirable approach. As in many industrialised countries, union density is steadily declining in Japan. The organisation rate had been about 35 per cent in the 1960s but has fallen to about 24 per cent in recent years (Ministry of Labour, various years). A tendency to avoid coalition and collective regulation, despite the benefits these bring to the protection of their own interests, is becoming notably visible among the younger generation. Managerial, professional and service workers show a preference for more individualistic treatment based on ability and performance rather than conventional egalitarian treatment backed up by unions.

Many of the new type of individualistic workers are equipped with sufficient vocational ability to be assessed in the marketplace as an individual and are willing to bear the risks of making their own choices there. Although the quantity or proportion of this type of worker is yet to be empirically recognised, they are apparently increasing in number. It also seems that the labour force, in general, is gradually disseminating sympathy or conscious support for such workers. While a sector of workers will always remain the absolute weaker party in an employment relationship and will continue to need traditional collective protection, a new sector of workers who clearly request individual autonomy and choice will expand. The majority, at present, may be the sector of workers between the two extremes who require careful consideration for the delicate balance between collective protection and individual autonomy.

These changes seem to be taking place in most post-industrial societies. But the uniqueness of Japan as compared to Europe is that, even during the recent prolonged recession, Japan has been maintaining a comparatively lower level of unemployment resulting from the long-term employment system and the government's active employment policies (2.9 per cent on average during 1994, which gradually increased to 3.4 per cent at the end of 1995). Of course, with management carrying out rationalisation and reorganisation there is great concern for how to prevent massive unemployment in the process of large-scale industrial restructuring to adapt to the new global competition. The traditional protection of workers by labour law and trade unions is still very necessary in this context. However, the emergence of individual workers seems to have acquired more weight in labour policy discussions which are addressing how to adapt industry to the new competitive environment than in the society where the methods to combat existing structural unemployment dominate people's concern. Moreover, there seems to be a growing consensus that, even for the goal of revitalising industries without sacrificing employment, the reform of labour market systems for the utilisation of individual workers' talent and energy is vital.

The new goals of labour law

The socio-economic changes discussed above appear to necessitate significant modification of conventional labour law. The traditional role of labour law to protect the workers *en masse* as weaker parties in the market needs to be maintained, but given the diversification of workers in educational status, qualification, job type and job content, such regulations should be made more flexible and diverse to meet the needs of different types of workers. More fundamentally, a new body of legal systems should be developed for the support of individual workers who possess the vocational skills and talents and are prepared to trade on more beneficial terms in the market. Such support should aim at two major goals: (1) the reorganisation of labour market systems to improve their functions for individual workers; and (2) the reinforcement of individual workers' bargaining power.

The first goal for labour law is to introduce reforms for a more smoothly functioning labour market for individual workers. The Japanese labour market with its segmentation has been characterised by its the highly developed internal labour markets and underdeveloped external labour market systems. If exchange in the external labour market is not made easier, workers will continue to be confined in the internal labour market, and will be prevented from exercising their bargaining power. New public policies are needed for promoting job opportunities in the external labour market and for realising easier access to them through reliable information and exchange services.

As regards the internal market, the traditional aspects of employment systems that have been artificially impeding mobility in the external labour market need to be reformed.[4] Treatment in the internal labour market should be harmonised with opportunities in the external labour market. From this perspective, highly collective and uniform career and remuneration systems emphasising length of service and promotion in managerial ladders are already being replaced by more pluralistic systems placing more importance on workers' professional talent and choice. In terms of law, management prerogatives in personnel deployment have to be more and more restricted by concrete agreements in individual employment contracts.

As individual workers become more conscious of job changes, employers will become less positive in furthering in-firm education and training programmes and will increasingly seek necessary talents in the external labour market. Employees themselves will more often take up initiatives for enhancing their vocational skills through extra-firm education programmes. Thus, there will be a growing need for public policies to promote skill development opportunities for individual workers.

The second goal of expanding individual workers' freedom and opportunity requires the reinforcement of individual bargaining power. Despite the support of individual activities through the reorganisation of labour market systems and expansion of skill development opportunities, bargaining power will no doubt remain unequal between employers and workers. Unless changes are introduced the discrepancy in specialised knowledge and skill will continue to exist between the worker and the employer's bargaining representative, and the power of an employer as an institution will continue to overwhelm the power of workers as individuals. Furthermore, while it will be relatively easy for employers to receive specialised support from experts, workers will still experience difficulties in finding similar support structures. Consequently, any expansion of individual dealings will give rise to an increased number of grievances and disputes for which such support structures are needed.

The opportunity to organise labour unions should therefore be kept as a fundamental requirement of a democratic market economy. However, due to the diversification of working styles and worker attitudes and the difficulties in harmonising individual workers with the union's collective mentality, it is imperative to examine the propriety of public policy to formalise other systems to give efficient support in individual dealings and grievances.

ISSUES OF CHANGING LABOUR LAW

In response to the changes that confront it, labour law's future tasks include the reorganisation of conventional regulations which have become unsuitable for present conditions, and the creation of a new framework to meet the new demands for the support of individual workers. More concretely, the major issues are as follows.

Issues relating to the external labour market

With the development of internal labour markets in post-war industrial relations, labour law systems in Japan have been shaped by its distinctive features based upon the long-term employment system. As regards the underdeveloped external labour market, labour law did not go beyond establishing the basic framework of labour standards and social insurance systems together with strictly regulating labour exchange services. There have been few policy measures to vitalise the external labour market. Yet, the need for management to promote the restructuring of enterprise under the tougher business conditions calls for the external labour market to function better. From the worker perspective, the diversification and individualisation of working styles and personnel systems are generating the growing need for enhanced mobility across enterprises. From the viewpoint of strengthening the bargaining power of individual workers *vis-à-vis* their employers, employment opportunities with other employers must be available in terms of both quality and quantity. The scarcity of favourable job change opportunities generated the saturation of middle-aged and older workers in the internal labour market and their disadvantageous treatment in enterprise restructurings. Hence, for the creation of a support system for 'workers as individuals' it is vital to create systems to enable job changes when it is so desired by the worker.

From this perspective, the reform of employment placement agencies is imperative to assist workers in their ability to participate in market exchanges. Private or public, intermediary agencies not only perform a matchmaker function in market interactions, but also provide workers with valuable information and consultation services which can reinforce their bargaining incentive and power. Such support not only facilitates workers finding jobs suitable to their skills, but also helps them improve the terms and conditions of employment.[5] Such functions of employment placement institutions should be strengthened.

As discussed before, the Employment Security Law endowed monopolistic power in employment exchange services to the Public Employment Offices (PEO) and restricted the activities of private agencies very strictly. The PEO had played a significant role for a few decades after World War II in correcting past exploitative practices and facilitating the moves of the workforce from farming to urban industries. However, their services have not been sufficient in many respects in meeting current social demands. This is manifested in the fact that only about 20 per cent of workers who obtain employment utilise these offices,[6] and that more and more enterprises and workers are relying on other channels and media for recruitment. The job-matching services provided by such agencies have been characterised by a quantitative adjustment of labour. They have been insufficient in dealing with sectors containing professionals and managers in which individual quality is a vital issue. Also, placements for women and older workers have especially lagged in the public agencies. Moreover, although improvements brought about by computerisation are underway, labour referral services encompassing broader regions are not yet sufficiently established. The agencies would not be able to respond effectively to the massive movement in labour which it is anticipated will occur as a result of large scale industrial restructuring.

Hence, the employment exchange system should be better tailored to the dramatic environmental changes that are taking place. In particular, the division between public and private sectors needs to be re-evaluated. The PEO must continue to act as the core institution in the employment services, but the framework of Employment Security Law should be reformed so as to give greater room for manoeuvre for the private institutions and services.

To this end, the PEO should assume the role of monitoring the labour market, providing assistance services to enterprises and workers, and preventing deviant behaviour in the realm of employment placement.[7] The public offices need to continue to have responsibility for the administration of employment insurance systems including the provision of unemployment benefits and the implementation of various subsidy programmes. Moreover, much is expected of public sector activity in counselling services involving career choice, re-employment, job changes, mid-career hires and education and training. Grievance resolution procedures involving employment placement also fall within the province of the public offices. It is desired that public agencies play a more active role in these arenas by fully utilising electronic job information systems.

However, there is a growing need to weed out those individual services which are not problematic even if entrusted to the private sector. The human resource services which are better effectuated by private sector activities must be identified and delegated to private businesses with the proper social regulation. Trends in international standards such as the re-evaluation of the ILO Convention No. 96 should be considered in this regard.[8] For such a reform it is necessary to proceed in stages, with prudence, as a rough revolution carries with it the danger of injurious results.

As for worker leasing businesses (temporary employment services), there are some countries which place no restrictions on the kind of jobs for which workers can be leased, but restrict those businesses in that the workers can be leased only on a temporary basis. Such a regulation tends to carry the consequence that leased workers are relegated to a lower social status and are regarded as temporary assistants to regular workers. In contrast, the Worker Leasing Business Law of 1985 places strict limitations on the kind of jobs for which workers are leasable to emphasize their specialised nature,[9] while not restricting the dispatching period strictly. The system contributed to raising the dispatched workers' wage levels, thereby elevating their social status. Despite such positive aspects, the dispatchable jobs have been too limited, especially in light of the needs for expanding employment opportunities for older and white-collar workers and the growing demand for specialised skilled labour. Thus, a gradual expansion should be pursued beginning in those areas where there would be least abuses and where socio-economic demand is the greatest.[10]

With respect to skill development, there is a tendency in European countries to depend upon vocational training provided by labour organisations or public institutions. In contrast, vocational education and training in Japan has been heavily undertaken by firms, with public training institutions playing only supplementary roles. Within such a framework, Japanese employment policies have actively supported in-firm training while also providing public training and testing services.

Nevertheless, in Japan, the entire training system has been geared towards on-site labour in manufacturing industries and has not coped with the expansion of professional, managerial and artistic work as well as service sectors. There are growing needs to facilitate the skill development of part-time and other flexible workforce members, on the one hand, and professional workers on the other. The former type of employment is undertaken mainly by women, and younger and older workers for whom sufficient training by the employer cannot be expected. For part-time workers, in particular, the establishment of a training system and the opening up of career development has become imperative. The latter type of workers are those who, instead of leaving their skill development entirely to their employers, have taken the initiative for enhancing their professional skill. A new policy agenda to assist those individual workers will require a new concept of a vocational education system that is different from the conventional policies towards supporting employers' in-firm education and training.[11]

Issues for the internal labour market

In the internal labour market, the agenda is also how to establish systems for supporting workers' more individualistic career and skill development while defending their stable employment. In this regard, there have been accumulated case law rules which were constructed on the basis of the long-term employment system to accord workers comprehensive employment security and which afforded employers the right to manage employment relations flexibly. The court has been imposing strict requirements for disciplinary and economic dismissals while recognising a comprehensive management right to human resource cultivation and deployment. These comprehensive management rights were premised on the collective and uniform treatment of workers in accordance with critical standards of age and length of service. However, such rules are challenged by the increasingly individualised merit-based employment relationships. There are four significant issues:

The first is the establishment of rules for employment contracts which are needed in response to the mobilisation of the labour market under industrial restructuring and worker individualisation. It is necessary for this perspective to have the basic rules of dismissal spelt out in the Labour Standards Law; that is, the general rule of just cause for dismissals and the requirements for economic dismissals,[12] both of which had been established by case law. In this respect, the introduction of the concept of 'constructive dismissal' should be considered which deems a worker resignation induced by the employer's excessive pressure to be a dismissal. Moreover, the case law rule requiring a valid reason for an employer's termination of a fixed-term employment contract that had reasonably been expected to be renewed should be set down in the basic statute. The requirement of an individual worker's consent for transferring employment to related firms (*tenseki*) is also a basic rule that should be expressed in the statute. At the same time as the establishment of such rules, when the individualisation of workers and diversification of working styles is taken into consideration, Article 14 of the Labour Standards Law, which sets forth a maximum term of one year for fixed-term contracts, should be made more flexible to enable specialist workers to experience more than one year's employment at an establishment in the process of their career development.

The second issue concerns the legal rules of the human resource deployment within the internal labour market. As mentioned above, recognition of broad personnel management rights in job assignment, education and training, promotion, transfers and relocation has been established both in law and in practice. Management has also been endowed the critical right to make reasonable changes in terms and conditions of employment by rewriting work rules when necessary to accommodate any drastic changes in business conditions. Those rights have made up a comprehensive management prerogative in employment relationships which was afforded to the employer in return for a high level of employment security for workers. However, one can foresee the dilution of such cohesive employment relationships as the labour market becomes more mobile. More predictably, the encompassing right to management of personnel will become more limited due to the increase of individualistic personnel management systems. For example, job assignments, transfers and career development will be increasingly implemented on the basis of workers' consent and choice. Employment forms, career tracks, working time and location will become more pluralistic and flexible. Salary and promotion will be further linked with individual evaluations and negotiations. One resulting legal change will be the individualisation of the employment contract, or the limitation of comprehensive employment relationships with individual agreements.

The individualisation of employment relationships will also necessitate the modification of rules for reconciling conflicting interests. For example, the critical issue of to what extent and by what means management is allowed to make reasonable changes in working conditions will no longer involve the simple question of how to balance the interests of management and the worker group, but will become a more complex one of how to reconcile management's demand for flexibility and the diversified interests of individualised workers. The test of how reasonable these interest claims are will have to take into account conflicts of interest and differences in choice among workers. With the changes of working conditions clearly stated in individual contracts, a new legal framework such as the German system of contract cancellation for the alteration of its conditions will be needed.

The third issue concerns the deregulation of white-collar workers' working time. The Labour Standards Law exempts directors and managers ('persons in positions of supervision and management') from its 8-hour day and 40-hour week standards. The Law also allows the employer to define working time of certain categories of specialists as a certain number of hours fixed by a written agreement with a majority union or a majority representative in the undertaking, regardless of the length of their actual working hours. Yet there is an increasing number of professional and managerial workers who are not covered by these special exemptions, but perform their jobs with ample individual initiative and discretion. They are the employees for whom both management and workers prefer more individualistic treatment in remuneration and promotion by way of goal setting and performance assessment. For them the tight regulation of working time relating the amount of remuneration to the quantity of work carried out came to be regarded as highly out-dated. Thus, there have been arguments for new exemptions from working time regulation for this other group of expert workers. This matter requires prudent investigation for it touches upon the fundamental issue of working time regulation and the accompanying possibility of abuse (such as its exploitation in order to evade overtime pay). However, where a high level of individual discretion is required as a result of the creativity and speciality of jobs in which they are involved, it is necessary to exempt such workers from the statutory regulation of working time. Such exemption should be compensated for by advantageous remuneration and vacation arrangements. Moreover, individual consent should become a fundamental requirement for professional exemption in the introduction of such exemption.[13]

Fourth, a fundamental issue in the more individualised labour market is to ensure gender equality in employment and the support of parental responsibility. For this purpose, the Equal Employment Opportunity Law of 1985 needs to be developed to bring about stronger regulation of discriminatory treatment of female workers throughout the career development process (*inter alia*, in recruitment and hiring, and job assignment and promotion). For enhancing equal opportunities, the restriction of women workers' night work should, under the Labour Standards Law of 1947, either be eliminated or made subject to an individual worker's decision to opt out.[14] On the other hand, in order to implement gender equality in the workplace and to enhance career development for both male and female workers, systems to assist workers to harmonise their working and parental responsibilities are imperative. In this context, the enactment of childcare leave legislation (the Child Care Leave Law of 1992) is commendable. The subsequent institutionalisation of parental care leave by the 1994 legislation (the Child and Parental Care Leave (Consolidation) Law of 1995) is also remarkable. The immediate goal is to fully implement and strengthen such new measures.

Related issues

The reform of dispute resolution systems

To facilitate implementation of the labour law reform explained above, a few more issues still need to be tackled. First is the reform of grievance procedures and dispute resolution mechanisms providing support for individual workers in the more individualised labour market and employment relationships.

Post-war labour law established a highly sophisticated system for dealing with collective labour disputes: the labour dispute adjustment procedures (conciliation, mediation and arbitration) and the unfair labour practice remedial procedures undertaken by the Central and Local Labour Relations Commissions. Unions and management also developed joint consultation procedures within firms to discuss a wide range of managerial decisions affecting workers, which function as a mechanism for preventing and resolving collective disputes in the enterprise. Yet, regarding individual workers' grievances and assertion of rights, there is no effective system for grievance procedure as found in the USA or the labour court in Europe. Individual workers' complaints are dealt with either informally by their supervisors and managers or by the unions through joint consultation. Disputes that are not resolved by such mechanisms can be taken to inspection agencies or an ordinary civil court if they involve a violation of statutes or legal rights. Workers who take such legal actions tend to be regarded as disloyal dissidents in the workplace community. However, recently a growing number of cases have been brought to legal counselling services offered by labour lawyers, labour organisations and prefectural governments. Such cases typically involve middle-aged and older white-collar workers whose jobs are threatened under the enterprise restructuring, women workers who face discriminatory treatment in their career development, and part-time and dispatched workers whose contractual rights are not fully implemented.

As explained above, more individualistic and merit-based personnel management such as goal setting and performance assessment is in the process of being introduced. In addition to such changes in core employment relationships, there are a growing number of non-core workers whose working styles and forms of employment are increasingly diversified. These trends signify increased individual dealings in the process of employment relationships for which there should be new systems for prompt and fair resolution of grievances other than the existing informal and collective mechanisms. To support individual workers in their efforts to obtain fair dealings, it is not only necessary to establish substantial rules for fair treatment but also to create procedural systems to facilitate the prompt resolution of disputes involving negotiation, interpretation and implementation of the individual employment contract.

The greatest needs lie in the fulfilment of the legal rules concerning dismissals and job changes as mentioned above, for which a new third-party institution is necessary to exercise two types of function. One is counselling through which dismissed or resigned workers have the opportunity to understand their legal position and obtain advice on the actions they can take. The other is a mediatory function to hear the content of disputes from the parties involved and to offer them mediation and arbitration services. From a practical viewpoint, it seems quite unfeasible to create a completely new institution such as a German type labour court or a British type industrial tribunal in the current tide of administrative reform. Thus, the most practical way is to add the above mentioned functions to the jurisdiction of the existing Labour Relations Commission. Due to the stabilisation of union management relations, the Commission has, in recent years, faced a drastic decline of collective disputes being brought before it. It seems quite practical for the Commission to use its expertise and human resources in the growing area of rights disputes. The Labour Dispute Adjustment Law of 1946 should be revised in that direction.[15]

As regards the grievances which are anticipated to increase under the more individualistic and merit-based employment relationships, a new in-firm system needs to be designed, in which the individual with a grievance can obtain advice and mediatory aid from a third party with expertise in personnel management. This is exactly the function the newly developing American corporate ombudsman is performing (Silver 1967, pp. 77–8, Rowe 1991, pp. 353–62). Thus far in Japan, such a function has been performed by human resource staff, superiors and union officials, but in light of the rise of individual interest such in-community systems need to be supplemented by an in-firm procedure undertaken by an independent mediator. Grievances involving contractual issues can also be brought to the Labour Relations Commission's newly created mediation services when they are not resolved by in-firm procedures. The last resort for such disputes will of course be the existing civil court which has jurisdiction over all kinds of disputes.

Public policies for reinforcing collective representation of worker interest

Established mostly in enterprises, the Japanese unions function both as trade unions for gaining higher wages and improving working conditions in negotiations with enterprise management and also as employee representative bodies to promote participation in and cooperation with management. Enterprise unions in Japan have also developed webs of super-enterprise organisations in enterprise groups, respective industries, industrial sectors and regions to engage in industrial relations and civic activities. Unions have also established a national organisation to participate in national politics and governments. Particularly noteworthy as the activities of such a national organisation are the nation-wide synchronisation and coordination of wage negotiations by the Shunto (Spring Wage Offensive) system and the heavy involvement in the government's policy-making processes. Thus, despite their enterprise-based nature, Japanese unions have performed many of the corporatist functions of industrial unions as well as employee representation functions of works councils in Europe. Because of such multi-faceted functions, unions have become significant public institutions in Japanese socio-economic systems. The problem is that such public functions are now at risk due to the unions' waning density in the society as mentioned in the previous section.

The declining union density raises two significant policy issues. The first is the issue of whether there should be legislation establishing works councils in unorganised firms. Concerned by the growing number of non-union firms, many scholars now argue that this should occur. However, since Japanese unions are enterprise based, it is difficult to distinguish 'unions' and 'works councils' in organisational and jurisdictional terms. Even if such a technical difficulty is overridden, one can raise the question as to whether such a new attempt of collective banding of workers can function well in the tide of individualisation and diversification. A further weak point of works council arguments is that such a workplace system cannot substitute the significant social functions unions perform at industrial, regional and national levels which need to be maintained even in the more individualistic society.

Because of the social nature of their functions in contemporary industrial relations, unions in Japan seem to be facing a dilemma in being both the promoters of worker interests and the institutions with social responsibilities. Of course, it is the unions themselves that should respond to underlying organisational challenges with their vigorous and ingenious efforts. In particular, unions should redefine and reorganise their functions in the changing labour market and develop new measures to defend workers' individualistic interests. Unions should strengthen their functions to assist and represent workers in their individual dealings and grievances. Assuming unions' new efforts, the second and more fundamental issue is whether there should be a new type of policy for reinforcing unions as a subsystem in a free democratic market economy and whether this can be done without sacrificing freedom of association, their essential nature as independent organisations. For example, considering the importance unions place on human resources with the high level of professional expertise, it seems desirable to develop public systems to assist unions to cultivate such resources.[16] Also worth examining is the nature and extent of benefit unions provide to their members in countries with high union density.

CONCLUSION

As in many industrialised countries, Japan is experiencing socio-economic transformations represented by the drastic ageing of the population, intensified global competition and industrial restructuring, individualisation and diversification among workers, and the advent of an information society. All of these structural changes have a significant impact on labour relations and require their systems to be reformed. This is particularly so when a shift is occurring from 'collective labour' to 'individual workers', past regulatory measures need to be reconsidered by re-examining the conventional and yet contemporary question of how to reconcile collectivity with the individual. Labour law systems need to be supplemented with new measures and policies to assist the individual worker to effectively participate in market exchanges.

In essence, the authors regard labour law as a 'legal system that provides an array of support mechanisms to facilitate worker transaction in the labour market'. As such, labour law makes a significant subsystem in the market economy. Since the subordinate nature of the worker *en masse* had been dominant in the general situation of class division, labour law of the nineteenth and twentieth centuries developed as a social law protecting a weaker social class. Such conventional labour law utilised many elaborate regulatory means against market transactions and labour–management autonomy. The state directly controlled the labour market by establishing statutory standards for terms and conditions of work and by strictly regulating intermediary services in the labour market. The state did not expect much of the private services which were still underdeveloped and whose potential dangers for abuse were significant. Instead, legal recognition was given to the strengthening of bargaining power through trade unions which were based upon worker solidarity.

Such were the choices made in public policy in accordance with the realities of that period. Under the current socio-economic transformations, the basic premise of the subordinate nature of the worker *en masse* is changing with the emergence of workers who want to, and who are qualified to, act in the labour market as individuals. Such structural changes require a reform of the conventional measures to support worker transactions. Measures that have become in large part unnecessary for worker protection and those that have become potential disruptions for market transactions need to be amended by the revision of the obsolete parts. Furthermore, new methods need to be developed for those policies that have become essential.

Even in the new situation of a labour market with more qualified and independent individuals, workers will face potential vulnerability when exposed to market mechanisms without the appropriate support systems. The gap in bargaining power that will remain will make market transactions unfair and distort both supply and demand adjustment, and resource distribution. Hence, various public policies that assist 'the individual worker as the weaker party' become essential. A new mission of labour law is to provide this function. In this sense, there will be no change in its fundamental concept of 'assisting workers' transactions in the labour market'.

As specific elements of the new support system, the following are three crucial points among various issues. First is the substantiation of 'employment contract' law to make treatment of the worker as an individual more stable and fair; second, the development of efficient services for providing individual workers with consultation, advice, grievance procedure and dispute resolution; and third, the reorganisation of the institutions and services to support worker mobility in the external labour market (employment placement and vocational skill development systems). All of these issues are mutually complementary, and the lack of any one could impede the attainment of a balanced working society in the next generation.

NOTES

1   In the 1993 survey of 851 top managers by Keizai Doyu Kai (Japan Committee for Economic Development), 41.3 per cent stated that the system would inevitably face broad reform, and 41.0 per cent said that the system would be

maintained. In the 1994 survey of 354 firms by Nikkeiren (the Japanese Employers Federation) focusing on larger and medium sized enterprises, 30.4 per cent of respondents said that the system would be maintained, 58.0 per cent said it would be able to be maintained if it was altered in part, and only 7.7 per cent responded that they would not be able to preserve the system. In the 1993 'Survey of the Future of the Lifetime Employment Practice' by the Japanese Productivity Centre (304 listed companies' human resources managers), opinions supporting the maintenance of the long-term employment practice were overwhelming at 89.3 per cent. As for opinions on the labour side, the 'Survey on Workers' Attitudes' undertaken by the Life Insurance Culture Centre in 1993 (2,978 workers of both sexes between the ages of 20 and 59 employed by enterprises with more than 10 employees), 69.1 per cent replied that lifetime employment was desirable or somewhat desirable, and likewise in the Japanese Research Institute's survey (657 company employees) in 1993, 71 per cent said that they supported the lifetime employment system.

2   For example, in the Nikkeiren Survey (see note 1), 97.9 per cent of those surveyed said that the seniority wage system should be re-evaluated, and the Japanese Productivity Centre Managing Ethics Survey (636 company managers and 150 union leaders) (1992) 89.5 per cent of the managers and 80.7 per cent of the union leaders responded that they support an ability-based rather than a seniority-based wage system. The survey on wage systems by the Rengo Research Institute (342 unions) (1992) revealed that only 10.9 per cent of unions surveyed would maintain the seniority wage system, and also in the 'Workers' Opinion Survey' by the Office of the Prime Minister (1992) 64.6 per cent responded that a shift from seniority-based wages to that of ability-based wages would be favourable, and only 12.2 per cent responded such a system not to be desirable, indicating that there is much support for ability-based wages from the labour side as well.

3   For example, the Labour Standards Law of 1947 maintains such obsolete regulations in the contemporary employment relationships, as the protection of minors from their parents' and employers' economic exploitation, standards for workers' dormitories to secure their freedom and health, and the protection of workers in the old apprentice system. However, the case may vary according to country as shown in the case of Germany and Austria which still have apprentice systems that function well.

4   A typical aspect of long-term employment that has hampered worker mobility is the retirement benefit system maintained by most firms. The amount of benefit is set forth progressively with the increase of service years so as to encourage employees' continuous service. The company pension system which is in most cases set up by reorganising the retirement benefit fund lacks cross-firm portability.

5   Private human resource services not only serve to expand employment opportunities for workers but also contribute to the improvement in their terms and conditions of employment. For example, when the hourly wage of dispatched workers and part-time workers are compared, the average hourly wage for the job of 'filing' for dispatched workers which is more or less comparable to the part-time office job was estimated to be ¥1,090 to ¥1,220 (as calculated by the authors based upon the Labour Ministry's compilation of Dispatched Business Reports, 1992), while that of part-time office work was ¥729 to ¥943. Functionally speaking, the dispatching business which collects labour market information and intermediates supply and demand, contributes to the support of the external labour market bargaining power of dispatched workers who would otherwise remain dispersed and be less favoured in terms of market transactions.

6   According to the Labour Ministry's 'Basic Survey on Working Structure' (1992), only 16.3 per cent of both men and women surveyed replied that 'Application to a Public Employment Security Office' was a method for searching for employment for those who usually do not work but are looking for jobs (22.2 per cent of men, 13.4 per cent of women, and older workers, 13.4 per cent).

7   Troubleshooting and counselling regarding unfair practices in job advertisements, recruitment, private employment placement, and worker dispatching projects are important functions for the Public Offices.

8   So far, only in Anglo-American law countries have private institutions for employment placement been the dominant actor. But even in tightly-regulated European labour markets there is an increasing tendency for re-examining the relationship between civil and public (administrative) means. For example, in 1992 Germany opted out from the ILO Convention No. 96 which provided that profit-making employment agencies be strictly regulated by the state, and is now embarking on an attempt to rearrange employment placement systems. Moreover, Sweden, which had been under a typical system of public employment placement, also quitted from this Convention and introduced, in 1993, a policy of broad deregulation (except for the regulation of the fees for such private agencies, the reform abolished the requirement for administrative permission and other supervisory mechanisms for private job reference agencies (Fahlbeck 1995).

9   The Law adopted the position that the newly institutionalised worker leasing projects should be designed so as not to erode the long-term employment system. It therefore defined the jobs for which workers are leasable as those which are difficult to be cultivated under the long-term employment system because of their speciality. The government designated 16 jobs by the end of 1995, such as software programmers, OA machine operators, interpreters, filing, secretaries to this category.

10   The Central Employment Security Council recommended to the Labour Minister that 12 jobs such as OA instruments instruction, interior co-ordinator, management planning, research and development, should be designated as dispatchable jobs. The author (Suwa) chaired the subcommittee of the Council which discussed the issue. The 12 jobs were designated in the Ordinance in 1996.

11   From this viewpoint, the recent supportive measures provided to middle-aged and older workers have been laudable, but more creativity is necessary in view of the long-term perspective. Other measures worth examining are the ideas of a standard 10 hours of training and education for every 1,000 hours worked, education and training leave for workers with long periods of service, preferential treatment in social insurance and subsidies for firms that invest in education and training, accounting standards that reflect human resources circumstances, tax exemptions for individual investment in education, and so forth.

12   Based on the pattern of employment adjustment in larger firms established during the economic adjustments after the 1973 Oil Crisis, the court formulated the following four requirements for economic dismissals: (a) a sufficient need to resort to the personnel curtailment measure which gave rise to the economic dismissals; (b) that every effort is made to avoid dismissal as a means of achieving necessary personal curtailment, i.e. the exhaustion of alternative means such as the reduction of overtime work, suspension of hiring new workers, relocation of workers, *kurzarbeit*; (c) the use of reasonable criteria to select dischargees; and (d) sufficient communication and consultation with workers and their representatives. These are quite similar to the requirements of economic dismissals manifested in the ILO's

Termination of Employment Recommendation, 1963, which evolved into the Termination of Employment Convention, 1982, and its accompanying Recommendation.
13 The author (Sugeno) chaired a study group set up in the Labour Ministry to discuss the issue of working time regulation for professional and managerial workers. In May 1995 the group recommended the reform of the Labour Standards Law along the lines stated in this paragraph.
14 Discussions along the lines of this paragraph are held in the Women and Minors Council in the Labour Ministry. Yet there is resistance from the labour side to the elimination of the overtime and night work protection and from the management side to the strengthening of the equality regulation.
15 The reform of the individual dispute resolution system has been discussed in the Central Labour Standards Council to which the authors belong. There seems to be an emerging consensus among labour law experts for the reform proposed in this paragraph.
16 Union officials' professional positions to provide various services to labour union members should not be underestimated. From such perspectives, one should take note of examples of a public education system, such as in Australia, for their professional skill development for union leaders (education of labour law, economic analysis, negotiating skills, grievance handling), or of professional skill development programmes in graduate schools as in the USA.

REFERENCES

Araki, Takashi (1994a) 'Flexibility in Japanese Employment Relations and the Role of Judiciary', in Oda, Hiroshi (ed.), *Japanese Commercial Law in an Era of Internationalizations*, London: Graham & Trotman, pp. 249–74.
—— (1994b) *Promotion and Regulation of Job Creation Opportunities, National Report: Japan,* in *International Society for Labour Law and Social Security, Promotion and Regulation of Job Creation Opportunities*, Proceedings of XIV World Congress of Labour Law and Social Security, Theme I, pp. 385–403.
—— (1994c) 'The Japanese model of employee representational participation', *Comparative Labor Law Journal*, 15(2), pp. 143–54.
Brinton, M. (1993) *Women and the Economic Miracle: Gender and Work in Postwar Japan*, Berkeley: University of California Press.
Economic Planning Agency (ed.) (1994) *White Paper on the Economy 1994*, Ministry of Finance Publishing Centre, p. 322.
Endo, M. (1955) *New Developments in Employment Policy*, Study Group on Contemporary Labour Economics, pp. 209.
Fahlback, R. (1995) 'Employment Exchange and Hiring-out of Employees in Sweden', *The Monthly Journal of the Japanese Institute of Labour*, 36(12): 16–30.
Hanami, Tadashi A. (1979) *Labour Law and Industrial Relations in Japan*, Deventer: Kluwer.
—— (1979b) *Labour Disputes in Japan*, Tokyo: Kodansha-International.
Inagami, Takeshi, Sugeno, Kazuo, Suwa, Yasuo and Seike, Atsushi (1995) 'Nihon gata koyo shisutemu no henka to rodo ho no kadai' ('Changes in Japanese Employment System and Labour Law Issues'), *Jurisuto* (Jurist), No. 1066, pp. 12–40.
Japan Institute of Labour (ed.) (1989) *In Search of a New System of Labour-Management Relations*, Tokyo: Japan Institute of Labour.
Kezuka, Katsutoshi, Yamakawa, Ryuichi, Hamamura, Akira, Ishii, Yasuo, Nakamura, Kazuo, Koakutsu, Masafumi, Takada, Masaaki and Yamashita, Koji

(1995) *Kobetsu Funso Shori Shisutemu no Genjo to Kadai* (*Present Situations of Individual Labour Dispute Resolution System*), Tokyo: Japan Institute of Labour.

Kurokawa, Michiyo (1995) 'The harmonization of working life and family life: Japan', *Bulletin of Comparative Labour Relations*, vol. 30, pp. 45–59.

Lam, A. (1992) *Women and Japanese Management: Discrimination and Reform*, London: Routledge.

Ministry of Labour (ed.) (1994) *White Paper on Labour 1994*, Tokyo: Japan Institute of Labour, p. 100.

Ministry of Labour (various years) *Basic Survey on Trade Unions*, Tokyo: MOL.

Nakajima, A. (1988) *History of Administrative Employment Security*, Study Group on Employment Issues.

Oosawa, M. (1993) *Economic Changes and Female Workers*, Nihon Keizai Hyoronsha, pp. 99, 262.

Rodosho Rodo Kijun Kyoku (Labour Ministry Labour Standards Office) (ed.) (1993) *Rodo Kijun Ho Kenkyu Kai Hokoku Sho* (Report of Study Group on the Labour Standards Law: the Future of Labour Contract Law Systems), Tokyo: Japan Institute of Labour.

Rowe, M.P. (1987) 'The corporate ombudsman: an overview and analysis', *Negotiation Journal*, April, pp. 127–40.

—— (1991) 'The Ombudsman's Role in a Dispute Resolution System', *Negotiation Journal*, October, 353–62.

Saito, M. (1993) *Law for Vocational Ability Development*, Sakaishoten, p. 123.

Sako, M. and Dore, R. (1988) 'Teaching or testing: the role of the state in Japan', *Oxford Review of Economic Policy*, 4(3), pp. 72–81.

Silver, I. (1967) 'The corporate ombudsman', *Harvard Business Review*, 45(3), pp. 77–8.

Small and Medium-sized Enterprise Agency (ed.) (1994) *White Paper on Small and Medium-sized Enterprises 1994*, Ministry of Finance Publishing Centre, p. 107.

Soya, N. (1993) *New Developments in Policies for Workers in the Coal Mining Industry*, Rodo Shinbunsha.

—— (1995) 'Changes in the Japanese employment system and issues for the reform of labour law' Special Issue, *Jurisuto* (in Japanese) (May) p. 1066.

Sugeno, K. (1992) *Japanese Labor Law*, Seattle and London: University of Washington Press.

—— (1994) 'Unions as Social Institutions in Democratic Market Economies', *International Labour Review*, 133(4), pp. 511–22.

—— (1995) *Rodo Ho* (Labour Law), 4th edn, Tokyo: Kobundo.

—— (1996) *Koyo Shakai no Ho (Employment Society and Law)*, Tokyo: Yuhikaku.

Sugeno, Kazuo and Suwa, Yasuo (1994) *Hanrei de Manabu Koyo Kankei no Hori (Case Law of Employment Management)*, Tokyo: Sogo Rodo Kenkyusho.

Suwa, Yasuo (1990) 'Flexibility and security in employment: the Japanese case', *The International Journal of Comparative Labour Law and Industrial Relations*, 6(4), pp. 229–67.

Takanashi, Akira (1989) *Aratana Koyo Seisaku no Tenkai (The Development of New Employment Policies)*, Tokyo: Romu Gyosei Kenkyusho.

Ujihara, Shojiro (1988) *Nihon Keizai to Koyo Seisaku* (The Japanese Economy and Employment Policy), Tokyo: University of Tokyo Press.

Yamakawa, Ryuichi (1995) 'The Role of the Employment Contract in Japan', in Lammy Betten (ed.) *The Employment Contract in Transforming Labour Relations*, pp. 105–28.

3 Corporate strategy and human resource management

Takashi Kawakita

The purpose of this chapter is to discuss the following three issues by drawing evidence from questionnaire surveys conducted by Kawakita *et al.* between 1985 and 1994: (1) how the corporate strategy of leading Japanese companies has changed; (2) how their organisation and human resource management strategy have changed; and (3) how human resource management strategy is related to corporate strategy.

CHANGE IN THE CORPORATE STRATEGY OF THE JAPANESE COMPANY

The extent to which the corporate strategy of the Japanese company has changed over the last ten years can be seen by examining the results of three surveys in which the author was involved. These surveys were carried out for leading Japanese companies in 1984,[1] 1989,[2] and 1995.[3] Table 3.1 shows the results of the surveys and in particular the changes in the main strategic areas tackled by the companies. These changes will be explained in the rest of this section by putting them in the context of the economic and business climate at the time of each survey.

Corporate strategy in the low-growth period just before the 'bubble economy'

After the two oil crises in 1973 and 1979 which brought about global recessions, Japanese manufacturing industries such as shipbuilding, steel and chemical industries fell into a deep recession and were forced to introduce employment adjustments on a large scale. Some companies experienced mass job losses for the first time, apart from the aftermath of World War II. Most, however, avoided such cut-backs wherever possible while the workers continued in their efforts to improve their productivity to help overcome the recession. The corporate behaviour to emerge during this recovery process was later to be called 'Japanese-style management' and was to win the admiration of the world.

Table 3.1   The main strategic issues of the leading Japanese companies 1985–94 (multiple responses allowed)

Choice	1995 (%)	1989 (%)	1984 (%)
1 Enhancement of ability and quality of employees	66.0	67.2	n/a
2 Development of human resources	n/a	n/a	85.1
3 Expansion of sales network, strengthening of sales force	60.0	62.7	72.8
4 Rationalisation of indirect functions	59.4	30.2	n/a
5 Enhancement of financial ability	n/a	n/a	59.0
6 Development of new products and services	55.2	52.9	63.8
7 Improvement of existing products and service quality	54.5	49.8	45.0
8 Corporate streamlining and downsizing	52.4	22.4	29.7
9 Computer system networking of intra-company information, integration of advanced communication systems	44.4	43.2	n/a
10 Introduction of new machinery and technology	n/a	n/a	44.4
11 Commitment to customer-oriented and market-driven management	42.1	33.0	n/a
12 Rationalisation of production departments	38.0	34.1	n/a
13 Stabilisation of labour–management relations	n/a	n/a	36.2
14 Enhancement of research and development departments	35.7	40.7	43.1
15 Long range business planning	35.7	43.0	n/a
16 Clarification and settlement of corporate strategy	34.3	40.3	n/a
17 Establishment and renewal of corporate culture	29.6	32.6	n/a
18 Deployment of corporate groups and coordination among group companies	26.4	22.0	32.4
19 Opening of new business ventures, diversification, and changes to business structure	25.8	30.7	n/a
20 Multinationalisation and globalisation	17.6	17.4	19.4
21 Recovery from the Dinosaur syndrome (Big Business syndrome or Empire-building mentality)	16.3	8.1	n/a
22 Recruitment of staff for new business ventures	13.3	29.7	n/a
23 Selection and training of corporate elite	12.3	9.1	n/a
24 Enhancement of information network among group companies	11.6	13.8	n/a
25 More production overseas	9.3	4.9	n/a
26 Other	1.5	0.3	1.1

Notes: 1. Items that have almost the same meaning but worded slightly differently in the surveys are combined.   2. n/a indicates the item is not available in the survey.

While the manufacturing industries of other developed countries were going into a decline, those in Japan showed a quick recovery by the early 1980s. Exports increased steadily. High-technology equipment (such as robots, computer numerical control machines) with built-in micro-electronic devices was widely adopted in order to reduce the cost and improve the quality of manufacturing products. Having assigned the mass production of standard products to the newly emerging Asian NIEs (Newly Industrialised Economies) such as Taiwan and Korea, the Japanese companies started to develop and manufacture a wide range of high quality products. However, the increase in exports to Western countries caused the yen to appreciate and gave added support to the calls to boost the domestic market. Reflecting the steady increase of domestic consumption, general merchandising stores, department stores and supermarkets were growing rapidly. However, the periods following the oil crises were generally recognised as a 'low-growth period' in comparison to the 'high-growth period' of the 1960s and 1970s.

The 1984 survey was conducted during a 'low-growth period' and identified the following attitudes within the leading Japanese companies (see Table 3.1):

1. 'The development of new products and services' (63.8 per cent) is given higher priority than the 'improvement of existing products and service quality' (45.0 per cent).
2. With investment increasing at a fast pace while the economy continued to grow, they have had to depend heavily on loans to supplement the shortage of capital throughout the low-growth period. The 'enhancement of financial ability' (59.0 per cent) was, therefore, an urgent requirement.
3. The enhancement of financial ability was also aimed at raising funds to promote the 'introduction of new machinery and technology' (44.4 per cent).
4. Companies were aware of the importance of developing original advanced technology instead of importing it from the Western developed countries ('enhancement of research and development departments' (43.1 per cent)).

Companies were not sure if their workers could successfully keep their skills up-to-date for the new technology and equipment which had been introduced. Since some companies had just experienced employment adjustments after an interval of twenty years, the 'stabilisation of labour–management relations' (36.2 per cent) was of great importance. This is a good example contradicting the commonly held opinion that Japanese labour–management relations had always been smooth.

The idea emerged that Japanese companies should decelerate their expansion plans and should be reorganised into a conglomerate consisting of business units dealing with a wide variety of specialised products instead of mass producing basic goods. This is reflected by 32.4 per cent of the companies insisting on 'deployment of corporate groups and coordination among group companies'.

Of the companies surveyed in 1984, 72.8 per cent strongly supported the 'expansion of sales network, and strengthening of sales force'. Companies hired a great number of college graduates not only as researchers and engineers, but also as sales personnel. The number of workers with academic qualifications grew and the percentage of white-collar employees in the Japanese workforce increased drastically. To cope with these new trends in the mid-1980s, 85.1 per cent of the companies showed renewed interest in the 'development of human resources'.

Corporate strategy in the 'bubble economy' period

Let us verify the condition of the Japanese economy around 1989. The manufacturing industries benefited from the strong yen in the form of cheap imported raw materials and components. Combined with the remarkable growth in the materials industry, trading companies, retailers and manufacturers succeeded in developing new products at lower cost and in expanding exports. While Western developed countries were going through a downward trend, the Japanese economy continued to boom for almost all industries. The value of property owned by Japanese companies swelled with the steep rise in share and land prices. There suddenly emerged a growing cluster of people called the 'new rich'.

Under the slogan of 'Make it more luxurious', manufacturers launched one new luxury product after another and their inventory turned over rapidly. Companies simultaneously adopted the two strategies of 'development of new products and services' (52.9 per cent) and 'improvment of existing products and service quality' (49.8 per cent). As a result, the strategy concerning the 'enhancement of research and development departments' (40.7 per cent) stayed as important as ever.

Among management, a bullish attitude prevailed that the newest product they put on the market would sell without question. Therefore, the 'expansion of sales network and strengthening of sales force' (62.7 per cent) was still regarded as high priority.

The introduction of computerised equipment had swept through the manufacturing sites, and as this technology reached the head office and sales offices in the form of word processors, intelligent terminals, and mini- and desktop computers, there was a call for 'computer system networking of intra-company information, and the integration of advanced communication systems' (43.2 per cent). In the preceding low-growth period, much rationalisation had been made as a result of workers' activities for continuous improvement. While the 'rationalisation of production departments' still continued (34.1 per cent), some pointed to the necessity of 'rationalisation of indirect functions' though this was still a minority opinion (30.2 per cent).

During this period, leading companies, supported by ample funds, were striving for 'new business venture openings, diversification, and changes to business structure' (30.7 per cent). For such companies, the 'recruitment of staff for new business ventures' (29.7 per cent) was of great importance. Diversification, however, could turn against Japanese companies as a centrifugal force. Therefore, many companies tried to redefine their corporate identity to keep the centripetal force among their employees. To tie corporate members to the traditional bond, Japanese companies focused on 'long range business planning' (43.0 per cent), 'clarification and settlement of corporate strategy' (40.3 per cent), or 'the establishment and renewal of corporate culture' (32.6 per cent). Such trends, however, might in the final analysis have sometimes ended up as empty gestures.

In proportion to the growth of Japanese companies, the demand for workers increased. Facing a sudden labour shortage, many companies (67.2 per cent) recognised that the 'enhancement of ability and quality of employees' was an important corporate strategy. It is a remarkable characteristic of Japanese companies that they regard the development of human resources as a primary strategic objective.

Corporate strategy after the bubble economy burst: the situation in the 1990s

What happened to the Japanese economy in the early 1990s before the survey in 1995? Economic prosperity suddenly came to an end and the sharp decline in stock and land prices deflated the value of assets and caused a drastic decline in corporate demand.

Luxury goods were no longer in demand and consumers swarmed into the discount outlets. Advocating price reduction, the superstores strategically entered into partnership with manufacturers to cut distribution costs. This caused a reduction in the number of wholesalers. A steep appreciation of the yen led to production being shifted overseas in pursuit of lower production costs. As subcontractors, small-scale manufacturers were severely affected by this production shift. The tone of self-praising of Japanese-style management during the bubble economy dejectedly quietened. There were plausible arguments that judged Japanese-style management as the chief cause of triggering this recession by overgenerous treatment of their managers and employees.

In the context of this economic situation, the 1995 survey reveals that the two strategies of 'development of new products and services' (55.2 per cent) and 'the improvement of existing products and service quality' (54.5 per cent) have progressed simultaneously as in the preceding bubble economy periods. The difference is that 'new products' here means 'cheaper products', and 'new services' the provision of 'simplified services by fewer people'. By rejecting the arrogant idea of a manufacturer-driven market, Japanese companies have made 'commitment to customer-oriented and market-driven management' (42.1 per cent) a higher priority. The 'expansion of sales network, and strengthening of the sales force' remains of importance (60.0 per cent). Japanese companies seem to have shifted their focus more directly to discovering their customers' demands and needs.

In order to compete with foreign-made goods, the 'rationalisation of production departments' continued to be mentioned (38.0 per cent). However, it was outnumbered by the companies which identified the 'rationalisation of indirect functions' (59.4 per cent) as being of central importance to management.

Japanese companies came to review the administrative departments which became over-staffed during the bubble economy period when their head offices recruited a lot of white-collar workers. Many companies pointed out the necessity for 'corporate streamlining and downsizing' (52.4 per cent). To raise the productivity of clerical and administrative work, companies introduced information technology instead of increasing staff. As a result the 'computer system networking of intra-company information, and the integration of advanced communication systems' (44.4 per cent) remained as important as before. In contrast to this unwanted excess of clerical workers, those white-collar workers specialising in technical and research fields continue to be in high demand.

To compete with cheaper and thus more affordable products from the developing countries, most companies in the manufacturing industries have continued to emphasise the 'enhancement of research and development departments' (35.7 per cent). On the other hand, the 'recruitment of staff for new business ventures' (13.3 per cent) has ceased to be important. Many new business ventures started in the bubble economy period, and the withdrawal from these is a rather urgent subject for Japanese companies.

Some companies are driven by the necessity to revise the management plan or corporate strategy, 'long range business planning' (35.7 per cent), and the 'clarification and settlement of corporate strategy' (34.3 per cent). Under these conditions, so completely different from those previously experienced, the 'enhancement of ability and quality of employees' is as high a priority for management as ever (66.0 per cent).

Change in corporate strategy (1989–95)

Let us examine how corporate strategy had changed between the height of the bubble economy period in 1989 and the deepest trough of the recession in 1995.

The strategy which declined in popularity most remarkably was that for 'recruitment of staff for new business ventures' (from 29.7 per cent to 13.3

Table 3.2 Patterns of business restructuring

	Corporate resource allocation for traditional business area (Per cent of total companies)		
	Expansion	Status quo	Downsizing
Corporate resource allocation for new business area			
Expansion	6.6	n/a	31.4
Status quo	n/a	38.7	n/a
Downsizing	4.2	n/a	7.8

Source: Nikkeiren and Nissankun (1995)

Note: n/a indicates that the category was not asked in the survey. The percentages add up to 88.5%. The rest (11.3%) did not respond to this question.

per cent). Japanese companies started new business ventures during the bubble economy period in order to facilitate the readjustment, integration and shedding of excess labour. Existing excess staff have been reassigned to new product and service operations.

Further, management put greater emphasis on the following four strategic areas in 1995 than in 1989:

- Corporate streamlining and downsizing (22.4 per cent → 52.4 per cent)
- Rationalisation of indirect functions (30.2 per cent → 59.4 per cent)
- Commitment to customer-oriented and market-driven management (33.0 per cent → 42.1 per cent)
- Recovery from Dinosaur syndrome (8.1 per cent → 16.3 per cent).

From the above figures, Japanese companies seem to prefer the strategy of downsizing to the strategy of growth in the 1990s.

The 1995 survey shows that 43.4 per cent of the companies have been driven to reduce the scale of their entire business, or at least the main business or new business ventures (see Table 3.2). In short, almost half of them are found to be in severe difficulty. On the other hand, 42.8 per cent of the companies expect to expand their new business ventures. It therefore seems to be an urgent requirement for Japanese companies to convert their employees' specialist ability within the main business to those required for the new business ventures.

Corporate strategy patterns

Factor analysis was conducted in order to find out how different management priorities of leading Japanese companies correlate with each other (see Table 3.3). This analysis showed that the companies could be classified into the following five clusters:

(a) A cluster consisting of companies which are trying to clarify corporate strategy, settle their long range plan and renew their corporate culture. This type of company also has a strong desire to enhance the ability of the employee.
(b) A cluster consisting of companies that open new business ventures and recruit staff for them, as well as quickly introduce multinationalisation and globalisation. This type of company also tends to tighten coordination among subsidiary companies.
(c) A cluster consisting of companies that intend to enhance their research and development departments for the development of new products in addition to improving the existing ones. They also consider it important to increase the sale of those products.
(d) A cluster consisting of companies that aim to flatten and downsize their organisation in order to make labour-saving adjustments while rationalising both production and indirect functions.
(e) A cluster consisting of companies whose urgent problem is to overcome the Dinosaur syndrome and devote themselves to focus on customer-oriented and market-driven management.

CHANGES IN ORGANISATION AND HUMAN RESOURCE MANAGEMENT STRATEGY

Optimising the company scale

It is almost impossible to quantify the number of small businesses in Japan. But a large number alone could provide a favourable environment for the so-called 'flexible specialisation'. Large companies that grew at a fast pace have to downsize to an optimal size in the 1990s (see Table 3.4).

Generally speaking, larger Japanese companies tend to have more managerial problems than smaller companies. This is partly because, as mentioned earlier, the current circumstances surrounding smaller companies are too dire for them to survive. It is also because larger companies are more conscious of excess labour, particularly in the indirect functions. One third of companies of 3,000 or more employees mention the rationalisation of indirect functions and corporate streamlining and downsizing as top priority. One out of three large companies emphasises the importance of overcoming the Dinosaur syndrome.

Corrective action against over-staffed administrative function is recognised as an important managerial priority. A recent audit on labour demand mainly within firms revealed a strong perception of an excess of middle managers (see Table 3.5).

Evaluation of employees' skills under restructuring

It has already been noted that the enhancement of ability and quality of employees is given a high priority by management. Table 3.6 shows the result of the audit on what change is found in employees' skills.

Japanese companies do not always take the immediate necessity to reduce company size or the recession as negative factors in the development of employees' capabilities. Most companies think that such circumstances could give employees a chance 'to develop new skills' and 'to raise the standards of excellence in their skill by surviving the recession, business shutdown and organisational change' (Nikkeiren and Nissankun 1995).

The requisite skill of the employee has a strong correlation with restructuring in the 1990s (see Table 3.7). In Japanese companies experiencing a reduction in their main business or new business ventures, the workload of an employee expands cross-functionally as a result of downsizing. However, their expertise and skills are becoming obsolete as the challenging work helpful for expanding skills decreases. If an employee attempts to search for a job with another company, he may just find that his skills are outdated or different from those required. In contrast, employees will have more chance to give full scope to their abilities in the growing company in its main business or new business ventures operations.

Training strategy under restructuring

The extent to which the restructuring is taking place has a great influence on the company's present human development strategy (see Table 3.8).

Japanese companies which have been forced to reduce their entire business cannot afford the expenses associated with human resource development. Although they regard the education of their employees as important, once they fall into financial difficulties, such cost will be a primary target for cutbacks.

Growing companies invest a great deal in human resource development which is focused upon the education of young employees in their main and new businesses. Such companies have also seen their managers' capability to nurture the young employees to improve.

Change in the main strategy of human resource management

Corporate downsizing is the primary managerial directive in taking corrective action against overstaffed indirect functions and excessive managerial positions. Almost two out of three companies emphasise the enlightenment of managers as the means to change their negative attitudes towards the adoption of the merit system as the main element in human resource management.

Table 3.3 Factor analysis on the priority areas in corporate strategy (principal components analysis with Varimax rotation)

	Factor 1 Visionary management	Factor 2 New business/ globalisation	Factor 3 Product development/ sophistication of sales pitch	Factor 4 Rationalisation and downsizing	Factor 5 Recovery from Dinosaur syndrome
Factor 1					
Long-range business planning	**.60601**	.12368	.02387	.18099	-.01650
Enhancement of employee's ability	**.60505**	-.06076	.05688	.08785	-.11224
Clarification and settlement of corporate strategy	**.53407**	.03898	.07880	.30717	.08231
Establishment and renewal of corporate culture	**.45091**	.00254	.19876	-.09025	.30490
Factor 2					
Enhancement of information network among group companies	.37154	**.25004**	.14822	-.09414	.22226
Opening of new business ventures, change of trade	.18809	**.65516**	-.06850	.02051	-.17306
Multinationalisation and globalisation	-.12826	**.59162**	.15100	.13566	.10309
Overseas shift of production	-.20552	**.53272**	.21491	.24132	.12184
Recruitment of staff for new business	.33157	**.48350**	-.10342	-.13450	.05617
Coordinated teamwork among subsidiary companies	.24177	**.43721**	-.11781	.02179	.31826
Selection and training of elite	.20153	**.23437**	.23414	.13106	.22408

Table 3.3 (continued)

	Factor 1 Visionary management	Factor 2 New business/ globalisation	Factor 3 Product development/ sophistication of sales pitch	Factor 4 Rationalisation and downsizing	Factor 5 Recovery from Dinosaur syndrome
Factor 3					
Development of new products	.02822	.15635	**.64258**	-.04424	-.06008
Enhancement of research and development departments	-.07394	.36838	**.51690**	.14691	-.28674
Computer-system-networking and integration of intra-company information system	.35049	.10971	**.43618**	-.00813	.10946
Improvement of existing product	.05550	-.11818	**.42764**	.13893	.10626
Expansion of sales network, strengthening of sales force	.27225	-.10772	**.38360**	.03288	.07910
Factor 4					
Rationalisation of indirect functions	.17215	.11169	.05524	**.69419**	.12299
Rationalisation of production departments	.03256	.12333	.29363	**.64190**	-.23604
Corporate streamlining and downsizing	.13127	-.01385	-.10188	**.63314**	.31675
Factor 5					
Recovery from Dinosaur syndrome	.01832	.11607	-.05589	.18572	**.64396**
Commitment to customer-oriented and market-driven management	-.00558	-.04277	.43480	.01696	**.55902**

90   *Takashi Kawakita*

Table 3.4 Variation in strategic areas of importance, by size of company (column per cent)

| | Size of companies (number of employees) | | | |
	Less than 299	300–999	1,000–2,999	3,000+
Multinationalisation and globalisation	9.2	13.3	16.8	26.8
Commitment to customer-oriented and market-driven management	29.9	38.1	43.1	51.6
Opening of new business ventures/change of trade	18.4	24.8	22.8	34.6
Rationalisation of indirect functions	48.3	59.3	56.9	68.6
Corporate leaning and meaning and downsizing	33.3	46.0	55.1	64.1
Deployment in conglomerate, coordinated teamwork among subsidiary companies	13.8	18.6	23.4	42.5
Recovery from Dinosaur syndrome	3.4	8.8	13.2	33.3

Source: Nikkeiren and Nissankun (1995)

Note: The table shows only those strategic areas whose importance varied greatly by company size.

Table 3.5 Labour demand by rank and occupation (row per cent)

	Heavily short	Fairly short	Appropriate	Fairly excess	Heavily excess	No reply
Rank						
a. Bucho (Department (Manager)	0.4	5.9	46.7	39.1	4.4	3.6
b. Kacho (Section Manager)	0.8	5.9	35.3	46.5	8.0	3.6
c. Shunin or Kakaricho (Group Chief)	1.3	15.6	43.3	30.9	3.2	5.7
d. Hirashain (rank and file)	0.4	16.1	54.1	23.7	2.1	3.6
e. Newly recruited employees	3.8	25.6	56.7	8.3	0.9	4.6
Occupation						
f. Engineer and technician	2.1	29.2	43.1	10.4	0.9	14.2
g. Production worker	0.6	20.7	43.1	14.0	0.9	20.7
h. Administrator and clerk	0.2	6.8	40.2	43.3	2.5	7.0
i. Sales staff	0.8	29.6	47.8	0.4	0.0	11.4
j. Professional staff	1.9	35.3	38.3	11.0	0.4	13.1

Source: Nikkeiren and Nissankun (1995)

Table 3.6 Management view on employees' requisite skills in the company (multiple responses allowed) (per cent)

1 The worker is required to carry an increased workload as the downsizing continues	57.7
2 Surviving the recession, business shutdown, and organisational change could be a chance for the employees to raise the standards of excellence in their skills	44.6
3 Because of the decrease in the chance to commit to a big business, the pace of skill enhancement is slowing down	17.8
4 Chances are increasing to put the accumulated knowledge and skill into practice	15.6
5 Though the employees have useful skills and knowledge, the business size is too small to afford enough positions	15.4
6 Different skills and knowledge are required at the new workplace after retirement or outplacement	14.6
7 The accumulated expertise and knowledge become rapidly obsolete	13.3
8 With no idea of what sort of skills will be required in the future, we have not discovered in which skills the employees should be retrained	6.3
9 The employee is overqualified for the business operations at hand	4.9
10 Improving employees' capability is out of the question because they feel dissatisfied with restructuring	1.1

Source: Nikkeiren and Nissankun (1995)

Table 3.7 Evaluation of situation concerning employees' skills by restructuring policy (multiple responses allowed) (row per cent)

Corporate resource allocation pattern	7 Outmoded skill	4 Increased chance to make use of existing skills	6 Requirements of new skills at new workplace	1 Increased workload	3 Slower skills acquisition with less challenges
Reduction in all the business areas	**17.1**	9.8	**22.0**	**90.2**	**24.4**
Steady in traditional business areas but downsizing in new business areas	18.2	4.5	27.3	72.7	22.7
Downsizing in traditional business but upscaling in new business areas	**18.8**	12.7	24.2	70.9	20.0
Maintaining the present condition	9.3	15.7	6.4	45.1	**18.1**
Expansion both in main and new business areas	6.7	**35.0**	8.3	40.0	8.3

Notes: The table selected the management views in Table 3.6 that differ greatly by corporate restructuring pattern in the 1995 survey. The numbering at the top of the table correspond to the numbering in Table 3.6.

92   *Takashi Kawakita*

Table 3.8 Trends in employee education and training by corporate restructuring pattern (multiple responses allowed) (row per cent)

Corporate restructuring pattern	More spending on job training	Focusing on educating younger employees	Improving managers' skills to educate subordinates
Reduction in all the business areas	7.3	48.8	24.4
Steady in traditional business areas but downsizing in new business areas	31.8	40.9	31.8
Downsizing in traditional business but upscaling in new business areas	26.1	46.1	33.9
Maintaining the present condition	29.4	45.6	35.8
Expansion both in main and new businesses	35.0	60.0	46.7

Source: Nikkeiren and Nissankun (1995)

Note: The table selected only those trends that differed greatly.

Let us discuss how Japanese companies' human resource management pattern changed alongside the change in corporate strategy by comparing their present positions to those in the 1984 survey. This was done by comparing items with almost the same meaning between the two surveys (see Table 3.9).

The 'enhancement of education and training programmes', the top priority in the 1994 survey, becomes less important in 1995. This means that companies have cut their education budgets, at least for off-the-job training, as a result of the downward trend in the economy. Also, the number of companies supporting the 'adoption of the merit-oriented personnel system' has reduced. However, this policy still remains one of the most important issues.

Similarly, support for the 'full-scale application of the specialist career system' fell by almost the same degree as the 'adoption of the merit-oriented personnel system'. The specialist career system, is one way in which employees can be promoted up tracks other than the line management hierarchy, such as a gold collar track, a professional staffer track, a local hires track, and a 'mom track' (*ippan shoku*) (see Chapter 4 for details). Since this system has been adopted by large companies for some time, it may be taken for granted to place a priority on it. The multi-track human resource management system, targeted for core employees, is the keystone of the merit-oriented personnel system.

Few companies selected 'expansion of the welfare system' in 1995. One reason is that the benefit package had already been well arranged during the bubble economy period. Another is that the labour market has become advantageous to companies. Companies no longer need to sell an attrac-

Table 3.9 Change of main themes in human resource management (multiple responses allowed) (per cent)

Ranking in 1995	1995	1989	1984
1 Motivation skills and leadership training of managers	71.2	67.5 (1)	n/a
2 Adoption of the merit-oriented personnel system	66.8	49.8 (4)	78.9
3 Empowerment of older workers	40.4	31.8 (12)	42.4
4 Enhancement of education and training programmes	40.0	57.0 (3)	86.6
Encouragement of small group activity such as quality control circles	n/a	n/a	47.1
5 Shortened working hours	38.1	34.4 (8)	n/a
Improvement of wage and shortening of work hours	n/a	n/a	29.4
6 Dealing with employees' diverse values	36.2	36.0 (6)	n/a
Employment of labour with various working styles	n/a	n/a	38.3
7 Flexible redeployment of labour within the company	34.3	20.3 (15)	33.9
8 Employment and promotion of female regular employees	30.2	35.2 (7)	n/a
9 Flexible redeployment of labour in group companies	30.0	15.4 (18)	n/a
10 Corrective action against labour surplus	28.5	n/a	n/a
11 Redeployment for new business ventures or by restructuring	26.2	15.1 (19)	n/a
12 More personal customised management	25.8	20.0 (16)	n/a
13 Preparation for globalisation	24.7	20.9 (14)	n/a
14 Flattening of organisation by abolishing sections, etc.	20.9	5.5 (22)	n/a
15 Full-scale application of the specialist career system	20.5	5.5 (20)	29.6
16 More active employment of part-timers and temporary workers	20.3	33.4 (11)	n/a
17 Expansion of welfare benefit programmes	20.1	34.1 (9)	30.0
18 Improvement of wage levels	19.2	33.8 (10)	n/a
19 Countermeasure against labour shortage	17.5	64.9 (2)	n/a
20 Stabilisation of labour–management relations	15.0	17.2 (17)	35.3
21 Securing research and development staff and engineers by offering better terms and conditions of employment	13.9	38.5 (5)	29.6
22 Selecting and developing star employees (gold collar)	11.6	5.8 (21)	n/a
23 Recruiting mid-career professionals	7.8	27.9 (13)	n/a
24 More active employment of foreign staff	3.6	4.9 (23)	n/a
25 Others	0.4	0.5 (25)	n/a

Notes: Sorted in descending order based on the percentages in 1995. Figures in ( ) indicate ranking in 1989. n/a indicates the item is not asked in the survey. Unnumbered items are the closest corresponding items in the 1984 survey.

tive welfare system to hire good quality employees. This buyer's market can be seen in the fact that fewer companies now place 'securing engineers with better treatment' as a priority. It has become easier than ever for companies to recruit and retain engineers.

'Stablisation of labour–management relations' has also lost its influence in human resource management. This is because a basic consensus was reached in the recessions following the oil crises that both labour and management would strive to improve business performance by protecting job security even at the expense of sacrificing an improvement in working conditions.

To find what impact the burst of the bubble economy gave on the human resource management policy, the 1995 ranking may be compared with the one in the 1989 survey. 'Countermeasure against labour shortage' is given a significantly lower ranking (2 → 19) in 1995. The labour shortage in 1989 quickly turned into a labour surplus by 1995. There was, therefore, no more need for 'securing research and development staff and engineers by offering better terms and conditions of employment' (5 → 21). 'Recruiting mid-career professionals' has also declined in ranking (13 → 23) as has 'more active employment of part-timers and temporary workers' (11 → 16). These results changed companies' attitudes towards employees, with less priority being given to the 'improvement of wage levels' (10 → 18) and the 'expansion of welfare benefit programmes' (9 → 17).

In contrast, there are human resource strategies which are ranked higher in 1995 than in 1989 such as 'redeployment for new business ventures or by restructuring' (19 → 11). Companies have given up the expansion of their organisation and have started the 'flattening of their organisation by abolishing sections, etc.' (22 → 14), and promoting the 'flexible redeployment of labour within the company' (15 → 7) instead of hiring other employees. If the positions for surplus workers are still short, companies will promote 'flexible redeployment of labour in group companies' (18 → 9).

The workforce, having aged at the fastest pace in the world, came to be perceived as a burden to companies. Seeking the utilisation of older workers is now considered to be the most urgent problem ('empowerment of older workers' (12 → 3)). Japanese companies cannot afford to promote all their older employees further. The double-track human resource management system consisting of two types of promotion for the generalist and the specialist is strongly supported ('full-scale application of the specialist career system' (20 → 15)). The companies' demand for the selection and cut-back of older employees is good evidence of how worn attitudes were towards the group-oriented tradition. Surely Japanese companies will tend towards emphasising 'more active employment of part-timers and temporary workers' (11 → 16) in human resource management. However, in spite of all the changes taking place, the same strategies remained at the top of the list of the main human resource management policies: 'motivation skills and leadership training of managers' (1 → 1), 'adoption of the merit-oriented personnel system' (4 → 2), 'enhancement of education and training programmes' (3 → 4), and 'dealing with employees' diverse values' (6 → 6).

Human resource management in companies of different sizes

The main strategy adopted appears to differ greatly depending on the size of the company (see Table 3.10). Larger companies focus on the following areas:

(a) Slimming down of the company: 'Flattening of organisation by abolishing sections, etc.' and 'corrective action against labour surplus'.
(b) Deployment of business: 'Redeployment for new business ventures or by restructuring', and 'preparation for globalisation'.
(c) Older employees: 'Empowerment of older workers'.
(d) Flexible redeployment: 'Flexible redeployment of labour within the company', and 'flexible redeployment of labour in group companies'.
(e) Double-track human resource management system: 'Selecting and developing star employees (gold collar)' and 'full-scale application of the specialist career system'.

Small companies with less than 1,000 employees place higher priority on the following subjects compared with larger companies:

(a) Recruitment: 'Countermeasure against labour shortage'.
(b) Improvement of labour condition: 'Securing research and development staff and engineers by offering better terms and conditions of employment' and 'expansion of welfare benefit programmes'.
(c) Development of managers: 'Motivation skills and leadership training of managers'.

Strategic patterns in human resource management

Japanese companies can be classified into five clusters following the factor analysis of the main human resource management strategies adopted by each company (see Table 3.11):

(a) A cluster consisting of companies that consider flexible redeployment of labour not only within the company but the entire company group for new business ventures or global business. They also aim to correct for labour surplus and to flatten the organisational structure.
(b) A cluster consisting of companies for which the main strategies are stable labour–management relations, improvement of wage levels, the expansion of the welfare benefit programmes and shorter working hours. They also tend to utilise part-timers and temporary workers.
(c) A cluster consisting of companies placing a high priority on the introduction of the merit-oriented personnel system of human resource management. This includes the full-scale application of the specialist career system, treatment on an individual basis, and the selection and development of star employees (gold collar).

Table 3.10 Main themes in human resource management by company size (multiple responsibilities) (column per cent)

	Company size (Number of employees)			
	Less than 299	300–999	1,000–2,999	3,000+
Corrective action against labour surplus	16.1	19.5	30.5	41.2
Countermeasure against labour shortage	24.1	27.4	12.6	11.8
Redeployment for new business ventures	14.9	18.6	24.0	41.2
Preparation for globalisation	11.5	19.5	27.5	34.0
Flattening of organisation	12.6	16.8	20.4	28.8
Motivation skill and leadership training of managers	75.9	76.1	67.7	68.6
Selecting and developing star employees (gold collar)	4.6	8.8	12.0	17.0
Full-scale application of the specialist career system	10.3	18.6	22.8	25.5
Empowerment of older workers	24.1	39.8	42.5	46.6
Securing research and development staff and engineers by offering better terms and conditions of employment	16.1	21.2	11.4	9.2
Flexible redeployment of labour within the company	26.4	30.1	33.5	42.5
Flexible redeployment of labour in group companies	6.9	15.9	29.9	53.6
Shortened working hours	23.0	23.9	48.5	45.8
Expansion of benefit and perks programme	27.6	27.4	19.2	11.8

Source: Nikkeiren and Nissankun (1995)

(d) A cluster consisting of companies intending to utilise women and older employees. In order to deal with the diversified workforce, they also provide intense education and training of employees, especially managers, to develop their motivation and leadership skills.

(e) A cluster consisting of companies having to deal with staff shortages in areas such as engineers and specialists. They consider it important to recruit mid-career personnel and utilise foreign employees and to provide them with higher salaries or benefit packages.

THE LINK BETWEEN CORPORATE STRATEGY AND HUMAN RESOURCE MANAGEMENT STRATEGY

Corporate strategy: human resource management strategy linkages

In the previous section, corporate strategies and human resource management strategies were categorised into five factors respectively. In this section, we discuss how the human resource management strategy is associated with the corporate strategy. Using each factor loading coefficient as a variable, a further factor analysis was carried out, as shown in Table 3.12. The results are as follows.

1. Companies oriented towards new business ventures and global business tend to give priority to the traditional way of improving labour conditions, such as wages and hours. Companies with traditional management techniques are also predominantly in the domestic market where there is little or no fear of restructuring. These latter type of companies, however, will decline in number as the recession continues. Management, which provides its employees with favourable labour conditions and stable labour–management relations, will be transformed in the globalisation age.
2. Companies focusing on visionary management tend to adopt multi-valued personnel administration. Their use of female workers, formally regarded by most Japanese companies as being second-rate workers, and older employees is expected to swell rapidly in the near future. These companies tend to be strongly education-minded as well as oriented toward the future. They are following the same path as the advanced Western multinational corporations which thrive on multi-culturalism within the company.
3. Recruiting professionals is a tendency found in companies trying to overcome the Dinosaur syndrome by attention paid to the front line. Such a company does not wish to increase the number of non-professional workers who have no real concern for what kind of jobs they are assigned to or for rising in the corporate hierarchy.
4. Companies emphasising rationalisation and downsizing, as corporate strategies, tend to consider the merit-oriented personnel system and selection of corporate elite as the important human resource management strategy.
5. No particular human resource management policy was found in the company emphasising sophistication of products and expansion of sales network.

Industry and corporate strategy: human resource management strategy linkages

Table 3.13 indicates which industrial sectors are most applicable to each cluster, based on the mean value of each set of factor loading coefficients by industry. Those sectors for which the mean value is above average are listed in the 'most applicable' column, those sectors with below average mean value are in the 'least applicable' column.

In the high-growth period after World War II up until the 1970s, process-automation and machine-intensive type manufacturing industries (textile,

Table 3.11 Factor analysis of main human resource management strategies (principal components analysis with Varimax rotation)

	Factor 1 Downsizing	Factor 2 Improvement in accordance with traditional methods	Factor 3 Merit oriented selective system	Factor 4 Diversity in labour management	Factor 5 Recruiting and retaining professionals and experts
Factor 1					
Redeployment for new business ventures	**.70107**	.10533	-.06124	-.01991	.04583
Flexible redeployment of labour in group companies	**.64298**	-.07625	.10035	.14254	-.1180
Corrective action against labour surplus	**.63401**	.02682	.13750	-.03973	.01246
Flattening of organisation	**.51711**	.02161	.10198	.09216	.12700
Preparation for globalisation	**.48291**	-.21844	.17494	.06864	.14692
Flexible redeployment of labour within the company	**.46308**	.27364	.07100	.06065	-.14324
Factor 2					
Stabilised labour–management relations	.14749	**.59956**	-.07767	-.10868	-.06760
Improvement of wage level	.01322	**.59917**	.07725	.08894	.13948
Expansion of benefit and perks programme	-.11581	**.53250**	.09008	.22929	.21565
Shortened working hours	.04525	**.47992**	.05272	.20037	-.23590
More active employment of part-timers and temporary hand workers	-.06304	**.36119**	.16386	-.06332	.25689

Table 3.11 (continued)

	Factor 1 Downsizing	Factor 2 Improvement in accordance with traditional methods	Factor 3 Merit oriented selective system	Factor 4 Diversity in labour management	Factor 5 Recruiting and retaining professionals and experts
Factor 3					
Full-scale application of the specialist career system	.08455	-.02904	**.61765**	.12097	.13514
More personal customised management	.03175	.00069	**.57281**	.26365	-.01074
Selecting and developing star people (gold collar)	.25287	.04457	**.55666**	-.00028	.05942
Adoption of merit-oriented personnel system	.14177	.23416	**.47602**	-.17256	-.12104
Factor 4					
Utilisation and promotion of women regular employees	-.03737	-.00231	-.02377	**.72610**	.06751
Empowerment of older workers	.21283	-.13436	.14343	**.48742**	-.02409
Deal with employee's diverse values	.08389	.20089	.07868	**.43701**	-.15064
Enhancement of education system	-.02742	.34196	-.07738	**.40462**	.17416
Motivation skill and leadership training of managers	.08979	.26225	.16492	**.33136**	-.0151
Factor 5					
Recruiting mid-career professionals	.09125	.01203	.08389	.02128	**.64883**
More active employment of foreign staff	.18916	-.16803	-.25799	-.01626	**.60031**
Countermeasure against labour shortage	-.16913	.27515	.11266	-.01479	**.47754**
Securing research and development people and engineers with better treatment	.01094	.17565	.25710	.01561	**.31177**

Source: Nikkeiren and Nissankun (1995)

Table 3.12 Factor analysis of corporate strategic patterns and human resource management patterns (principal components analysis with Varimax rotation)

	Factor 1	Factor 2	Factor 3	Factor 4	Factor 5
Factor 1					
New business/globalisation	**.78069**	−.10663	.05624	.05992	.01791
Improvement in accordance with traditional management methods	**.47721**	.14483	.34546	.34642	.45104
Restructuring	**−.46203**	−.38529	.34836	.26395	.12203
Factor 2					
Visionary management	.10015	**.77783**	.03491	−.07134	.05274
Diverse values in personnel	−.37855	**.65212**	.10195	.20870	−.02872
Factor 3					
Recovery from Dinosaur syndrome	−.02722	.03038	**.75590**	.05315	.08829
Recruiting professionals and experts	.13327	.08574	**.56127**	−.20584	−.38077
Factor 4					
Rationalization/ downsizing	−.02581	.06522	.01703	**.75089**	.05305
Merit oriented personnel system	−.14523	.14097	.11172	**−.54917**	.45748
Factor 5					
Product sophistication/ sales networking	.04953	−.01849	−.05038	−.04308	**.74814**

chemical, petroleum, ceramics, pulp, paper, steel and non-ferrous metal), as well as the supply of raw materials, had grown to be key Japanese industries. However, these companies now find themselves under severe pressure. In their search for an opportunity to start new business, they try to promote simplification and downsizing in their main businesses. As a result, restructuring is going on throughout industry. With no hope for traditional means to improve basic labour conditions, employees are facing cutbacks and selection. Companies, once the leaders in labour–management matters, now appear to have lost their positions.

In the 1980s, the manufacturing industry of the machine assembly type (for example, machinery, electric appliances, precision machines, automobiles and auto parts, and shipbuilding) has grown rapidly. This industry is seriously threatened by rivals from developing countries in the 1990s. There is pressure from Western companies to transfer production overseas to correct for trade friction. This industry is facing a serious wave of 'de-industrialisation'. All it can do is to manage precariously on a day-to-day basis, since to search for a corporate strategy is out of the question.

Table 3.13 Most applicable industrial sectors for each corporate strategy–human resource management strategy linkage

	Most applicable sectors	*Least applicable sectors*
1 Personnel management focused on new business development and globalisation along with restructuring. Less focused on improvement of basic labour conditions	Manufacturing industry: process-automation and machinery-intensive type	Financial, insurance, real estate
2 Emphasis on visionary management. Diversity in personnel management	Financial, insurance, real estate	
3 Recovery from Dinosaur syndrome and front line-orientated management. Recruiting of professionals		Manufacturing industry: labour-intensive type
4 Simplification and downsizing. Promotion by merit system	Manufacturing industry: process-automation and machinery-intensive type	Commercial, restaurant

Transferring production offshore in order to reduce costs is considered more advantageous than utilising flexible labour.

Large companies belonging to the labour-intensive manufacturing industry (such as, marine products, food, apparel, timber, furniture, stone, moulding, pressing, plating) were defeated by global competition, and shrank in the 1970s. Small businesses, which are still operating domestically, contribute to 'flexible specialisation' with their agility. These small companies are free from the Dinosaur syndrome in which large companies are trapped.

Financial, insurance and real estate businesses grew rapidly in the bubble economy period. However, they have a hard time paying up for the hopelessly huge debts. They are too heavily involved in withdrawing from this situation to be able to extend business. Far from globalisation, they have started quitting business overseas. In this industry, companies are looking to survive while cutting down costs by the utilisation of contingent labour.

Service industries such as commercial, restaurant and hotel businesses devoted to customer satisfaction make efforts to recover from the Dinosaur syndrome, listen to the opinion from the front line, and recruit professional service personnel. They value human resource development and revitalisation of the organisation through streamlining and flattening of the organisation structure.

CONCLUSION

As in other countries, the human resource management strategy of Japanese companies changes in accordance with their corporate strategy. This corporate strategy is a product of the companies' independent action to anticipate and respond to the kaleidoscopic changes surrounding them. It has been emphasised frequently that in the strategy for human resource management, the Japanese-style employment practices are unique. However, this focus mistakes a temporary phenomenon for a permanent one. Depending on changing circumstances, the Japanese style of employment may become intensified, or turn around and fall apart.

However, no matter what the circumstances, the following three themes have been the keystone of Japanese corporate strategy; the shaking up of managers' consciousness to improve their motivation and leadership skills, the gradual introduction of merit systems, and the everlasting effort to develop human resources.

NOTES

1 Ministry of Labour, Policy Research Department (1987) *Nihonteki Koyokanko no Henka to Tenbo* (*Changing Japanese Employment Practices*). Out of 1,500 randomly sampled companies with 100 or more regular employees, 629 companies responded (41.9 per cent). The author was a research director.
2 Nikkeiren and Nissankun (Japan Federation of Management and Japan Association of Industrial Training), (1990) *Dai Nanakai Sangyo Kunren Jittai Chosa* (*Seventh General Survey of Industrial Training*). Out of 3,974 large or middle-sized companies, 616 companies responded (15.5 per cent). The author was a research adviser.
3 Nikkeiren and Nissankun (Japan Federation of Management and Japan Association of Industrial Training) (1995) *Dai Hachikai Sangyo Kunren Jittai Chosa* (*Eighth General Survey of Industrial Training*). Out of 3,463 large or middle-sized companies, 527 companies responded (15.2 per cent). The author was a research adviser.

REFERENCES

Chusho Kigyo Chosa Kyokai (Small Business Research Association) (1990) *Keiei Senryaku Jittai Chosa* (*Survey on Corporate Strategy*).
Keizai Doyukai (1994) *Kigyo Hakusho* (*White Paper on Japanese Corporations*), Tokyo: Keizai Doyu Kai.
Ministry of Labour, Policy Research Department (1987) *Nihonteki Koyokanko no Henka to Tenbo* (*Changing Japanese Employment Practices*), Tokyo: Okurasho Insatsukyoku.
Mizuguchi, Koichi (ed.) (1994) *Shintenkai saguru Nihon Kigyo: Human Capitalism*

e no Shido (*In Search of New Management: Human Capitalism*), Tokyo: Toyo Keizai Shinposha.

Nikkeiren and Nissankun (Federation of Management and Japan Association of Industrial Training) (1990) *Dai Nanakai Sangyo Kunren Jittai Chosa* (*Seventh General Survey of Industrial Training*), Tokyo: Nikkeiren and Nissankun.

—— (1995) *Dai Hachikai Sangyo Kunren Jittai Chosa* (*Eighth General Survey of Industrial Training*), Tokyo: Nikkeiren and Nissankun.

Okubayashi, Koji *et al.* (1994) *Jukozo Soshiki Paradaimu Josetsu: Shinjidai no Nihonteki Keiei* (*Flexible Organization Paradigm; New Generation of Japanese Management*), Tokyo: Bunshindo.

Tokyo Chamber of Commerce and Industry (1994) *Nijuisseiki ni Mukete Motomerareru Keiei Kaizen no Hoko* (*Business Change Strategy for the 21st Century*), Tokyo: Tokyo Shoko Kaigisho.

4 Human resource management systems in large firms
The case of white-collar graduate employees

Hiroki Sato

INTRODUCTION

This chapter examines the characteristics of human resource management systems in large firms with reference to the case of white-collar employees with university education. It analyses two specific topics, promotion and employment management, rather than considering the entire field of human resource management. This focus lies at the heart of the customary interpretation of the Japanese employment system.

The current system of promotion is undergoing change against a background of slower rates of organisational expansion, a flattening of structures within organisations, and growth in the number of graduate employees. This has led to re-examination of the principles of promotion, and this study considers the ways in which promotion rules are likely to evolve. Two aspects of employment management are considered. One is the question of possible changes in the practice of continuous employment to retiring age; the other is the current state of career development within enterprises.

PROMOTION MANAGEMENT: CURRENT STATE AND MAJOR ISSUES

Promotion and means of selection

Generally speaking, promotion means movement from a lower to a higher post, both in level of managerial rank and in 'skill qualification' (*shokuno shikaku tokyu*, hereafter 'grade'). Promotion in managerial rank and promotion in grade are distinguishable, but here they are both considered as promotion. Grades are based on a classification which corresponds to an individual's capacity to perform a job. In firms where this grade system is in force a part of employees' salaries is determined on the basis of grade level and is known as capability-based pay (*shokunokyu*) or qualification-based pay (*shikakukyu*).[1]

These grades resemble 'pay grades' of white-collar staff of large British or American firms, but there is a fundamental difference. Japanese grades are not based on the job actually being performed as in the case of a pay grade, but on a classification of an employee's performance capacity. Accordingly, even where there is no promotion in terms of managerial rank or responsibilities, if there is an increase in an employee's capability, the system provides for promotion in terms of job qualification grade.[2]

For employees, promotion brings rewards in the form of better pay, increased responsibility and authority, and enhanced social prestige. Promotion not only provides improved rewards, but also brings with it a higher level of managerial responsibility and tasks, and thus provides an opportunity for skill development. In other words, closing promotion opportunities also deprives employees of opportunities to develop their abilities. Since promotion provides opportunities for rewards in the form of qualification-based pay and skill development, employees are extremely interested in promotion. Consequently the way in which promotion is managed is an important determinant of employees' motivation.

Since the organisational hierarchy is usually pyramidal in structure, there are fewer senior posts, in terms of managerial rank, than junior ones. Therefore if the structure does not change it becomes essential to be selective in making promotions to higher rank. On the other hand promotion in terms of *grade* is not subject to the same systematic restriction. However, even when one is promoted to a higher grade, if there is only a limited number of jobs which require the ability level corresponding to that grade, it may be that one cannot be assigned a higher-level position. Yet for the enterprise, a cost is incurred in increasing an employee's salary in accordance with promotion in grade without being able to move him to a post where he can generate a corresponding increase in value added. For this reason firms must attempt to maintain a balance between the numbers of employees at different grades and the numbers of jobs which require the degrees of skill corresponding to these grades. In the short term it is not necessary to achieve a balance between the two, but in the medium term it will become essential.

The implication of the foregoing is that, if there is no change in other relevant circumstances, large Japanese firms cannot continue to practice the promotion management system, whereby rank and grade automatically rise in accordance with the length of continuous employment (the so-called seniority-based promotion system) in the medium to long term. What alternatives do large Japanese firms have to promotion based on age and seniority? Before examining the current state of promotion management, let us consider a number of models of promotion management and selection procedures.

Rosenbaum (1979) describes the principle of intra-organisational selection as 'tournament mobility', in a model derived from Turner's (1960) 'sponsored mobility' and 'contest mobility'. Sponsored mobility involves a division between the elite, to whom promotion opportunities are guaranteed at the initial stage of their career, and the non-elite who are excluded from such future opportunities. A very small number of individuals are selected at this initial stage and are promised subsequent promotion. The motivation of non-elite to participate in the competition for promotion is problematic, but a small number may be selected for education and training, in which a cost-effective investment may be made. In the case of contest mobility, the organisation provides opportunities to compete for promotion at every stage in a career course, and preserves these opportunities well into the second half of a career. This can sustain motivation over a long period, but since it is not possible to select and train a small elite at an early stage, the efficiency of investment in education and training is impaired. In the case of tournament mobility, on the other hand, as distinct from sponsored mobility and contest mobility, promotion may be considered as a process of continuous selection whereby at every stage it is necessary to continue to succeed at each successive selection in order for promotion to continue. Tournament mobility is a selection procedure which gradually squeezes out the participants in the competition for promotion.

The main points of difference between tournament mobility and sponsored mobility or contest mobility are as follows. First, in the case of tournament mobility, but not contest mobility, the loser at any stage of the promotion contest is excluded from the opportunity to compete at the next stage. Second, in contrast to sponsored mobility, tournament mobility enjoins that the victor at one stage is not guaranteed victory at the next stage, but in order for promotion to continue must succeed in competition at that stage too. Tournament mobility, by providing victors with the opportunity to compete at the next stage, can have a motivating effect; and at the same time, since education and training for the next stage of promotion can be confined to an already selected group, it is possible to concentrate and increase the efficiency of the investment in training. Tournament mobility thus has the twin effect of motivating employees and enhancing the efficiency of investment in training (Yashiro 1995).

According to Rosenbaum (1984), the tournament mobility model applies and is appropriate to American firms. But it may be asked whether it is a model which also applies to Japanese firms. Before considering the reality of promotion in Japanese firms, we first turn to the methods of selection for promotion in large Japanese firms.

Koike (1991a, 1991b) on the basis of case studies of some 60 companies, has proposed a model of 'late selection' for large firms' promotion selection procedures. 'Late selection' differs from the three models discussed above: it may be contrasted with the 'early selection' which occurs in tournament mobility whereby at an early career stage selection determines who may be eligible for later promotion to senior executive positions at the level of division manager and above. Rosenbaum's model of tournament mobility is termed 'early selection' because his analysis of promotion patterns found that those who were promoted early on had a high probability of later promotion, particularly if the initial stage occurred within the first three years after joining the company. In the case of tournament mobility, as distinct from sponsored mobility, there is no guarantee of promotion to an elite selected at the start of their career, but future promotion prospects are strongly influenced by selection at an early stage. In both cases future career prospects may be decisively affected at an early stage.

On the other hand, according to Koike's concept of late selection, promotion to key senior executive posts at division manager level and above depends on selection at quite a late stage in the course of a career, about 15 years after joining the firm in the case of his large-firm study (Koike 1991a).

On the basis of assessments of an employee's performance and approach to work which have been built up over a long period, selection for onward promotion is made at a relatively late stage. At this stage employees are divided into, (A) those who will not reach management-level posts, (B) those who will reach section manager level, but rise no further and (C) those destined for divisional management and top management posts.

In the case of late selection, between the early stage of employment and the point at which decisive selection takes place, of those who joined the company at the same time (cohort fellows) a small number may fall behind, but almost all are promoted at roughly the same pace.

It must be noted that at the point where decisive selection begins the members of the cohort have not all been promoted or received pay increments at exactly the same rate. Subject to the performance appraisal not only may annual pay increments differ, but there is also variation in rank advancement terms and in many cases in grade promotion. However, the degree of divergence is not large and there is a strong possibility of its being reversed in the light of subsequent performance. Up to the point at which decisive selection occurs it is possible for those who have been lagging to recover their position.[3]

Although divergence in promotion on the basis of performance appraisal is small, there is a strong competitive consciousness among members of the same recruitment cohort. This is because, since the number of those who drop out of competition for promotion is small, the number of those who continue to compete is large and does not rapidly decline after entering the company; and since when divergence occurs in the speed of promotion the process of catching up again takes a long time, the will of many members of a cohort to continue to compete until the point of decisive selection is maintained.

Takeuchi has produced a model of promotion based on an elaboration of Koike's 'late selection' (Takeuchi 1995). Takeuchi's model classifies modes of selection on the basis of two measures: the proportion of members of a recruitment cohort promoted to each level of rank; and the divergence between the times it takes members of a cohort to be promoted to a higher rank. Within a cohort, divergence between time to promotion for a given rank is indicated by the difference between the shortest and longest times between the promotion to that rank of the earliest and the latest individuals to reach it. If all members of a cohort reach a rank simultaneously, promotion time divergence is zero. In Figure 4.1 promotion selection is classified in four ways according to probability of promotion and promotion time divergence. These four selection processes are referred to as simultaneous promotion, divergent promotion, selection and discrimination. The meanings attached to these are as follows.

- Simultaneous promotion = a large proportion of a cohort is promoted in rank or grade at the same time (high promotion rate and same promotion time).
- Divergent promotion = there are variations in the time at which promotion occurs but a large proportion of the cohort are promoted (high promotion rate but differing promotion times).
- Selection = a small proportion of a cohort are promoted to the relevant level but the time at which promotion occurs is roughly the same (low promotion rate, but promotion occuring roughly simultaneously).
- Discrimination = a small proportion of a cohort are promoted to the relevant level and there are variations in the time at which promotion occurs (low promotion rate, differing promotion times).

It is necessary to apply this fourfold classification to promotion at each level of rank and grade. As stated above, according to Koike, during the first 15 years no decisive divergence in career path arises, implying that simultaneous or divergent promotion occur only after the elapse of a

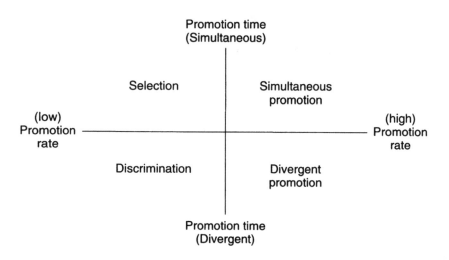

Figure 4.1 Classification of promotion patterns
Source: Takeuchi (1995)

comparatively long period from a cohort's year of entry. In addition Takeuchi's analysis of large-firm 'career trees' reveals a promotion pattern which, with the passage of time from entry, evolves from simultaneous promotion, to divergent promotion, and subsequently to discrimination or selection; this constitutes the nub of the 'late selection' model.

A concrete example of 'late selection'

A concrete example of 'late selection' is represented by Takeuchi's study of the 'career tree' of a large company in the finance and insurance sector (Takeuchi 1995). Figure 4.2 shows the promotion record, at the point when the study was conducted in 1988, of 67 employees who graduated from university in 1966 and joined the firm in April of that year. Figure 4.2 should be read as follows. The number of years after joining the firm at which promotion to the relevant level has occurred is shown in brackets. The number of individuals promoted to each level is shown inside the squares. For example, the rank of assistant section manager (*kacho dairi*) was reached after 8 years by 56 staff, after 9 years by a further 9 staff, and after 10 years by 2 others. According to the figure, therefore, there has been little divergence in promotion to assistant section manager and the situation is, broadly speaking, one of simultaneous promotion. In the case of the rank of senior staff member (*shunin*), all employees were promoted simultaneously, and at the next stage of promotion to group manager (*kakaricho*) 66 out of 67 staff were promoted simultaneously 5 years after entry. Even in the case of promotion from group manager to assistant section manager, 56 staff were promoted at the first occasion of selection (termed 'first selection'), and 9 at the second occasion (or 'second selection') one year later, so almost all the cohort were promoted within one year of each other. Many of those who were promoted to assistant section manager one year late were able to catch up at the next stage. Moreover the number of staff unable to progress beyond assistant section manager was very small (only two). It may thus be considered that up to assistant section manager the practice is one of simultaneous promotion.

Although the rate of promotion from assistant section manager to junior section manager (*kacho I*) is high (82 per cent), a significant divergence can be seen in the time at which promotion occurs. A small number of staff (five) were promoted to junior section manager after 12 years, so that in contrast to promotion at earlier stages, only a small minority were promoted at the first selection. Moreover, and importantly, promotion to the next level (senior section manager or *kacho II*) is very difficult if one has not achieved promotion to junior section manager within 14 years after entry (that is, at the first, second or third selections for promotion to junior section manager or *kacho I*). One individual, having been promoted to junior section manager after 16 years, was subsequently

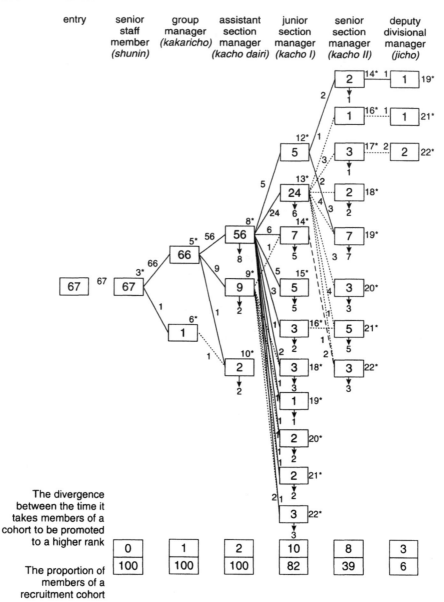

Figure 4.2   Career tree

Source: Takeuchi (1995)

Note: * Denotes number of years employment before promotion to that rank.

promoted to senior section manager, but it seems that this should be considered an exceptional case. In other words, those who did not achieve promotion to senior section manager within 14 years were effectively excluded from the competition for promotion to higher posts. It may be said that this level is the point at which tournament mobility begins. In this company those staff for whom promotion to key executive positions at divisional manager level and above is a possibility are henceforward selected by a decisive 'squeezing-out' process, which begins 14 years after entry. Moreover, among those who are promoted to senior section manager more than 14 years after entry (that is at the second and third selections), there is a possibility of catching up at the 'return match' which is constituted by the opportunity to compete for promotion to higher levels.

Although there is a negligible possibility of promotion to posts higher than senior section manager for those who have failed to reach senior section manager by the third selection, that does not mean that competition between this group ceases once the third selection has taken place. What then happens is that competition centres on the time of eventual promotion to senior section manager, and younger staff from later cohorts also become competitors for this promotion. Consequently competition for promotion continues on a long-term basis. Since the promotion rate from senior section manager to deputy divisional manager (*jicho*) is low, discrimination or selection occurs.

The above account demonstrates the promotion pattern of company A, proceeding from simultaneous promotion, through divergent promotion, to discrimination and selection. This is the core of the mechanism of Koike's 'late selection'.

Promotion management: macro-data

Koike's late selection model of promotion in large firms derives from a number of case studies, but Takeuchi's characterisation of the promotion process is based on a single company. To what extent is late selection actually implemented by large firms in Japan? It is not possible to produce data on a large scale to confirm the widespread use of 'late selection', but there are survey data on the extent of simultaneous promotion as defined by Takeuchi. According to this survey, for white-collar university graduate employees joining the firm in a given year, 64.5 per cent of firms stated that, 'After entry for a fixed period promotion is simultaneous'. In larger firms this response was more frequent, rising to 71.6 per cent for firms with more than 5,000 employees (Nikon Rodo Kenkyu Kiko 1993). The survey examined 'simultaneous promotion' but also strongly suggests the widespread use of 'late selection'.

Other data provide information on the age at which promotion occurs. Table 4.1, from the Ministry of Labour *Basic Survey of Wage Structure*

Table 4.1   Ranks of graduate male employees in large firms (over 1,000 employees) classified by age (per cent)

Age	Total	Divisional manager (bucho)	Section manager (kacho)	Other manager	Group manager (kakaricho)	Non-manager
55–59	100.0	30.7	13.4	19.3	2.8	33.8
50–54	100.0	35.0	19.3	22.1	2.8	20.8
45–49	100.0	15.5	32.4	20.7	6.3	25.0
40–44	100.0	3.5	33.5	17.8	12.3	32.9
35–39	100.0	0.4	13.0	14.8	21.2	50.5
30–34	100.0	0.1	1.4	9.2	12.1	77.2
25–29	100.0	–	0.1	2.5	0.8	96.6
20–24	100.0	–	–	1.2	0.1	98.8

Source: Rodosho (1994a)

Note: Other manager includes deputy divisional manager and assistant section manager.

shows figures on promotion of male university graduate white-collar workers in large firms (with more than 1,000 employees). Figures are aggregated for different firms and so do not provide information on the promotion practice of individual firms. It is also necessary to bear in mind that the figures shown only cover promotion in level of rank, not grade, and that they do not extend to specialist jobs or to positions other than those in line management. From the table the following points emerge.

(1) Promotion for employees in their twenties is exceptional.
(2) In the early thirties the first selections for group manager (*kakaricho*) begin, but promotion to section manager (*kacho*) is extremely rare. The first selection for section manager may begin in the later thirties, and promotion to section manager may take place in the later forties. Thus there is considerable divergence for promotion to this rank.
(3) It is difficult to estimate the promotion rate to group manager or section manager, since other ranks may also exist such as assistant section manager (*kacho hosa*). If one supposes that about half of the intermediate posts are of assistant section manager and half are of deputy divisional manager (*jicho*), the proportion of staff who are promoted to section manager or above is about 65 per cent. The rate of promotion to group manager is about 80 per cent. The rate would probably be higher if one included promotion to grades corresponding to the relevant ranks. In other words there is a high rate of promotion to the ranks of group manager and section manager, and to the corresponding grades.
(4) Promotion to posts higher than section manager takes place between the later forties and early fifties. The rate of promotion to division manager (*bucho*) is low, about 30 per cent.

To sum up the above results: employees in their late twenties, some seven years after joining the company, are liable to be promoted roughly simultaneously up to just before the move to group manager level (*kakaricho*); at the start of their thirties there is a first selection for the first round of promotions to group manager; then, in the later thirties, there is a first selection for section manager (*kacho*). Promotion rates for both ranks are quite high (although that to section manager is of course lower than that to group manager), but within a cohort, divergence in the date of promotion becomes quite substantial. For promotion to division manager (*bucho*), the promotion rate is low, and selection or discrimination come into effect. Promotion management of white-collar employees of large firms tends to be simultaneous for the first seven years, with divergence emerging thereafter, and there is divergent promotion, but with a high rate of eventual promotion, to the comparatively high rank of section manager. These findings support the promotion model derived from Koike's and Takeuchi's case studies.

Pros and cons of late selection

Here we consider the advantages and disadvantages of the system of late selection and of simultaneous and divergent promotion (Koike 1991a, 1991b, Yashiro 1995, Takeuchi 1995, Sato 1995a).

The first advantage is that, because selection which is decisive for one's subsequent career occurs a considerable time after entering the firm, a large number of employees are able to continue to compete over a long time, and they therefore have long-term motivation to develop and improve their skills. Second, when decisive selection takes place, reference is made to the appraisals which an employees' superiors have made to the personnel management section over the long period when simultaneous promotion has been practised. This means that, compared with a system of early selection, the assessment of ability on which selection is based is likely to be more accurate and selection is more convincing and acceptable to employees.

On the other hand there are disadvantages to late selection. First, because of the fact that decisive selection of top managers occurs late, the training and preparation of core senior executives is not only time-consuming but involves a considerable waste of investment in training costs. Second, because late selection involves the inculcation of strongly competitive attitudes over a long time, this produces an excessively competitive environment.

On balance, considering these pros and cons of late selection, the net effect as a source of the competitiveness of the enterprise itself may be judged positive in so far as the system contributes to the skills and morale not only of the top and senior managers but also of middle managers, who constitute the larger part of the organisation.

Conditions for existence of late selection

Many large firms in Japan implement late selection, but in order for the system to function several conditions must be satisfied. If not, other selection systems may be applied. If the basis on which the system rests changes, a change in selection system is required.

First, a high rate of promotion to quite senior levels must be maintained in order for decisive selection to take place at a late stage. If other conditions do not vary, in order to sustain an increasing number of such senior posts the size of the company must also increase. There are a large number of employees who face limited opportunities for promotion, or the chance of promotion only to fairly low levels (for example high school graduates, female employees), and the restriction of management posts to white-collar university graduates is necessary (Sato 1995a, Takeuchi 1995).

Second, although divergences in promotion and salary are small, employees are conscious of them, and a reference group is necessary for the purposes of comparison (Sato 1987, Takeuchi 1995). Such a group is made up of the employees who joined in the firm in the same month of the same year. A sense of cohort consciousness is fostered by the simultaneous recruitment of new graduates every April and the provision of new recruit training for each year's crop of new graduates. Against the background of the cohort as reference group, employees develop a competitive consciousness of 'not wanting to lag behind the cohort', and an awareness even of small divergences in promotion.[4]

Third, it is necessary that, in view of the fact that decisive selection occurs late, up to that point wide discrepancies do not exist in skill levels or performance. It is difficult to maintain late selection if there is a major divergence in levels of competence. This is because highly competent employees will react against a system which gives similar promotion, pay and other rewards to those whose performance is drastically inferior. For this reason it is necessary to give thought at the time of initial recruitment to avoiding a wide divergence of ability levels, and subsequently to ensure that skill development and job allocation is done so as to prevent major divergence in competence from arising. Job proficiency is developed through on-the-job training (OJT), so skill development is largely determined by the nature and level of jobs which are allocated to employees. It is therefore necessary to allocate jobs requiring similar levels of competence to members of an entry cohort. Moreover, since the guidance and instruction of superiors and senior colleagues has a major influence on skill development, a similarly homogeneous character is also required in this instruction.

The fourth necessary condition is that the group of employees who are subject to such a system of promotion management should have a shared aspiration to rise in the ranks of management. If the rewards of promotion are not attractive to employees, they cannot be motivated to compete for promotion. According to surveys of the promotion hopes of employees in large firms, almost all of them hope at least to become section managers and over 70 per cent wish to reach the level of divisional manager or above. This applies not only to employees generally but also to younger ones in their twenties (Rodosho Seisaku Chosabu 1995b).

The above conditions for the functioning of late selection are currently declining, and changes in promotion systems are increasingly going to be necessary.

Changes in the conditions of promotion systems

First, it is increasingly difficult to maintain high rates of promotion. Factors tending to diminish promotion rates include decelerated growth in the numbers of management positions, caused by slackening of corporate growth and flatter, less hierarchical, organisational structures, and a rise in the proportion of employees who are university graduates and assume that they stand a good chance of promotion. The growth in numbers of female graduate employees is also a factor tending to restrict further the prospects for male graduates.

Second, growth in the numbers of graduates recruited has increased the difficulty of avoiding major divergence in training possibilities, particularly since the decline in companies' growth means that there is increasing variance in the level and nature of the jobs to which employees are posted. In other words, there is increasing difficulty in achieving a fair allocation of posts which can give new employees similar opportunities to display their potential, and consequently there arises increased divergence in the extent to which employees' skills are developed (Sato 1995a).

These changes mean that firms are shortening the period of simultaneous promotion and indeed of divergent promotion, and bringing forward the onset of selection (Sato 1995a). At the same time, in order to preserve promotion opportunities, many firms are introducing a system of maximum age for each managerial rank (*yakushoku teinen seido*) and promoting secondment of employees to other workplaces. These topics are now examined more closely.

Table 4.2 shows the results of a study on measures for utilising middle-aged white-collar workers in enterprises. It shows that the number of firms seeking to preserve the promotion system by delaying opportunities for promotion is extremely small, and that a large number of firms do not wish to alter the timing of promotion to section or divisional manager level. If promotion opportunities decline but the tempo of promotion is not changed, the rules of promotion must inevitably alter. The first such change is the creation of a climate in which, through expansion of the system of specialist jobs, promotion is less confined to managerial positions (56.1 per cent). This seeks to alleviate the pressure for management promotion by establishing a 'multi-track career system' in which there

116   *Hiroki Sato*

Table 4.2 Conditions making continuing employment of middle-aged white-collar company employees possible (percentages of number of firms so responding)

Creation of an organisational climate in which, through expansion of the system of specialist jobs, promotion is less confined to managerial positions	56.1
Thorough implementation of meritocratic promotion, becoming able resolutely to implement selection and demotion in personnel management	46.8
Reduction in pay level beyond a certain age, following a normal continuously rising seniority pay profile	41.6
Planning to apply or expand the system of maximum age for managerial posts (*yakushoku teinen seido*)	35.0
Introducing large differentials in pay between employees of the same age after a certain age	21.4
Planning a fundamental transformation in methods of human resource development	24.3
Expansion of the quota of secondments outside the firm for employees between a given age and retiring age	12.8
General delaying of the period at which promotion occurs	6.8
Current practice is satisfactory	6.4
Impossible to continue employment until retiring age	2.1

Source: Rodosho Seisaku Chosabu (1995b)

Note: Up to three responses permitted.

are good prospects other than through promotion in line management positions.

The second change is the implementation of meritocratic promotion (selective personnel management and demotion) (46.8 per cent). This involves a reduction in the proportion of those who are promoted in grade or rank at the same time on the basis of accumulated years of service, diminution of the number of opportunities for promotion, and an attempt to apply a selective system.

The third change is the preservation of the career point at which promotion occurs by applying or extending a time-limiting rule whereby a post may be held for only a limited number of years (35.0 per cent).

It can therefore be expected that the future will see the introduction and expansion of more time limitations for managerial posts and of prospects for specialist posts outside the line management career track. The extent to which the development of systems of specialist jobs can be effected without friction will depend on the nature of promotion opportunities and mechanisms.

EMPLOYMENT MANAGEMENT

The current state of continuous employment

Customarily it has been common to characterise Japanese employment practice as one of 'lifetime employment', but recently it has come to be described as 'continuous employment to retirement'. It is worth considering to what extent this description corresponds to reality.

According to a comparative international study by OECD, there are considerable differences between the degree of employees' job tenure in firms (that is, the extent of continuity of employment) in different countries (OECD 1993). From an international point of view Japanese firms have a high level of employee job tenure (see Chapter 1 for details). Moreover, the trend over time has been for the proportion of employees with long continuous service within a given enterprise to grow. For example, according to the Ministry of Labour *Basic Survey of Wage Structure*, in firms in the manufacturing sector with over 1,000 employees, the average number of years of continuous service of male managerial, clerical and technical staff aged 45–49 was, in 1973, 21.4 for university graduates and 23.1 for high school graduates; whereas in 1993 the corresponding figures had risen to 23.0 and 27.3 respectively, thus confirming the trend towards longer-term continuity of employment. This trend is also shown by statistics broken down by firm size and by sex of employees (Koyo Joho Sentaa 1993).

However, although the trend is a general one, there are substantial differences in the extent of employee job tenure between firms of different sizes and between male and female employees. Job tenure is longer in large firms than in smaller ones, and longer for male than for female employees (Koyo Joho Sentaa 1993). Let us look at these differences in job tenure between larger and smaller firms in terms of retention rates. Retention rate is defined here as the proportion of employees who, having been employed in a given firm at a given time, remain continuously employed there up to a given later time. Figure 4.3 shows the proportion of male employees who remain in the same firm after the age of 27. The following points emerge.

For employees in their thirties and forties, if one compares small and medium enterprises (SMEs, firms with between 10 and 999 employees) with large firms (those with 1,000 or more employees), there is a rapid fall in retention rates. In SMEs the rate at which employees in their thirties and forties leave is high compared with employees of large firms. In large firms, on the other hand, retention is high for employees in their forties, remaining at 67.8 per cent at age 49. However, rates fall sharply for employees in their fifties, particularly the later fifties. Rates for employees between 50 and 59, the year before retiring age, are 65.5 per cent for 50-year-olds, 57.4 per cent for 53-year-olds, 41.9 per cent for 56-year-olds, and 24.5 per cent for 59-year-olds – a figure not very different

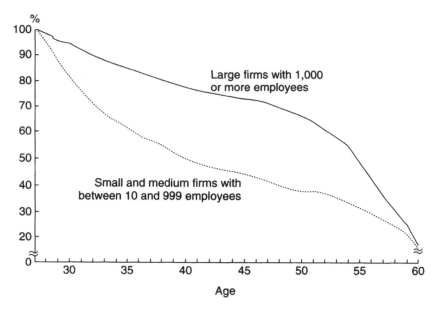

Figure 4.3 Retention ratio (male employees' entire education level)
Source: Rodosho (1994b)
Note: Estimated ratio calculated from Ministry of Labour (1987, 1992) *Basic Survey of Wage Structure.*

from the rate of 21.5 per cent in SMEs. For both large firms and SMEs, the proportion of employees who at 59 are still in the same firm as they were in at 27 is in the range 20–25 per cent.

Since almost all large firms have a retirement age of 60, there is a systematic guarantee of continous employment up to that age. Yet for employees in their fifties retention rates fall rapidly. One reason for this is that around that age it is common for employees, particularly in management grades, to be transferred to subsidiaries or other related firms. In many cases transfer takes place after an initial period of secondment. The process of transfer involves facilitation, by the existing employer and with the consent of the individual concerned, of the opportunity of alternative employment at the firm to which he is transferred.

According to the *Employment Management Survey* (Rodosho Seisaku Chosabu 1995a), among firms with over 5,000 employees (almost all of which have a retirement age of 60), the greatest number of employees who leave (including those who are transferred) between 45 and 60 are those aged between 55 and 60.[5] These cases of early departure include employees who leave under schemes which involve special payments to those who elect to leave early, but they are a small proportion of the total

(Rodosho Seisaku Chosabu 1995b), although 42.5 per cent of firms with over 5,000 employees have introduced such a system of severance payments (Rodosho Seisaku Chosabu 1995a).

The main reasons firms have for the practice of transferring staff are to preserve employment opportunities for staff once they are over 60, and to reduce the number of staff employed. The former objective is based on the fact that it is easier to preserve employment opportunities for those in their early sixties by arranging for their transfer while still in their fifties to firms which have a retirement age of 65 or which permit postponement of retirement, rather than waiting till they have reached the age of 60 before seeking such jobs. This is because even where the possibility might exist of recruitment after 60, the time necessary to learn the new job would be long in proportion to the total time of employment, and the opportunity to be useful to the new employer accordingly circumscribed.

The second objective, reduction in total employee numbers, achieved by the movement of managerial staff out of the firm by transferring them to other employers, includes both the creation of promotion opportunities for remaining employees and a reduction of the excessive absolute number of managerial staff. The practice of transfer or secondment is linked with the policy of introducing a rank-related maximum age system for managerial staff (*yakushoku teinen seido*) as a means of eliminating a shortage of managerial posts. Such a system involves the determination of a specified maximum age for a given level of post, and has been introduced by 35.8 per cent in firms with over 5,000 employees, and 34.6 per cent in those with 100–4,999, according to Rodosho Seisaku Chosabu (1995a). For example, although the company retiring age may be 60, the maximum age for divisional manager may be set at 55 and 50 for section manager. In such a case if a section manager has not achieved promotion to divisional manager by 50 he must leave his post. In firms which have introduced a grade system, a section manager may retain the corresponding grade even after leaving his section manager post. In almost all firms such a system is applied on the uniform basis of age, irrespective of performance or capacity. After reaching the designated age, in some cases employees may remain within the firm and in others they may be liable to secondment or transfer to subsidiaries or other firms (Rodosho Seisaku Chosabu 1995b). In the latter case, the number of employees being transferred is increasing. Of course, there are many firms which do not have such a maximum age system which none the less are encouraging transfer, especially of management staff.

Detailed study of retention rates in large firms shows that rates of continuous employment up to the age of 50 are high compared with SMEs, but fall rapidly thereafter. Rapid decline in the level of continous employment of those aged over 50 is due to the promotion of transfer and other forms of exit from the firm. Does this mean that the practice in large firms of continous employment until retiring age has collapsed? Transfers are not unilateral termination of employment by firms for their exclusive convenience, but facilitation of voluntary re-employment. In general, when the new job carries with it inferior conditions, particularly lower pay, the original firm provides a subsidy until the employee reaches that firm's retirement age to ensure that the employee is not disadvantaged by the change. Moreover, in many cases the new employer provides the opportunity of employment after the employee reaches what would have been his date of retirement in the original firm. In other words, it may be said that the practice of continuous employment in one firm to retirement age has changed to one of continuous employment within the group of companies comprising the original firm, its subsidiaries and other related firms (and in some cases in unrelated firms).

Excluding the small number who proceed to top management positions, the careers of white-collar graduate employees may lead in one of the three following directions:

(1) transfer or secondment within the same group of firms; or
(2) under a system of maximum ages for specific posts, losing managerial rank but remaining within the same firm until retirement age; or
(3) leaving the firm under a severance payment scheme and developing a new career.

So far, for employees in management positions in their fifties the first two are more common, particularly the first, and will probably remain so, but the first route is becoming progressively harder as it becomes more difficult to find firms to which secondment or transfer is possible. Finding such a means of secondment or transfer is increasingly becoming a matter of concern.

CAREER MANAGEMENT: THE CURRENT SITUATION AND EMERGING ISSUES

The breadth of 'narrow' careers

Our examination of promotion management has focused on vertical career structures, involving increase in level of rank. We now proceed to consider horizontal career structures, that is to say the breadth or range of kinds of work which employees get to experience within the firm. The point at issue when career breadth is the subject of debate is the appropriate means of measuring the scope of a range of jobs. If jobs are classified in a precise and detailed way, the number of different jobs which employees experience, and therefore the breadth of their careers, will tend to increase. Conversely, a classification of job types into larger groups will decrease the number of job types that employees experience. It is helpful to use the results of a survey of individuals, concerning new developments in working life, conducted by the Rengo union research institute (Rengo Sogo Seikatsu Kaihatsu Kenkyujo 1995).[6] This survey classifies areas of work into 13 job categories: management planning; legal; accounting, finance and budgeting; personnel, labour relations and training; general administration and secretarial; advertising and publicity; information systems; sales and marketing; international trade and overseas operations; materials, purchasing, distribution and process management; production technology and production management; product development and planning; research and development. These categories may be termed fields of work.

This classification of job types was applied, in order to examine the breadth of careers within the firm, with reference to two parameters, the field of work in which an employee's current post lies, and the total number of years during which an employee has worked in the field of work in which his experience is longest (within the company where he is currently employed). The following points emerged from the analysis.

First, for a large number of people, the field of work in which their experience is longest is also the field in which their current post lies. Comparing employees whose current work lies in various fields, in those cases where there were more than 100 respondents, those for whom the current field is also the one where their experience is longest comprise 80 per cent or more of those in information systems, sales and marketing, production technology and production management, product development and planning, and research and development; and the figure is 60 per cent or more for those currently working in accounting and finance, personnel and labour relations, and materials, purchasing and process management.

Second, if one compares the total number of years continously employed with the total number of years in the field where an employee's experience is longest, the two figures gradually diverge with increasing age, but for employees in their forties the average difference is still not very big (Table 4.3). In other words, a large number of employees remain more or less continuously in the same field throughout their careers. If one classifies career paths in terms of the range of fields in which an employee gets to work, three types of pattern can be distinguished: (a) employees whose careers are entirely within one field; (b) those with experience of more than one field, but who spend almost all their career within a single field; and (c) those whose experience is in more than one field and who do not spend a particularly long period in any of them. If one applies this classification to the subjects of the survey, cases of type (c) careers seem to be infrequent and types (a) and (b) predominate. Thus for a large proportion of the survey subjects the scope of their careers falls within a single field of work. If one defines 'generalists' as those whose careers encompass experience across a large number of fields of work, this category of employee is a minority.

Table 4.3   Years of continuous service and total number of years in the field of longest experience (male employees)

Age group	Age on entering the firm	Current age	Length of service (years)	Years in the field of longest exposure	Proportion whose experience is entirely in one field (%)
All ages	22.6	35.8	13.2	10.2	77.2
–24 (n = 88)	20.7	23.3	2.6	2.7	103.8
25–29 (n = 526)	22.8	27.9	5.1	4.5	88.2
30–34 (n = 759)	23.1	32.4	9.3	7.3	78.5
35–39 (n = 482	22.9	37.4	14.5	11.2	77.2
40–44 (n = 333)	20.9	42.3	21.4	16.5	77.1
45–49 (n = 197)	22.4	47.2	24.8	19.6	79.0
50–54 (n = 114)	21.6	52.2	30.6	22.2	72.5
55– (n = 40)	25.5	56.9	31.4	20.2	64.3

Source: Sato (1995b), raw data from Rengo Sogo Seikatsu Kaihatsu Kenkyujo (1995)

Notes: Length of service = Current age minus age on entering the firm. For employees up to 24 years old the number of years in the field of longest experience exceeds the number of years of continuous service; this is because some subjects did not give responses to the question asking for the former figure and the total figure does not therefore completely correspond to the figure for years of continuous service.

We now proceed to consider the scope of work which falls within the field in which the employee's working experience is longest. In the survey quoted above, three possible responses were offered in relation to this question, namely (a) 'I have had a deep experience of doing one job within this area'; (b) 'I have had the experience of doing various jobs within this area'; and (c) 'I have had a broad range of experience within this area'.

Excluding those men who did not respond, the proportions of responses were: (a) 43.7 per cent, (b) 31.5 per cent and (c) 24.8 per cent. With only about a quarter offering the third response, and the first two predominating, with (a) getting nearly 45 per cent of all responses, it is clear that in the field where work experience is longest it is very common for employees to have careers with a narrow range of work. Moreover, if one looks at the responses in terms of age of respondent, omitting the under-24s (whose period of employment is still short) and the over-55s (of which the sample size is small), for each age group the distribution is broadly similar. Thus there is no reason to foresee an increase in future proportions of those who have broad experience of types of work within a specific field.

Although overall the range of types of work within the field of longest service is narrow, there are variations between fields. Leaving out areas for which there were fewer than 50 respondents, in the field of personnel, labour relations and training only about 25 per cent of those surveyed gave response (a) above, whereas in product development and product planning, research and development, and sales and marketing, the response rate for (a) was over 45 per cent. In the fields of accounting, finance and budgeting, information systems, production technology and production management, and materials, purchasing, distribution and process management, the rate was intermediate between these two poles. It may be concluded that careers which are narrow in scope are common within the fields of product development and product planning, research and development, and sales and marketing, particularly when compared with the field of personnel, labour relations and training.

The above shows that, irrespective of age or years of service, a large number of employees spend their careers in a single field of work. Moreover, within the field of work where all or most of their careers are spent, although there are some whose work ranges widely, a large proportion of employees do work which covers only a narrow range. Thus the typical career structure within the firm is not one involving movement between a number of different fields of work, but rather one in which a narrow range of types of work is experienced within a specific field. The skills required of employees are not those of generalists, but of specialists.

Initial job posting and long-term field of work

Since for so many employees their careers are structured within a particular field of work, it is worth asking how decisions are taken on assigning employees to specific fields. The survey cited above asked individual respondents about what they felt to be the important factors in the decision to assign them to the field in which they had longest experience. They were invited to state the factor which they thought most influential, and the second most influential factor. Table 4.4 shows the results. The most important factors were judged to be the section in which employees had been initially assigned and the intentions of the company or of the personnel department. Much less weight was attached to the individual's own preferences. If one adds together the figures for the section of initial assignment and for the field of work experienced in the first three to five years after entry, it is clear that the field in which an employee will spend most of his career tends to be decided relatively soon after entering the company. In general the intentions of the company or its personnel section, in determining the field of work of the initial job assignment, also determine the likely field in which subsequent career formation will take place. This of course raises the question of how the initial assignment is decided.

In response to the question of how their initial posting was determined, 9.9 per cent of the men sampled in the survey already cited responded

Table 4.4 Decisive factors in assignation to principal (longest total experience) field of work (male employees)

Decisive factor	Index of degrees of influence
Section of initial job posting	109.8
Intentions of firm or of personnel section	106.9
Own wishes	62.8
Superior's intention	61.1
Field of work experienced 3–5 years after joining	41.6

Source: Sato (1995b). The raw data are from Rengo Sogo Seikatsu Kaihatsu Kenkyujo (1995)

Note: Index of degree of influence = (2 × Response rate for factor judged strongest) + (Response rate for factor judged second strongest).

'By my own expressed preferences', 48.3 per cent responded 'By the company but with reference to my preferences, which I was given an opportunity to express' and 40.7 per cent 'By the company without my having an opportunity to express my preferences'. Relatively few employees were able to choose their own initial assignment, and in most cases it was decided by the company with or without reference to the individual's wishes. Even in those cases where employees had the opportunity to express a preference, it is open to question to what extent companies ultimately provided fulfilment of these wishes.

When asked whether their initial job assignment met their wishes, 32.5 per cent of the male employees questioned answered 'Yes', 45.5 per cent 'To some extent', and 21.1 per cent 'Hardly at all'. Thus one-fifth of employees feel that their wishes were hardly met at all; when it is considered that the initial posting may have long-term impact on subsequent career development, the possibility that employees are thus obstructed from manifesting their abilities and aptitudes is a cause for misgiving. If one analyses the relationship between the method of allocating the initial post and the extent to which the individuals concerned feel their wishes were met, those who answered 'Yes' to the latter question were most numerous among those whose initial post was decided 'by my own expressed preferences', and fewest among those whose first posting was decided 'by the company without my having an opportunity to express my preferences'.

In 56.4 per cent of cases an opportunity occurred to express a wish for a change of posting within two to three years after the initial posting, and in 45 per cent of these cases the wish was satisfied. In 38.5 per cent of cases there was no such opportunity and in 30.9 per cent the opportunity occurred but the wish was not met, a total of 69.4 per cent of cases, or

Table 4.5 Scope of experience in career and kinds of work which employees would like to have done (per cent)

	Kinds of work which employees would like to have done					
	Experience of a variety of jobs within the same field	*Deep experience of a single kind of work within the same field*	*Experience of work in a different, but related, field*	*Experience of work overseas*	*Experience of work in a related company*	*No reply*
(1)	40.4	17.4	31.5	5.0	2.1	3.6
(2)	32.2	22.0	33.3	6.5	3.1	2.9
(3)	23.6	25.3	37.2	7.4	1.9	4.5

Source: Sato (1995b)

Notes: (1) I have had a deep experience of doing one job within this area. (2) I have had the experience of doing one job within this area. (3) I have had a broad range of experience within this area.

nearly seven-tenths. This situation also applies to those whose initial placement corresponded 'hardly at all' to their wishes.

In a large proportion of cases initial posting is made without consideration of the individual's wishes, and cases where such wishes are hardly met at all and where after a number of years it is possible to express a wish for a change of assignment and for such a wish to be granted are comparatively infrequent. The breadth of employees' careers is largely confined within a single field of work, and that field is frequently determined by the initial job allocation. The employees themselves have only very limited opportunities to express their own wishes in the matter.

CAREER BREADTH: EMPLOYEES' PREFERENCES

As we have seen, not only is the scope of most employees' careers largely confined to a single field of work, but it covers a narrow range of work within that field. To what extent are employees satisfied with this structure, and to what extent would they prefer a different career structure?

Table 4.5 shows kinds of work which employees surveyed would like to have experienced in the course of their careers hitherto, classified according to the breadth of those careers. Among those whose careers have involved deep experience of one kind of work in their field (the largest group of the overall sample), the two commonest experiences which they would like to have had are 'Experience of a variety of jobs within the same field' (40.4 per cent) and 'Experience of work in a different, but related, field' (31.5 per cent). In other words, a large proportion of those who have had a narrow range of job experience, largely in a single field, would prefer to have had a wider range of work in the same or a related field.

Among those who have indicated that they have had the experience of doing a wide range of jobs within a single field, the proportion of those who would like to have had is slightly higher than the number of those in the previous paragraph (i.e. those with deep experience of one kind of work) with the same preference. However, in both cases, the total of those who would have liked 'experience of a variety of jobs within the same field' or 'experience of work in a different, but related, field' exceeds those whose preference is for 'deep experience of a single kind of work within the same field'.

It thus appears that, irrespective of the breadth of career hitherto in a given field of work, most respondents would prefer to have had a broader range of job experience than they have actually had.

Similarly, among employees with differing patterns of experience within their principal field, a large proportion would like the scope of their work to widen in the future, either in the form of a wider range of work within their field, or of work in a related field.

As we have seen, the careers of white-collar employees tend not only to be largely confined over the long term to a single field of work, but to be restricted to a fairly narrow range of work within that field. The allocation of the employee's initial post within the firm has a major impact on the subsequent form which his career takes, but employees have little influence on such matters.

Many employees wish the scope of their work to be broader, and to have increased opportunities to express their preferences in terms of career path, which is a determinant of opportunities for skill development. For example, according to the survey, when asked about their requirements of the personnel management system, 52 per cent replied that they would like to see 'an increase in opportunities for individuals to express future career path preferences' and as many as 28.5 per cent expressed a wish for 'a system of application for jobs within the company and increased opportunities for individuals to express preferences'.

In addition, since the system of allocation of jobs determines the opportunities for skill development and the possibilities of displaying skills and aptitudes, a mechanism which provides for the aspirations of employees concerning their career patterns is called for. It is worth noting that according to the survey, compared with the extent to which aspirations in other spheres are reflected, the level to which wishes concerning future career paths is reflected is low ('reflected to a considerable extent' being the view of 9.3 per cent, 'reflected to a limited extent' of 59.4 per cent, and 'hardly reflected at all' of 29.3 per cent). What is required is a system of career management which moves from one administered unilaterally by employers to one which is based on discussion and mutual agreement by the firm and the individual employee.

SUMMARY

The following changes are taking place in the promotion and employment systems in large firms. Hitherto 'late selection systems' have been customary in large firms, but there is now a move towards shorter periods of simultaneous promotion and of divergent promotion, and towards earlier onset of discriminative and selective promotion. However, this does not seem to constitute a move towards a system of 'early selection' whereby decisive selection is made at an early stage in an employee's career.

Employment practice is already changing, from one of continuous employment to retiring age, to one whereby employment is preserved by means of secondment or transfer within the group of firms. Because of the shortage of positions within company groups, the system will increasingly call for secondments or transfers to firms which do not belong to the group.

The long-term career patterns of white-collar workers in large firms have been not only confined largely to specific fields of work, but have been narrowly concentrated on the particular kinds of work within each field. Staff may be regarded as specialists rather than generalists. However, in future personnel management must broaden the range of work which employees experience in the course of their careers. This is not only because employees desire such a broader range of work, but also because in the medium term it can contribute to employees' ability to adapt to changing skill requirements and to their productivity (Dentsu Soken 1995).

NOTES

1 In many cases, basic pay is composed of capability-based pay and age-related or 'livelihood' pay. The proportion of basic pay which is based on capability-based pay varies between companies, and varies within companies across grades. For each grade, there is a fixed range of possible levels of pay.
2 The capability-based pay system serves the function of providing an incentive to employees to improve their skills. See Koike (1994), Chapter 3, and Imano (1995).
3 There have been a number of case studies applying the concept of tournament mobility to promotion management in Japanese firms (Hanada 1987, Wakabayashi 1986, 1987, Pucik 1985). However, as noted below, in all cases the period of decisive selection is considerably later than the third year after entry as posited by Rosenbaum. Wakabayashi (1986, 1987), in a survey of male university graduate employees of a department store, conducted 3, 7 and 13 years after entry, found a significant relationship between performance assessments and relationships with superiors in the first three years and promotion in the seventh year. However, the assessments at three years did not have a strong impact on subsequent job allocations or other aspects of career management, and after seven years, when promotions to group manager (*kakaricho*) began, the divergence between dates of promotion was only six months to one

year. Hanada (1987) established 'career trees' for male graduate employees who entered five companies in different business sectors in the same year. In the different firms the period when divergence in rate of promotion began to emerge was 4, 5, 6, 10 and 12 years after entry. In the first of these firms, although divergence began in the fourth year, 89 per cent were promoted in this year, so the squeezing-out process affected only a few at this stage. In the second firm 21 per cent were promoted in the fifth year, but losers at that stage were able to catch up subsequently and the stage of decisive selection occurred considerably later in this firm. In the third firm, 29 per cent were promoted in the sixth year and some of this group were promoted fairly rapidly to higher management positions, but this is still quite late compared with the third year by which Rosenbaum's research implies decisive selection will have taken place. Pucik's (1985) analysis of a general trading company found selection taking place 14 years after entry, which may indeed be considered late selection.

4   According to a survey of male employees of large firms, only 18.3 per cent 'are not at all worried' about the speed of promotion of the cohort. Moreover, when asked at what point one would cease to compete with the top group of a cohort whose promotion had begun to diverge, 29 per cent answered '3 to 4 years', 27.9 per cent '5 or more years', 24.8 per cent 'would definitely not give up' and 13.1 per cent responded one year or two years; (non-respondents constituted 5.2 per cent). Comparing the latter two, there was no great difference when results were analysed by age of respondent (Rodosho Seisaku Chosabu 1995b). The survey, which covered firms with 1,147 or more employees and their male employees, was conducted between mid-January and mid-February 1994. Valid responses were returned by 535 firms and 4,351 individuals.

5   A survey in January 1993 found that the largest age-group of employees subject to transfer in firms operating such a system were those aged 55–59 (30.1 per cent in all firms, 41.7 per cent in firms with 5,000 or more employees), the next largest 50–54 (26.2 per cent and 37.5 per cent respectively) (Rodosho Seisaku Chosabu 1993). For details on secondment and transfer, see Nagano (1989).

6   A survey of 5,000 union members in November 1994 was conducted by the Rengo General Livelihood Development Research Centre, with 2,778 replies received.

REFERENCES

Dentsu Soken (General Telecommunications Research Centre) (1995) *Howaito Karaa no Chuto saiyo no Jittai ni kansuru Chosa, Howaito Karaa no Tenshoku no Joken seibi ni kansuru Chosa: Hokokusho* (*Survey reports on mid-career white-collar recruitment and white-collar job mobility*), Tokyo: Dentsu Soken.
Hanada, Mitsuyo (1987) 'Jinji seido ni okeru kyoso no jittai: shoshin, shokaku no shisutemu kara mita nihon kigyo no jinji senryaku' ('Competition in personnel systems: promotion systems and strategy in Japanese firms'), *Soshiki kagaku*, 21(2), pp. 43–53.
Imano, Koichiro (1995) 'Atarashii jinji kanri no choryo: "Noryoku kaihatsu shugi" no saihen' ('New currents in personnel management: Re-organising "skill-developmentism"'), *Nihon rodokenkyo zasshi*, September, 426, pp. 2–14.
Koike, Kazuo (1991a) *Howaito Karaa no Jinzai Kaihatsu* (*Human Resource Development of White-Collar Workers*), Tokyo: Toyo Keizai Shinposha.
—— (1991b) *Shigoto no Keizaigaku* (The economics of work), Tokyo: Toyo Keizai Shinposha.

—— (1994) *Nihon no Koyo Shisutemu: Sono Fuhensei to Tsuyomi* (*The Japanese Employment System: Its Generality and Strength*), Tokyo: Toyo Keizai Shinposha.

Koyo Joho Sentaa (Employment Information Centre) (ed.) (1993) *Utsuriyuki Koyo to Chingin* (*Changing Employment and Wages*), Tokyo: Koyo Joho Sentaa.

Nagano, Jin (1989) *Kigyo Guropunai Jinzai Ido no Kenkyo: Shukko wo Chushin to Shita Jisshoo Bunseki* (*Job Movement of Human Resources Within the Enterprise Group: An Analysis of the Evidence of Secondment*), Tokyo: Taga Shuppan.

Nihon Rodo Kenkyo Kiko (Japan Institute of Labour) (1993) *Daikigyo no Howaito karaa no Ido to Shoshin: Howaito karaa no kigyonai haichi, shoshin ni kan suru jittai chosa: Kekka hokoku* (*Job Assignment and Promotion of White-Collar Workers in Firms: Survey Report*), (Chosa kenkyo hokoku 37), Tokyo: Nihon Rodo Kenkyo Kiko.

OECD (1993) *Employment Outlook*, Paris: OECD.

Pucik, V. (1985) 'Promotion Patterns in a Japanese Trading Company', *The Columbia Journal of World Business*, 20(3), pp. 73–79.

Rengo Sogo Seikatsu Kaihatsu Kenkyujo (Rengo General Livelihood Development Research Centre) (ed.) (1995) *Atarashii Hatarakikata no Sozo wo Mezashite* (*Imagining New Ways of Working*), Tokyo: Rengo Sogo Seikatsu Kaihatsu Kenkyujyo.

Rodosho (1994a) *Chingin Kozo Kiban Tokei Chosa* (*Basic Survey of Wage Structure*), Tokyo: Ministry of Labour.

—— (ed.) (1994b) *Heisei 6-nen Han Rodo Hakusho: Koyo Antei wo Kiban to Shita Yutaka na Rodosha Seikatsu e no Kadai*, Tokyo: Nihon Rodo Kenkyu Kiko (Japan Institute of Labour).

Rodosho Seisaku Chosabu (Policy and Research Department, Ministry of Labour) (ed.) (1993) *Koyo Kanri no Jittai (Heisei 5-nen han)* (*Employment Management in 1993*), Tokyo: Romu Gyosei Kenkyojo.

—— (1995a) *Koyo Kanri no Jittai (Heisei 6-nen han)* (*Employment Management Survey*), Tokyo: Romu Gyosei Kenkyujo.

—— (1995b) *Nihonteki Koyo Seido no Genjo to Tenbo* (*The Japanese-style Employment System: Current State and Prospects*), Tokyo: Okurasho Insatsu Kyoku.

Rosenbaum, J. (1979) 'Tournament Mobility: Career Patterns in a Corporation', *Administrative Science Quarterly*, 24, pp. 220–41.

—— (1984) *Career Mobility in a Corporate Hierarchy*, Orlando, FL.: Academic Press.

Sato, Hiroki (1987) 'Rodosha no ishiki, kachikan no henka' ('Workers' changing consciousness and values'), in Rododaijin Kanbo Seisakuchosabu (ed.) *Nihonteki Koyo Kanko no Henka to Tenbo (Kenkyu Hokoku Hen)* (*Japanese Employment Practices: Changes and Prospects*), Tokyo: Okurasho insatsu kyoku.

—— (1995a) 'Shoshin, shokaku no kikai to ruru no genjo to yukue: iwayuru nenko joretsu shoshin wa do kawaru ka' ('The changing rules of promotion opportunity systems: how is so-called seniority promotion changing?'), in Nihon Gata Koyo Shistemu Kenkyu Kai (ed.), *Nihon Gata Koyo Shistemu Kenkyu Kai Hokokusho* (*Survey Report on Japanese-style Employment System*) Tokyo: Policy and Research Department, Ministry of Labour.

—— (1995b), '*Atarashii Hatarakikata to Jinji Kanri*', (New Ways of Working and Personnel Management), in Rengo Sogo Seikatsu Kaihatsu Kenkyujo (ed.).

Takeuchi, Hiroshi (1995) *Nihon no Merittokurashii: Kozo to Shinsei* (*Japan's Meritocracy: Structure and Character*), Tokyo: Tokyo Daigaku Shuppankai.

Turner, R. (1960) 'Models of Social Ascent through Education: Sponsored and Contest Mobility', *American Sociological Review*, 25, pp. 855–67.

Wakabayashi, Mitsuru (1986) 'Daisotsu shinnyosha no kyaria keisei katei wo saguru' ('A study of the careers of new graduate company recruits'), *Gekkan Rekuroto*, February and March, pp. 15–19.

—— (1987) 'Kanrishoku e no kyaria hattatsu: nyusha 13-nenme no forouappu' ('Career progress into management: a follow-up 13 years after entry'), *Soshiki Kodo Kagaku* 2(1), pp. 1–13.

Yashiro, Atsushi (1995) *Daikigyo Howaito Karaa no Kyaria: Ido to Shoshin no Jissho Bunseki* (*Careers of White-Collar Workers in Large Firms: A Substantive Analysis of Movement and Promotion*), Tokyo: Nihon Rodo Kenkyu Kiko.

5 Women at work

Akira Wakisaka

The Classical Japanese Model is characterised by 'lifetime employment'. This form of stable employment is considered necessary for the firm to invest in firm-specific skills. Because employees are required to stay in a company for a long time, and because women tend to quit due to marriage or childbirth, companies exclude women from core jobs. It is said, therefore, that female workers are not members of the firm as community.

This chapter addresses the following questions. What changes can be seen in the female labour market since 1980? What impact has the Equal Employment Opportunity Law (enacted in 1985) had on the nature of this labour market? Given that female part-time workers are growing in number in Japan as in European countries, how can these part-time workers be conceptualised in the Japanese context? Are dual labour market theories and the core-periphery model relevant and sufficient to explain the Japanese part-time labour market?

GENERAL TREND – DISCRIMINATION AND PROMOTION

Increasing women employees

There is an amazing increase in the number of working women in Japan, which is growing faster than men. In 1960 there were 18.1 million, in 1980, 21.4 million and in 1992, 26.2 million. The proportion of women who were employed increased from 40.8 per cent in 1960 to 75.4 per cent in 1992. However, the self-employed among working women decreased from 15.8 per cent to 10 per cent, and unpaid family workers decreased from 43.4 per cent to 14.3 per cent during 1960–92.

Modernisation has caused a decrease in the number of self-employed and unpaid family workers. By 1975, the rate of female labour force participation (LFP) steadily decreased to 45.7 per cent. Since then the LFP rate has steadily increased to 50.7 per cent by 1992. When considering the rate of paid employee participation (that is, the number of paid employees divided by the members of the population who are 15 years old and over), it can be seen that there has been a consistent increase from 8.8 per cent in 1960 to 33.6 per cent in 1990.

As represented in Figure 5.1, the female LFP rate was still M-shaped (double-peaked) in 1992. Despite the low rate in LFP for females in their late twenties and early thirties, the major feature of the period 1982–92 was that there was an overall increase in the LFP rate for all ages. These increases were caused by the growth in number of middle-aged part-time female workers, women tending to marry later, and the number of working mothers.

Wage differential by sex

It is said that the wages of Japanese working women are very low. For example, in 1992 a female's total earnings were 50.7 per cent of her male counterpart. (These figures are calculated from the wage levels reported in the Monthly Labour Statistics which cover establishments employing five or more workers.) According to unadjusted International Labour Organisation (ILO) statistics, wage differentials in advanced countries, except Japan, were between 70 per cent and 80 per cent. Thus Japanese women workers seem to face very severe labour market conditions. But

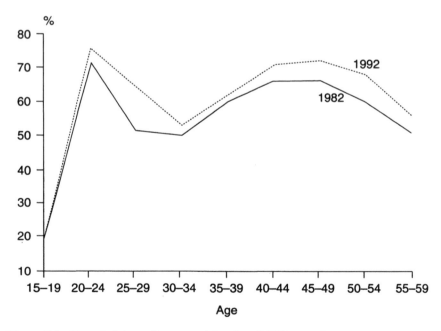

Figure 5.1   Female labour force participation (LFP) rates by age

Source: Sorifu Tokeikyoku (1992)

these arguments are based on unadjusted and average data.

In an international comparison, Koike (1988a, pp. 111–15) found that wage differentials in Japan, Germany, France and the UK were about the same for women in their twenties. However, large wage differentials occur in Japan for middle-aged employees depending on their sex. Koike pointed to two reasons for these wage differentials. First, major differences between wages received by male and female employees resulted from an individual's length of service. Middle-aged women employees in Japan are shown to have a relatively shorter length of service than their male counterparts. Second, the age-wage profile of Japanese male workers has a sharper slope in middle age than that of their European counterparts.

Koike's comparisons were based on reliable data in the mid-1970s. Higuchi (1990), using the same data, emphasised that the length of service of Japanese women was not short when compared with European countries, and that the length of service of Japanese men was much longer than their European counterparts. Higuchi asserted that this was another reason for the differential in wages.

In Japan, women's average length of service increased from 4.5 years in 1970 to 7.4 years in 1992. In view of this, it might be anticipated that the wage differential according to sex will rapidly shrink. However, improvement will be a slow process. The wage gap was 51.5 per cent in 1970, 55.3 per cent in 1980, 57.1 per cent in 1990, and 58.9 per cent in 1992 (figures are calculated from wages in the Basic Survey of Wage Structure (Rodosho 1992a) where firm size is ten employees and over). These results were based on data which included overtime payments. If we excluded overtime payments the wage gap shrinks to 61.5 per cent in 1992. The reduction in the wage gap is not a rapid, but gradual trend. Part of the reason for this slow shrinkage is the lengthening of service for Japanese men. Their average tenure increased from 8.8 years in 1970 to 12.5 years in 1992.

As represented in Table 5.1, if we control various characteristics such as age, length of service and education, the wage gap is considerably diminished. In their early twenties, male and female employees with the same number of years of schooling received about the same wages. However, owing to factors such as discrimination in the workplace, the number of women employees who were promoted was very limited. Therefore as women aged, they gradually earned less in relation to their male counterparts.

The table also shows that the contrast in wages for standard workers was fairly narrow when compared with those calculated from average wages. Standard workers, for example 35-year-old workers with 17 years of service in the case of high school graduate employees, are nearly equal to those who are hired immediately after graduation and who continue working at the same company. For example, average differences in male and female workers' wages, depending on their education, were consid-

Table 5.1   Comparison of wages in relation to education and age of standard worker*

Education level	Age	Monthly** ('000 Yen)		Gap (Male wage = 100)
		Male	Female	
Primary school	total	318.5	191.7	60.2
	−17	135.7	121.9	89.8
	18–19	155.6	137.8	88.6
	20–24	195.1	147.8	75.8
	25–29	234.7	182.5	77.8
	30–34	254.8	183.1	71.9
	35–39	293.5	212.2	72.3
	40–44	333.8	230.0	68.9
	45–49	371.1	247.9	66.8
	50–54	401.0	281.9	70.3
	55–59	381.2	284.8	74.7
High school	total	298.4	183.1	61.4
	18–19	160.1	148.8	92.9
	20–24	185.3	165.7	89.4
	25–29	230.3	195.6	84.9
	30–34	278.3	225.2	80.9
	35–39	335.3	262.6	78.3
	40–44	390.4	289.4	74.1
	45–49	472.4	340.0	72.0
	50–54	512.8	350.0	68.3
	55–59	498.3	368.5	74.0
University	total	356.9	226.8	63.5
	20–24	206.2	196.5	95.3
	25–29	248.0	225.4	90.9
	30–34	316.1	271.0	85.7
	35–39	386.6	325.1	84.0
	40–44	483.5	389.2	80.5
	45–49	556.8	466.5	83.8
	50–54	630.3	491.4	78.0
	55–59	643.3	506.7	78.8

Source: Rodosho (1992a)

Notes: * The standard worker's wage is nearly equal to that for a worker who was hired immediately after graduation and has been working at the same company.   ** Wages are basic wages excluding overtime payment.

erably lower than the differences in wages due to age. This is because female standard workers are concentrated in the younger short-tenured group, and because many women exit and re-enter the labour market after childbearing.

It can therefore be noted that the problem of the gap in wages between sexes is linked both to promotion (as can be seen by the relatively small number of female managers) and to women's behavioural patterns. I shall deal with these issues in the next two sub-sections.

Promotion possibilities

It is said that women managers are seldom seen in Japan (Lam 1992). However, since the mid-1980s, the number of women managers has been steadily increasing (see Table 5.2). From 1982 to 1992, their number has doubled, but the number of women promoted is still low and is particularly so at senior management levels.

Internal labour markets in Japan are more prevalent than in other countries. It was not until 1985, when the Equal Employment Opportunities Law (EEOL) was enacted,[1] that most of the large firms started to hire female university graduates (Cannings and Lazonick 1994). It will therefore take time for the number of women managers to increase substantially.

In Japan, firms give their employees many chances to be promoted by means of a sophisticated personnel system: the grading system (*shokuno shikaku seido*). As will be discussed later, this system plays a pivotal role. According to a 1993 survey, 27 per cent of firms have a grading system (Rodosho 1993). In large corporations with 5,000 or more workers, 90 per cent brought grading systems into use. The fact that only a few small firms have a grading system is not surprising as it is not as necessary to grade or rank when relatively few workers are employed. The average number of grades in a grading system is ten. The criteria for grading or ranking is almost always based on 'job performance ability' (*shokumu suiko noryoku*) which includes not merely employees' performance on current jobs, but also their future potential for related jobs.

Clearly where examinations are not held, as is the case in many Japanese firms, there is room for promotions to be affected by a supervisor's arbitrary appraisal. But the existence of a grading system is more favourable to competent women. Under a system where the criteria for ranking is based on simple job performance or on official qualifications, women are forced to do time-consuming activities to undertake expensive study programmes. That is disadvantageous to women because of domestic responsibilities and so on. Under the Japanese grading system, however, women are basically ranked on their performance and their potential ability. In this way, unless they experience arbitrary appraisals by their bosses, women are dealt with more fairly by being saved from short-term, cut throat competition between rivals. But the arbitrary appraisal of a subordinate's daily activity is not persistent, since frequent transfers of managers create the fair personnel assessment system proposed by Koike (1988b).

There are five possible reasons for the barrier which prevents women from being promoted.

1. Inferiority of women's ability, including physical strength.
2. Difficulty in relocating women because of their resistance to changing residence when they find themselves constrained by their domestic responsibilities.
3. Difficulty in assigning overtime work to women.
4. Men's prejudice towards women.
5. Higher probability of women leaving the company because of marriage or childbearing.

I shall comment on each of these explanations in the light of studies discussed further in the section Women on the shop-floor (see p. 138).

Women's inferiority   Nowadays in Japan, physical strength is not a necessity in either white- or blue-collar jobs so gender differences are not relevant. Potential ability (unlike physical strength) is basically the same between sexes.

Relocation problems   This reason is based on the assumption that the variety of job experience acquired through relocation is indispensable to skill formation for managers. But because it depends on the job, this reason is generally rejected. For example, a career within a general merchandise store typically involves moving to the same type of sales shop when changing to a different store so, in this situation, working in many stores does not necessarily raise the skill level of the sales clerk. Of course, there are some jobs for which experience of different regions is necessary to develop the requisite skill.

Overtime   When regarding the efficiency of skill formation, the difference between sexes can be considered to be negligible. For example, the important overtime work duties of retail clerks involve changing the layout of shops, designing important schemes, and so on. This type of overtime work is only done once or twice a month so these duties are not high hurdles for women to overcome.

Table 5.2   Distribution of female managers (per cent)

	1982				1992			
	Total	*Senior bucho*	*Middle kacho*	*Junior kakaricho*	*Total*	*Senior bucho*	*Middle kacho*	*Junior kakaricho*
Women's share*	2.2	1.0	1.5	3.4	4.1	1.7	2.9	6.6

Source: Rodosho (1992a)

Notes: * The number of women managers divided by the number of all managers in each category. These figures are based on firms with 100 or more employees.

Prejudice   Prejudice against women was rarely observed in my investigation of the shop-floor. Also from a theoretical point of view, the 'taste' hypothesis of discrimination (that is, the taste for discriminating against women) put forward by Becker (1957) cannot explain the persistent discrimination pointed out by Arrow (1972).

The higher probability of women leaving the company   Of the five reasons, this one represents a real hurdle for the female worker possessing the will to work as well as the ability to work. This reason can often be explained by an economic theory referred to as the Statistical Discrimination Theory put forward by Phelps (1972) and Thurow (1975). According to this theory, employers are not prejudiced against women. However, on average, more women tend to leave the company than men, as many women consider their work as a 'stop gap' before marriage. As employers cannot predict an individual woman's future potential and duration of service, they cannot identify which women will work throughout their lifetime. Whatever the outcome will incur a personnel training investment cost. As can be seen in Table 5.3 the separation rate for women is much higher than for men, particularly in large establishments.

These differences in separation or quit rates between the sexes in large firms lead employers to assign only men to key jobs, or job slots with good prospects for internal promotion. Also, when making the decision of whom to promote, women are less likely to be promoted than men because if a female supervisor quits there will be a great loss to the company. So employers assign men to career-tracked jobs, and women to dead-end jobs. I shall refer to this type of workplace as a 'gender-segregated workplace' and will return to this topic later. This form of job allocation is not, therefore, generated by an employer's prejudices, but results, rather, from rational appraisal of the situation. The Statistical Discrimination Theory is considered the most convincing means of explaining the phenomenon of discrimination.

Table 5.3   Separation rates by sex and by establishment size

Size of establishment	Separation rates %			Quit rates %		
	Male	Female	F/M	Male	Female	F/M
1,000–	7.1	20.3	2.84	4.4	18.4	4.18
300–999	9.3	19.2	2.06	6.7	17.1	2.54
100–299	13.0	19.6	1.51	10.0	17.0	1.71
30–99	13.2	19.0	1.44	9.4	15.3	1.62
5–29	14.7	18.6	1.26	10.9	15.6	1.44

Source: Rodosho (1991a)

Marriage and birth

Despite emphasising the importance of the statistical theory of discrimination, the findings of my fieldwork cannot be fully explained by that theory. First of all, in many cases both sexes are hired for the same job slots and are given the same on-the-job training (OJT) and off-the-job training (Off-JT). This type of workplace is referred to as a 'gender-equal workplace'. Such gender-equal workplaces are created by severe labour shortage.

Second, selection for promotion is often done through a rigid ranking system and an objective examination. Executives have relatively little discretion over promotion, so statistical discrimination is less likely to occur when being promoted than when being hired. However, almost all middle-managers and upper-managers are men even in gender-equal workplaces.

This situation can be explained by considering women's behaviour concerning marriage and birth. Generally the age at which a single woman becomes a lower-manager or middle-manager is the same as the age for her final chance of marriage. In 1992, the average age of a Japanese woman getting married for the first time was 26. About 90 per cent of women get married before the age of 30, so a woman must decide at this age whether to either stop working and get married and have a baby or to continue working. In Japan the Childcare Leave Act came into force in 1992. As a result, in 1993, 50.8 per cent of establishments employing more than 30 regular workers had a childcare leave programme compared with 14.3 per cent in 1981, and 21.9 per cent in 1990. However, it takes time for childcare leave programmes to induce women to continue working and thereby be promoted.

The other reason why there are so few career-track women is that there are insufficient day-care services for children under three years of age. So, it is still difficult for a woman, competent in business, to be a working mother.

WOMEN ON THE SHOP-FLOOR

This section uses previous studies to present a concrete image of working women on the shop-floor. First of all a typology of workplaces is explained from the viewpoint of gender segregation and then this typology is discussed with reference to two representative cases, banks and super-markets. Finally, the impact of EEOL on female workers is examined, including the introduction of the so-called 'double-track personnel management' system (*ko-su betsu jinji seido*).

Typology of workplaces

It is useful to investigate the problems of working women from the view-point of gender segregation where workplaces are divided into four types. The first two workplaces are male-dominated and female-dominated respectively. The other two employ both men and women. One is a gender-segregated workplace where tasks between sexes are completely different. There, men are given important and challenging tasks, while women are allocated mundane and repetitive tasks. Men progress through a related series of jobs while women are unable to progress higher because of the dead-end jobs they occupy. Men and women are also given different OJT and Off-JT. The other type of gender-mixed workplace is a gender-equal workplace where tasks and jobs are basically the same for both sexes. Men and women have an equal opportunity of gaining access to OJT and Off-JT, as a result of which they have the same promotion opportunities.

There are a few surveys, for example Denki-Roren (1991) and Chubu-Sanseiken (1992), from which we can estimate a distribution of the types of workplaces just defined. Estimates based on these two surveys show that the distribution of workplace types vary greatly in occupation (Wakisaka 1993). Gender-equal workplaces are mostly seen where sales clerks or engineers are employed. Gender-segregated workplaces are typically found in clerical/office work. There are relatively few female-dominated workplaces in Japan, but sometimes these can be seen in electronic production work and in clerical/office work.[2] Many male-dominated workplaces can be found in manufacturing, for example in the car industry. Two typical cases which can be examined in more detail are banks as gender-segregated workplaces, and general merchandise stores (GMS) often called supermarkets in Japan as gender-equal workplaces.

Gender-segregated workplaces: banks

In all of the advanced countries, banks have internal promotion systems. As Morris (1986, pp. 24, 119) pointed out, British banks have an informal agreement not to recruit from each other's staff and they place emphasis on OJT and job rotation. Muramatsu's (1988) comparison of Japan and EC countries revealed that internal labour markets (ILMs) are the most prevalent in the Japanese banking industry where the ILM is an 'integrated' type in which there is only one port of entry and exit as opposed to the 'separated' type that has a double promotion ladder.

According to my fieldwork on two typical Japanese banks in 1988, bank clerks were given initial training for one week after they entered the bank. Both men and women took the same course. After that they were allocated to branches where they learnt bank clerk skills by OJT. New employees underwent two-day Off-JT at two or three monthly intervals. This consisted of training to increase their skills to do particular jobs as well as reception work. Gender-based differences occurred as follows: while men's careers developed towards work in the Lending Section and in the Customer Section (the Customer Section is found only in Japanese banks), women's careers generally stopped at the level of a teller. Even the job of teller was monopolised by men until the 1960s. Before then, female clerks had to take 'back office' jobs. Now, almost all tellers are women. A similar change occurred in the USA (see Strober and Arnold 1987).

Both banks interviewed had a grading system, but only one of them set an examination. These were taken three times; twice as a written paper only when being upgraded and once as a written examination and an executives' interview when being promoted to the first (lowest) management level. It is, in general, normal practice for Japanese banks to only conduct examinations.

Though the proportion of females employed in banks has rapidly declined since 1980 as a result of computerisation (for example electronic banking), clerks' work has never been routinised and 'downgraded'. As a result the bank clerk's role has developed into an increasingly complex occupation. Despite certain jobs becoming very simplified, the careers of individual men and women simply enlarged vertically and horizontally, The banks' employment practices may lead towards equal opportunity for women and men despite wide differences in the career prospects for men and women. However, the diversified personnel management, which many banks have introduced since 1985, may, as will be explained later, bring banks to recreate gender-segregated workplaces by employing a dual labour market strategy.

Gender-equal workplaces: general merchandise stores

During my fieldwork in 1985 on general merchandise stores (GMS), two shops, a fruit and vegetable shop and a women's garment shop, were investigated in detail. First, in the fruit and vegetable shop, division of labour based solely on gender was investigated. It was a typically gender-segregated workplace. For example, as represented in Table 5.4, part-time workers worked from 9 a.m. to 4 p.m. except for Ms E who worked from 8 a.m. to 4 p.m.

There was a complete division of labour between the sexes, and between full- and part-time workers. There were no female full-time workers in the shop. The important tasks were all carried out by male full-time workers. The tasks of the female part-time workers were basically to supplement the male workers.

In the women's garment shop, where female employees outnumbered male employees, there were many female supervisors. Many of the managerial positions occupied by women were that of the lowest manager, called a chief. The chance of a woman becoming a middle-manager, a *kacho*, was rare, but in this shop, there was no sexual discrimination regarding one's training and promotion opportunities. In fact, with regard to training, sexual discrimination hardly existed either in formal Off-JT, or informal OJT.

Table 5.4 Grading of workers in a fruit and vegetable shop

Name	Grade*	Status**	Sex	Age	Length of service (years)	Educational qualification
A	5	F	M	35	13	College
B	3	F	M	25	3	College
C	2	F	M	20	1	High school
D	1	F	M	19	0	High school
E		P	F	35	7	
F		P	F	37	5	
G		P	F	33	1	
H		P	F	38	2	
I		P	F	43	3	
J		P	F	45	6	
K		P	F	21	1	

Note: * The grading system in this firm is 13 ranks. Managerial position is Grade 5 and above. Part-timers are not graded. ** F = Full-timer, P = Part-timer.

The important tasks in both of the shops were as follows: ordering; pricing and price reduction; supervising part-time workers; display; and judging which items would sell well (*ure suji*) and which items would not (*shini suji*), the latter task being a key one in my view.

Table 5.5 shows that, with the exception of A, every sales clerk in the garment shop had his or her own goods for which he/she was responsible. Judgements on sales projection and quick ordering were made by all the woman workers in both shops. Even part-time workers in the garment shop had their own goods and often made orders by phone. It can be seen, therefore, that in this shop, there was no job segregation by sex.

Grading systems have been introduced in every GMS company. This system of ranking by merit rating, which determines the degree of competence by types of job group and tests for upgrading by written examination and/or by interview by executives constitute the two main pillars of the personnel management system.

The impact of Equal Employment Opportunities Law on Japanese companies

The 1986 Equal Employment Opportunities Law (EEOL) prohibits employers from discriminating against women in terms of the provision of vocational education to new recruits, dismissal, retirement, and fringe benefits. Since the EEOL came into effect, many female workers have been hired, particularly female university graduates, as pointed out by Cannings and Lazonick (1994). It is difficult to estimate what effect the EEOL had because the latter half of the 1980s was a period of severe labour shortage.

Table 5.5   Tasks in women's garment shop

Name	A	B	C	D	E	F	G
Grade*	4	4	4	3	2	1	1
Sex	F	M	M	F	F	F	F
Age	29	30	27	22	24	23	21
Tenure	7	15	4	4	5	1	1
Educational qualification**	C	H	C	H	H	C	JC
Task*							
1 In charge of selecting and ordering goods	Y	Y	Y	Y	Y	Y	Y
2 Selecting and ordering goods not under one's own charge	N	Y	Y	Y	Y	N	N
3 Selling goods not under one's own charge	Y	Y	Y	Y	Y	Y	Y
4 Dealing with client's complaints (e.g. returned goods)	Y	Y	Y	Y	Y	Y	Y
5 Training new people and part-timers	Y	Y	Y	Y	Y	O	O
6 Making out a working schedule	Y	Y	O	Y	Y	N	Y
7 Determining the display and priority of goods in the shop	Y	Y	Y	Y	O	O	O
8 Judging which items will and will not sell and analysing the cause	Y	Y	Y	Y	O	O	O
9 Keeping account of sales and profit on sales	Y	Y	Y	O	O	O	O
10 Determining clearance goods and clearance prices	Y	Y	Y	N	O	O	O
11 Participating in designing branch sales tactics	O	O	N	N	N	N	N
12 Consulting with subordinates	Y	Y	O	O	O	N	N
13 Voicing one's opinion concerning manning policy	Y	O	O	N	N	N	N
14 Appraising subordinates	Y	Y	N	N	N	N	N

Source: Tomita (1986), Wakisaka (1990)

Notes: A–G are all full-time workers.   * The grading system in this firm is 13 ranks. Managerial position is Grade 5 and above. Part-timers are not graded.   ** C = College graduate, JC = Junior College graduate, H = High school graduate.   *** Y = Perform this task, O = Sometimes perform this task, N = Do not perform this task.

According to a special survey (Rodosho 1991b) on female workers and the personnel management of women by the Ministry of Labour in 1991, 36 per cent of women reported that they had experienced a change in employment policy since the introduction of the EEOL, while 40 per cent responded that nothing had changed. Changes were mostly seen in 'an increase of promotion opportunities', 'an increase of women managers', 'the assignment of women to tasks with responsibility' and the introduction of a programme supporting women.

One change which was triggered by the EEOL was the introduction of the 'double-track personnel management' system (DPM). The traditional personnel management practice of many large firms was to hire 'core' white-collar employees (mainly male university graduates) for the head office, and blue-collar and female white-collar workers for local branches. The former were expected to work anywhere in Japan or in the world, and were to be promoted to higher levels. Conversely the latter were expected to work at the site where they were hired, and were to be promoted within a certain level.

Regardless of the introduction of DPM and the enactment of the EEOL, there has been a growing number of highly educated women employed particularly for white-collar jobs. Despite an awareness that in wishing to hire a competent woman with a diploma, companies always have to face the risk that many highly-educated women might leave their workplace before the company can recoup its investment, the firms nevertheless offer them valuable Off-JT and OJT.

In response to such risk, some corporations have created a double-track system known as DPM. One track is referred to as the *sogo shoku* where progress is made along a career track with unrestricted potential for promotion. Mostly men and a few competent women are hired as *sogo shoku*. The other track is referred to as the *ippan shoku* where the potential for promotion is limited. Cannings and Lazonick (1994) suggested that *ippan shoku* looked very similar to the 'mommy track' in the USA. Many women are hired as *ippan shoku* as firms wish to distinguish a career-oriented woman from a woman who regards work as a temporary job until marriage.

According to a Ministry of Labour survey in 1995, 4.7 per cent of firms had a DPM system (Rodosho 1996). The larger the firm, the more likely it is that they will have DPM. For example, 52.0 per cent of firms with over 5,000 employees implemented the DPM system. Of firms in finance and insurance, 34.0 per cent had DPM.

It is doubtful that the DPM system will operate well or become more prevalent in future, for the following reason. The DPM system is based on the premise that from the time she enters a company a woman will never change her intentions regarding what she wants to do in life. In other words, a career-oriented woman will work throughout her life and a home-oriented woman will leave a company as soon as she gets married or has her first baby. However, this premise is not accurate according to a survey of about 7,000 women workers conducted in 1991 (Wakisaka 1993). The survey reveals that women workers had changed their attitudes to their lifecourse from those they had had when they first joined their companies. For example, about 20 per cent of women with five to nine years' tenure, who had intended to work until retirement age, had decided to work only until marriage or the birth of their first child. Only 28 per cent of the 7,000 women workers had not changed their minds. On the other hand, about 10 per cent of women with five to nine years' tenure who intended to work only until marriage decided to work until a mandated age. Thirty-six per cent of those did not change their intentions. Even among women managers, beginning their first jobs, only about

30–40 per cent intended to work throughout the course of their life (Wakisaka 1993). Many women change their intended career course as their work experience influences their attitudes or commitments to the firms. Overall, DPM fails to utilize competent women in the company.

PART-TIME WORKERS

Previous sections focused mainly on full-time women workers. But many women also do part-time jobs. In Japan it is difficult to define accurately what we mean by part-time workers (often referred to as *paato*). If we consider such workers as those who work less than 35 hours per week, in 1992 there were 8.68 million part-time workers. But in 1993 there were 5.65 million workers who were defined by their workplaces as *paato*, half of whom worked more than 35 hours. The reason for the difference between the two figures is partly as follows. In Japan there are many *arubaito* workers. *Arubaito* is standard terminology for student part-time work, whereas *paato* is the standard term for working housewives. Moreover, *paato* is often regarded as referring not to working time but to status by both employers and workers. The situation of these *paato* workers is a central issue in Japan.

Whichever definition we may take, the number of part-time workers has grown faster than full-time workers, and the majority of part-timers are women, particularly married women. The second peak in the labour force participation rates in Figure 5.1 reflects this group's growth. Using the above definition of less than 35 hours of work per week, part-time workers represent 17.3 per cent of total employees. In 1992 the number of female part-time workers was 5.92 million, which is 68.2 per cent of the total number of part-time workers and 30.7 per cent of the total number of women employees. Further, of the 8.68 million part-time workers employed in 1992, 5.38 million of them worked in establishments with more than five employees.

In 1993, the Government enacted the Part-time Workers Law which aims to improve personnel management practice towards part-time workers.

Stereotypes

Some stereotypes of part-time workers in Japan are that:

(i)   Housewives have to work in order to improve their living standards. However, they cannot work full-time because of domestic responsibilities, so they have no choice but to hold a part-time job.
(ii) Part-time jobs mean low wages. Part-time jobs mean cheap labour.
(iii) Part-time jobs are routine, repetitive, monotonous and the level of skill required is minimal.

(iv) Employers utilise part-time workers as a means of obtaining numerical flexibility. In other words, part-time workers are used as a shock absorber, allowing a degree of flexibility in adjusting to the business cycle.

(v) The part-time workforce is unstable. Workers often move from one firm to another, and job tenure is very short.

(vi) Housewives do not generally want to join unions because of (i) and (v). This partly leads to low wages in part-time jobs.

The theoretical background for explaining these stereotypes is as follows. Many scholars have stressed that the wages of part-time workers are very low in comparison to those of full-time workers, and that these part-time workers are the principal actors of the 'peripheral sector', as contrasted with the 'core sector'. In the core sector, long-term, stable employment, often called lifetime employment, is promoted, while in the peripheral sector, employment is short-term for repeated short-term periods. Moreover, recent technological changes have tended to lead to a relative reduction in the size of the core sector and a corresponding growth in the size of the peripheral sector (see Kumazawa and Yamada 1989). Hence it is said that more fluid labour markets are emerging and that the size of a less stable workforce (that is, part-time workers) is increasing.

The empirical background for these stereotypes is based on the following data. The average wage of part-time workers is about 70 to 80 per cent of that for female full-time workers. Moreover, this wage gap widened from 80.6 per cent in 1976 to 71.9 per cent in 1987. Most part-time workers are paid at an hourly rate, while full-time workers are paid a monthly salary. (The above figures are adjusted to the hourly rate.) The length of service for part-time workers is also short in comparison with that for full-time workers of both sexes. Commentators argue that the number of such 'low-wage and short-tenure' workers is increasing, that the size of the peripheral sector is growing, and the dual structure of the Japanese economy has been re-established. However, these data are merely based on averages and are examined in more detail in the next sub-section, which also shows that most of these prevailing notions regarding part-time workers are incorrect.

Job attachment by part-time workers

Not only has there been an increase in the average length of service for full-time workers of both sexes but also in that for female part-time workers. The average length of service for this group has increased from two years in 1970 to 4.9 years in 1995. This increase can be seen in every age category and in every industry. Therefore, even where part-time workers are concerned, labour markets are not becoming more fluid but, rather, more stabilised. In 1990, 12.5 per cent of female part-timers had

Table 5.6   Job tenure of part-time workers*

Job tenure	Male (%)	Female (%)	Total (%)
Less than 6 months	20.2	14.0	15.2
6 months but less than 1 year	19.9	12.5	14.0
1 year but less than 3 years	30.8	25.8	26.8
3 years but less than 5 years	14.3	14.2	14.2
5 years but less than 7 years	7.0	11.5	10.6
7 years but less than 10 years	3.9	9.4	8.3
10 years but less than 20 years	3.3	11.1	9.6
20 years or more	0.7	1.4	1.3
Total	100.0	100.0	100.0
Average job tenure (years)	2.6	4.3	4.0

Source: Rodosho (1992b)
Note: * A part-timer is a worker whose contracted working hours are shorter than those of normal workers.

been working at a single company for over 10 years, and 33.4 per cent for over five years (see Table 5.6).

In fact many of the part-timers are to some extent 'permanent employees' as can be observed in the United Kingdom (Gallie and White 1994). For example, 60 per cent of part-timers are hired on contracts without a time limit. Why do so many 'long-tenure' part-time workers exist? What kind of jobs do these workers perform? Are their jobs simple and repetitive, and are their wages constantly low throughout their working lives?

Information on the wages of part-time workers according to their length of service has been available in the Wage Structure Survey since 1985. These statistics reveal that the wages of part-time workers increase according to their length of service by at least eight per cent per annum, excluding bonuses, and by about 15 per cent in total earnings including bonuses. There is an insignificant difference in the rate of wage increase between female part-time workers and female full-time workers when the effects of tenure are considered (Ichino 1985, 1989). According to a detailed analysis of the 1990 survey on part-time workers by the Ministry of Labour (Kantani 1994) general wage increases (including bonuses), based on tenure, for female part-time workers can be seen, but this pattern is not observed for those part-timers who adjusted their working time when faced with the income tax threshold. If employers merely utilised part-time workers as unskilled cheap labour, they would not need to raise the wages of part-time workers. Why do employers raise wages of part-time workers even though they are not faced with union pressure? In order to judge the question of part-time workers more accurately, we need to examine the skill content of their jobs in more detail.

Independent part-time worker verses assistant part-time worker

In Japan there are some studies regarding part-time workers from their skill perspective. Nakamura (1990) made a distinction between core part-time workers (*kikan gata paato*) and supplementary part-time workers (*hokan gata paato*). The latter do monotonous and repetitive jobs, with no possibility of wage increases irrespective of job tenure or effort. Their jobs are basically supplementary to jobs held by full-time workers. In contrast, the *Kikan-gata paato* perform highly skilled tasks, acquiring their skills by OJT. They generally begin with easier tasks and gradually move to more difficult ones.

Further studies by Mitsuyama (1991) and Honda (1993) have revealed that core part-time workers are important and essential to retail companies. The result of my fieldwork on general merchandise stores referred to earlier is now presented. As mentioned before, there are two types of workplaces found in general merchandise stores. One is a gender-segregated workplace, as seen in the fruit and vegetable shop, the other is a gender-equal workplace, as seen in the women's garment shop.

In the former case, the tasks of part-time workers are basically supplementary to those of the male full-time workers. A major task of part-time workers is the cutting and wrapping of vegetables and fruit. Ms E (see Table 5.4), who has the longest tenure, is in charge of the other part-time workers. She cuts vegetables and teaches the tasks to new part-time workers. Everyone except Ms E in this shop is a supplementary part-time worker.

In the latter case, all the employees at the garment shop, including the part-time workers, have their own sale items. In other words, all male full-time, female full-time and female part-time workers have their own goods such as casual sweaters, formal suits, etc. for which they are responsible. Part-time workers who have worked for a long time in this shop can often make orders at their own discretion. Most of the part-time workers are 'core part-time workers'.

Generally speaking, part-time workers are most likely to quit during the first three months but this is less likely thereafter. Part of the reason for this is that they will have just begun to acquire skills and will have begun to find their work interesting. As expected, a part-time worker in the women's garment shop is less likely to quit than one in the vegetable/fruit shop because she is trusted with relatively more important tasks. However, in both shops, there are some 'core' part-time workers who have worked in their particular shop for a long time and whom employers would find difficult to fire, for without them the shop would not operate so efficiently.

Results of fieldwork on part-time workers included in the study imply that some part-time workers are, to some extent, internalised within the same shop. Quasi-internal labour markets are seen among part-time workers and thus provide us with the crucial reason for stability among some part-time workers. It should therefore be noted that the view that all part-time workers are 'peripheral workers' or 'marginal workers' is often misleading.

However, it is also incorrect to say that all part-time workers are 'regular employees' or internalised. It is a fact that some part-timers are utilised as shock absorbers. Following on from Nakamura's (1990) proposal that we should divide part-timers into two types, 'core part-time workers' and 'supplementary part-time workers', the opportunity should be given to some of the latter group to move into the core part-time group, with the rest of the workers remaining in the supplementary part-time workers group. However, it should be emphasised that while this provides us with a stereotype for part-time workers, this image is correct only for those remaining in the group of supplementary part-time workers.

CONCLUSION

This chapter has shown that in Japan, female labour participation rates by age are still double-peaked, with quite a few women withdrawing from the labour market at marriage or childbirth and re-entering it in their middle ages. However, female labour force participation has risen since 1975, and the average job tenure has become longer over time. The female–male wage gap has also narrowed, particularly if controlled for age, tenure and education.

Therefore, some women are becoming members of the firm as community even if they are not high-level managers of whom there are only a few. In Japan, male-dominated and female-dominated workplaces are relatively few. There are many gender-segregated workplaces, however, and quite a few gender-equal workplaces. Women working in gender-equal workplaces are clearly members of the firm community and some women in gender-segregated workplaces can also become members as they switch from dead-end jobs to mainstream jobs.

One of the notable changes brought about by the Equal Employment Opportunity Law is the introduction of the double-track personnel system by large companies. But the analysis in this chapter has cast a doubt on the success of this system. There is evidence that not all women stick to their initial career intention even if they are recruited for the general managerial (*sogo shoku*) track.

Lastly, this chapter has shown that part-time workers are growing in number, and more importantly that their job tenure has been growing. The author's fieldwork also shows that part-time workers may be divided into core and supplementary groups. Thus, both the longer tenure of part-time workers and the fieldwork evidence suggest that the simple core-periphery model, with all part-timers categorised in the periphery, is inadequate to conceptualise the part-time labour market in Japan. In fact, quasi-internal labour markets are being established for some part-time workers in Japan.

NOTES

1 See Lam (1992) Chapter 5.
2 Compared to results contained in British surveys such as the *Women and Employment Survey* (1980) (Martin and Roberts 1984) or the *British Social Attitudes Survey* (1987) (Jowell *et al.* 1988) there are, in my opinion, definitely fewer female-dominated workplaces in Japan. For example, according to a survey in 1991 in Japan, 48 per cent of female full-time workers worked in jobs where men outnumbered women, 18 per cent in jobs where the number of men and women were nearly equal and 34 per cent in jobs where women outnumbered men (Rodosho 1991b).

REFERENCES

Arrow, Kenneth J. (1972) 'Models of job discrimination', in A.H. Pascal (ed.) *Racial Discrimination in Economic Life*, Lexington, MA: Lexington Books.
Becker, Gary S. (1957) *The Economics of Discrimination*, Chicago: University of Chicago Press.
Cannings, Kathleen and Lazonick, William (1994) 'Equal employment opportuinity and the managerial woman in Japan', *Industrial Relations*, 33(1), pp. 44–69.
Chubu-Sanseiken (1992) 'Josei jugyoin no kyaria keisei ishiki to sapoto seido no jittai ni kansuru chosa' ('A survey on women's attitudes towards career development and on conditions of support programmes for women'), JIL Report Series, No. 21, Tokyo: The Japan Institute of Labour.
Denki-Roren (1991) 'Josei kumiaiin ishiki chosa kekka' ('Opinion survey on women's members'), *Monthly Bulletin* No. 248.
Gallie, Duncan and White, Michael (1994) 'Employer policies, employee contracts, and labour market structure', in Rubery, J. and Wilkinson, F. (eds) *Employer Strategy and the Labour Market*, Oxford: Oxford University Press.
Higuchi, Yoshio (1990) *Nippon Keizai to Shugyo Kodo (Japanese Economy and Workers' Behaviour)*, Tokyo: Toyokeizai Shinposha.
Honda, Kazunari (1993) 'Paatotaimu rodosha no kikan rodoryokuka to shogu seido' ('Utilization of part-time workers and their compensation programs') *Studies of The Japan Institute of Labour* No. 6, Tokyo: Japan Institute of Labour.
Ichino, Shozo (1985) 'Joshi paato rodosha no koyo chingin kozo', (Employment and wage structure of women part-timers'), *Monthly Labour Statistics and Research Bulletin*, 37(1), pp. 7–20.
—— (1989) 'Paatotaimu rodosha no henbo katei', (Transformation process of part-time workers), *Nihon Rodo Kenkyu Zasshi (Monthly Journal of the Japan Institute of Labour)*, 31(5), pp. 16–30.
Jowell, Roger, Witherspoon, Sharon and Brook, Lindsay (eds) (1988) *British Social Attitudes: the 5th report*. Aldershot: Gower.
Kantani, Takayuki (1994) 'Joshi jikankyu paatotaimu rodosha no nenkan-chingin', ('Yearly wage of hourly paid female part-time workers'), *Nihon Rodo Kyokai Zasshi* (Monthly Journal of the Japan Institute of Labour), 36(9), pp. 13–32.
Koike, Kazuo (1988a) *Understanding Industrial Relations in Modern Japan*, London: Macmillan.
—— (1988b) 'Futatsu no michi' ('Two ways of women's skill formation'), in K. Koike and Y. Tomita (eds) *Shokuba no Kyaria Uman (Career Women at Work)*, Tokyo: Toyo Keizai Shinposha.
Kumazawa, Makoto and Yamada, Junzo (1989) 'Jobs and skills under the lifelong nenko employment practice', in Stephen Wood (ed.) *The Transformation of Work*, London: Unwin Hyman.

Lam, Alice (1992) *Women and Japanese Management*, London: Routledge.
Martin, Jean and Roberts, Ceridwen (1984) *Women and Employment; A Lifetime Perspective*, London: HMSO.
Mitsuyama, Masako (1991) 'Paatotaima senryokuka to kigyonai kyoiku', (Utilization of part-time workers and training within firms), *Nihon Rodo Kyokai Zasshi* (*Monthly Journal of the Japan Institute of Labour*), 33(3), pp. 28–36.
Morris, Timothy (1986) *Innovations in Banking; Business Strategies and Employee Relations*, London: Croom Helm.
Muramatsu, Kuramitsu (1988) 'Kinzokubetsu kyuyo kozo kara mita naiburo-doshijo no ruikeika' ('A classification of internal labor markets from the aspect of seniority-structure), *Nanzan Journal of Economic Studies*, 3(1), pp. 77–97.
Nakamura, Megumi (1990) 'Patotaimu rodo', ('Part-time Labour'), *Nihon Rodo Kyokai Zasshi* (*Monthly Journal of the Japan Institute of Labour*), 32(1), pp. 40–1.
Phelps, E.S. (1972) 'The statistical theory of racism and sexism', *American Economic Review*, 62(4), pp. 659–61.
Rodosho (Ministry of Labour) (1991a) *Koyo Doko Chosa* (*Survey on Employment Trend*), Tokyo: Rodosho.
—— (1991b) *Joshi Koyo Kanri Kihon Chosa – Joshi Rodosha Rodo Jittai Chosa* (*Special Survey on Employment and Management of Women Workers*), Tokyo: Rodosho Fujin-kyoku (Women's Bureau, Ministry of Labour).
—— (1992a) *Chingin Kozo Kihon Chosa* (*Basic Survey of Wage Structure*), Tokyo: Rodosho.
—— (1992b) *Paatotaima no jittai* (*Report on the Status of Part-time Workers*), Tokyo: Okurasho Insatsukyoko.
—— (1993) *Koyo Kanri Kihon Chosa* (*Survey of Employment Management*), Tokyo: Rodosho.
—— (1996) *Joshi Koyo Kanri Kihon Chosa* (*Survey on Employment and Management of Women Workers*), Tokyo: Rodosho.
Sorifu Tokeikyoku (Statistics Bureau, Management and Coordination Agency (1992) *Rodoryoku Chosa* (*Labour Force Survey*), Tokyo: Sorifu Tokeikyoku.
Strober, Myra H. and Arnold, C.L. (1987) 'The dynamics of occupational segregation among bank tellers', in Clair Brown and J.A. Pechman (eds) *Gender in the Workplace*, Washington DC: Brooking Institution.
Thurow, Lester C. (1975) *Generating Inequality*, New York: Basic Books.
Tomita, Yasunobu (1986) 'Ogata kourigyo ni okeru gino keisei' ('Skill formation in large supermarket companies'), in Kazuo Koike (ed.) *Gendai no Jinzai Keisei*, Kyoto: Minerva Shobo.
Wakisaka, Akira (1990) *Kaishagata Josei* (*Women in the Workplace*), Tokyo: Dobunkan.
—— (1993) *Shokuba Ruikei to Josei no Kyaria Keisei*, (*Types of Workplaces and Women's Career Formation*), Tokyo: Ochanomizu.

6 Ageing workers

Atsushi Seike

INTRODUCTION

The population of Japan is now rapidly ageing. This ageing population has two conspicuous features. First, when this phenomenon reaches its peak, the proportion of older people in Japan will reach an unprecedented magnitude. It is expected that the proportion of people aged 65 years old and over will reach more than 25 per cent by the year 2020. This will be the highest proportion of older people in the world at that time.

Second, the speed at which the ageing population has increased in Japan has been faster than that of other OECD countries, and it will accelerate still further in the future. This rapidly ageing population will increase the necessity for the employment of older people for several reasons. In order to keep the public pension system financially healthy, we need to keep an adequate ratio between the number of pensioners and the number of pension contributors within the public pension system. The increase in employment of older people will ameliorate this problem. Furthermore, the size of the younger workforce will decline proportionately after the mid-1990s. To cope with the future labour shortage resulting from the declining younger population, the labour supply from the older population must be increased.

This chapter examines the possibilities for promoting the employment of older people. The feasibility of this will depend fundamentally upon the supply and demand for such labour.

On the labour supply side, the labour force participation rate of older people in Japan is the highest among OECD countries. Although there has been recent upward change, this rate has been declining for a quarter century up to the end of the 1980s. Will older people in Japan increase their participation in the labour force in the future?

On the labour demand side, employers have been reluctant to employ older people so far. Will employers change their attitude and increase their employment of older people in the future? What reforms are necessary to the employment system and to the government policy to promote the employment of older people hereafter?

These questions will be discussed in the following sections. Before discussing these key issues, however, the next section will briefly describe the ageing population itself in Japan.

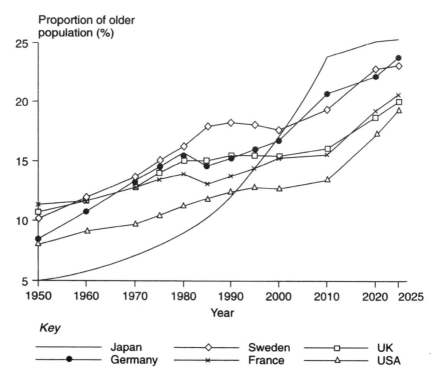

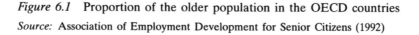

Figure 6.1   Proportion of the older population in the OECD countries

Source: Association of Employment Development for Senior Citizens (1992)

THE AGEING POPULATION IN JAPAN

Figure 6.1 shows the past trend and the future projection of the ageing population among OECD countries. The degree of the ageing is measured by the proportion of the population who are 65 years old and over. As seen in Figure 6.1, Japan has had a relatively low proportion of older people so far, although it has caught up with other countries in recent years.

In the future projection it can be seen that the proportion of older people in Japan will soon rise above other countries around the year 2000. After that point, the proportion of older people in Japan will increase quite rapidly and will reach more than 25 per cent of the whole population in 2020, which will make it one of the highest proportions of older people among OECD countries.

Figure 6.1 also shows that the speed at which the population is ageing is faster in Japan than in other countries. Japan has increased its proportion of older people by 10 percentage points within the past four decades, while its European counterparts increased this proportion by 5 percentage points in the same period of time. In other words, the speed of ageing in Japan has been double that of other OECD countries. And because the proportion of older people will increase another 10 percentage points within the coming 25 years, the speed of ageing in Japan will accelerate even more.

This ageing population has already had an effect on Japanese society. The number of pensioners who receive the public pension, *kosei nenkin* (social security for employed workers), has increased from 0.5 million in 1970 to more than 5 million in 1993 (Social Insurance Agency 1993). This, of course, is expected to increase more rapidly in the years to come given the projection of an increasingly older population in Japan.

While this sector of the population increases as described above, the opposite side of the coin is the drastic decline in the number of the younger population. Figure 6.2 shows the past trend and the future projection of the older and younger population in Japan. The number of people aged 20 to 29 was about 19 million in 1995, an increase of 2 million from 17 million in 1990, mostly because of the children of the babyboomers. It will then drastically decline by almost 7 million to just 12.5 million by

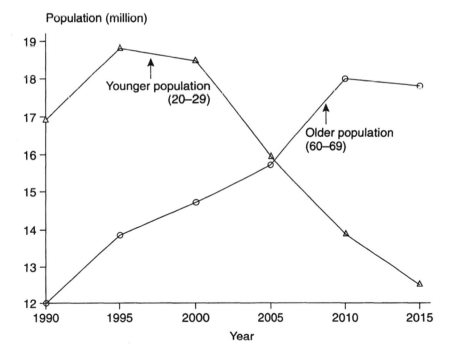

Figure 6.2 Trend of the older population and the younger population

Source: Population Research Institute of the Ministry of Welfare (1992)

2015. This will mean a decline of one-third of the level of the population for this age group in 1995. In contrast, the number of people aged 60 to 69 was about 14 million in 1995 and will increase by 4 million to 18 million by 2015.

As the younger population declines, the younger labour force is expected to decline unless, correspondingly, there is an unlikely social change such as, for example, a drastic reduction in the college attendance rate among younger people which causes a jump in labour force participation.[1] It is therefore important to promote the employment of the older population in the business community since companies will need to utilise older workers to cope with the shortage of a younger workforce, and society as a whole will need to ensure a financially healthy pension system.

THE LABOUR SUPPLY OF OLDER PEOPLE IN JAPAN

The employment of older people is determined by the interaction of their labour supply and demand. It is therefore essential to know about the labour supply of older people to analyse the feasibility of promoting their employment.

The following two sections will describe the basic characteristics of the labour supply of older people in Japan. Although the labour supply of older women is by no means negligible, the focus here will be on that of older men for statistical reasons. Woman of the older generation have limited experience of working as full-time employees. Therefore the number of older women who are fully eligible for employed workers' public pension benefit is correspondingly small. It would thus be difficult to include the labour supply of older women to examine the effect of the public pension (*kosei nenkin*) on employed workers, which is the main theme of the next section. The historical fact that women's opportunities to work as company employees have been limited is an important issue, however, and is examined in Chapter 5.

The labour supply of older people in Japan has special characteristics compared to their counterparts in other OECD countries. Table 6.1 shows the labour force participation rate of men aged 60 to 64 in the OECD countries. It is clear that the participation rate of older people in Japan is far higher than that of other OECD countries. The rate for Japanese males aged 60 to 64 years old is 75 per cent, whereas the rate for its USA and UK counterparts is around 55 per cent, and its European counterparts is 20 to 40 per cent. The level of labour force participation among older Japanese people is about 1.5 times that of the USA and the UK and 3 to 4 times that of Germany and France. It could be said that Japanese older men have a much higher willingness to continue working beyond the age of 60.

Note that the pension eligibility age of 60 for employed workers in Japan is even earlier than that for most other countries, where it is usually

Table 6.1 The labour force participation rate of men aged 60–64 in the major OECD countries

Country	%
France*	18.0
Germany*	35.0
Italy*	37.2
Japan**	75.0
UK**	54.2
USA**	55.1

Source: ILO (1993)

Notes: * As of 1991.   ** as of 1992.

65 years old (although in these cases there are special options to receive benefit earlier than the formal eligible age).[2] In recent years the Japanese public pension system has provided at least the same dollar value benefit as other OECD countries (Ministry of Welfare 1995). Therefore the high labour participation rate of older people in Japan cannot be blamed on the poor pension benefit in Japan.

The natural interpretation of the internationally high participation rate of Japanese older people is that they have a greater desire or willingness to continue working despite having the same pension benefits for retirement as their counterparts in other OECD countries. This can be viewed as fortunate for Japanese society, in a sense, because older people in Japan wanting to stay in the workforce create added value for society, whereas if they retired, the increased pension benefit they would claim would cause more burden on society.

The proportion of older people in the Japanese workforce has declined, however, in the past three decades. The labour force participation rate of men aged 60 to 64 has declined from 84 per cent in the 1960s to 71 per cent at the end of the 1980s, a 13 per cent decline within three decades. In the past five years however, this downward trend seems, yet again, to have been reversed. The labour participation rate of men aged 60 to 64 has increased from 71 per cent in 1988 to 75 per cent in 1993. If this change in trend continues, Japan should expect to keep its internationally higher labour force participation rate of older people in the future.

Suppose this rate of men aged 60 to 64 were to remain at its current level of 75 per cent in 2015. The expected labour supply is calculated by the product of the expected population and the estimated labour force participation rate. There will be about 3.1 million men aged 60 to 64 in the workforce in 2015. If the labour force participation rate of men aged 60 to 64 increases 80 per cent that year, then the labour force for that age group would be about 3.3 million. If the rate declines again to the level of the late 1980s, however, there would be 2.9 million in the workforce. This means that a 10 percentage point difference in the labour force participation ratio would result in an approximate difference of 0.4 million men in the labour force aged 60 to 64 in 2015.

On the other hand, it is expected that the male workforce aged 20 to 24 will decline from 3.8 million in 1995 to 2.3 million in 2015, a decline of 1.5 million, if their current labour force participation rate of 75 per cent keeps stable. From this point of view, it is desirable for Japan to keep or to increase the higher level of labour force participation of its older population in the future, even though it will not be enough to compensate for the decline of the younger workforce. Of course, whether this scenario will be realised or not will depend upon the labour supply behaviour of older people in the future.

THE IMPACT OF PUBLIC PENSIONS AND LABOUR SUPPLY

There are many factors that determine the labour supply behaviour of older people including preference for leisure time and such labour conditions as wage rate and working hours. One of the most important factors that has determined the labour supply of older people in recent years, however, is their public pension. This is also important in the context of the debate about whether society should provide more jobs or more social security in order to maintain the well-being of the relatively younger group of older people in their early sixties.

In order to examine the impact of public pension scheme, let us look at the trend of labour supply and public pension benefit as seen in Figure 6.3. The longitudinal labour force statistics divide the age groups of the older population into 60–64 years old, and 65 years old or over. Since there is a 'natural declining trend' for the age group 65 years old or over because of the inclusion into this group of the extremely aged who would not be working anyway, use of this age group would not produce clear data. The focus is therefore on the age group 60–64 years old who are less affected by the 'natural decline'.[3] Figure 6.3 shows that, up to the end of the 1980s, there was a decline in the labour supply of men aged 60–64 for at least a quarter of a century in Japan, which has already been mentioned in the previous section. There are several reasons which can explain this downward trend of labour force participation for older people. One is the decline of self-employed workers among the older population. Self-employed workers are not forced by mandatory retirement to leave the workplace and are able to make their own decisions about adjusting their working schedule depending on their preference for leisure time. This group thus tends to continue working until a later age than employed workers.

The decline in the proportion of the self-employed among the older population therefore reduces older people's participation in the workforce. In fact, the proportion of self-employed among the older population

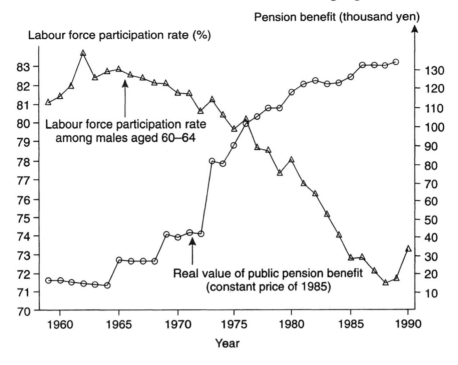

Figure 6.3 Trend of the labour force participation ratio of older men and public pension benefit

Source: Social Security Agency, *Annual Report*, and Management Coordination Agency, *Labour Force Survey* (1959–90)

declined particularly in the 1960s, mainly because of the drastic drop in the farming population.

After the mid-1970s, however, there was a more important factor which contributed to the downward trend. Japan substantially improved public pension benefits for employed workers (*kosei nenkin*) in 1973, when it made a major revision of its public pension system. Indexation was introduced for the retiring workers' past wages to determine the amount of their pension benefit at retirement. Following the determination of benefit level at retirement, benefits were index-linked in order to maintain the benefits' real value.

This revision caused a significant jump in pension payments as can be seen in Figure 6.3. Because the average benefit seen in the figure still includes beneficiaries with very low benefits being paid as a result of their short period of contributions, standard workers are receiving more benefit than shown in Figure 6.3. In fact, the so-called 'model' benefit available to the career worker who continues working from the age of 18 through to 60 is higher now, at about 220,000 yen per month.

As can also be seen in the figure, there is a sharp contrast between the downward trend of older people in the labour force and the substantial improvement in the public pension benefit. This suggests that people who used to be unable to retire if this meant relying only on public pension benefit became able to retire through these improved benefits. Of course, this is arguable because this contrast could just be a historical coincidence. It is therefore necessary for us to conduct a more rigorous analysis to test the effect of the public pension on the labour supply of older people in Japan.

In order to examine this, the author conducted an econometric analysis with cross-sectional micro data[4] using the Heckman-type model of standard labour supply functions to estimate the labour force participation and the market wage equation together. The data used here comes from *The Employment Status Survey of the Elderly* (1993) by the Ministry of Labour.

Table 6.2 shows the results of the labour supply function (probit estimation of the participation function). The coefficient of the indicator variable of the public pension eligibility (public pension eligibility dummy), which, from estimates, has been shown to be statistically significant, reveals a negative effect on the probability of labour force participation in the participation function. The magnitude of the effect shows that eligibility for public pension reduces the participation probability by 15 per cent. The negative impact which public pension has on the labour supply is quite consistent with micro-economic theory and with previous results found in the USA and in the UK.

Table 6.2 also shows the impact of other variables on labour supply. The negative coefficients of the age variable (Age), and the health variable (Health dummy), which are the two most significant, and the mandatory retirement variable (Mandatory retirement dummy), can be attributed to the increasing preference for leisure time and the reduction in market wage. Coefficients of the education variables (High school dummy, College dummy) and the variable for residence in the Tokyo metropolitan area (Tokyo Metropolitan residence dummy) show a positive effect on the labour supply because they increase the market wage of older people.

In addition to the pension benefit effect, one aspect of the public pension scheme itself has an impact on the decision of workers eligible for a pension to continue working, particularly on those aged 60 to 64. This is the earnings test scheme which accompanies the public pension benefit for working beneficiaries aged 60 to 64. The scheme asks pension-eligible workers aged 60 to 64 to give up a proportion of benefit in relation to their earnings. In the previous earnings test scheme, eligible workers who earned more than 250,000 yen per month had to give up all the benefit given to them. Even for workers who were earning less than 250,000 yen a month, the pension benefit was reduced depending on their

Table 6.2 Estimated results of the labour supply model

Variables	Participation function	Market wage function
Constant	4.145	1.263
	(11.348)	(4.321)
Age	−0.017	−0.028
	(−8.378)	(−5.803)
Health dummy	−0.331	−0.282
	(26.861)	(−4.935)
High school dummy	0.037	0.391
	(2.745)	(11.438)
College dummy	0.087	0.670
	(2.616)	(12.333)
Public pension elegible dummy	−0.153 (−11.429)	
Other non-earned income	−0.0002	
	(−4.386)	
Mandatory retirement dummy	−0.177 (−13.103)	−0.361 (−8.298)
Tokyo Metropolitan residence dummy	0.056 (3.688)	0.211 (7.338)
Lambda		0.544
		(5.143)
Sample size	7014	4559
Log likelihood	−3859.3	
Adj-R-Square		0.1273
		(F = 96.073)

Source: Seike (1989)

Notes: The data used in this analysis were extracted from the *Employment Status Survey of the Elderly*; which was conducted by the Japanese Minstry of Labour in 1983. The sample population surveyed was chosen as representative of persons 55 to 69 years old by a two-phase sampling method. Participation: 1 if employed; 0 otherwise. Working Hours = [(daily hours worked) × (days worked per week) × 52]/12. Market Wage = (monthly earnings)/working hours. Age: Each individual's actual age. Health dummy: 1 if health problems exist; 0 otherwise. High school dummy: 1 if completed high school; 0 otherwise. College dummy: 1 if received college degree;) 0 otherwise. Public pension eligible dummy: 1 if eligible to collect public pension; 0 otherwise (this includes all those who satisfy the months-of-contribution requirements). Other non-earned income: Non-wage income except public pension benefit. Mandatory retirement dummy: 1 if had experienced mandatory retirement; 0 otherwise. Tokyo Metropolitan residence dummy: 1 if living in the Tokyo metropolitan area; 0 otherwise. Lambda: Inverse of the Mill's ratio. Figures in parentheses are t-values.

earnings to the extent that ultimately, workers were only able to receive 80 per cent of their full pension if their earnings had become as low as 95,000 yen per month.

Figure 6.4 shows the effect of this scheme on the labour supply of men aged 60 to 64. A quarter of pension-eligible workers are working just at the point where their monthly earnings are about 95,000 yen, while those workers in this age group not eligible for pensions do not show such an earnings distribution.[5] This means that these pension-eligible workers

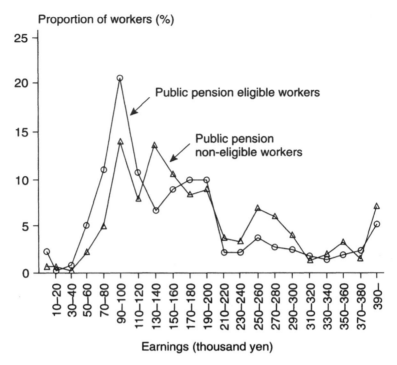

Figure 6.4 Earnings distribution for public pension eligible workers and non-eligible workers

Source: Seike (1989)

reduce their labour supply so as not to exceed the ceiling of earnings that allows them to receive 80 per cent of their pension benefit.

Thus the labour supply of older people is clearly dependent on their eligibility for the public pension and its related earnings test scheme, as well as on available wage levels and their preference for leisure. Given this information, let me briefly forecast the future trend of the labour supply of older people in Japan.

In 1994, the Japanese government revised the public pension system to include a moderation of benefit level, an extension of eligible age from 60 to 65, and a relaxation of the earnings test. The moderation of benefit level will be done by changing the method of indexing past wages of retiring workers. The system now indexes past wages based on the after-tax earnings of public pension tax payers instead of before-tax earnings, which was the previous practice. The extension of the eligible age has been accomplished by introducing a new partial pension for those between the ages of 60 and 64 which provides about a half the full pension for those who would like to retire before age 65. As for the relaxation of the earnings test, the new scheme lifts the ceiling for collecting pension benefit from 250,000 yen per month to 350,000 yen. Furthermore, under this new ceiling, the total income, that is earnings plus pension benefit, does not decrease as earnings increase.

This revision of the public pension system is expected to increase the labour supply of older people. Both moderating the pension benefit and raising the eligible age level will increase the probability of labour force participation. The relaxation of the earnings test will help those pension-eligible workers who have previously reduced the number of hours they work in order to avoid a large reduction in their benefit, and will thus increase the labour supply of pension-eligible workers.

The educational level of and the health care for older people will improve in the future. These, along with the extension of the mandatory retirement age, will bring about a rise in their market wage. This improvement in wages for older people will also increase their labour supply.

THE LABOUR DEMAND FOR OLDER WORKERS

On the labour demand side of the employment of older workers, there has been a substantial improvement in employment opportunities for workers up to the age of 60 in the past decade. As seen in Table 6.3, the age for mandatory retirement, which on average used to be 55, became 60 years old in part because of a strong campaign by the Ministry of Labour. Now, more than 90 per cent of firms have mandatory retirement systems set or are scheduled to set 60 years old as the mandatory retirement age.[6]

Continuation of employment in the same firm beyond the mandatory retirement age of 60, however, has not been practised so far. Only 10 per cent of firms have a mandatory retirement age over 60. Table 6.4 shows the proportion of firms that have any kind of employment continuation after the mandatory retirement age or a re-employment programme beyond the age of 60. Although the proportion of firms with programmes is not small, the proportion decreases as the size of firms increase. Furthermore, even among firms with these programmes, many of these keep the right to select who can remain. There are very few firms which automatically accept applications for job continuation or re-employment programmes by workers.

There are too few opportunities for full-scale continuation of jobs for workers beyond the age of 60 to satisfy their labour supply, and therefore the labour market for older workers is more difficult than for other groups of workers. For example, the applicants for jobs/vacant ratio for workers aged 60–64 was 0.08 per cent at the beginning of 1995 while the average ratio for all workers is 0.66 per cent. The unemployment rate for men aged 60–64 is more than 6 per cent, over double the average unemployment rate for all men.

162   *Atsushi Seike*

Table 6.3 The age of mandatory retirement (per cent)

Age of mandatory retirement	Year			
	1980	*1985*	*1993*	**1993*
–54	0.2	0.1	0.2	
55	39.5	27.0	9.7	2.3
56–59	20.1	17.4	10.3	3.3
60	36.5	51.0	73.9	83.6
61–64	0.7	2.1	1.6	3.0
65	2.5	1.8	4.4	7.8
66–		0.5	0.0	
60 and over	39.7	55.4	80.0	94.4

Source: Ministry of Labour (1993)
Note: * 1993 includes firms which have not yet revised the mandatory retirement age, but are planning to do so in the near future.

Table 6.4 Proportion of firms with continuation of employment after mandatory retirement or re-employment programmes (per cent)

Size of firm (no. of employees)	Continuation of employment	Re-employment	Both programmes	Total
Total	18.1	39.9	15.0	72.9
5,000 or more	2.7	44.9	3.3	50.9
1,000–4,999	6.9	44.6	9.5	61.0
300–999	10.4	45.5	13.3	69.2
100–299	16.4	42.9	17.0	76.3
30–99	20.0	38.0	14.7	72.7

Source: Ministry of Labour (1993)

Table 6.5 Wage decline after mandatory retirement from first job

Age	Length of service	Firm size	Monthly wage (thousand yen)
55–59	30 years	All	460.2
60–64	0 years	All	232.8
55–59	30 years	Large firm	500.1
60–64	0 years	Small firm	234.6
55–59	30 years	All	460.2
60–64	Part-time 0 years	Large and small	137.8

Source: Ministry of Labour (1993)

Under these circumstances, even those workers who find a 'second job' after mandatory retirement from in the first job cannot utilise their full ability and have to accept a sharp decline in wage level. Table 6.5 shows the wage gap for men that exists between the money they are paid before and after the mandatory retirement age of 60. Comparisons are made between men aged 55–59 with 30 years length of service and men aged 60–64 with zero years length of service because when they are hired for the second job they are starting from zero.

As seen in Table 6.5, the wage level declines sharply by 50 per cent after age 60. Because there are very few job opportunities for older workers in large firms, one typical job change at age 60 is from a large firm to a smaller firm. In this case, wages decline by almost 60 per cent after the age of 60. Another is a job change from full to part-time, when monthly wages decline by two-thirds. Whatever the case, the labour conditions of older workers drastically change at the age of mandatory retirement.

The current situation could be changed if a concerted effort were to be made to promote the employment of older workers. This will be particularly so after 2000 when the Japanese Government will gradually start to extend the pension eligibility age from 60 to 65, and it will be important to extend the mandatory retirement age to 65. What are the obstacles to extending the mandatory retirement age, and what kind of reform of employment practices should be undertaken to cope with the problem?

WHY EMPLOYERS ARE RELUCTANT TO EMPLOY OLDER WORKERS

There are several reasons for employers' reluctance to substantially expand employment of their older workers by extending the mandatory retirement age.

First of all, particularly in recent years, there has been little necessity for employers to expand employment of older workers. Unlike the economic boom period of the 'bubble economy', employers have actually been trying to reduce the total workforce, including those below the age of 60. And at least up until 1996, the number of young workers will continue to grow as described in the section on 'The Ageing Population in Japan' (see p. 153). There will be no urgent necessity for employers to rush to employ older workers.

The other factors are institutional obstacles. The factor which most impedes employers from expanding the older workforce is the seniority wage system. It is certainly costly for employers to extend the age of mandatory retirement beyond 60 with a seniority wage scheme in which the wage levels are increased in part either by age or by length of service.

With the seniority wage system, employers and workers have made an implicit long-term contract.[7] This system, in which the company hires new school graduates, trains them and keeps them until mandatory retirement, is intended to balance the relationship between contribution and total wage in the long run. The company pays wages even to young people fresh from school while they undergo training programmes. In return, they are asked to work for a lower wage, relative to their contribution or productivity from their late twenties onward, thus returning the training costs the employer has invested in them. Furthermore through their thirtes, as they maintain their productivity, they in effect lend funds to their employers by continuing to receive lower wages. Subsequently, however, the employer pays them higher wages relative to their actual contribution when they become middle-aged and older. This 'balance sheet' between employers and workers is designed to be equal at the age of the current mandatory retirement age.

In order to extend the retirement age to 65 from the current 60 years of age, it is important to reduce the gap between the productivity and wages of middle-aged and older workers. Table 6.6 shows the results of a survey which asked firms about the feasibility of extending the mandatory retirement age to 65 depending on whether a gap existed between the productivity and the wage of their employees at the age of 55. As seen in the table, firms without a gap between productivity and wage for employees aged 55 say that they are more willing to extend their mandatory retirement age to 65 than those with such a gap. It is important, therefore, to make the wage profile less steep in order to extend the mandatory retirement age to 65.

Related to the seniority wage scheme is the seniority promotion scheme, in which most older workers take managerial positions. This creates another obstacle, because employers need to ask older employees to retire to create room for the promotion of younger employees. Human resource training practice in many firms allots most of the training resources to younger workers, which may also discourage older workers from retraining, and lead to their being perceived as less attractive as workers in the job market.

Nevertheless, these obstacles for promoting the employment of older workers look as though they will decrease in the future. First, as mentioned

Table 6.6   Feasibility of retirement at age 65 and the gap between productivity and wage at age 55

Is it possible to extend retirement age to 65?	Percentage of firms with positive, zero and negative gaps between wage (W) and productivity (P) at age 55		
	W > P	*W = P*	*W < P*
Possible	39.90	49.71	59.38
Not possible	60.10	50.29	40.62
All firms	100.00	100.00	100.00

Source: Association of Employment Development for Senior Citizens (1995)

earlier, the age population structure will change. There will be a sharp decline in the younger population in the coming decades. Employers will need to depend more on older workers to cope with the decline in a younger workforce.

Seniority wage and promotion schemes will also change, partly because of the change in the age population structure, but also because of the change in the industrial structure. In the new industrial structure, employers will need more professional workers who move between employers depending on the wages offered to them. Employers will have to pay for workers' contributions or abilities in the short run, instead of using the seniority wage scheme which equalises workers' contributions and wages over their lifetime's employment with that company.

As long as there is this fundamental restructuring of wage and employment systems in the long run, the employment of older workers will expand automatically. In this case, the private sector would be the engine promoting the employment of older people in Japan as an integral part of each company's human resource strategy.

POLICY IMPLICATIONS

Taking into account all the situations relating to the employment of older workers both on the labour supply side and the labour demand side, it is very difficult to see the employment of older workers expanding immediately. However, the possiblity that circumstances will change in the future gives us a more optimistic view of the employment of older workers in future decades.

Different kinds of policies to promote the employment of older people should be applied to different time-spans. For the relatively short-term period up to the end of this century, labour market conditions for older workers will not change. Motivation to employ older workers will not increase enough and the wage and employment system preventing the employment of older workers will not change completely during this short period of time. It is therefore important for the Government to encourage reluctant employers to expand the employment of older workers by, for example, paying wage subsidies to firms that employ older workers.

In the mid-term, which would be the first decade of the twenty-first century, more substantial policies to promote the employment of older people will be needed. In this decade, the public pension eligible age will be lifted gradually to 65. The population structure will have changed drastically and employers will be facing a sharp decline in the younger labour force.

Under these circumstances, wage scheme and employment practices in many firms will change to utilise the workforce of older people. Policies will be needed to support these favourable trends towards the employment of this group. Although the Ministry of Labour already has a policy to require employers to have a mandatory retirement age of at least 60 or above, and to encourage employers to extend the retirement age up to 65, it will be necessary to require employers to set the mandatory retirement age at 65 when this becomes the public pension eligible age.

In the long run after the first decade of the twenty-first century, when market forces fully promote the employment of older people, policies that intervene in the market (paying subsidies for example) should be minimised as much as possible. The most important policy for the Government under these circumstances is to eliminate obstacles, which may prevent market forces from expanding the employment of older workers.

The ageing of the population itself is one result of the 'economic miracle' of post-war Japan. The fact that older people are still willing to continue working in Japan is fortunate for our society. If we can construct a society in the future where the willingness of older people to continue working is fully utilised, surely this would be an achievement matching our economic miracle of the past.

NOTES

1 Although the college attendance ratio has been stable in the past 15 years, it started to increase again in recent years according to the Ministry of Education (1995).
2 In Europe, France keeps its pension eligible age at 60.
3 In fact, the labour force participation ratio of men aged 65 years and over has declined from 56.4 per cent in 1963 to 37.7 per cent in 1993 as the proportion of very old increased among the age group.
4 For details, refer to Seike (1993) in Japanese or Seike (1989) in English. For Heckman's theory, see Heckman (1974).
5 The pattern of distribution between that of pension-eligible workers and that of non-eligible workers is significantly different by statistical test.
6 Mandatory retirement is defined as company enforced retirement from one's first job, and does not necessarily mean retirement from the general workforce.
7 This explanation about seniority wage here is based on the theory of Lazear (1979).

REFERENCES

Association of Employment Development for Senior Citizens (1992) *Korei Shakai Tokei Yoran* (*Statistical Handbook of Ageing Society*), Tokyo: The Association of Employment Development for Senior Citizens.
—— (1995) *Koreika Shakai ni Tekigo Shita Chingin Taikei Model ni Kansura Chosa Kenkyu Hokoku Sho* (*Report on Wage Models for an Ageing Society*), Tokyo: Association of Employment Development for Senior Citizens.
Heckman, J.J. (1974) 'Shadow wages, market wages and labour supply', *Econometrica*, 42(4), pp. 679–94.
ILO (1993) *Yearbook of Labour Statistics*, Geneva: ILO.

Lazear, E.P. (1979) 'Why is There Mandatory Retirement?', *Journal of Political Economy*, 87(6), pp. 1261–84.

Management and Coordination Agency (1959–90) *Annual Report*, Tokyo: Government of Japan.

Ministry of Education (1995) *Monbu Tokei Yoran* (*Statistical Handbook of Education*), Tokyo: Dai'ichi Hoki Syuppan.

Ministry of Labour (1993) *Koreisha Syugyoto Jittai Chosa* (*The Employment Status Survey of the Elderly*), Tokyo: Ministry of Labour.

Ministry of Welfare (1995) *Koteki Nenkin ni Tsuiteno ILO heno Hokoku* (*Report to ILO on Public Pension*), Tokyo: Ministry of Welfare.

Population Research Institute of the Ministry of Welfare (1992) *Nihon no Shorai Jinko Suikei* (*Population Projection for Japan*), Tokyo: Ministry of Welfare.

Seike, Atsushi (1989) *The Effect of the Employee Pension on the Labour Supply of the Japanese Elderly, A Rand Note*, No. 2862, Santa Monica: RAND Corporation.

—— (1993) *Koreika Shakai no Rodoshijo* (*Labour Market of the Ageing Society*), Tokyo: Toyo Keizai Shinposha.

Social Insurance Agency (1993) *Jigyo Nenpo* (*Annual Report on Social Insurance*), Tokyo: Social Insurance Association.

7 Internationalisation of the labour market
Foreign workers and trainees

Koichiro Imano

INTRODUCTION

The internationalisation of the labour market in Japan, which can be defined as the mobility of workers between Japan and other countries, has recently made remarkable progress in two aspects. First, the flow of foreign workers into Japan has increased, especially since the second half of the 1980s, and has emerged as one of the main pools supplying a labour force to Japanese industry.

Second, and very closely related to the internationalisation of business activities of Japanese companies, is the increase both in the number of Japanese employees sent to overseas subsidiaries and in the number of local employees sent by overseas subsidiaries to parent companies for training and introduction of new technology. This chapter will focus on the latter category, 'the foreign trainee'. Foreign trainees are unique in terms of the schemes set up for them in Japan compared to those found in other advanced countries. It is not only the local staff of overseas subsidiaries who received training in their parent companies. Some trainees may be taken on by a company as part of Japan's international aid to developing countries, while others may be there to meet its own labour demands.

In this chapter, foreign workers and trainees will be examined from two points of view: the schemes set up to receive them, and their present situation of employment and training. The discussion will then turn to what impact they have on the labour market and how effective the Japanese trainee system is in terms of the development of human resources in developing countries.

THE LEGAL SYSTEM: IMMIGRATION AND FOREIGN WORKERS

The legal system and the administration of immigration

Entry into and continued stay in Japan of all foreign nationals, including foreign workers, are both controlled by the Immigration Control and

Refugee Recognition Act (ICRRA).[1] The list of residential statuses, as stipulated by the ICRRA, is shown in Table 7.1. Any foreign nationals entering Japan have to acquire one of these statuses, and their activities while in Japan are limited to those determined by the status they have acquired.

Therefore, foreign nationals (foreign workers) seeking employment are required to obtain work-related statuses, denoted by asterisks in Table 7.1. The exception to this regulation is that there is no limitation on activities for the status of 'Permanent resident', 'Spouse etc. of Japanese nationals', 'Spouse etc. of permanent resident' and 'Long-term resident'. As will be mentioned later, many foreign nationals of Japanese origin acquire the status of 'Spouse etc. of Japanese national' or 'Long-term resident' to engage in work.

Table 7.1 List of resident statuses and the number of new entrants in 1991

Residence status	New entrants
Diplomat/Official	22,318
* Professor	750
* Artist	52
* Religious activities	2,073
* Journalist	401
* Investor/Business manager	1,523
* Legal/Accounting services	7
* Medical services	4
* Researcher	823
* Instructor	2,651
* Engineer	3,166
* Specialist in humanities/International services	6,416
* Intra-company transferee	3,780
* Entertainer	89,572
* Skilled labour	2,381
Cultural activities	3,097
Temporary visitor	2,979,547
College student	9,620
Pre-college student	20,654
Trainee	43,649
Dependent	12,739
Designated activities	5,173
Permanent resident	–
Spouse etc. of Japanese nationals	22,820
Spouse etc. of permanent resident	260
Long-term resident	4,398
Total number of new entrants	3,237,874

Source: Ministry of Justice (1992(A))

Note: * Work-related status.

Government policy regarding foreign workers

The legal system regarding foreign workers mentioned above, is based on the principle policy of the Japanese Government introduced in 1988 that foreign workers engaged in jobs requiring a high level of expertise, such as engineers and other professional, should be permitted to enter the country as much as possible, but that unskilled workers should not. The ICRRA was amended in the 1990s based on this policy so that the range of jobs foreigners were allowed to engage in was expanded, and the punishment for illegal work was increased.

The present employment situation for foreign workers is, as a result of the legal system and the new Government policy, more complicated than expected. Foreign nationals entering Japan with work-related status represent a small proportion of all foreign workers. However, not all foreign workers without work-related status are illegal. What is clear is that there are several types of foreign worker who enter Japan by legal and illegal means other than by acquiring this status. In addition, some of the foreign trainees or students may complicate the situation by also working, legally or illegally, in spite of the fact that, in principle, they are not allowed to work. I would therefore like to begin by exploring an outline of each type of foreign worker.

FOREIGN WORKERS IN THE LABOUR MARKET

Foreign workers with work-related status

Needless to say, the first type of foreign workers are those with work-related status. As of 1992, they totalled 11,000 in terms of new entrants and 86,000 in terms of residents. As shown in Table 7.2 the number of new entrants has fluctuated, but residents have increased steadily. In particular, the increase of residents in the 1990s is remarkable partly because of the amendment of the ICRRA.

Regarding the composition of new entrants by residential status (see Table 7.1), the most notable feature is that about 80 per cent of new entrants are foreign workers who fall within the category of 'Entertainer', working in theatres, show business, and so on. Interestingly, the number of those falling within the categories of 'Engineer', 'Specialist in humanities/international service' and 'Intra-company transferee', whom larger companies are very likely to employ as regular workers, is about 13,000 which is much lower than that for the 'Entertainer' category.

Foreign nationals of Japanese origin

The second type is the foreign national of Japanese origin who acquires the status of 'Spouse etc. of Japanese nationals' or 'Long-term resident'. The majority come from South American countries, especially Brazil,

Table 7.2   Number of new entrants and residents

Year	New entrants	Residents
1986	54,736	30,645
1988	81,407	40,398
1990	94,868	67,983
1992	108,143	85,517
1993	97,101	95,376

Sources: Ministry of Justice (each year (A)) and Ministry of Justice (each year (B))

where many foreigners of Japanese origin live. This second type of worker is unique in that their activities are not constrained as are other statuses. As a result, most of them engage in work.

The number in this group of workers residing in Japan increased quickly in the 1990s as a result of the abolition of the restrictions on their activities in 1990. According to estimates made by the Ministry of Foreign Affairs, the number of this group of residents had reached about 145,000 by 1992, which is almost five times as many as in 1989 when there were 29,000.

Foreign students

Foreign students are the third type of foreign worker, and acquire the status of 'College student' or 'Pre-college student' which enables them to study at colleges, vocational schools and other educational institutions. The reason why they are classed as workers is that many of them also work, legally and illegally. The ICRRA stipulates that students can engage in work only when they get permission in advance and when their working hours do not exceed the legal limit. However, many of them work without permission or for more than the prescribed working hours. As of 1992, the number of this type of workers is estimated to amount to about 62,000 people. Of the 103,000 students staying in Japan about 60 per cent of them are thought to be employed (Koyokaihatsu 1989).

We also need to pay attention to foreign trainees with the status of 'Trainee'. This is because foreign trainees are similar to foreign students in the sense that some of them work legally or illegally, in spite of only being permitted to reside to acquire industrial knowledge and skills. The Government has been sensitive with regard to accepting them, because many of them are trained in companies as part of on-the-job training (OJT) schemes which makes it difficult to distinguish the tasks these involve from straightforward work. Therefore, strict regulations apply to the receiving companies. The details of these restrictions are explained later.

Illegal workers

The last type is the illegal worker. This group can be classified into two types:

(1) 'Foreign workers with overstay' who remain in Japan for longer than the period permitted. Most of them are thought to reside illegally to earn an income.
(2) 'Foreign workers without work-related status' who engage in work other than that permitted by their residential status. A typical example is that of foreign nationals who acquire the status of 'Temporary visitor' and then engage in work.

According to the Ministry of Justice, the number of foreign workers with overstay, as of 1992, amounted to 279,000 (see Table 7.3). However, as the exact number of foreign workers without work-related status is not known this is represented by 'α' in Table 7.4.

The Ministry of Justice statistics are the most useful source of data on the composition of illegal workers and their change over time, though they do not cover all the groups. As shown in Table 7.3, illegal workers increased very rapidly in the 1990s. In 1994, 61 per cent of these workers were male and this proportion had grown since the 1980s. One reason for this lay in the main occupations traditionally held by this group which

Table 7.3(a)   The number of foreign workers with overstay 1990–4

Date of survey	Number of workers
July 1990	106,000
May 1991	160,000
May 1992	279,000
May 1993	299,000
May 1994	294,000

Source: Ministry of Justice (1995)

Table 7.3(b)   The distribution of foreign workforce with overstay, by country of origin (May 1994)

Country	%
Thailand	17.1
Korea	14.8
China	13.5
Philippines	12.8
Iran	7.1
Malaysia	6.9
Pakistan/Bangladesh	4.9
Others	22.9

Source: Ministry of Justice (1995)

Table 7.4 Composition of foreign workers residing in Japan – 1992

Types of foreign workers	Number of workers
Foreign nationals with work-related statuses	86,000
Students	52,000
Foreign nationals of Japanese origin	145,000
Illegal workers:	
Foreign workers with overstay	279,000
Foreign workers without work-related status	α
Total	562,000 + α

had changed from female-dominated roles such as barmaid to male-dominated roles such as factory and construction workers. As to their composition by country of origin, most of them came from the East Asian countries such as Thailand, Korea, China and the Philippines.

Estimates of the total number and composition of the foreign workforce

Table 7.4 summarises the composition of foreign workers by type, as defined above. The total number of foreign workers, as of 1992, was estimated to amount to 562,000 plus 'α'. One further important finding here is that foreign nationals of Japanese origin and illegal workers are the two main groups of foreign workers. Therefore, attention needs to be paid not only to the foreign workers with work-related status who usually work as regular employees, but also to these other two groups who are mainly employed as temporary workers.

Employment structure of foreign workers

Following on from the above examination of where foreign workers originate, the supply aspect, this discussion will now focus attention on the demand side of foreign workers. In 1993 the Ministry of Labour introduced an administrative system called the Reporting System on Employment of Foreign Workers (*Gaikokujin Koyo Hokoku Seido*) which aims to collect information from companies on the employment of foreign workers. The resulting report is published yearly and provides the most comprehensive statistical data available on employment.

According to the 1994 report, the manufacturing (especially automotive) and service industries are the two main sectors which employ foreign workers: 61 per cent and 21 per cent respectively. Table 7.5 shows details of this group's employment by occupation. As can be seen, professional, technical and managerial workers, who are supposed to be foreign workers with work-related status, make up only 17 per cent of the foreign

Table 7.5   Employment of foreign workers by occupation – 1994

Occupation	%
Professional, technical, managerial workers	17.1
Sales, clerical workers	4.0
Service workers (cooks, waiters etc.)	7.8
Production workers	59.1
Construction workers	1.7
Transportation workers	2.0
Others	8.3

Source: Ministry of Labour (1994)

workforce. In comparison, production workers form the largest sector, making up about 60 per cent. In addition, the total proportion of production, construction, transportation and service workers who are regarded by the Government as holding unskilled occupations reaches 70 per cent. This shows that most foreign workers are employed in unskilled jobs, despite the Government's adoption of the policy that unskilled foreign workers should not be permitted to enter the country.[2]

FOREIGN TRAINEES AND THE INTERNATIONALISATION OF JAPANESE COMPANIES

The legal framework of the training system

The Japanese training system is very complex. This is mainly because the legal requirements vary to a great extent according to the receiving organisation involved, the training method adopted and the receiving channel used. Therefore, an explanation regarding the legal framework will have to be focused on cases closely related to our main concern, that of private companies receiving trainees and where OJT is included in the training.

The requirements for qualification to take part in this system can be summarised in three points. First, receiving companies should not only provide adequate training conditions (training facilities, trainers, etc.), but also accommodation, training allowances, accident insurance and so on. Second, with regard to the training schedule, at least one-third of the training should be allocated to off-the-job training. Third, the organisations which send trainees should be subsidiaries of the receiving companies, or organisations which have had close dealings with the receiving companies. These requirements also apply to the training channels mentioned below, in which private companies are involved and where OJT is used. There is one exception, however. The requirements regarding the second and third points are relaxed to a great extent in the latest scheme, 'The Practical Skills Training System', which was developed in 1993.

The traditional system – up to the 1980s[3]

The training system reached a turning point at the beginning of the 1990s. The first channel to offer access to this before then was the 'Inter-Government Based Channel' through which the Japanese government mainly received public officers as trainees. The government in principle bore all the training costs using the ODA's public budget. This channel is also seen in other advanced countries but the rest of the channels mentioned below are specific to Japan.[4]

The second channel is the 'Private Channel With Subsidies' in which private, non-profit-making organisations which offer technical aid, are permitted to receive trainees. This channel was originally developed by the government to encourage Japanese companies to expand export and direct investment in other countries. Trainees are therefore mainly sent from subsidiaries of Japanese companies or local companies which have close dealings with them. Besides, receiving companies can receive a public subsidy for each trainee which, in the case of representative training courses is equivalent to three-quarters of the direct training costs. Foreign trainees usually first learn the Japanese language together with a general knowledge of Japanese society in the non-profit-making organisations, followed later by practical knowledge and skills in their parent companies. The main occupations held by trainees are managers, engineers and foremen.

This particular channel has a high reputation abroad, particularly in Asian countries. The reason for this is that a number of young foreigners have received high quality training and, as a result, have entered good vocational careers after returning to their home countries, regardless of whether their positions were held inside or outside of Japanese subsidiaries.

The third channel, the 'Private Channel Without Subsidies', can be seen as a purely private channel in that Japanese companies receive trainees from foreign companies without any assistance from the government. A central concern of the Japanese government regarding this channel is that the quality of training might not be maintained or that the receiving companies might use trainees as ordinary workers. The government cannot have the same direct control over training in this channel as it can through the subsidies it provides for the first two. As a result, stringent requirements are stipulated in the legal framework in order to avoid abuses of the system.

What are the occupations of the trainees received by Japanese companies through this channel? No statistical data on this is available. However, from an estimate, based on evidence from the Japan Institute of Labour survey (1995) on human resource management in subsidiaries of Japanese companies, showing the occupational composition of local employees sent as trainees to Japan, the composition is similar to that for the Private Channel With Subsidies in that managers, engineers and foremen are dominant among them.

The training system, consisting of these three channels, continued to be used until the 1980s. The composition of channels had remained stable up to this period in spite of an increase in the number of trainees. In terms of numbers, the approximate proportions were 40 per cent for the Inter-Government Based Channel, 20 per cent for the Private Channel With Subsidies and 40 per cent for the Private Channel Without Subsidies. This situation, however, changed radically in the 1990s as a result of the development of new purely private channels.

Development of the Employers' Association Channel since the 1990s[5]

The 1980s system has been criticised as one designed for large, not small companies. In fact, most small companies could not use it because very few of them had established overseas subsidiaries or had dealings with foreign companies. The first reform of the system was carried out in response to this criticism and regulations were relaxed in several ways following the amendment by the ICRRA.

The most important part of the reform was to develop the new channel called the 'Employers' Association Channel' by relaxing the requirements placed on organisations sending candidates for training. As a result, companies were allowed to receive trainees from foreign companies ('unrelated foreign companies') rather than their subsidiaries or customers. In order to avoid potential abuses of this arrangement, the Government stipulated that employers' associations were to take responsibility for receiving the trainees, that the companies to which trainees were sent were affiliates of the associations and that training was to be conducted under the supervision of the associations with the assistance of public institutions such as local governments, public vocational training centres and so on.

As a result, even small companies have been able to make use of the training system and have received most of their trainees through this channel. Their occupational composition is very different from the existing large-company-dominated Private Channel Without Subsidies and Private Channel With Subsidies. This is essentially because most of these trainees receive training mainly for blue-collar jobs.

Establishment of the Practical Skills Training System

An additional system was developed in 1990 – the 'Practical Skills Training System'. Foreign nationals under this system were called 'Practical Trainees' to distinguish them from the existing trainees. The most important element of the new system was that restrictions on the training programme were relaxed and practical trainees were given statutory permission to work.

Practical trainees do not necessarily need to receive off-the-job training, which was mandatory under the existing training system, and they can learn practical skills primarily on an OJT basis under labour contracts with companies. They are, with a few exceptions, such as the lack of freedom to change companies, treated as legal workers. Almost all labour-related laws are applied to them and they are allowed to earn wages legally. However, new regulations have been introduced in order to distinguish them from the legal foreign workers, to maintain the quality of practical training and to avoid abuses of the system. The most important regulation is that trainees are only permitted to proceed to practical trainee status once they have passed skill assessment tests supplied by the Government which have to be taken following the completion of the training period. Additionally, the duration of this training has to be less than one and a half times that for a trainee and the length of stay as both trainee and practical trainee should be no more than two years in total. Practical trainees are, as yet, still quite rare as the system has only just started, but it should be noted that they are mainly to be found in blue-collar jobs in relatively small companies. This is explained by the fact that skill assessment tests are limited to blue-collar related jobs.

Why did the Japanese Government develop the new system, despite the problem that practical trainees might be viewed as a new type of foreign worker? On the one hand, it is a system which responds in part to the increasing demand by companies, especially small companies, for foreign workers. On the other, it has been developed as a new system for technical aid which is likely to make a greater contribution to the development of human resources of developing countries by the increased opportunities it offers for foreigners to receive OJT-based training. It should be stressed here that this idea is based on the experience of Japanese companies that discovered that with the introduction of OJT-based training came a higher level of productivity from their employees.

Composition and change of trainees over time

A result of the development of the new channels, combined with the increasing internationalisation of Japanese companies, is that the training system has entered into a new era since the 1990s. The number of trainees increased quickly during this period and reached about 44,000 in 1991, two and a half times as many as in 1987 (see Table 7.6). The sharp increase was mainly caused by the expansion of the Private Channel Without Subsidies which arose from the increasing internationalisation of Japanese companies and the formation of the Employers' Association Channel which was created in response to the entry of many small companies into the scheme.

Consequently, the composition of the different channels, which had remained stable until the 1980s, changed dramatically. The proportion of trainees in the Inter-Government Based Channel and the Private Channel With Subsidies fell to about half of the 1980s level. In contrast, there has

Table 7.6   New entrants to the foreign trainee schemes

Year	Number of new entrants
1983	12,612
1985	14,268
1987	17,081
1989	29,489
1991	43,649
1993	42,275*

Source: Ministry of Justice (each year (A))

Note: * estimated.

been a substantial increase in those taking part in the Private Channel Without Subsidies and the Employers' Association Channel, from about 40 per cent in the 1980s to about 70 per cent in the 1990s.

Such radical shifts of trainees between the channels have had an impact on their occupational composition. The proportion of government officials is decreasing due to the relative decline of the Inter-Government Based Channel. In comparison the occupations of managers, engineers and foremen are estimated to have increased rapidly in spite of the decline of the Private Channel With Subsidies which focuses on these particular occupations, as the Private Channel Without Subsidies has increased more quickly. What is more notable is the substantial increase in blue-collar workers resulting from the quick expansion of the Employers' Association Channel. This tendency is likely to be accelerated by the spread of the Practical Skills Training System.

The profile for the trainees' country of origin has also changed radically. In particular, trainees from China increased much more quickly than those from other countries during the 1990s. The main reason for this lay in the sharp increase in trainees which small companies had received from China via the Employers' Association Channel. It can therefore be seen that one result of the structural changes made to the training system in the 1990s was the rapid emergence of China as the leading country taking advantage of the training scheme.

CONCLUSION: THE IMPACT OF FOREIGN WORKERS AND TRAINEES

The social cost of foreign workers

Empirical studies to evaluate the impact of foreign workers on the Japanese economy, especially in the 1990s, have been conducted mainly by labour economists. They have focused on two topics; the estimate of the social cost which Japanese society will bear as a result of the entry of foreign workers and their impact on the labour market. Social cost is estimated by the Ministry of Labour (1992) to be in the region of between ¥6.2 billion to ¥29.1 billion and ¥80.6 billion by one of the leading private research institutes, Nihon Sogo Kenkyusho (1992). These estimates are based on the assumption that 500,000 foreign workers are admitted to the schemes. Such large differentials in estimates occur mainly as a result of what costs are considered to represent the social cost.

Nakamura (1993) estimates the social cost by using a macro-economic model, as opposed to the above two studies which calculate the various costs resulting from receiving foreign workers. According to his study, the social cost is estimated to be about ¥56 million. His estimate, based on data from 1986 can, if the rate of inflation is taken into consideration, be seen to be almost the same as the one by Nihon Sogo Kenkyusho. However, studies in this field are still at the trial stage and, as Nakamura stresses, it is very difficult to decide which of these estimates is the most accurate.

The impact of foreign workers on the labour market

Studies in this field focus on the impact of foreign workers on employment and Japanese workers' wages. The first approach uses a macro-economic model to clarify their effect on various economic variables selected to represent the national economy. According to Nakamura (1993), the entry of foreign workers into the Japanese labour market lead to an increase in the total workforce and, at least in the short or medium term, had a significantly positive influence on the growth of GNP in spite of a decrease in real wage. But, it is also made clear that the impact on these economic variables is dependent on what percentage of the income earned by forcign workers in Japan was sent to their home countries.

Research has been carried out to clarify the respective impact on skilled and unskilled workers with regard to employment and wage since it is held that foreign workers are supposed to have a more serious effect on unskilled workers. According to Ootake (Ootake and Oogusa 1993), skilled and foreign workers are complementary in that the increase of foreign workers leads to an improvement in employment and wage for skilled workers. In comparison, he found that with an increase in the number of foreign workers there follows a worsening in employment and wage for unskilled workers. He points out that as the supply of unskilled workers increases with foreign workers entering this sector of the labour force so too does the demand for skilled workers who are, in turn, employed to supervise the unskilled workers.

Mitani's work (1993) in this area made clear the possibility of substitution between part-time workers as unskilled workers and foreign workers. In addition, the following possibility is stressed in connection with this finding. Typical features of part-time workers in Japan are that the majority of them are female and in contrast to foreign workers, their supply changes flexibly in response to the fluctuations of the labour market. Therefore, if part-time workers were to be replaced by foreign workers the flexibility of the labour market might be lost and, as a result, the unemployment rate would be likely to increase to a higher level than it is in the mid-1990s, during a recession, when demand for labour shrinks.

These findings, while important, are still tentative. Lack of statistical data on the employment of foreign workers may need to be improved in order for the empirical study by labour economists to progress further.

Evaluation of foreign trainees

The training systems for both the 1980s and the 1990s need to be evaluated separately because of the differences that exist between them in all aspects of the receiving channel, the receiving and sending companies and the trainees themselves. With regard to the 1980s training system, comprehensive evaluations have already been carried out. Imano and Sato (1991) conducted a questionnaire survey of subjects who were ex-trainees attached to the Private Channel With Subsidies and who lived in their home countries at the time of the survey. Direct effects of training, such as the improvement of practical skills, were evaluated positively by the ex-trainees, about half of them responded that 'aims were achieved as planned' and 30 per cent reported that 'about half of the aims planned were achieved'.

Indirect effects were also evaluated very highly by ex-trainees. As shown in Table 7.7 trainees acquired various experiences by having close contact with Japanese workers in workshops and these experiences enabled them to understand problems which they would have to solve in their own companies. In particular, they felt impressed with 'work discipline', 'safety measures' and 'workers' consciousness of quality'. Further, many of them had made efforts to realise or introduce within their present companies aspects with which they had felt impressed.

Similar effects can be observed for trainees of the Private Channel Without Subsidies (Japanese Institute of Labour 1995). It can be concluded, therefore, that the 1980s training systems in which Japanese companies were involved, functioned very effectively in terms of the development of human resources of developing countries. In addition to this, the findings also show that Japanese companies placed great importance on the system as a method of training local employees of overseas subsidiaries. Several studies make it clear that many of the positions held by local core employees at all levels of management were occupied by ex-trainees in overseas subsidiaries. This comes about essentially because the training method had been widely applied not only to managers and engineers, but also to blue-collar workers. It should also be noted, however, that Japanese companies provided a high quality of training

Table 7.7 Evaluation of the indirect effects of training by ex-trainees

Work practices	*Which gave a favourable impression during training* (%)	*Which were introduced after training at home- country workplaces* (%)
Multiple answers allowed		
Work discipline	71.0	61.2
Safety measures	58.6	55.2
Workers' consciousness of quality	53.2	50.7
Working environment	49.4	40.3
Work ethics	48.5	31.5
Industrial relations	40.8	30.3
Communication within company and workshop	37.5	27.2
QC and Zero Deficit	35.2	32.4
Promotion of orderly and clean workshops	35.0	33.0
Mutual support between sections	30.0	25.7
Linkage between staff and line sections	25.7	20.0
Transfer of personnel	18.0	15.5
Others	4.0	2.4

Source: Imano and Sato (1991), p. 139

mainly because the system had been geared for the training of local employees of their overseas subsidiaries. The success of the 1980s training system, therefore, does not necessarily guarantee the same for the 1990s system which can be characterised by the number of trainees sent from 'unrelated foreign companies'.

Three points need to be taken into consideration when the prospects of the 1990s training system are discussed, irrespective of the Employers' Association Channel and Practical Skills Training System. First, what incentives do companies have to train foreigners? These can be summarised as: (1) to participate in providing technical aid; (2) to use trainees partly, or wholly, as workers; and (3) to prepare for establishing new business relations with the trainees' home countries. Between them, the first and third incentives show that companies do not necessarily expect a return in the short term.

Second, how likely are the incentives, especially the second one, to be satisfied by the existing 1990s system? It is too early to make a final judgement on this, but it can at least be shown that receiving companies experience difficulty in gaining enough benefits in the short term to exceed training costs. This may be mainly because a lot of initial investment is needed and the duration of training is short. As a consequence of this, many receiving companies hope to extend the duration of a trainee's stay.

Third, what kind of contribution can the system make to developing the human resources of developing countries? This is an important consideration, but there are insufficient data available to evaluate the system from this point of view. Therefore, further studies will be needed in order to evaluate and improve the 1990s system.

NOTES

1 For details of the legal system of immigration, refer to the guidebook for the Japan Immigration Association (1993).
2 Topics concerning working conditions and human resource management, which are very important to employment of foreign workers, are not dealt with in this chapter. For useful reading on these, see studies by Kokumin Kinyukouko (1992), Tokyo Toritu Rodo Kenkyusho (1991) and the Ministry of Labour (1991).
3 For details of the 1980s system, refer to Imano and Sato (1991).
4 Research programmes on the international comparison of trainee systems have recently been conducted by the Japanese Institute of Labour (1994) and Kuptsch and Oishi (1995).
5 For details of the 1990s system, refer to Kuptsch and Oishi (1995).

REFERENCES

Goto, J. (1990) *Gaikokujin Rodo no Keizaigaku* (*The Economics of Foreign Workers*), Tokyo: Toyo Keizai Shinposha.
Higuchi, Y. (1988) 'Gaikokujin rodosha mondai no keizaigakuteki sokumen – kokunai koyo eno eikyo' (Economic aspects of foreign workers – their impact on domestic employment), *Nihon Rodo Kyokai Zasshi*, No. 348.
Imano, K. and Sato, H. (1991) *Gaikokujin Kenshusei* (*Foreign Trainees*), Tokyo: Toyo Keizai Shinposha.
Japan Immigration Association (1993) *A Guide to Entry: Residence and Registration Procedures in Japan for Foreign Nationals*, Tokyo: Japan Immigration Association.
Japan Institute of Labour (1993) *Keizaishakai no Kokusaika to Rodomondai ni kansuru Kenkyu* (*A Study on the Internationalization of the Economy and Labour Problems*), Tokyo: Japan Institute of Labour.
—— (1994) *Igirisu, Furansu, Doitsu ni okeru Gaikokujin Kenshusei Seido* (*The Foreign Trainee Systems in Great Britian, France and Germany*), Tokyo: Japan Institute of Labour.
—— (1995) *NGO gata Hitozukuri Kyoryoku-III* (*A Report on International Co-operation for Human Resource Development by NGO-III*), Tokyo: Japan Institute of Labour.
Kokumin, Kinyukouko (1992) *Gaikokujin Rodosha o Senryokuka suru Chushokigyo* (*A Study on Human Resource Management of Foreign Workers in Small Companies*), Tokyo: Kokumin Kinyu Koko.
Koyokaihatsu Senta (1989) *Kigyo no Kokusaika to Gaikokujin Ryugakusei, Kenshusei* (*The Internationalization of Companies, Foreign Students and Trainees*), Tokyo: Koyo Kaihatsu Senta.

Kuptsch, C. and Oishi, N. (1995) *Training Abroad: German and Japanese Schemes for Workers from Transition Economies or Developing Countries*, Geneva International Labour Office.

Ministry of Justice (annual (A)) *Shutsunyukoku Kanri Tokei (Statistics of Immigration Control)*, Tokyo: Okurasho Insatsu Kyoku.

—— (annual (B)) *Zairyu Gaikokugin Tokei (Statistics of Foreign Residents)*, Tokyo: Nyukan Kyokai.

Ministry of Labour (1991) *Gaikokujin Rodosha no Syugyo Jittai Chosa (Survey on the Employment of Foreign Workers)*, Tokyo: Ministry of Labour.

—— (1992) *Gaikokujin Rodosha ga Rodomen nado ni oyobosu Eikyo nado ni kansuru Kenkyukai Senmonbukai Hokokusho (Report on the Impact of Foreign Workers on Employment)*, Tokyo: Ministry of Labour.

—— (1994) *Gaikokujin Koyojyokyo Hokoku (Report on the Employment of Foreign Workers)*, Tokyo: Ministry of Labour.

—— (1995) *Honpo ni okeru Fuho Zanryusha no Kazu ni tsuite (The Number of Foreign Workers Who Overstay)*, Tokyo: Ministry of Labour.

Mitani, N. (1993) 'Gaikokujin rodosha to joshi paatotaima rodosha' ('Foreign workers and female part-time workers'), *Kokusai Kyoryoku Ronshu*, 1, pp. 101–27.

Nakamura, J. (1993) 'Kokusai kan rodoidou ni tomonau makuro keizai teki eikyo' ('The impact of international labour mobility on the macro-economy'), in Japan Institute of Labour *Study on the Internationalization of the Economy and Labour Problems*, Tokyo: Japan Institute of Labour.

Nihon Sogo Kenkyusho (1992) *Gaikokujin Rodosha Ukeire ni tomonau Shakaiteki Kosuto ni kansuru Chosa Hokokusho (Report on the Social Cost of Foreign Workers)*, Tokyo: Nihon Sogo Kenkyosho.

Office of the Prime Minister (1990) *Gaikokujin Rodosha Mondai ni kansuru Seron Chosa (Opinion Survey on Foreign Workers)*, Tokyo: Office of the Prime Minister.

Ootake, F. and Oogusa, Y. (1993) 'Gaikokujin rodosha to nihon rodosha tono daitai hokan kankei' ('Complimentary and alternative relations between foreign workers and Japanese workers'), *Nihon Rodo Kenkyu Zasshi*, No. 407.

Shimada, Haruo (1994) *Japan's Guest Worker*, Tokyo: University of Tokyo Press.

Tokyo Toritu Rodo Kenkyusho (1991) *Tokyo ni okeru Gaikokujin Rodosha no Syuro Jittai (Survey on Work of Foreign Workers in Tokyo)*, Tokyo: Tokyo Toritu Rodo Kenkyosho.

Part II

8 Rengo and policy participation
Japanese-style neo-corporatism?

Toru Shinoda

What do Japanese trade unions do at the national level? How do they influence national policy making? In this chapter, the political activity of Japanese trade unions will be discussed from the viewpoint of the relationships among unions, political parties and governments. The first aspect to be dealt with will be the political characteristics of Japanese trade unions. Second, the transition of national centres and the relationship between unions and political parties will be traced. Third, the political activity of Rengo, the new national centre, will be described. Finally, the implications of Rengo's political activities in Japanese labour politics will be examined.

These aspects are considered with the following theoretical interest in mind. As is well known, the label of 'corporatism without labour' (Pempel and Tsunekawa 1979) had been widely accepted internationally in the 1970s and 1980s. This was devised to capture the characteristic in Japanese industrial relations and labour politics that not all major social groups were co-opted into the process of policy making and interest intermediation at the macro- and meso-levels; rather, only labour was excluded or marginalised in such a process. However by the late 1980s, there was a realisation particularly among Japanese scholars that labour politics in Japan was becoming more corporatist. This chapter is also based on this interpretation.

Much of the existing analysis of the move towards corporatism in Japan focuses on the developments since the late 1970s which is considered the starting point for 'corporatisation'. By contrast, this chapter goes further back in history to trace the changes in the essential characteristics of the labour movement. The examination of the issue from this angle makes it possible to understand more fundamentally how the structure of 'corporatism without labour' in Japan, as characterised in the following quotation, was transformed into 'corporatism with labour': 'Thus, by early in this century, the dominant coalition of the state and big business was expanded to include, as minor partners, the agricultural and small-business sectors. One of the major political strategies chosen by this coalition was to systematically exclude labour from the national-level organisations and to incorporate them at the individual plant level, thus neutralising their potentially disturbing influence' (Pempel and Tsunekawa 1979, p. 268).

Another aim of this chapter is to further our understanding of the concept of 'corporatism'. For example, in attempting to define 'corporatist arrangements', Ronald Dore (1990) raised the problems of sectoral clashes and the establishment of public interest, and emphasised the importance of the management of interest representation in the contemporary context. This chapter also pays much attention to this point, while at the same time providing a useful perspective for analysing future developments in 'corporatism' in Japan and elsewhere.

THE POLITICAL CHARACTERISTICS OF THE JAPANESE TRADE UNION MOVEMENT

In the past, foreign experts have interpreted Japanese labour politics as backward or peculiar and have regarded Japanese unions as marginal in the policy-making process.[1] Japanese unions have certainly had a history of unique political features.

The anti-establishment stance

Prior to and immediately following World War II, Japanese union leaders often had a tendency to regard their movement as an anti-establishment class struggle. As a result of this, the Japanese labour movement was influenced by radical ideologies committed to overthrowing the establishment. Some labour leaders reacted to this radical element by avoiding politics altogether. The conflicts which arose between radical groups and moderate apolitical groups led to divisions in the labour movement. In such a situation it became very difficult for pragmatic political reformists to move into leadership roles.

The strong central government which had controlled Japan since the Meiji Era was primarily concerned with preserving the peace and preventing civil disorder. Labour unions were thus viewed as a potentially disruptive element which had to be kept under strict control. The post-war government, led by the Liberal Democratic Party (LDP), inherited this tradition and tried to discourage the concepts of modern industrial relations which were introduced by the Supreme Commander of Allied Powers (SCAP) as a counter to the militaristic influences in Japanese society.

The history of industrial relations in the public sector after the war reflects the anti-establishment stance. In the early post-war years, basic union rights, such as the right to strike, were partially restricted by the government which wished to prevent public sector unions, controlled by the Communists, from radicalising the entire labour movement.[2] Unfortunately, due to the hegemony of public sector unions in the labour movement, the removal of the restrictions placed on public workers became virtually the only priority of labour politics after World War II. So much so, that only recently has it been made possible for the labour movement to take up problems faced by workers in the private sector. This is particularly true of the rights and work conditions of unorganised workers in small and medium-sized enterprises which have historically been underemphasized by the labour movement.

In these circumstances, the task of establishing institutions of industrial relations was entrusted substantially to the pro-labour bureaucrats in the Ministry of Labour who took over the traditions of liberalism cultivated by pre-war reformist bureaucrats in the Ministry of the Interior.[3]

Enterprise unionism

The anti-establishment stance of the labour movement had existed hand-in-hand with enterprise unionism. It is well known that Japanese unions are organised at the level of individual enterprises and working conditions are substantially determined by collective bargaining between each enterprise union and the employer. Japanese enterprise unionism is best characterised by the autonomy in personnel and financial affairs from higher-level labour organisations, and by a sense of the community sharing the fate of the enterprise (Shinoda 1989, pp. 13–18).

Unions at large firms in particular satisfied members' demands by bargaining for wage increases and better welfare programmes in return for increased productivity, and such bargaining took place on the understanding with management that employment security was guaranteed. Through the annual wage bargaining process, known as Shunto, enterprise unions have managed to improve their members' standard of living by obtaining fair and consistent wage increases during periods of high economic growth. In this way workers in the private sector lacked economic incentives to demand political solutions (Hiwatari 1991, p. 137).

By encouraging introversion and automony, enterprise unions restrained the influence of outsiders such as nationwide industrial federations and national union centres. The radical labour movement often promoted this trend, and as a result a large number of enterprise unions have either withdrawn from such outside organisations or remained completely unaffiliated. Additionally, employers who wanted to maintain a sense of community among their workers would sometimes intervene in union affairs and force the union to break away from having political connections with labour organisations outside the enterprise.[4]

Dependent unions

Another feature of Japanese unions is their political dependence on political parties. In order to compensate for the lack of personnel and financial resources of a mass movement in Japan, unions were often involved in organisations and activities of socialist parties. These political connections in turn brought about a situation of political dependence.

There were also circumstances where the unions themselves promoted such dependence. One such circumstance originated in the internal power structure of the unions. Since Japanese union leaders' power base is weaker than in Western unions, some union leaders, particularly those in the public sector, attempt to compensate for their weakness by raising the standard of political alliance with organisations such as the socialist parties. These standards would serve to protect the established leadership against the internal opposition groups such as radical socialists or communists in the unions (Yoshimura 1977, pp. 56–7, Yoshimura 1979, pp. 39–40).

Another circumstance sprang from the identity of unions. Enterprise unions looked for ways to show their members their ability to become a central force in areas not connected with business activities. Thus, unions frequently sought to gain influence within political parties. As a result, many veteran union leaders, particularly from unions at large firms and public corporations, ran for seats in the Diet. They also stood in local prefectural and municipal assemblies as candidates for those specific parties supported by the unions. The public sector unions had many socialist party members in the Diet in order to strengthen their ability to make better deals with the government about their working conditions.

As a result of these characteristics, unions led by public sector workers in post-war Japan developed anti-establishment struggles which took the form of national movements. This style of labour politics was effective in raising the political and social status of the labour movement until the early 1960s when the Japanese political and economic systems were still unstable and the public sector constituted a considerable portion of the Japanese workforce. In the middle of the 1960s however, when economic, political and social development was finally well under way, the labour movement began to search for new objectives and activities. The later half of the decade saw growing criticism from within the labour movement about this style of labour politics. This in turn gave birth to movements to unify the labour front and to lead the way towards the creation of a new national centre.

THE TRANSITION OF NATIONAL CENTRES AND THEIR RELATION TO POLITICAL PARTIES

Japanese unions followed a long and winding road to achieve a unified national centre and it was during this time that they developed their various relationships with political parties.

The pre-war period

From the 1890s to the 1930s the Japanese labour movement went through a long transformation that saw the moderate faction becoming gradually more and more radicalised, until finally splitting away and ultimately disappearing altogether under governmental oppression (Inagami 1988, pp. 99–100). Because of this, the total number of union members failed to increase smoothly with the largest membership of 420,000 achieved in 1936. The highest unionisation rate reached during this period was 7.9 per cent which was achieved in 1931. No strong national centre emerged during this time due to repeated splits in the labour movement.

In 1924, universal suffrage was finally realised and during this period the first proletarian parties were organised. These parties, however, could not gather a large enough vote at the three general elections which took place. The left-wing unions, influenced by communism and anarcho-syndicalism, often caused splits which brought about oppressive responses from the government. The right-wing unions, whose centre was the Japanese Federation of Trade Unions (Sodomei), the oldest national centre at that time and primarily influenced by US business unionism of the American Federation of Labour, were enthusiastic about making labour agreements with each company and organising mutual aid activities for their members. They restricted their political activity to lobbying for the Trade Union Bill which the Liberal-Conservative led government submitted to the Diet, but which was rejected in the end (Banno 1991, pp. 235–6).

Eventually, the government eliminated the left-wing unions, leaving the right-wing unions to work in cooperation with the government. The Japanese labour movement was finally disbanded by the militaristic government established at the end of this period.[5]

The post-war period

Japanese workers were granted labour's three major rights (the rights to organise, to collectively bargain and to take industrial action) when SCAP encouraged the growth of unions after the war. Membership increased rapidly, reaching 4.6 million within the first year and the unionisation rate reached its highest peak ever at 55.8 per cent in 1949. In this period, the Congress of Industrial Unions of Japan (Sanbetsu), composed primarily of radical public sector unions, led the labour movement. Sanbetsu was in virtually complete control of the Japan Communist Party (JCP) while the Japanese Federation of Trade Unions (Sodomei), to which moderate private sector unions were affiliated, became linked to the Japan Socialist Party (JSP).

Sanbetsu failed to go on general strikes aimed at overthrowing the Conservative government in 1947. The resulting criticism by radical elements from within Sanbetsu, especially the strong criticism from the Affiliated League for Democratisation (Mindo, a group which sought to break the control of the JCP), led to yet another split in Sanbetsu. The final death blow to Sanbetsu was dealt by the Red Purge, while Sodomei and Mindo, with support from the SCAP, formed the General Council of Trade Unions of Japan (Sohyo) in 1950 as a new national centre. Sohyo was expected to support anti-communist labour movements and to pursue affiliation with the US-controlled International Confederation of Free Trade Unions (ICFTU).[6]

The establishment of the four national centres

The issues of the US–Japan Security Treaty and the Korean War (1950–3), following the formation of Sohyo, changed Sohyo's character. It voted down the affiliation to the ICFTU because of the ICFTU's commitment to the Korean War. Furthermore, Sohyo opposed a separate peace treaty with Western countries and insisted that the overall peace treaty should also include Eastern countries. When the JSP split as a result of this issue, Sohyo wholeheartedly supported the left-wing JSP's insistence on an overall peace treaty.

After the change from its anti-communist stance to an anti-American stance, Sohyo, in the spirit of class struggle, stirred up a series of strikes against dismissals. At the same time it drew together the main forces in the political campaigns opposing the internal and foreign affairs of the government along with those aimed at overthrowing the government. These campaigns continued until the end of the struggle against the Japan–US Security Treaty and the defeat of the Mitsui-Miike strikes in the coalmining industry in 1960.[7]

The radicalisation of Sohyo, however, brought about splits within the organisation. In 1950, a part of Sodomei rejected joining Sohyo. In 1952, the National Federation of Industrial Organisations (Shinsanbetsu) withdrew from Sohyo as a result of the different views they held on labour politics. In 1953, the right-wing unions rejected Sohyo's decision on the peace treaty and the proposed affiliation to the ICFTU, and left to form the Japanese Trade Union Congress (Zenro). In 1962, Zenro and Sodomei combined to form the Congress of the Japanese Confederation of Labour (Domeikaigi). Meanwhile, those executives within Sohyo who had supported the eastern countries and who had shown commitment to the political struggles were replaced by a group which favoured neutrality and economic struggle. In 1956, amid the conflict between Sohyo, Sodomei and Zenro, the unaffiliated unions formed Churitsurokon, which was shortly thereafter renamed Churitsuroren, or the Federation of Independent Unions of Japan.[8] In this way the four national centres were established.

The formation of the blocs

During the same period, unions formed blocs with political parties. Sohyo considered political parties the arm of Sohyo in the Diet and entered into the bloc following its support for the left-wing JSP. By strengthening the political party, Sohyo's specific intention was to realise a socialist society through its own actions. This was brought about by extending the JSP membership, supporting the JSP in all of the elections and promoting the teachings of Marxism–Leninism.[9]

In 1956, after linking with the JSP, Sohyo formed the Sohyo–JSP Membership Council (SJMC) for the purpose of acquiring JSP members, establishing JSP workshops, mastering socialist theories and competing with the JCP. This council, in league with the JSP, played a key role in a variety of political campaigns. An increasing number of former union officers, particularly those from public sector unions, became JSP candidates in national elections, and by the middle of the 1960s, they represented more than 50 per cent of JSP members standing for election (Yoshimura 1979, pp. 51–7).

Sodomei and Zenro supported the right-wing factions within the JSP and together became committed to the formation of a new party, which they called the Democratic Socialist Party (DSP). When the DSP was formed in 1960, Zenro was responsible for the party's administration and set up the Liaison Conference for Diet Activity with Sodomei support. Furthermore, the Domeikaigi, renamed Domei in 1964, specified strengthening the DSP in its principles for action and this was realised following Sohyo's example.

However, although Domei sent its union officers as candidates for the DSP, the degree of actual support it offered was lower than that of Sohyo. The relationship between Domei and the DSP was developed superficially. The DSP was gradually moving away from its democratic socialist ideals which lay close to those of the British Labour Party and was instead linking up with big business employers. Increased complaints were received from the rank and file of Domei concerning the continual support for the DSP, specifically because the DSP remained a small party. Domei, however, expected the DSP to act as a check on the radicalisation of the JSP rather than a large party to replace the JSP (Takeda 1967, pp. 19–22). The relationship was most convenient for large enterprise unions because those unions which split or withdrew from Sohyo-affiliated industrial federations had to compete ideologically with minor opposition groups within the unions which included JSP and JCP members. These unions also needed connections within the opposition parties in order to counterbalance their employer's connections with the ruling LDP.

Although Sohyo was opposed to the JCP in the beginning because of its anti-communist principles, it was JCP's move away from radical principles in 1956 and its intent on integrating into Sohyo itself which led to

Sohyo joining the JCP in the ongoing power struggle between the JSP and JCP factions. This led to the formation of the SJMC as mentioned earlier, and the rejection of the right-wing unions. The JSP faction, disturbed by the formation of the Domeikaigi, switched Sohyo's focus to being economy-oriented, which led to it being opposed to the JCP once more (Yoshimura 1977, pp. 52–5).

Furthermore, the JSP faction had decided that Sohyo should formally support JSP and strengthen SJMC. After that, the relationship between Sohyo and the JCP continued to be strained over the issue of formal union support for specific political parties. On the other hand, the SJMC supported the hegemony of the JSP faction in Sohyo by accepting its agenda including personnel affairs (Yoshimura 1977). It was in this way that the Japanese labour movement was split in the middle of the 1960s.

THE LABOUR UNIFICATION MOVEMENT[10]

The labour unification movement, which created the new national centres, began in the middle of the 1960s when the deadlock in the labour movement appeared.

Prologue

The movement to unify labour was brought about at the initiative of private sector unions faced with the new economic environment (see Figure 8.1). In the 1960s, when the Japanese economy showed a high rate of growth and the national standard of living rose, private sector unions increased their membership. Domei absorbed a part of this increase, exceeding Sohyo's share while others unhappy with the established national centres became unaffiliated.

The ruling Liberal Democratic Party adapted to the environment by leading public attention away from debate over the selection of economic and political systems towards the realised high economic growth. The JSP failed to transform itself from a resistance-oriented party into a government-oriented party. The formation of the Clean Government Party (CGP), a centrist party supported by a huge new Buddhist organisation, together with the rise of the JCP in the city areas, further complicated the opposition party camp.

The formation of the Japanese Council of the International Metalworkers' Federation (IMF-JC) in 1964 was virtually the starting point of the labour unification movement. The metalworkers' unions, which affiliated separately into four national centres or remained unaffiliated, sought the realignment of the national centres to adapt to the new environment which found them confronting the internationalisation and realignment of key industries in Japan.

The IMF-JC also presented a new view of labour politics. It stressed the necessity of unions to engage in political activities, not in the normal sense of ideological politics but in the sense of interest politics. It emphasised the autonomy of unions in their activities and it declared the necessity for the development of more realistic opposition parties and for the support of such parties on all these points. This idea was later adopted by Rengo.

The first labour unification movement

The formation of the IMF-JC shook Sohyo and Domei. In 1967, Takaragi, the chairman of Zentei (the Japan Postal Workers' Union, which was a leading union in Sohyo) published an essay entitled 'On the unification of labour and the establishment of a Japan Socialist Party government' in a magazine and conspicuously began to discuss the issue of labour unification. He appreciated the formation of the IMF-JC and stressed the need for the establishment of a JSP government through the reunification of the JSP and the DSP.

Following the Takaragi proposal, the general secretaries of the major unions in the four national centres formed a liaison organisation. After the JSP suffered a crushing defeat, the JCP made remarkable progress and the LDP's supremacy built up in the 1969 general election. The big business unions of the IMF-JC aimed to create a new reformist group formed of various liaison organisations across the four national centres.

In 1970, the leaders of the major unions agreed basically on unification. The heads of the six private sector unions in the four national centres convened a meeting of agents in 1971 and the Conference of Twenty-Two Unions for Unification took place in 1972. The conference discussed unification and the new national centre. However, a deadlock was reached during the discussion over whether public sector unions should participate. This deadlock emerged because Sohyo was able to assert its opposition to unification when the JSP and the JCP made progress in the 1972 general election. The election saw a retreat by the LDP and a crushing defeat by the DSP and the CGP. As a consequence, the first labour unification movement failed and the conference was dissolved that same year.

The second labour unification movement

The second labour unification movement started when the private sector unions formed a Joint Action Council of Private Unions (JACPU) in order to preserve the possibility of unifying the labour movement after the dissolution of the Conference of Twenty-Two Unions. This organisation demanded positive government measures to deal with inflation when the oil crisis occurred in 1973. The four national centres struggled jointly on the subjects of prices and employment. The relationship between the four

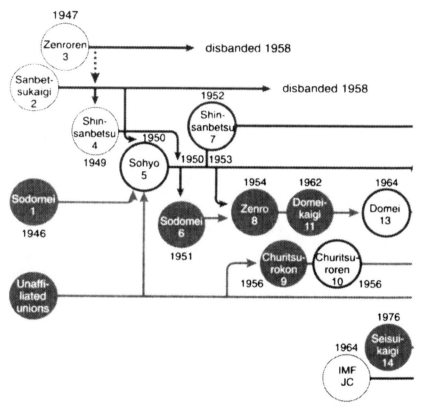

Figure 8.1 History of post-war labour organisations

Source: Japan Institute of Labour (1994), pp. 19–20

Note: Those in bold rimmed circles were centralised national labour organisations from 1964 to 1993.

① Sodomei: Japanese Federation of Trade Unions
② Sanbetsukaigi: Congress of Industrial Unions of Japan
③ Zenroren: Liaison Council of All Trade Unions of Japan
④ Shinsanbetsu: National Federation of Industrial Organisations
⑤ Sohyo: General Council of Trade Unions of Japan
⑧ Zenro: Japanese Trade Unions Congress
⑨ Churitsurokon: the former organisation of Churitsuroren
⑩ Churitsuroren: Federation of Independent Unions of Japan

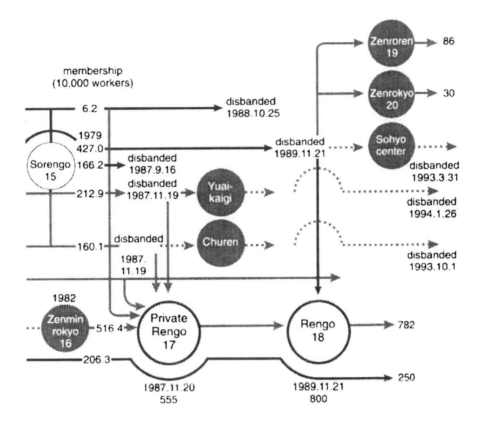

① Domeikaigi: Congress of Japanese Confederation of Labour
② IMF–JC: Japanese Council of International Metalworkers' Unions
③ Domei: Japanese Confederation of Labour
④ Seisuikaigi: Trade Union Council for Policy Promotion
⑤ Sorengo: National Federation of Trade Unions of Japan
⑯ Zenminrokyo: Japanese Private Sector Trade Union Council
⑰ Private Rengo: Japanese Private Sector Trade Union Confederation
⑱ Rengo: Japanese Trade Union Confederation
⑲ Zenroren: National Confederation of Trade Unions
⑳ Zenrokyo: National Trade Union Council

national centres worsened until the joint organisation dissolved to form the Trade Union Council for Policy Promotion (Seisuikaigi) in 1976 and the conditions for unification were once again present. As a result, the situation surrounding the Sohyo–JSP bloc changed. First, opposition parties began to realign at the defeat of the LDP in the 1976 general election. Second, after Sohyo's defeat in 1975 to win the public sector workers' right to strike, it lost its hegemony in Shunto to the IMF-JC and began looking for realistic ways to approach private sector unions.

In 1980, six unions of the four national centres formed the Conference for the Promotion of Unification whose aims were outlined in the Basic Plan for Unification. The provisions of the Basic Plan included the promotion of policy demands, affiliation to the ICFTU, the identification of anti-unification unions, which meant the virtual exclusion of JCP-related unions and preceding onward with the unification of the private sector unions. Following heated debates on the conference's aims, Sohyo entrusted each affiliated union with the decision of whether or not to affiliate itself with the new national centre. In 1981, the Preparatory Committee for Unification was formed, and in 1982 the Japanese Private Sector Trade Union Council (Zenminrokyo) was founded. By 1987, the Japanese Private Sector Trade Union Confederation (Private Rengo) was established as the new national centre for the private sector unions. It was at this time that Domei and Churitsuroren were disbanded, followed by Shinbetsu in the next year.[11]

After the formation of Private Rengo, the remaining task to be accomplished was unification with the public sector unions. Private Rengo revealed to the public sector unions affiliated to Sohyo and Domei what conditions were attached to unification. The conditions were: to respect Rengo principles; to accept affiliations to the ICFTU; and the identification and expulsion of anti-unification unions. The public sector unions consented to the conditions and Sohyo proposed that unification would be attained in 1989.

Following this schedule, the public sector unions affirmed their affiliation to Rengo at their respective conventions. However, the JCP faction of the National Prefectural and Municipal Workers' Union (Jichiro), along with the Japan Teachers' Union (Nikkyoso), expressed their opposition to unification by boycotting the conventions. In 1989, the convention marking the final unification of Private Rengo and the public sector unions was held and the Japanese Trade Union Confederation (Rengo) was inaugurated. Sohyo disbanded on the same day. Furthermore, Sohyo, Domei and Churitsuroren left to their respective successors, namely the Sohyo Centre, Yuaikaigi and Churen, the task of dealing with problems over political activities and local organisations which they deemed too complex to bring into Rengo immediately (Nitta 1990).

The labour unification movement managed to involve a lot of unions unaffiliated to the pre-existing national centres in one stroke. In 1963, when the competition between Sohyo and Domei was stabilised, those unions which did not affiliate to any of the four national centres totalled 31.3 per cent of total union membership. The proportion of members in unaffiliated unions rose to 40.7 per cent in 1987 just before the formation of Private Rengo. However, after Private Rengo was established, it fell to 34 per cent by 1989, and dropped again to 32.4 per cent in 1990 after the formation of Rengo (Shinoda 1992b, pp. 204–5).

The anti-Rengo movement

The JCP started a counter-unification movement when the labour unification movement turned against the JCP. Following the JSP's crushing defeat in the 1969 general election, the JCP made remarkable progress in expanding its influence. Shortly thereafter the pro-JCP unions formed the Conference for United Front Promotion which was renamed the Trade Union Conference for United Front Promotion (TUCUFP) in 1970. Sohyo's approach to the unification movement, and the Agreement on the JSP and CGP Coalition Government Plan in 1980 following the failure of the Shunto campaign for the right to strike in 1975, worsened the relationship between the JSP and the JCP. The JCP criticised Sohyo and the JSP for 'leaning to the right'. Sohyo labelled the TUCUFP a 'sect' and immediately broke off relations.[12]

After that, the TUCUFP criticised the Basic Plan, mentioned above, as 'the plan for right-wing unification' and labelled Zenminrokyo 'the pre-war Patriotic Industrial Labour Organisation'. Just before the establishment of Rengo, and just after the disbandment of Sohyo, the TUCUFP faction formally from within Sohyo proposed the formation of 'the class-conscious national centre'. In 1989, pro-JCP unions such as the Japan Federation of Medical Workers' (Iroren), the Japan Federation of National Service Employees (Kokkororen) and other pro-JCP members withdrew from Jichiro and Nikkyoso, and established the National Confederation of Trade Unions (Zenroren). In 1983, the left-wing JSP group critical of the labour unification movement formed the Centre for the Study of Labour Movements aimed at 'the regeneration of the left-wing Sohyo' and 'the prevention of the right-wing labour movement'. The centre established the National Trade Union Council (Zenrokyo) following the disbandment of Sohyo in 1989. The main unions of this council were the Federation of Tokyo Metropolitan Government Workers' Unions (Tororen) and the National Railway Workers' Union (Kokuro), whose membership had decreased sharply as a result of the division and privatisation of the National Railway Company.[13]

In this way, the labour unification movement was influenced by the situations surrounding the political parties. For example, the victory of the JSP in the general election caused the movement to stagnate, whereas the defeat of the JSP revitalised it. This explains why the key players in the movement, the private sector unions, sought to distance the labour movement from political parties.

THE DEMAND FOR POLICY CHANGES AND THE INSTITUTIONAL REFORM OF RENGO

As stated above, the labour unification movement provided Rengo with a new bottle. So how about new wine?

Demand for policy changes and institutional reform (*seisaku seido yokyu*)

The Demand for Policy Changes and Institutional Reform (DPCIR) is an annual document published by Rengo that contains demands and proposals concerning governmental policies. DPCIR is also used as a way of referring to a series of meetings Rengo uses to work together with cabinets, political parties and administrative bureaucracies in order to realise their annual goals. This is linked to the industrial and regional policy activities of the affiliated unions and local Rengos through the taking up of a part of their demands for change. The DPCIR is the main activity which Rengo took over from Seisuikaigi and has become firmly established within the Japanese labour movement.

DPCIR gives unions the ability to break away from traditional tactics by providing them with the tools to formulate and realise policies which benefit not only union members but also workers as a whole. This is a view which some elements of the labour movement have held since the 1960s. DPCIR is influenced less by the idea of political democracy, where unions seek to realise their policies through the expansion of the political party which they support, than by the idea of industrial democracy, whereby unions seek to influence the process of policy making and implementation through sending workers' representatives to administrative organisations. This is why it is often called 'policy participation' (Inagami 1980, pp. 158–63). DPCIR represents the embodiment of the unions' autonomous political activity as sought by the labour unification movement.

Background

There were six factors which led to the emergence of Rengo's practice of making demands for policy changes and institutional reform. The first was that unions came to realise the limit of industrial relations within companies. The private sector unions regarded consistency with the macro-economy and securing real wages as important factors in Shunto negotiations following the first oil crisis. But they were also aware of the profound impact government policies could have on the jobs and living standards of union members, an impact which surpassed that of even the most well-managed industrial relations practices at the enterprise level.

The second was the orientation of the labour movement's policies. Their awareness of the limit of an individual enterprise's industrial relations persuaded the private sector unions to redirect their movement from quantity-oriented aims such as wage increases to quality-oriented aims of changing economic and social structures by influencing policy making.

The third was the de-blocing of labour politics. As the private sector unions' concerns over policy grew, so did their complaints of bloc politics due to the way confrontations between the conservative and the progressive factions had long prevented the effective promotion of policy change.

The fourth was the unification movement. As noted earlier, the development of the DPCIR coincided with the introduction of the second labour unification movement. The DPCIR, therefore, became a symbol of overcoming past splits by gaining the mutual trust of the unions in the private sector and aiming for a new labour movement which would rectify the limits of enterprise unionism.

The fifth was the concern for unorganised workers. There was an awareness of the need for widening the labour movement beyond the existing union membership in order to improve the movement's constitution. It was for this purpose that unions called for economic and social policies which took account particularly of unorganised workers who tended to work in medium and small-sized enterprises.

The sixth was the development of policy participation at the industrial level. Many federations participated in formulating industrial policies for structural adjustment when faced with the first oil crisis. During that process, labour and management cooperation was strengthened, representatives were sent to serve on governmental advisory committees, direct communication with relevant authorities was opened and the political channels to the LDP widened.

Measures and contents

Rengo's DPCIR is implemented according to the following schedule every year. Rengo starts discussing the previous year's results and collecting demands from affiliated organisations in the spring. These demands are proposed to the cabinet, political parties and ministries in the summer when the demands for budgetary appropriations are considered. In the autumn, Rengo holds policy consultation meetings with various ministries. By this time, Rengo's demands are prioritised, and are proposed again when the governmental budget is formulated at the end of the year. Rengo continues to lobby in the Diet while the budget is being deliberated from the new year to the spring.

One feature of the measures adopted in Rengo's DPCIR is a broad consultation network involving cabinets, political parties, the administrative bureaucracy and associations built up from the time of Seisuikaigi. In particular, Rengo holds councils with each ministry to discuss policy matters. These policy councils consist of summit conferences, where top leaders of Rengo propose their demands to each minister, periodic conferences, where executive members discuss policy changes and institutional reform, and working meetings at which the content of the DPCIR is ironed out before the conferences. In addition, this network enables close relationships to be formed between the people who handle practical issues and offers an opportunity for them to meet any time. Depending on the results, Rengo's assistance in policy making is often appreciated by the bureaucracy.[14]

Regularly held policy talks reflect the private sector unions' view of DPCIR. They regard reaching a consensus with bureaucracy over the DPCIR important. This is in direct contrast to the public sector unions which take political bargains with the LDP, backed by the JSP, more seriously. Private sector union leaders believe that the Japanese political process is basically controlled by bureaucracy. This belief derives from the fact that university graduates and white-collar workers have increasingly become private sector union officials, making their organisation much more policy-oriented than that of the public sector unions, whose officers tend to be high school graduates and blue-collar workers.

Policy talks are also useful for the bureaucracy. First, a consensus is important for policy implementation. Second, if a ministry arrives at an understanding with Rengo about its policy, it can expect the support of the opposition parties which Rengo influences. Third, if the bureaucrats have trouble gathering support for non-labour policy matters, they can refer the issues to Rengo and request their assistance. This style of give and take also corresponds with the private sector unions' experience in raising issues with management from within the business sector (Shinoda 1989, pp. 129–31).

How original are the contents of DPCIR? The circumstances surrounding the unification process shed some light on this point. One of the principles of DPCIR is that in order to achieve cooperation it is sometimes best to 'begin from easy areas' and to 'avoid those subjects which make joint actions difficult'. The primary DPCIR policy arena relates to the interests of the affiliated organisations, so for Rengo to seek consistent policies, it has to coordinate those interests. Rengo, however, does not yet have enough power to do this. For example, although administrative reform was a main theme of DPCIR during the time of Private Rengo, the demand for this was toned down after unification with the public sector unions (Shinoda 1989, p. 131).

Development

DPCIR originated in the activity of regional liaison organisations which unions at large enterprises formed at the beginning of the first labour unification movement. One example was the policy demands which the Osaka Private Unions Council made about pollution, prices and taxes to the national and municipal governments. Before it was finally resolved, this issue gathered considerable attention from all over the country. DPCIR at the national level was started by the Joint Action Council of Private Unions (JACPU) which was formed in 1973. Although the JACPU was formed at the same time as the resurgence of the unification movement, its policy demands on price stabilisation and employment adjustment in the chaos following the first oil crisis showed the effectiveness of its activities. Afterwards, the practice of making demands for policy and institutional reform was firmly established by Seisuikaigi and the patterns that guide it were set in place during this period. This activity of Seisuikaigi was taken over by Zenminrokyo, and then finally by Rengo following the success of the second attempt at unifying the labour movement.

The performance of DPCIR was influenced by the political situation in each period. The success of Seisuikaigi was brought about by the good relationship between the private sector unions and the LDP which developed following the 1975 Shunto. The IMF-JC, acting as the centre of the private sector unions at the time, led the movement to voluntarily restrain the demands for higher wages when the LDP government urged employers to hold back wage increases in order to implement price controls more effectively. Private sector unions, struggling to move forward with labour unification and DPCIR, and the LDP, struggling to overcome the resistance of the opposition parties in the Diet, found themselves unexpectedly sharing a common interest in their mutual need to gather support from unconventional sources. This contributed to the realisation of joint government–labour talks on DPCIR at the national level and brought Seisuikaigi to an equal footing with the national labour centres.[15]

This relationship between the government and the private sector unions was deepened through the tripartite Round Table Discussion Meeting of Industrial Labour Problems (Sanrokon). This is the private advisory committee of the Minister of Labour modelled after the concerted action committee in Germany which encourages free discussions of current economic problems between the government, unions and employers. During this period, the number of active government participants in Sanrokon increased, and the private sector unions requested upgrading this informal private council of the Labour Minister to a more formal tripartite consultation forum.[16]

The private sector unions' commitment to administrative reform was a significant contributing factor to the success of DPCIR. Seisuikaigi stressed administrative reform because private sector unions were actively

complaining about lax public sector management, in contrast to the stren-
uous rationalisation efforts being made by both management and labour
in the private sector. It was after the government established the Special
Investigative Committee for Public Administration (Rincho) in 1981 that
the private sector unions sent representatives to Rincho and formed a
popular movement for administrative reform. In Rincho, the private sector
unions opposed the public sector unions by supporting the goals of recon-
structing public finance without tax increases, controlling the tax burden
in the social security system, along with the privatisation of public corporations such as Nippon Telephone and Telegraph, Japan Tobacco, and
Japan Railways.

The private sector unions' behaviour had a profound influence on the
wider political situation. To start with, unions in the private sector played
a key role in the formation of LDP domination in the Diet through the
success of the administrative reforms it helped them attain in the first half
of the 1980s (Tsujinaka 1987, pp. 60–5). When the second labour unification movement succeeded, the affinity of the private sector unions for
neo-liberalism was inherited by Rengo (Inagami 1992, p. 69). Secondly,
the private sector unions continued to send representatives to similar
committees set up to consider further administrative reforms, educational
reforms, and so on. This aspect of Rincho politics helped the private sector
unions overcome their status as political newcomers and gave them the
opportunity to be heard. And finally, because Rincho politics were created
by Prime Minister Nakasone, a neo-conservative, an alternative political
route had to be taken in order to counter the vested interests from the
top down (Shinoda 1992a, p. 274).

The influence of the political situation on the implementation of DPCIR
in the second half of the 1980s was also significant. There was a national
trend away from a 'production-oriented' economy towards a 'lifestyle-
oriented' economy as a new national goal with the publication of the report
compiled by the Research Council for Economic Structural Adjustment to
Aid International Co-operation (the Maekawa Report) in 1986. As a background to this report, there was widespread understanding that enhancing
productivity and competitiveness at the corporate level resulted in stronger
national economic power, but that this also exacerbated trade friction while
the fruit of economic achievement was not reflected in improvements in the
quality of life. The Maekawa Report, by advocating a conversion of the
Japanese economy from an export-oriented to a domestic demand-oriented
one, laid out a framework of new national goals for correcting the trade
imbalance and improving the quality of life. This meant that the government would have to take radical action to reduce the immense trade
surplus as quickly as possible without endangering the national economy.
In order to ensure a national consensus on the problem, the research council itself was composed of representatives from the unions, the employers
and the government (Inagami 1992, pp. 71–2).

This political trend toward reform has basically continued into the present day, stimulated in part by the rise and fall of the 'bubble economy', the strong yen and dramatic changes in the government power structure in the early 1990s. The unions in the private sector in particular sympathised with the contents of the Maekawa Report. Before it was disbanded, Zenminrokyo had originally planned to publish a similar report as the basis for DPCIR. When Rengo came into being, they took over these ideas as well, finally publishing them in 1993. At the same time, the private sector unions realised the limits of the LDP-dominated political situation and became one of the predominant forces in bringing about changes in the government.

This political trend toward reform actually began to grow in the late 1980s. Rengo, established in this period, was drawn into this trend, and the nature of the DPCIR was much influenced by it. This has been particularly true since LDP domination ended in the 1993 national elections.

In additon to a government-sponsored initiative to reduce working hours, there has been a new emphasis by Rengo on social values such as 'affluence', 'fairness' and 'comfort'. These new values were added to the 1990 Shunto and DPCIR in addition to the standard aims of wage increases and shorter hours. In 1992, Rengo succeeded in achieving the passage of new laws for a reduction in work hours and a standard five-day working week for civil servants. The government has also recently introduced a Rengo-backed Five-Year Plan for Advancing the Quality of Life.

The national elections in 1993 brought about the first non-LDP led coalition government in 46 years. Rengo fully supported the new government and as a result they quickly ironed out minor policy differences and also succeeded in obtaining a reduction in income tax. Conflicts within the ruling coalition led to two rapid changes in the structure of the government, while in 1994 the JSP and DSP parted ways, with the former siding with the new ruling coalition and the latter siding with the opposition. Rengo, however, using their influence in the national ballot, along with DPCIR as a platform for negotiation free of political infighting, achieved good results on tax and pension reform. Meanwhile, the tumultuous political situation externally led to internal conflicts in the political structure of Rengo itself.

RELATIONS BETWEEN RENGO AND THE POLITICAL PARTIES

DPCIR introduced Rengo and unions to the new world of politics, but it also added an element of confusion to the relationship between the unions, Rengo and the political parties.

The development of the relationship

The LDP, despite consolidating its power in the middle of the 1980s, fell into disfavour with the general public when it initiated and passed a 3 per cent consumer tax, fell into a scandal over the misuse of political funds, and then removed restrictions on rice imports, losing their majority in the House of Councillors in the 1989 election. The Private Rengo put 12 candidates up for election in the 1989 campaign while also supporting the JSP and DSP candidates, all with the intention of breaking the LDP hold on power and dissolving bloc politics. When Rengo's candidates unexpectedly won, Rengo was forced to formalise its standing as an officially recognised party within the House of Councillors. This success obliged the newborn Rengo to expand its strategy from one of mere policy recommendation to active participation in the turbulent national politics to bring about a change of government. In the 1990 general election Rengo again offered up candidates of its own, only to be defeated by JSP and LDP. Unfortunately, Rengo and DSP's loss also meant that reconciliation between the JSP and DSP was once again frustrated.

Rengo's Political Committee released an interim report in 1990 outlining its political policy including its desire to change the traditional relationship between unions and political parties while at the same time upholding the ideal of creating a new political force worthy of being entrusted with power. Rengo's first goal was to form a cooperative relationship with those legislators who supported their policies, in addition to maintaining their current relationships with political parties. To achieve this goal they launched an in-house conference to muster Diet members supported by their affiliated unions. They also launched the Rengo Political Forum which was designed to confer with Diet members who supported Rengo's polices in order to more extensively broaden their range of cooperative relationships. Second, Rengo was to promote the functional separation of the union from the political party. It was toward this end that Rengo formed a support network between political parties, politicians and individual union members as a means to challenge traditional arrangements based on support for a specific party (Nitta 1991, pp. 5–6).

In 1992, Rengo made preparations to campaign for a large number of seats in the upcoming House of Councillors election in the summer. Rengo's candidates did manage to win a few seats away from the LDP in the spring by-elections. The LDP in turn, aimed its attack at Rengo and lured the DSP and CGP into cooperation by focusing on issues such as Japan's role in the United Nations Peace-Keeping Operations. The schism between the JSP and the DSP caused the election to become a virtual battlefield between the LDP and Rengo, with Rengo ending up taking a sound beating in the polls. This defeat led the major affiliated unions to abandon the idea of a reconciliation between the JSP and DSP, focusing instead on a commitment to a more drastic party alignment.

In 1993, after the LDP split and the resulting formation of the New Party Herald (NPH) and the New Birth Party (NBP), a vote of no confidence was passed in the cabinet and the LDP lost their majority in the general election. The non-LDP coalition cabinet was composed of the JSP, the CGP, the DSP and the SDC (a splinter group that broke away from the JSP in 1977). The Japan New Party (JNP), which rose to prominence like a comet in the 1992 election, produced the prime minister with the support of the NPH and the NBP. During this process the major unions broadly supported non-LDP parties including the JNP, the NPH and the NBP, while Rengo worked behind the scenes to establish a coalition cabinet. The new cabinet succeeded in passing a bill on political reform, including the single member constituency system in the Diet. In the background, there was a drive for a Council for the Promotion of Political Reform which business leaders, Rengo, politicians and scholars formed jointly in 1992.

The government, however, was unstable and when the second coalition cabinet was formed in the spring, the JSP and the NPH left the cabinet. By summer, the JSP, the NPH and the LDP had established the third coalition cabinet with a JSP prime minister. Rengo had to follow a policy of judging matters on their own merits in both cabinets because the JSP and the DSP remained split. In the autumn, the first president of Rengo, who had played a key political role during this period, was replaced by a less politically active one. Furthermore, the NBP, the CGP, the DSP, the SDC and the JNP came together and formed the New Frontier Party (NFP) that winter. Meanwhile, the conflict between the reformers and the conservatives of the JSP grew, the former scheming to break up the JSP when relations among the unions supporting the JSP became hostile.

In 1995, two elections shook Rengo and its affiliated unions. First, the candidates who were supported by the local Rengo and most of the major political parties, were defeated by unaffiliated candidates in the nation-wide elections for prefectural governors. Second, the NFP achieved a great victory while the JSP suffered a crushing defeat in the House of Councillors election. As a consequence, the JSP-related unions pushed for the formation of a new party to replace the JSP. This resulted in a dead-lock in Rengo's political activities as it faced a distancing from existing political parties and into a situation where their affiliated unions defected to the NFP and the JSP just as the first general election under the new single member constituency system was about to take place.

The political activity of Zenroren and Zenrokyo

Zenroren advocated 'independence from capital, government, and political parties', and did not profess any support for or cooperation with any specific political party. However, it had a very close relationship with the

JCP. Even though Zenroren advocated free support of political parties in the Diet elections, in reality that usually meant coming out in support of JCP candidates and policies. For example, in local elections Zenroren candidates often ran under the banner of Progressive Unification Candidates (*kakushin toitsu koho*), a pseudonym commonly employed to disguise a candidate's affiliation with the JCP (Igarashi 1992, pp. 320–30). During this period of political development, Zenroren and the JCP remained critical outsiders.

Zenrokyo has always expected their member unions to support their affiliated political parties, even though they have never openly guaranteed the full support of individual members. Historically, Zenrokyo has affiliated itself with left-wing elements within the JSP, although recently it has come out in support of a more conservative splinter group which has formed to protect the current constitution.

JAPANESE NEO-CORPORATISM?

The emergence of Rengo and DPCIR certainly appears to have drastically changed the landscape of Japanese labour politics, but is it possible to interpret the current situation from a more theoretical perspective?

The change of political features

How have the political features mentioned at the beginning of this chapter changed? First, the traditional ideology with a revolutionary labour orientation has almost completely disappeared. Rengo maintains that a deep respect for the market-based economic model and full support of parliamentary democracy is fundamental to its party platform. DPCIR in its purest essence is based on the idea of working from within the current political structure toward a gradual reformation of the establishment. This willingness to work within the current political framework has helped to dramatically lessen the worries more conservative politicians usually have when dealing with labour unions. As a result, conservative parties such as the LDP and the NFP have eagerly sought out ways to cooperate and gain the support of Rengo-affiliated political elements.

Second, enterprise unions remain the key union organisation in Japan today. Enterprise-level industrial relations are generally far better today than historically, but at the same time, enterprise unions affiliated to Rengo still maintain high expectations in areas of tax breaks and secure pension plans. Furthermore, enterprise unions are still trying to expand their influence over the directions chosen by their employers through a more effective utilisation of Rengo's political network. On the other hand, Rengo does not intend to establish centralised control over its member unions; rather, its role occasionally appears almost as if the national centre were subservient to the affiliated unions. In accepting the strong autonomy of the affiliated unions, the managerial structure of Rengo has more in common with decentralised business associations than with centralised labour unions.

Third, the labour unification movement aimed at political autonomy for the unions, and thus Rengo's first major drives were aimed at breaking up large political blocs. But unions have not succeeded in coming out of the historical mode of supporting specific political parties. Although the JSP is forming a new party aimed at broadening the base of its support, the infrastructure of the new party remains JSP-related unions. On the other hand, although the DSP seems to have reached a new stage by dissolving itself to form the NFP, the unclear future direction of the NFP led ex-DSP-related unions to continue supporting what remains of the DSP rump organisation. The point which holds the key to union behaviour is how the composition of the political party system is expected to evolve in the future. In any case, the new political policy of Rengo aimed at establishing individual relations between unions and politicians has not yet been realised.

Japanese neo-corporatism

The debate over neo-coporatism in Japan as elsewhere has involved many social scientists. In Japan, it has developed with the labour unification movement and DPCIR since the 1980s. This argument has involved three different opinions along the way.[17]

The first opinion shows that the labour unification movement and DPCIR strengthened Japanese labour, regarded as weak before, and brought about a macro-corporatist arrangement in Japan (see Inagami 1986, 1992, Tsujinaka 1986, 1993). The second opinion, while agreeing with the trends shown in the first, then rejects it. It holds that Japanese political processes are pluralistic when considered in comparison with European corporatist countries (Ito 1988). The third opinion refutes the first, and asserts that the situation should be regarded as dualistic (Shinkawa 1993). This is due to the declining unionisation rate and the widening wage differentials, in spite of the corporatistic intention of unions.

Despite appearing to contradict each other, the three views coincided in pointing out the deviations from the ideal types in the Japanese system. In the 1990s, the argument shifted to solving the Japanese puzzle of the coexistence of inconsistent features in accepted theories. During that process, a Japanese neo-coporatist model possessing the following four features was constructed.

First, the total framework is corporatist. Second, the policy content includes neo-liberal factors. Third, the meso- or macro-corporatist arrangements at the industrial or national level are based on the decentralised micro-corporatist arrangements at the enterprise level. Fourth, the consensus process, where contexts and mutuality are taken very seriously, works in these mechanisms (Shinoda 1994, pp. 355–8). This model of Japanese neo-corporatism has a significant implication when compared to the recent trend towards decentralisation of industrial relations in some Western countries (Katz 1993). Instead of the extremes of centralised corporatism and the destruction of corporatism, the Japanese case points to the possibility of a viable intermediate form which maintains a balance between corporatist and decentralising forces.

Sectoral clashes

Another way to interpret Japanese labour politics is the clash between different sectors of society. Modern Japanese politics has witnessed some major sectoral clashes such as between agriculture and industry, and between the centre and the local areas. Japanese labour politics can be understood better through the sector politics approach rather than through the class politics approach. The development of the labour unification movement and DPCIR was based on the clash between the public and private sectors. It therefore follows that Rengo and DPCIR will be unable to avoid being exposed to the same clash in the future.[18]

For example, the deregulation issue discussed at home as well as abroad is a test of how Rengo might manage sectoral clashes in formulating its DPCIR. The private sector unions, particularly those at large enterprises in export-dependent industries which wish to increase imports in order to weaken the yen, are working with their employers in support of deregulation. However, the public sector unions, transportation unions and small and medium-sized enterprise unions are opposed to it. As deregulation became the national goal, no conspicuous clash between them has occurred yet. However, this conflict has shifted to other arenas.

The first is the relationship between unions and political parties. The difference in the evaluation of the LDP–JSP–NPH coalition government's passive attitude to deregulation is one reason why some unions have more reservation about this government than other unions. This situation is also reflected in the difference in unions' evaluation of the pro-deregulation NFP. Consequently, the NFP has gained support from unions in export-dependent sectors, and the LDP–JSP–NPH government from unions in protected industries and the public sector.

A second arena is Shunto. Recently, the 'self-determination of industrial federation' has appeared as a key principle in Shunto. Unions in export-dependent industries use this principle as a means of criticising those industries with a low productivity record of being given a free ride by adopting wage increases which are granted in the high productivity industries. Employers in the export industries place the blame for low wage increases on delayed deregulation.

The situation, of course, is not simply a case of public sector unions versus private sector unions. It is also a matter of large enterprise unions versus smaller enterprise unions. Public utility unions, protected by governmental regulation for large enterprises, are complex. At the same time, it is noteworthy that a large number of unions at small and medium-sized enterprises span across the ex-national centres. In 1993, these unions formed a liaison group to organise an amalgamation of the small and medium-sized unions once affiliated to Sohyo and those once affiliated with Domei in the metal industry. This amalgamation is planned to take place in 1997. The aim of the newly-formed union is to form a third force in Rengo, and to oppose both big business unionism and the enormous bias towards the public sector–private sector contrast within Rengo.

In this new situation Rengo appears almost to be a sector coalition. However, this begs the question, 'For whom will Rengo make demands for policy changes and institutional reform?' Whatever the case, the 1990s promises to be a period during which Rengo's management of the representation of interests will be sternly put to the test.

NOTES

1 See Taylor (1989). For details on Japanese labour politics until the 1970s, see Kawada and Komatsu (1973), and Kawada (1974, pp. 254–61). Also, Shirai (1977, pp. 254–5) and Shirai (1983) echo my opinion concerning the 'marginalisation of labour'.
2 On the transition of industrial relations in the public sectors see Harari (1973) and Koshiro (1977).
3 A good example of this is the labour policy during Ishida's term of office as the Minister of Labour in the 1950s. See Roseikenkyukai (1978).
4 This does not mean that industrial relations within enterprises are always peaceful. At one time or another almost every enterprise union has experienced fierce struggles with employers over the rights of management or discrimination concerning the status of employees. See Gordon (1988) or Nimura (1994). Also, Otake points out that there was a tendency towards syndicalism within the Japanese labour movement during the 1950s. See Otake (1994b, pp. 196–9).
5 For more on pre-war labour politics see Gordon (1991).
6 See Moore (1983) for further coverage of labour politics in this period.
7 On the radicalisation of Sohyo, see Shimizu (1982, pp. 317–40).
8 On the international relations of Japanese unions, see Williamson (1995).
9 On the influence of Marxism on Japanese unions, see Shirai (1983, pp. 339–42).
10 For details on the labour unification movement, see Rodoundoshi Kenkyukai (1988).
11 On the establishment of Private Rengo, see Nitta (1988).
12 The JCP had dreamed of its own national centre for a long time. See Izuka (1980).
13 For details on the anti-Rengo movement see Kinoshita (1992).
14 For details on the measures and proposals contained in the annual DPCIR, see Ohmi (1994, pp. 316–35).
15 For details on labour politics in this period see Shinkawa (1993, pp. 203–16) and Kume (1988).

16 See Inagami (1980, pp. 163–7) and Tsujinaka (1986, pp. 258–9).
17 The cause of the discussions was the thesis 'Corporatism without labour' by Pempel and Tsunekawa (1979).
18 On the sector clash in modern capitalism see Schmitter (1990).

REFERENCES

Banno, Junji (1991) 'Senzen Nihon ni okeru "Shakai minshushugi", "Minshu shakaishugi", "Kigyo minshushugi"' ('"Social democracy", "democratic socialism" and "enterprise democracy" in pre-war Japan'), in Tokyo Daigaku Shakaikagaku Kenkyujo (University of Tokyo, Institute of Social Science) (ed.) *Gendai Nihon Shakai 4 Rekishiteki Zentei* (*Modern Japanese Society: Vol. 4, Historical Conditions*), Tokyo: University of Tokyo Press.

Dore, Ronald (1990) 'Japan: a nation made for corporatism?', in Crouch, Colin and Dore, Ronald (eds) *Corporatism and Accountability: Organised Interests in British Public Life,* Oxford: Clarendon Press.

Gordon, Andrew (1988) *The Evolution of Labor Relations in Japan: Heavy Industry, 1853–1955,* Cambridge, MA: Harvard University Press.

—— (1991) *Labor and Imperial Democracy in Pre-war Japan,* Berkeley: University of California Press.

Harari, Ehud (1973) *The Politics of Labor Legislation in Japan: National-International Interaction,* Berkeley: University of California Press.

Hiwatari, Nobuhiro (1991) *Sengo Nihon no Shijo to Seiji* (*Market and Politics after Postwar Japan*), Tokyo: University of Tokyo Press.

Hosei Daigaku Ohara Shakai Mondai Kenkyujo (ed.) (1992) *'Rengo Jidai' no Rodo Undo* (*Labour Movements in the Rengo Era*), Tokyo: Sogo Rodo Kenkyujo.

Igarashi, Jin (1992) 'Seiji, seto to rodokumiai' ('Politics, political party and trade unions'), in Hosei Daigaku Ohara Shakai Mondai Kenkyujo (ed.).

Inagami, Takeshi (1980) 'Rodosha sanka to shakaiseisaku' ('Worker participation and social policy'), in Aoi, Kazuo and Naoi, Yu (eds) *Fukushi to Keikaku no Shakaigaku* (*Sociology of Welfare and Planning*), Tokyo: University of Tokyo Press.

—— (1986) 'Labor front unification and Zenmin Rokyo: the emergence of neo-corporatism', *Japan Labor Bulletin,* 25(5), pp. 5–8.

—— (1988) 'Seifu to roshi kankei' ('Government and industrial relations'), in Ko Takahashi, Ryuji Komatsu and Kyoichi Futagami (eds) *Nihon Romukanrishi 3 Roshi Kankei* (*The History of Japanese Labour Management: Vol. 3 Industrial Relations*), Tokyo: Chuo Keizai sha.

—— (1992) 'On Japanese-style neo-corporatism: era of a tripartite "honeymoon"?', *International Journal of Japanese Sociology,* 1(1), pp. 61–77.

Inagami, Takeshi, Wittaker, D. Hugh, Ohmi, Naoto, Shinoda, Toru, Shimodaira, Yoshihiro and Tsujinaka, Yutaka (1994) *Neo Koporatizumu no Kokusai Hikaku* (*International Comparative Research on Neo-corporatism*), Tokyo: Nihon Rodo Kenkyu Kiko (Japan Institute of Labour).

Ito, Mitsutoshi (1988) 'Daikigyo roshi rengo no keisei' ('The making of big business labour and management coalitions'), *Revaiasan,* no. 2, pp. 53–70.

Izuka, Shigetaro (1980) 'Kyosanto no sentaku to toitsurosokon' ('The strategy of the Communist Party and the choice of the Trade Union Conference for United Front Promotion'), *Gekkan Rodo Mondai,* no. 274, pp. 18–22.

Japanese Institute of Labour (1994) *Labour–Management Relations in Japan,* Tokyo: Japanese Institute of Labour.

Katz, Harry C. (1993) 'The decentralization of collective bargaining: a literature review and comparative analysis', *Industrial and Labor Relations Review*, 47(1), pp. 3–22.

Kawada, Hisashi (1974) 'Workers and their organizations', in Okochi, Kazuo, Karsh, Bernard and Levine, Solomon B. (eds) *Workers and Employers in Japan: The Japanese Employment Relations System*, Tokyo: University of Tokyo Press and Princeton: Princeton University Press.

Kawada, Hisashi and Komatsu, Ryuji (1973) 'Postwar Labor Movements in Japan', in Sturmthal, A. and Scoville, J.G. (eds).

Kinoshita, Takeo (1992) 'Taikoteki nashonaru senta no keisei ni tomonaru sangy-obetsu zenkoku soshiki no bunretsu to saihen' ('The making of oppositional national centres and the splits and realignment of industrial federations'), in Hosei Daigaku Ohara Shakai Mondai Kenkyujo (ed.).

Koshiro, Kazutoshi (1977) 'Kokyo kigyo no rodo mondai' ('Labour problems in public enterprises'), in Ichinose Tomoji *et al.* (eds) *Kokyo Kigyoron (On Public Enterprises)*, Tokyo: Chuokeizaisha.

Kume, Ikuo (1988) 'Changing relations among government, labor, and business in Japan after the oil crisis', *International Organizations*, 42(4), pp. 559–687.

Moore, Joe (1983) *Japanese Workers and the Struggle for Power 1945–47*, Madison: University of Wisconsin Press.

Nimura, Kazuo (1994) 'Sengo shakai ni okeru rodo kumiai undo' ('Trade union movements in postwar society'), in *Shirizu Nihon Kingendaishi 4 Sengo Kaikaku to Gendai Shakai no Keisei (Japanese Modern History: Vol. 4 Postwar Reform and the Making of Modern Society)*, Tokyo: Iwanami Shoten.

Nitta, Michio (1988) 'Birth of Rengo and Reformation of Union Organisation', *Japan Labour Bulletin*, 27(2), pp. 5–8.

—— (1990) 'The grand unification of Japan's labor movement: the formation of New Rengo', *Japanese Labour Bulletin*, 29(2), pp. 4–8.

—— (1991) 'Probing Rengo's political policy', *Japanese Labour Bulletin* 30(3), pp. 5–8.

Ohmi, Naoto (1994) 'Gendai nihon no makuro koporatizumu' ('The macro-corporatism in contemporary Japan'), in Inagami, Takeshi *et al.*

Otake, Hideo (1994a) *Jiyushugiteki Kaikaku no Jidai (The Era of Liberal Reform)*, Tokyo: Chuokoronsha.

—— (1994b) 'Rodo sogi no jissho kenkyu – shaken "Rodo Sogi Kenkyukai" no keifu' ('Empirical research of labour disputes: the genealogy of the institute of social science's "study group on labour disputes"'), in Hideo Otake *Sengo Seiji to Seijigaku (Post-war Politics and Political Science)*, Tokyo: University of Tokyo Press.

Pempel, T.J. and Tsunekawa, Keiichi (1979) 'Corporatism without labour?' in Philippe C. Schmitter and Gerhard Lembruch (eds) *Trends Towards Corporatist Intermediation*, London: Sage.

Rodoundoshi, Kenkyukai (ed.) (1988) *Shiryo Rodosensen Toitsu – Sohyo, Domei kara Rengo e (Data on Labour Front Unification: from Sohyo and Domei to Rengo)*, Tokyo: Rodo Kyoiku Centre.

Roseikenkyukai (1978) *Ishida Rosei: Sono Sokuseki to Tenbo (The Labour Policy of the Minister of Labour, Mr Ishida: Past and Future)* Tokyo: Romu Gyosei Kenkyujo.

Schmitter, Philippe C. (1990) 'Sectors in Modern Capitalism: Modes of Governance and Variations in Performance', in R. Brunetta and C. Dell' Aringa (eds) *Labour Relations and Economic Performance*, London: Macmillan.

Shimizu, Sinzo (1982) 'Sohyo 30 nen no baransu shito' ('The balance sheet of sohyo's three decades'), in Shimizu, Sinzo (ed.) *Sengo Rodo Undoshi Ron (Views of the Post-war History of Trade Union Movements)*, Tokyo: Nihon Hyoronsha.

Shinkawa, Toshimitsu (1993) *Nihongata Fukushi no Seijikeizaigaku* (*The Political Economy of Japanese-style Welfare*), Tokyo: Sanichi Shobo.

Shinoda, Toru (1989) *Seikimatsu no Rodo Undo* (*The Labour Movement at the End of the Century*), Tokyo: Iwanami shoten.

—— (1992a) '"Rengo" jidai ni okeru "seisaku sanka" no genjo to tenbo' ('The present situation and prospects of policy participation in the "Rengo" era'), in Hosei Daigaku Ohara Shakai Mondai Kenkyujo (ed.).

—— (1992b) 'Chiho soshiki no saihen – sono bunseki shikaku ni tsuite' ('The Realignment of local organisations: an analysis'), in Hosei Daigaku Ohara Shakai Mondai Kenkyujo (ed.).

—— (1994) 'Ima mata koporatizumu no jidai nanoka – mezo koporatizumu to sono nihonteki tenkai' ('Another era of corporatism? Meso-corporatism and the style of Japanese development'), in Takeshi Inagami *et al.*

Shirai, Taishiro (1977) 'Rodokumiai no seijikatsudo' ('The political activities of trade unions'), in Shirai *et al.* (eds) *Rodokumiai Dokuhon* (*Textbook on Trade Unionism*), Tokyo: Toyo Keizai Shinposha.

—— (1983) 'Japanese Labour Unions and Politics', in Shirai, Tashiro, (ed.) *Contemporary Industrial Relations in Japan*, Madison: University of Wisconsin Press.

Sturmthal, Adolf (1973) 'Industrial relations strategies', in Adolf Sturmthal and James G. Scoville (eds).

Sturmthal, Adolf and Scoville, James G. (eds) (1973) *The International Labour Movement in Transition: Essays on Africa, Asia, and South America*, Urbana: University of Illinois Press.

Takahashi, Hikohiro (1993) 'Seiji kaikaku ron no sai kosei' ('A reconstruction of the argument for political reform'), in Hikohiro Takahashi, *Sayoku Chishikijin no Riron Sekinin* (*Theoretical Accountability of Left Wing Intellectuals*), Tokyo: Madosha.

Takaragi, Fumihiko (1967) 'Rodosensen toitsu to shato seiken no tameni' ('On the unification of labour and the establishment of a Japan Socialist Party government'), *Gekkan Rodo Mondai*, February, pp. 11–22.

Takeda, Masakazu (1967) 'Minshato no wakagaeri wa kano ka' ('Can Democratic Socialist Party restore its youth?'), in *Gekkan Rodo Mondai*, June, pp. 18–31.

Taylor, Andrew J. (1989) *Trade Unions and Politics: A Comparative Introduction*, London: Macmillan.

Tsujinaka, Yutaka (1986) 'Gendai nihon seiji no koporatizumuka – rodo to hoshu seiken no hutatsu no senryaku no kosaku' ('Corporatization of modern Japanese Labour politics: a mixture of Labour and Conservative government strategies', in Man Uchida (ed.) *Koza Seijigaku III Seiji Katei* (*Lectures on Political Science III: The Political Process*), Tokyo: Sanrei Shobo.

—— (1987) 'Rodokai no saihen to 86 nen taisei no imi' ('The realignment of labour and the significance of the 1986 regime'), *Revaiasan*, Autumn, pp. 47–72.

—— (1993) 'Rengo and its osmotic networks', in G. D. Allinson and Y. Sone (eds) *Political Dynamics in Contemporary Japan*, Ithaca: Cornell University Press.

Williamson, Hugh (1995) *Coping with the Miracle: Japan's Unions Explore New International Relations*, London: Pluto Press.

Yoshimura, Yosuke (1977) 'Sohyo shakaitoin kyogikai no kozai' (Pluses and minuses of the Sohyo-JCP council), *Gekkan Rodo Mondai*, no. 240, pp. 51–7.

—— (1979) 'Iincho ron – ketsudan o wasureta kozetsu no totachi' ('On chairmen of words and inaction who forgot their determination'), *Gekkan Rodo Mondai*, no. 257, pp. 39–44.

9 The public sector and privatisation

Naoto Ohmi

It is well known that in Japan, industrial relations in the public sector is quite different from industrial relations in the private sector. This chapter analyses the ways in which industrial relations at public corporations changed after privatisation in the 1980s, by examining two contrasting cases, the privatisation of the Japan National Railway Corporation, and the Nippon Telegraph and Telephone Corporation.

INDUSTRIAL RELATIONS IN THE PUBLIC SECTOR IN JAPAN

While cooperative industrial relations were well-established in the private sector, especially in big enterprises, those in the pubic sector had been confrontational until the latter half of the 1980s. The reasons for this were as follows:

1. The basic workers' rights in the public sector were restricted and the government did not recognise public sector unions as legitimate representatives of the workforce.
2. The government and public corporations were not empowered to conclude collective labour agreements.
3. Since ultimate decisions on working conditions for public sector workers were made by the Diet or the local governments, the public sector union movement gave priority to political activities, which resulted in a movement opposed to the ruling party, the Liberal Democratic Party (LDP). This created an unfavourable reaction to the union movement by the LDP.
4. There were many leftwingers among the trade union leaders who aimed at a class struggle and whose activities therefore were focused on ideology.

For the public sector trade union movement, coupled with the political campaigns was the restoration of basic workers' rights, especially the right to strike. This had been a big issue between the labour force and management (i.e. public employees and the government) for a long time. From the latter half of the 1950s, especially, the unions appealed to the International Labour Organisation (ILO) on the following issues: the ratification of ILO Convention No. 87 (the Freedom of Association and

Protection of the Right to Organise Convention), the rejection of government agencies concerned with negotiations with the national railways unions and Zentei (the Japanese Postal Workers' Union), and finally the cessation of the disciplinary action being taken against workers who joined strikes. This provoked arguments in the Diet and the issues of industrial relations in the public sector and the related industrial disputes were brought before the ILO Committee on Freedom of Association.

In order to solve these issues, the ILO Governing Body proposed to establish the Fact-Finding Commission Concerning Persons Employed in the Public Sector in Japan. This was led by Mr Erik Dreyer, former Permanent Secretary to the Danish Ministry of Social Affairs, and former Chairman of the State Mediation Board of the ILO. He sent the Commission to Japan to analyse the labour laws on the public sector and the Japanese government received the mission. Subsequently, in 1965, the Dreyer Commission submitted a report to the ILO Secretariat in which it said that:

> The problems reviewed above arise in part from a failure both by the government and the trade union organizations to distinguish between the Government as government and the Government as employer. The Government in its capacity as employer has been inclined to assert an authority which it can properly claim in its capacity as government but which is inconsistent with the establishment of harmonious labour-management relations. Conversely, the trade unions have sought to extend the practice of negotiation which is a proper basis for their relations with the Government as employer to matters which lie within its authority as the Government.
>
> (ILO 1966, p. 2133)

When the Dreyer Commission visited Japan in 1965, it indicated the necessity for regular meetings between the leaders of the government and the unions to eliminate distrust among them. While the government was ready to accept the proposal, Sohyo (the General Council of Trade Unions of Japan) rejected it, and this led to the deterioration of industrial relations in the public sector (Kameyama 1976).

In May 1965, ILO Convention No. 87 was finally ratified and the related laws were amended accordingly. However, the confrontation between labour and management in the public sector became gradually more acute and many appeals were brought to the Labour Relations Commission and the ILO. At the same time, the struggle to restore the right to strike had been intensified by Sohyo in the first half of 1970. The peak of this struggle took place in November 1975 when a strike was led by the public sector unions under Sohyo to restore government employees' right to strike. Public corporation employees took part for eight days and affected the daily lives of many Japanese people by the stoppage of the Japanese National Railway during that period. The strike was not supported by the unions in the private sector and coolly received by people in general. The government totally opposed the unions' demands and the strike ended voluntarily without achieving any success.

Changes in industrial relations in the public sector were brought about both by administrative reform and the privatisation of public corporations in the first half of 1980s and by the formation of Rengo (the Japanese Trade Union Confederation) in 1989.

Before the establishment of Rengo, the Japanese trade union movement had been split into two groups resulting from a confrontation in ideology. The formation of Rengo eliminated the union movement oriented to class struggle and a trade union movement based on a market economy became the mainstream. Thus the previously adversarial relationship between the government and the trade unions diminished. Now, the Prime Minister and the President of Rengo meet to discuss matters such as the basic rights of public workers and the full implementation both of a recommendation made by the National Personnel Authority and an arbitration given by the Central Labour Commission to raise the wage of public corporation employees. In 1993, the LDP, which had been in power for 38 years, became the opposition party and the Hosokawa Coalition Government, supported by the non-Liberal Democratic Parties, was born. With the change in political situation a meeting between the Education Minister and President of Nikkyoso (Japan Teachers Union) was resumed on 22 October, 1993. In July 1994, the LDP succeeded in regaining power by forming a coalition government with the Social Democratic Party (SDP) with whom the LDP had previously had confrontation over every issue. However, following the changes in attitude of both the LDP and the public sector unions, there is now a dialogue between them.

WHY PRIVATISATION?

In the 1980s, a big change occurred in public sector industrial relations. This was due to the privatisation of the Japanese National Railway Corporation (JNR), the Nippon Telegraph and Telephone Public Corporation and the Japanese Tobacco and Salt Public Corporation.[1]

The Japanese public corporation system was established under the occupation forces after World War II and was modelled upon American public corporations. Originally a public corporation was an independent organisation which undertook economic and social roles on behalf of the government, had considerable autonomy in management with minimal governmental supervision, and was responsible to the people through the government and the Diet. Public corporations held independent assets, and provided goods and services to people while taking into consideration the same element of profitability found in private enterprises. There were two reasons for setting up such public corporations as opposed to private companies. The first was that the government tried to invest in the areas where private companies could not provide goods and services for practical and technical reasons. The second was that by taking ownership of public sector goods and services, the government was attempting to avert the possibility of a potentially hazardous monopoly being set up by private enterprises.

Von Mises pointed out, on the issue of public corporations, that:

> Public administration, the handling of the government apparatus of coercion and compulsion, must necessarily be formalistic and bureaucratic. In the absence of an unquestionable yardstick of success and failure, it is almost impossible for the vast majority of men to find that incentive to utmost exertion that the money calculus of profit seeking business easily provides. It is easy for an observer to indict the bureaucratic apparatus for extravagance. But the executive with whom the responsibility for perfect service rests sees the matter from another angle. He does not want to run too high a risk. He prefers to be on the safe side and to be doubly sure.
>
> (von Mises 1944, p. 122)

Before World War II, the government had run the railways, postal services and telecommunications (the Ministry of Railways and the Ministry of Post and Telecommunications) directly. With the restructuring which took place after the war, the Japanese Tobacco and Salt Public Corporation, established to sell cigarettes and salt, and the JNR to succeed the formerly government-run railways, were set up in 1949. These were followed in 1952 by the Nippon Telegraph and Telephone Public Corporation which was to maintain and expand telecommunication facilities and to provide services to the people.

Through the 1950s and 1960s these three public corporations made considerable contributions to the strengthening of the transportation capacity of the railway, the increased usage of telephones in the national communication network, a guaranteed salt supply, and a secure income for the government through the monopolistic sale of cigarettes. However, the JNR went into the red in 1964 and the financial situation continued to deteriorate since then. In 1980, the debt amounted to more than one trillion yen and the railways were virtually in a state of bankruptcy. Gradually, the voice of the people demanding that a solution to the problem should be sought became louder.

In 1980, Mr Masayoshi Ohira, who had died suddenly, was succeeded by Mr Zenko Suzuki as Prime Minister. Prime Minister Suzuki announced that he would concentrate his efforts on administrative reform and would establish the Provisional Commission for Administrative Reform (PCAR) as an advisory body to the Cabinet. The PCAR was established in March 1981 with Mr Toshio Doko chairing the committee for a term of two years. Mr Toshio Doko was the former President of Keidanren (Japan

Federation of Economic Organisations) where he exerted his influence to reform the management of the electrical manufacturing company, Toshiba. The PCAR was composed of nine members, namely, the Chairman, two representatives each from labour and management, and one from the press, a former government officer, a local government officer and an academic. Later it was learned that Mr Doko made Prime Minister Suzuki agree to the following conditions before taking up his chairmanship:

1. PCAR reports must be implemented.
2. Financial restructuring should be conducted without any tax increases.
3. Administrative reform should be implemented and include the local governments.
4. The 3K debts (Kome (rice), Kenkohoken (national health insurance), Kokutetsu (the Japanese National Railways)) should be eliminated and public corporations should be privatised (Kanbara 1986).

Thus, privatisation was on the agenda at the initial stages of the formation of the PCAR.

The PCAR, in its deliberations, gave priority to the privatisation of the public corporations in the administrative reform and in July 1982, the PCAR submitted a report pointing out the following problems:

1. Intervention in the public corporations by outside bodies, such as the Diet and the government.
2. The abnormal industrial relations based on the public corporation system, in which the corporations would never go bankrupt.
3. The over-expectation by the people of the services provided by public corporations.

In order to solve these problems, the PCAR proposed: release from outside intervention; establishment of financial autonomy; correction of the existing abnormal industrial relations; and necessary reforms to enable the labour force and management to make efforts to improve efficiency and to develop new forms of business. The PCAR's report, submitted to the Cabinet, pointed out that the public corporation system should be fundamentally reformed and the corporations should be privatised or changed to a similar form (Tanaka and Horie 1995). Further, the final report of the PCAR, submitted in March 1983, concluded that:

> For the three public corporations, efforts should be made to manage them in a financially independent and innovative manner. The Japanese National Railway should be divided and privatized and the Nippon Telegraph and Telephone Public Corporation should be reorganized and privatized, and the Japanese Tobacco and Salt Public Corporation should be privatized and fair competitive conditions should be set.
>
> (PCAR OB Kai 1991)

As for the JNR, whose organisation had became huge and suffered from many problems including accumulated debt, the PCAR requested that following a typical procedure for bankruptcy in the private sector, the Japanese National Railway Reconstruction Supervision Committee (RSC) should be established as a sort of a trustee to make concrete plans for the division and privatisation.

PRIVATISATION OF THE JNR

As mentioned earlier, the PCAR pointed out several problems in the public corporations system. The JNR, as compared to other corporations, suffered most from these problems.

The first problem, resulting from the excessive interventions by the Diet and government, was that the JNR Corporation could not decide its budget, fares and other charges for itself. The budget was decided by the Diet after approval of the agency concerned, the Ministry of Transport. Considerable influence over the process of drafting a budget to be submitted to the Diet was exerted by the then ruling party, the LDP and *zoku giin*[2] were also involved. The JNR, suffering from a worsening financial situation, needed the political power of the LDP members in order to seek financial assistance from the government. The JNR and *zoku giin* were therefore mutually dependent upon each other and it was no wonder that *zoku giin* asked for some facilities and cooperation from the JNR for an election campaign and for the purchase of materials from companies related to them or their supporters. It was revealed that when the plan for the division and privatisation of the JNR was made, the construction companies and the traders concerned made a petition to the LDP and *zoku giin* to stop the plan (Kusano 1989). Since only the Diet had the authority to decide the budget, the President of the JNR could not decide fares or other charges. Further, the President as a chief executive officer had to report to the Diet several dozen times a year, rather than devoting his time to rebuilding the JNR's financial status. However, it could not be denied that the lack of authority to decide the budget invited loose financial management of the JNR since it was the government who would take final responsibility for the debt.

The second problem identified by the PCAR, namely the abnormal industrial relations where public corporations would never go bankrupt, was clearly shown in the case of the JNR. Before its division and privatisation, there were four major unions, namely Kokuro (the National Railway Workers' Union), Doro (the National Railway Locomotive Engineers' Union), Tetsuro (the Japan Railway Workers' Union) and Zenshiro (the National JNR Facilities Workers Union), of which Kokuro was the largest having a membership of 600,000 at the peak in 1948 (245,000 in 1981). Kokuro was a major union affiliated to Sohyo (General Council of Trade Unions of Japan) and conducted a trade union movement oriented to class struggle as was expressed in its platform declaration, 'We shall fight for the liberation of the working class'. Doro, which had 44,000 members in 1981, was a craft union composed of locomotive drivers. There were new left-wing activists within Doro, which was said to be more militant than Kokuro in the 1970s. However, at the final stage, Doro changed its attitude in order to support the division and privatisation of the JNR. In contrast, a moderate and right-wing union, Tetsuro, was affiliated to Domei (Japanese Confederation of Labour) which believed that trade unionism's basic principle was labour-management cooperation. Because of the ideological differences between Kokuro, Doro and Tetsuro, there were many sharp confrontations. These reached their peak at the introduction of the productivity movement (Kokuro called it the Marusei Movement) which started in 1970.

This movement was based on the idea that in order to achieve economic progress, cooperation between labour and management was essential, and that this would, in turn, bring about an improvement in workers' economic and social status. The movement was proposed by the Japanese Productivity Centre (renamed in 1994 the Japanese Productivity Centre for Socioeconomic Development) which was a tripartite body with representatives from labour, management and the third party (e.g. academics). The productivity movement was well received by labour and management in the private sector. However, as for the JNR, participation in the Marusei Movement triggered confrontation among the unions. Kokuro and Doro tried to poach the union members from each other at workshops, which resulted in worsening individual relationships in the workplace (Watanabe 1994).

Industrial disputes occurred between the managerial staff of the JNR who tried to promote the productivity movement, and Kokuro and Doro. The unions appealed to the Labour Relations Commission claiming that the JNR was forcing the disaffiliation of members from the unions which were not cooperative towards the productivity movement and that there was discriminatory treatment of members in promotion matters. The Central Labour Relations Commission admitted that the reported cases were unfair labour practices and demanded that the JNR management make an apology. Since then, the Marusei Movement promoters have come from the core personnel administration and the JNR's personnel policy has begun to take into greater consideration the views expressed by Kokuro, which was strongly against the rationalisation (Kusano 1989). Because of this, the rationalisation of the JNR lagged behind, while, at the same time, discipline at the workshops was loosened.

In January 1982, no sooner than the PCAR started its deliberation of the JNR case, it was revealed that the train inspectors of the JNR in the Tokyo area had, by making false reports that they had worked on night trains, received allowances for work which had not been performed. The sum involved amounted to several million yen per year over the previous 10 years (*Asahi Shinbun*, 23 January 1982). An immediate investigation by the JNR found this practice in other areas and that ¥100 million had been paid per year illegally. The fact that this was a practice tacitly approved by labour and management shocked the Japanese people. This investigation triggered further revelations of the slack discipline at workshops, such as performing no work during working hours, absenteeism, taking baths in working hours, placing posters in the workshops and scribbling on trains. Additionally, in March 1982, a drunken night train driver caused a train crash. In response to these discoveries, public opinion demanded an improvement in discipline at workshops and normalisation of industrial relations.

THE TRADE UNIONS' RESPONSE TO THE PRIVATISATION OF THE JNR

Because of the differences in ideology and composition of union membership, the unions were divided between those who were for and those who were against the PCAR's report, which stated that public corporations should be fundamentally reformed and privatised.

Sohyo, the majority of the affiliated unions whose members were the employees of government agencies and the public corporations, expressed the following opinion on the PCAR's third report which recommended the division and privatisation of the three public corporations: 'Sohyo is against the PCAR's report, since it ignores the public nature of the public corporations'. (Sohyo 40 Nenshi Henshu Iinkai 1993, vol. 2). In contrast, Domei, most of the affiliated unions whose members were in the private sector, said: 'Domei highly values the report which is compatible with its (Domei's) opinions and meets the expectation of the people' (Domeishi Kanko Iinkai 1993, vol. 2).

In July 1985 when the RSC submitted the report, Sohyo issued a statement of protest saying that 'The report intends to destroy the JNR and divide the unions through the division and privatisation', and established the Struggle Committee for the Reconstruction of the JNR to campaign against the division. However, Mr Magara, then Secretary General of Sohyo, did not clearly state his intention to maintain the public corporation system and showed flexibility towards management reform. Domei's General Secretary issued a statement saying that 'There is no other way but to divide and privatize the JNR in order to secure employment', which was in sharp contrast to Sohyo's position.

Sohyo in its campaign against division and privatisation decided to collect 50 million signatures. At the same time, it considered that mere opposition to 'division and privatisation' would not gain the people's support and was deliberating on an alternative strategy which would put the emphasis on being against division but with flexibility towards privatisation. However, opinions emerged from the Sohyo affiliates in the private sector in support of division and privatisation and they rejected the signature collection campaign. In contrast, the communist-oriented Sohyo affiliates were critical that Sohyo's position was not clear on its opposition to privatisation and some of the unions started to promote a signature collection campaign separately from Sohyo. The result was confusion among the Sohyo affiliates on this issue (Sohyo 40 Nenshi Henshu Iinkai, 1993).

What were the opinions of the public corporation unions which were targeted for privatisation? Kokuro, from start to finish, was against the RSC's report on division and privatisation. In August 1985, immediately after the RSC submitted their report, Kokuro staged a one hour strike. Further, when the bills for the reform of the JNR were submitted to the Diet, Kokuro's Convention, in July 1986, decided the following policies: (1) Kokuro opposes the enactment of the reform bill and will make every effort to rebuild the JNR; and (2) Kokuro shall protect railway workers from selective 'dismissals' and fight to secure their employment.

In response to this, the management of the JNR took disciplinary actions, such as admonition, against both those union members who joined the strike and who wore badges opposing 'division and privatisation', and those who worked without name tags, on the grounds that these were violation of the work rules. This was a change in management attitude, since, up until then, the JNR personnel policy had been based on cooperation with Kokuro and it had never taken disciplinary action against union members wearing protest badges. As a result of this, the relationship between management and Kokuro gradually worsened.

Doro, which, together with Kokuro, had been against the division and privatisation, changed its position and stated, at its Convention in July 1986, that: 'There is no future in the JNR trade union movement centered around Kokuro. For a radical resolution to the JNR's problems, it is necessary to seek clarification of the questions concerning the proposed law' (Tokyoto Rodo Keizaikyoku 1990, pp. 30–3), and it disaffiliated from Sohyo in August of the same year.

Tetsuro basically agreed with the PCAR report, and clearly expressed its position at its Convention in August 1985, stating that 'There was no way other than by division and privatisation'. In response to these unions' attitudes, the JNR authority concluded the employment security agreement with the three unions, Kokuro, Tetsuro and Zenshiro in November 1985. Further, in January 1986, the President of the JNR and the three unions, excluding Kokuro, signed the 'Labour and Management Joint Statement' (the first version), which described the points for their cooperation based on mutual trust between labour and management. The statement resulted from the recognition that 'In reforming the JNR, employees who were willing to work diligently should not lose their jobs'. In the following August, the second joint statement was signed, the content of which included the point that 'The unions, even in the event that they are given the right to strike, will refrain from exercising this right until the management of the railways is stabilized' (Ariga 1989).

In this situation, Kokuro members, one after another, disaffiliated from Kokuro worrying that they may not be employed by the newly established railway companies if they remained in Kokuro. Kokuro's executives, afraid of isolation, convened the Extraordinary Convention in October 1986 and proposed new policies, changing the previous ones, to cooperate in the rationalisation of the JNR, to normalise industrial relations and to conclude the employment security agreement. However, left wing delegates strongly opposed the proposal, saying that it was a humiliation and the proposal was rejected. As a result, all the executives resigned and the division of Kokuro resulted.

Before April 1987, when the JNR reform was due to be implemented, Tetsuro and Doro amalgamated to form JR Soren (Japan Confederation of Railway Workers' Unions) and became affiliated to Rengo. The reformists (the former main group) in Kokuro established Tetsusan Soren (The Japanese Railway Industrial Workers Union) which also affiliated itself to Rengo. (See the section 'An Evaluation of the Privatisation' (p. 226) for further realignments among the railway unions.)

THE PRIVATISATION OF NIPPON TELEGRAPH AND TELEPHONE

While, in case of the privatisation of the JNR, the aim was to eliminate its deficit, the aim for Denden Kosha (Nippon Telegraph and Telephone) was deregulation, the opening of the market and the revitalisation of the industry by the introduction of private companies.

Japanese policy on telecommunications after the war had two goals. One was to spread the use of telephones and the other was to enable spontaneous telephone calls at a national level, both of which were almost implemented by the latter half of the 1970s. In the 1980s, the main tasks were how to meet the various needs of users and responding to the technological revolution in telecommunications, for example the developments in electronics, and the use of fibre optics and communications satellites. These technological innovations made it extremely difficult to distinguish between information equipment and telecommunications. Demands from private companies to abolish the Denden Kosha monopoly of telephone circuits and to allow other companies to obtain and use these circuits became stronger. Also from the other side, Denden Kosha was making requests to be released from public corporation regulations, such as the budget system and restraints on business jurisdiction, and for investment to be increased. At the same time, the introduction of free competition through the division of AT&T in the USA and the privatisation of BT in the UK activated arguments on the Denden Kosha reform.

The third report of the PCAR, submitted in 1981, pointed out the inefficiency of the Denden Kosha administration and recommended its division and privatisation together with the introduction of free competition. There were differences of opinion inside the LDP over the report and it took time for the Ministry of Post and Telecommunications to achieve a consensus among government-related authorities. During this process, the proposal concerning the division was deleted and the decision was made mainly to privatize the corporation.

In the case of the JNR, the unions were divided into those who supported division and privatisation and those who opposed them, which led to vehement confrontation. In contrast, the trade unions' response to the privatisation of Denden Kosha was quite different. The union of Denden Kosha, Zendentsu, is the largest enterprise based union, having a membership of 280,000, and supporting the right wing of the Social Democratic Party. Zendentsu officially announced its opposition, in principle, to the proposal for the privatisation of Denden Kosha, which stressed economic liberalisation. The reasons for its opposition were: (1) The telecommunications business was indispensable to people's livelihood; (2) Privatisation meant selling the people's common asset in pieces. (3) Division and privatisation might create unfair discrepancies in charges and services which might, in turn, harm the public interest.

Thus Zendentsu was against privatisation, preferring to support a management system based on priority being given to the public nature of its service, unitary ownership and administration of the network, and the maintenance of the public corporation system while having more authority over its management with less intervention from the government (Zendentsu 1984).

Zendentsu expressed its strong dissatisfaction that its members' wages were decided at the same level as other public organisations such as the JNR and the National Forestry department in spite of its cooperation with the rationalisation process and its contributions to increase productivity and profitability. Zendentsu did not, at that time, have the authority to negotiate wages and working conditions. In order to improve the situation it submitted a proposal on the reform of the public corporation system at its Annual Convention in August 1980, seven months before the PCAR started discussions on the matter (Zendentsu 1984).

During the PCAR's deliberations on the reform of the public corporation system, Zendentsu officially opposed privatisation. However, after the PCAR submitted the bill on the privatisation to the Diet, it changed its position and decided to cooperate, enabling the Act to be passed, while at the same time demanding its amendment. Mr Akira Yamagishi, the then President of Zendentsu appealed to the members, saying that

> The all or nothing stance of sticking to the policy of absolute opposition to privatization and the government's proposal would finally allow the Act to be passed in its original form at the Diet. Rather, by seeking the co-operation of the four opposition parties, it would be better to fight for its amendment.
>
> (Yamagishi 1989, p. 79)

Thus Zendentsu changed its policy of opposition and demanded the amendment of the Act on four points: (1) To maintain the public nature of telecommunications business; (2) To secure the right to negotiate on wages and working conditions; (3) To regain the right to strike; and (4) To secure conditions for fair competition.

Zendentsu was a main supporter of the SDP and had several Diet members from its membership on the Socialist Party ticket. In the process of the Diet discussions on the amendment, it gained the support of other parties (Komeito (Clean Government Party), the Democratic Socialist Party and the Social Democratic Federation), except for the Communist Party and made further approaches to the LDP both officially and unofficially. In this way, Zendentsu succeeded in amending the proposal. At the final stage of voting on the proposal, Zendentsu, having the same interests as the management, now actively promoted privatisation.[3] From April 1985, the NTT (the Japanese Telephone and Telecommunication Company) started its operation as a private company.

Zendentsu, in contrast to Kokuro, coped with privatisation, maintaining its position as the sole union of the NTT, and successfully achieving its aim for the privatisation of the NTT to be implemented with no dismissals.

AN EVALUATION OF THE PRIVATISATION

The aim of the reform was to eradicate the idea that public corporations had the national flag behind them, which encouraged the notion that no matter how badly they performed, this would never lead to bankruptcy. In order to change the situation, therefore, the responsibility for management needed to be transferred to individual corporations so that they ran more efficiently through the development of business initiatives.

An evaluation of privatisation follows, which looks at corporate earnings, service to customers, wage levels, industrial relations and personnel systems.

The effect of the reform was immediate. As Figure 9.1 shows, after the reform in 1987, the total transport mileage increased steadily every year from 198.3 billion passenger-km in 1986 (the last year of the JNR) to 250 billion passenger-km in 1993 for the six Japanese Railways (JRs). Even though the growth rate decreased between 1992 and 1993 as a result of the recession, the average increase during the seven-year period was 3.4 per cent. In the two years after the reform the total passenger transport mileage for the six JRs exceeded the highest figure of the former JNR, 215.6 billion passenger-km in 1974 (see Figure 9.1). As is shown in Table 9.1, the total operating profit for the seven JRs (the Six Japanese JRs and the JR Freight Company) also increased to ¥908.0 billion in 1992 from ¥352.3 billion in 1987 with an average annual increase of 20.3 per cent.

In case of the telegraph and telephone sector, the three companies, including Dai ni Den Den Incorporated (the Second Telegraph and Telephone Company) entered the market which had previously been

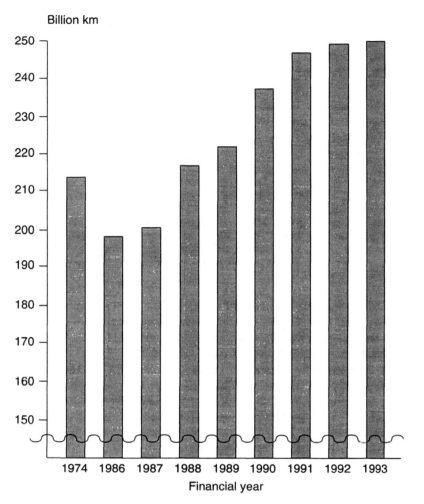

Billion km

Figure 9.1   Total passenger transport mileage of the six JR companies

monopolised by the NTT. This led to a price war over long distance calls
between the major cities. While streamlining the business, NTT established more than 150 related and subsidiary companies to absorb the
redundant employees and tried to cut down the costs. As a result, the
charge for a telephone call decreased more than eight times from 1980
and the charge for a long distance call between Tokyo and Osaka, lasting
three minutes, went down to ¥240 from ¥720. In the public corporation
period, it was taken for granted that if a cost increased, then there would
be an increase in the rate charged for a telephone call. The fact that the
charge decreased by more than half proved that privatisation had been a

Table 9.1   Financial conditions of the seven JR companies* (billion yen)

	1987FY	1988	1989	1990	1991	1992	1993
Operating income	3,633	3,899	4,053	4,354	4,531	4,454	4,560
Operating profit	3,523	4,228	4,025	4,727	6,914	9,080	8,624
Ordinary profit	1,515	2,118	2,684	3,876	3,063	2,480	2,210

Source: Ministry of Transport (1992)

Notes: FY: Financial year.   * Six passenger companies and one freight company.

Table 9.2   Financial condition of the NTT (billion yen)

	1985FY	1986	1987	1988	1989	1990	1991	1992	1993
Operating income	5,091	5,354	5,662	5,653	5,769	5,968	6,056	5,892	5,809
Operating profit	684	723	830	705	665	579	528	391	230
Ordinary profit	316	358	497	426	485	414	353	249	110

Source: NTT official data

benefit to consumers. The number of telephone subscribers per employee increased to 248 by the end of 1992 from 142 at the time of privatisation. As for business performance, profits tended to shrink as a result of the streamlining of the headquarters (see Table 9.2).

Table 9.3 shows the number of employees in the NTT, JRs and JT for the period 1985–95 following privatisation. A big reduction in employment is seen for the NTT. By rationalisation and the transferral of some departments' work to related companies, the number of employees at NTT decreased from 310,000, before privatisation, to less than 200,000 in 1995, without compulsory redundancies.

Even though privatisation faced the joint problems of reduced income and profit resulting from the recession and streamlining, generally speaking, it created good effects. But some problems remain. Though the JRs have been privatised, they still need approval and licences from the agencies concerned in deciding on charges and routes, while politicians intervene in the planning and construction of new railway routes. Additionally, JRs are trying to eliminate the operating deficit for the companies in the three islands Hokkaido, Shikoku and Kyushu.

In the case of the NTT, not only did they have to contend with strict regulations in the communications industry but also the government's approval was needed for the appointment of officers and business plans. Further changes in the company's articles have hampered the NTT from taking full advantage of privatisation (Kano 1991).

After privatisation, industrial relations have been generally stable. Both labour and management welcome the situation in which they can voluntarily negotiate wages and other working conditions. Table 9.4 shows the wage increases after privatisation. In order to eliminate the wage

Table 9.3 Number of employees in the NTT, JRs and JT after privatisation

	1985	1987	1989	1991	1993	1995
NTT	313,600	297,596	257,627	232,198	196,500	194,700
JR*	307,000	199,185	198,424	192,888	192,131	193,542
JT	34,216	29,321	26,464	23,865	23,808	23,216

Sources: NTT, JR and JT unpublished official data

Notes: NTT and JT were privatised in April 1985 and the JRs in April 1987. Figures for the NTT and JT are as of the end of March and for the JRs as of the beginning of April.
* The figures are the totals for the six passenger companies and a freight company.

Table 9.4 Average wage increases after privatisation (yen)

	1987	1988	1989	1990	1991	1992	1993	1994
Major companies in private sector	8,275	10,573	12,747	15,026	14,911	13,662	11,077	9,118
Average %	3.56	4.43	5.17	5.94	5.65	4.95	3.89	3.13
NTT	11,600	14,200	14,200	17,000	17,000	14,800	12,400	10,800
%	4.94	5.73	5.46	6.37	6.03	4.98	3.99	3.36
JR: East Japan	7,582	10,119	12,741	15,724	16,503	16,509	14,009	12,122
%	3.17	4.20	5.06	6.06	6.01	5.57	4.51	3.77
JR: Hokkaido	7,582	10,118	12,719	15,315	15,100	14,500	10,900	9,200
%	3.17	4.10	4.94	5.84	5.44	4.92	3.60	2.98
JR: Kyushu	7,582	9,862	12,443	15,199	15,195	14,538	11,963	9,759
%	3.17	4.10	4.96	5.92	5.58	5.00	3.97	3.16
JT	8,950	11,050	13,400	15,170	15,550	14,210	12,200	9,900
%	3.91	4.64	5.33	5.80	5.62	5.01	4.05	3.20

Sources: For major companies in the private sector, Rodosho (various years). For NTT, JRs, JT, Rengo (1987–94)

differences which had occurred during the public corporation period, the NTT and JT received wage rises surpassing the average of those given in major companies in the private sector. The wage increases for the JRs have also been commensurate with the average rises in the private sector.

Privatisation brought a big change in the wage structure. In 1986, immediately after the privatisation, the NTT's wage system, based on length of service, was changed to include performance-related pay. In its new form, half of the basic wage is calculated on age and the other on work performance. In April 1989 the JT also introduced the new wage system which took performance evaluation into consideration. This new system allows a manager at each workshop to evaluate the work performance of employees, and according to the evaluation, there is a difference in wage increase of between 20 and minus 10 per cent of the basic wage increase. When this plan was proposed by the management, the union agreed to it on condition that the basic wage in the manufacturing sector should not be decreased. The JRs have also changed their promotion system from one based on length of service to a qualification system in which employees are promoted through examinations and work performance evaluation. While the former, adopted in accordance with personnel systems within government offices, did not reflect daily work performance and ability in the wage structure, the new system did. In the private sector, many companies have already introduced the new wage system.

Zendentsu, as mentioned earlier, has maintained its position as the sole union of the NTT following privatisation. It amended its platform in February 1985 for the first time in 30 years since it was drawn up in 1955. The former platform included the phrase 'The democratic working class is the only power which can prevent fascism'. In the new version it says 'Efforts should be made to establish mutual trust between labour and management based on the principle of equality between them' (Tokyoto Rodo Keizaikyoku 1990, pp. 115–16). This is followed by a commitment to 'maintaining collective bargaining as a priority', and a statement that 'in exercising the right to strike, efforts should be made to pursue the struggle rationally so that public support and cooperation could be gained', both of which conform to the union's basic principles. When the new privatised company was established on 1 April 1985, the agreement concerning industrial relations was concluded. The agreement confirmed that:

> The company's industrial relations should be based on equality between labour and management and should aim to establish mutual trust between them through responsibility and independence to maintain both parties' self-autonomy. In collective bargaining, both labour and management should do their best to act responsibly.
>
> (Yamagishi 1989, pp. 135–41)

It further says that 'a management council should be established to discuss important issues, over and above the issue of collective bargaining, such as a basic management policy' (Yamagishi 1989).

Working from the basic agreement, the Central Management Council and the Local Management Councils were established as forums for the exchange of opinions between labour and management on business plans, personnel plans and business administration. At the same time, by Zendentsu seconding a former union officer as an auditor to the company, they were able to participate at the management level.

After privatisation, the JT union, Zen Tobacco (the Japanese Tobacco and Allied Workers' Union), with a membership of 21,000, became affiliated to Shokuhin Rengo (the Japanese Federation of Food and Tobacco Workers' Union). Since then, Zen Tobacco has sought labour and management collaboration and has shown itself cooperative towards rationalisation plans resulting from privatisation including the closure and merger of plants.

In the railways, the former Doro group gradually strengthened its influence in JR Soren. In response, union members at JR West, JR Tokai, JR

Shikoku and JR Kyushu, objected to Doro's dominance and disaffiliated from JR Soren. They amalgamated with Tetsusan Soren to establish JR Rengo (Japan Railway Trade Unions Confederation). As a result, single union companies were not achieved, and JR Soren with a membership of 77,000 and JR Rengo with 75,000, coexist. However, there is a division of power; JR Soren's jurisdiction is Eastern Japan and Hokkaido and JR Rengo's is Tokai, Western Japan, Shikoku and Kyushu.

The former employees of the Japan National Railway, who were not taken on by the JRs, took their case to the Labour Relations Commissions claiming that the loss of employment was an unfair labour practice. Several local Labour Relations Commissions including those in Hokkaido and Osaka, judged in the workers' favour. At the outset, the Central Labour Relations Commission encouraged labour and management to reach an amicable agreement on this matter. However, since neither were willing to do so, the Central Labour Relations Commission gave a ruling for the case in Hokkaido, held in December 1993, that unfair labour practices were experienced by some Kokuro members.[4] Kokuro, while pleased that some of its members' cases were approved, was dissatisfied with the ruling since the majority of its members' cases were rejected. It appealed to the court demanding the Commission's ruling to be changed. The court case is expected to be prolonged. However, the dispute is not whether privatisation itself is right or wrong, since privatisation has now become a reality.

This is not the end of the privatisation argument in Japan. Some issues remain to be resolved. The first is privatisation of the postal service. This includes not only mailing and parcels delivery, but also postal savings and life insurance. However, its financial structure has not been revealed. In 1994, postal charges were increased successively. Parcel deliveries compete with private companies, which deal with more parcels than the public postal service. Taking these situations into consideration the argument is made that the postal service ought to be privatised.

The second issue is the full privatisation of the three former public corporations. Even though they are privatised in part, because their service to the public has to be maintained, they are still supervised by the government.[5] Both the authority concerned and politicians sometimes intervene or advise on their policies and measures. To keep a balance between the public nature of their service and profitability is a difficult task. However, through the relaxation of governmental regulations such as the control over the adjustment of supply and demand, the new system should be developed to take the greatest advantage of privatisation.

SUMMARY AND CONCLUSIONS

This chapter has shown that industrial relations in the public sector had been generally confrontational until the latter half of 1980s. Changes in the relationship since then were triggered by both the privatisation of public corporations and other organisations in the latter half of 1980s, which brought changes in the framework of industrial relations, and by the formation of Rengo (the Japanese Trade Union Confederation) in 1989. Further, the end of the East–West Cold War as well as the fall of the ruling party in Japan, the Liberal Democratic Party (LDP), in the 1990s weakened the effect of left-wing ideology, and resulted in the transformation from confrontational to dialogue-oriented industrial relations.[6]

In 1981, talks on the privatisation of public corporations started in Japan. Privatisation took place as follows:

1. The public corporations were transformed into special companies, a majority of whose stocks continued to be owned by the government.
2. The stocks of the special companies were sold to the public gradually.
3. Since the reform of the public corporation system was coupled with the drastic reform of industrial relations in the public sector, strong resistance to the plan came from the unions.

The Japanese National Railway (JNR) unions' responses to the plan contrasted with those of Zendentsu (Telecommunication Workers' Union of Japan). The JNR was divided into four major unions, the largest of which was Kokuro (the National Railway Workers' Union), which was led by the left and had been opposed to the privatisation from beginning to end. As other unions supported the plan, Kokuro was isolated and gradually became disunited. General public opinion also supported privatisation and the JNR was divided and privatised in April 1987. Since then, mergers and disbandments have occurred among the former JNR unions, which subsequently led to the creation of two unions, JR Soren (Japan Confederation of Railway Workers' Union) and JR Rengo (Japan Railway Trade Unions Confederation). Kokuro, which became a minority union, is now appealing to the court on the discrimination against its union members in job recruitment. However, the case does not address whether privatisation is right or not.

In contrast to the above, Zendentsu, the sole union of the NTT (the Nippon Telegraph and Telephone Public Corporation) which originally opposed privatisation, changed its policy to support it after some amendments were made to the government's plan. At the final stage of deliberation at the Diet, it was actively involved in passing the law for privatisation. As a result, there were no dismissals following privatisation, which took place in April 1985, and Zendentsu maintained its position as the sole representative union of NTT.

The privatised corporations actively conducted business to increase corporate earnings. At the same time, the number of employees was reduced through rationalisation and personnel transfer to related companies. Wage systems were restructured to reflect employee's performance and ability, all of which were implemented with the consensus of the unions. Both labour and management welcomed the situation in which privatisation now allowed them to decide working conditions for themselves through voluntary negotiations.

The public response to privatisation was good in general. They had the impression that sales assistants' attitudes became polite and that there were no fare increases. This favourable effect partly resulted from the unprecedented economic boom immediately after privatisation. However, since 1991, the Japanese economy has stagnated and some of the privatised companies went into the red. The overall effects of privatisation are therefore unclear.

NOTES

1 Privatisation has various meanings such as changes of ownership from the public to the private sector, or transformation of main undertakings in the public sector into private companies. Here, 'privatisation' means the transformation of public corporations into joint stock companies.
2 Zoku Giin are the Diet members who have belonged to the industrial policy department of the LDP (in areas such as construction, transportation, agriculture and forestry) for a long period and are directly involved in policy making. This arrangement had been formed during the LDP's 38-year monopoly. Some of them were involved in political scandals and their corrupt relations with certain business dealers over concessions were all pointed to as problems (Iwai 1987).
3 According to the analysis of Hideo Otake on the active attitude of NTT's labour force and management towards the reform, the prediction of future problems is regarded as a preventive measure and as an advanced form of corporatism at the micro-level (Otake 1992).
4 In the unfair labour practice case at JR West Japan, the company had not hired two Kokuro members when the company was newly set up on 1 April 1987. At the first ruling, the Osaka Labour Relations Commission ruled it to be unfair labour practice since the union members had been discriminated against as a result of the union they belonged to. Dissatisfied with the ruling, the company applied to the Central Labour Relations Commission for a re-examination of the case. The Commission rejected the application for relief measures requested by the union saying that the six month suspension applied to the Kokuro members and since this was the cited reason for the company's rejection of employment their decision was rational (15 December 1993).
   In the JR Hokkaido unfair labour practice case, Kokuro claimed that the company discriminated against the union by not hiring 1,704 Kokuro members. At the first ruling, the Hokkaido Labour Relations Commission ruled that it was unfair labour practice and ordered JR Hokkaido and JR Freight to hire the men and backdate their employment to 1 April 1987. Both companies were dissatisfied with the ruling and applied for a re-examination of the case. On 15 December 1993 the Central Labour Relations Commission changed the first ruling and judged that among those who had been ordered to be retired, only those who had to leave the National Railways Settlement Corporation and were willing to work for the companies should be reconsidered for employment. Those offered employment should then be regarded as having held their position from 1 April 1987 (Central Labour Relations Commission 1994).
5 In the privatisation of the public corporations, the government was supposed to own the stocks of NTT, JR and JT for a fixed period and after that these

234   *Naoto Ohmi*

stocks were to be sold to the public. Of the corporations privatised, the stocks for NTT, JR East Japan and JT were listed and sold to the public in February 1987, October 1993 and October 1994 respectively. The profits gained from the sale were to be put in the government bond management fund to finance the budget deficit. The profit was also to be used as part of the national general account. Since the national budget was revised in 1987, the profits gained by selling the NTT stocks have been lent, interest free, for local government public works.

6 According to Mochizuki, one possible reason for the privatisation of Japanese National Railway Corporation and Nippon Telegraph and Telephone Public Corporation was to change the unions' left-wing ideological stance to a cooperative one (Mochizuki 1993).

REFERENCES

Ariga, Sokichi (1989) *Kokutetsu Minshuka eno Michi* (*Towards Democratization of the JNR*), Tokyo: Testsuro Yuai Kaigi.
Central Labour Relations Commission (Chuo Rodo Iinkai) (1994) *Bessatsu Chuo Rodo Jiho* (Extra edition, Central Labour Current Report), No. 1140, 1141, Tokyo: Roi Kyokai.
Domeishi Kanko Iinkai (Publishing Committee of Domei History) (1993) *Domei 23 nen Shi* (*23 Year History of Domei*), 2 vols, Tokyo: Yuai Kaigi, vol. 2, pp. 410–415.
ILO (1966) 'Report of the fact-finding and conciliation commission on freedom of association concerning persons employed in the public sector in Japan', *ILO Official Bulletin*, XLIX(1), pp. 481–531.
Iwai, Tomoaki (1987) *Zoku Giin no Kenkyu* (*Study on Zoku Giin*), Tokyo: Nihon Keizai Shinbunsha.
Kameyama, Hisashi (1976) *Roshi Kankei* (*Industrial Relations*), Tokyo: Gyosei.
Kanbara, Masuru (1986) *Tenkanki no Seiji Katei* (*Political Process in Transition Period*), Tokyo: Sogo Rodo Kenkyujo.
Kano, Yoshikazu (1991) *Mineika ga Nihon o Kaeru* (*Privatization Will Change Japan*), Tokyo: PHP Kenkyujo.
Kusano, Atsushi (1989) *Kokutetsu Kaikaku* (*The Reform of the National Railways*), Tokyo: Chuo Koronsha.
Ministry of Transport (1992) *Kokutetsu Kaikakugo Gonenkan no Seika to Kodai* (*Result and Evaluation of Five Years After the Privatisation of Japanese National Railway Corporation*), Tokyo: Ministry of Transport.
Mochizuki, M. (1993) 'Public Sector Labour and the Privatisation Challenge: the Railway and Telecommunication Unions', in Gary D. Allinson and Yasunori Sone (eds) *Political Dynamics in Contemporary Japan*, Cornell: Cornell University Press.
Otake, Hideo (1992) 'Jiyushugiteki kaikaku no nakano koparatizumu – denden kosha mineika ni okeru Zendentsu no yakuwari' ('Japanese corporatism in liberal reform: the role of the trade union in the privatization process of the Japan Telegraph and Telephone'), extra edition, *Leviathan* Summer, Tokyo: Bokutaku Sha, pp. 122–40.
PCAR OB Kai (1991) *Nihon o Kaeta Junen* (*Ten Years that Changed Japan*), Tokyo: Gyosei Kanri Kenkyu Sentaa.
Rengo (1987–94) *Toroku Kumiai Shunki Seikatsu Toso Kekka* (*Rengo Affiliates' Wage Negotiation Results*), Tokyo: Rengo.
Rodosho (Ministry of Labour) (various years) *Shiryo Chinage no Jittai* (*Survey on Wage Increases*), Tokyo: Ministry of Labour.

Sohyo 40 nenshi Henshu Iinnkai (Editing Committee of Sohyo 40-Year History) (1993) *Sohyo 40 nen shi* (*40-Year History of Sohyo*), 3 vols, Tokyo: Daiichi Shorin.

Takagi, Yoshio and Hayakawa, Seiichiro (1993) *Kokutetsu Rodo Kumiai* (*JNR Trade Unions*), Tokyo: Nihon Hyoron Sha.

Tanaka, Kazuaki and Horie, Masahiro (1995) 'Privatisation of the Big Three' in Toshiyuki Masujima and Minoru Ouchi (eds) *The Management and Reform of Japanese Government*, Tokyo: Gyosei Kanri Kenkyu Centre, pp. 214–30.

Tokyoto Rodo Keizaikyoku (1990) *Kokyo Kigyo tai Mineika ni Kansuru Shiryoshu* (*Data Concerning Public Corporations and Privatisation*), Tokyo: Tokyoto Rodo Keizaikyoku.

Von Mises, L. (1944) *Bureaucracy*, New Haven: Yale University Press.

Watanabe, Susumu (1994) 'Restructuring of the Japanese National Railways: Implications for Labour', *International Labour Review*, vol. 133, pp. 92–4.

Yamagishi, Akira (1989) *NTT ni Asu wa Aruka* (*Is There any Future for NTT?*), Tokyo: Nihon Hyoron Sha.

Zendentsu (1984) *Kosha Seido Kaikaku wa Mizukara Chosen Shitekita Michi de Aru* (*The Reform of the Public Corporations is the Path We Have Chosen to Take*), document distributed at the 37th Zendentsu Convention, Tokyo: Zendentsu.

10 Shunto

The role of employer and union
coordination at the industry and
inter-sectoral levels

Mari Sako

Since the 1980s, decentralisation of collective bargaining is said to have
become a common trend among major advanced industrialised countries
(Katz 1993). In nearly all cases, the driving force behind the shift towards
enterprise-level bargaining is the employer who had regarded national-
and industry-level bargaining as an obstacle to introducing flexibility at
the workplace (Dore *et al.* 1994, pp. 11–12). In Japan, however, enterprise-level bargaining has been firmly in place for several decades. And
yet, much coordination takes place between and among employers and
unions at the industry and national levels in the process of wage
bargaining, known as Shunto, or the Spring Offensive. Despite the impression that employers are gaining an upper hand over unions in Japan as
elsewhere, there is no move towards dismantling the institution of Shunto
which was after all initiated by unions. Why should this be the case?

Shunto means different things to different observers. For some, it is
simply a highly decentralised system of collective bargaining in which
'market forces' and the firm's ability to pay are fully taken into account
in enterprise-level negotiations (Calmfors and Driffil 1988). For some
others, Shunto is a type of incomes policy with a corporatist tripartite
involvement (Shimada 1983, Ohmi 1994). In fact, over time, Shunto has
become more of a learning process in which all actors in the industrial
relations system participate, and increasingly the traditional focus of
collective bargaining over wages has become subsumed under a holistic
approach to determining people's living standards (see Chapter 8).

While being sensitive to policy and political developments at the
national level, this chapter focuses on industry-level coordination for
collective bargaining. The chapter aims to evaluate the functions of coordination among employers as well as among unions at levels higher than
the enterprise – the usual focus of study on the management of industrial
relations in Japan.

In order to fully understand the functions of higher-level coordination,
this chapter will attempt to answer the questions: (a) how does a consensus
on wage increases which is compatible with sustaining the international
competitiveness of the Japanese economy emerge in the process of Shunto

discussions? and (b) why do employers and unions have an incentive to establish and observe such a norm? Universally applicable reasons, such as a principle of fairness for 'equal pay for equal work' may account for (b) but not for (a).

What makes Japanese wage settlements compatible with international competitiveness? The reason appears to lie in the institutional nexus between labour and product markets. In particular, actors in the Japanese industrial relations system are embedded in stable networks of labour relations (in the form of lifetime employment ideals) and corporate relations (in the form of long-term buyer–supplier relationships). Predictability of mutual behaviour is a main beneficial outcome of such labour and corporate institutions. Employer coordination over wage determination in Japan – identified by Brown (1986), Layard (1990) and Soskice (1990b) as perhaps more important than union coordination – fulfils the role of enhancing predictability not only of overall wage levels in the economy, but also of wages in the supply industry which translates into greater predictability of input prices. It is argued here that employers and unions have coordinated at levels higher than the enterprise with a clear understanding of how such links between labour and product markets affect the competitiveness of leading sectors in the Japanese economy.

This chapter is structured as follows. First, the 1993/4 Shunto round is described briefly with a view to clarifying the main collective bargaining institutions which exist above the enterprise level (see Figure 10.1 for a summary). Next, the origin of Shunto and its subsequent developments is traced. An evaluation is made of the major features and mechanisms of Shunto which contributed to the flexible adjustments of wages to external economic shocks of 1973 and subsequent recessions in the 1980s. The section on labour and product markets takes a more detailed look at certain segments of the Japanese economy. In particular, the role of inter-employer coordination in the four leading metal industry sectors and coordination within corporate groupings in the automobile sector is examined. The chapter concludes by summarising the interaction between management's motives and unions' incentives to continue participating in the Shunto process.

THE CENTRALISATION–DECENTRALISATION DEBATE

Collective bargaining systems are of interest to many people because of their impact on macro-economic performance. In particular, according to the Olsonian logic of collective action, decentralised collective bargaining structures are likely to make actors less concerned about the wider implications of their pay settlement and to cause pay leapfrogging and hence wage-push inflation (Olson 1982). By contrast, if bargaining takes place at the national level by all-encompassing organisations, they are less likely

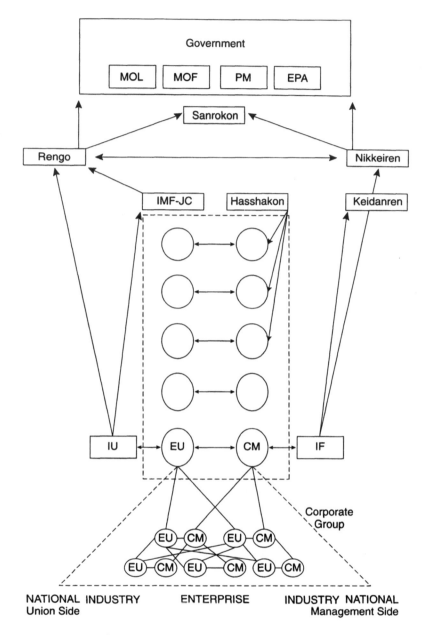

Figure 10.1 Coordination mechanisms in Shunto

Notes:

EU: enterprise union
CM: company management
IU: industry federation of enterprise unions
IF: industry federation of companies
MOL: Ministry of Labour
MOF: Ministry of Finance
PM: Prime Minister
EPA: Economic Planning Agency
Sanrokon: Tripartite Policy Consultation
 Meeting

Rengo: Japanese Trade Union
 Confederation
Nikkeiren: Japan Federation of Employers'
 Associations
Keidanren: Japan Federation of Economic
 Organisations
Hasshakon: Eight Company Round Table
 Meeting
IMF-JC: International Metalworkers'
 Federation – Japan Council

to behave as free riders because they have an incentive to take full account of the implications of pay settlement for nation-wide inflation and unemployment.

Various studies have been carried out to test this proposition. Consensus exists on the best measures of performance (unemployment or employment rates, or Okun's 'misery index' – the sum of unemployment and inflation rates – being the most popular). But due to different measures used for the degree of centralisation, there are disagreements over the link between bargaining structures and performance. In particular, a debate exists between those who found a linear relationship (the more centralised the better the performance) (for example Bruno and Sachs 1985) and those who found a non-linear relationship (both highly centralised and highly decentralised economies perform better than intermediate economies) (Calmfors and Driffil 1988). Moreover, a particular relationship which applies in one period has been found to break down in another (Crouch and Traxler 1995, p. 12, Pierce 1994).

The corporatist literature (for example Crouch 1985) suggests a measure of centralisation to be a combination of dimensions such as (a) the coverage of collective bargaining, (b) the level of collective bargaining, (c) the degree of coordination among unions, (d) the extent of employer coordination, and (e) the nature of interaction between unions and employers. However, depending on how these aspects are combined into an index, and depending also on subjective judgement in scoring particularly the coordination (rather than the structural) dimensions, the ranking of countries differs in various studies. For example, Calmfors and Driffil (1988) considered Japan to be one of the least centralised, ranking it fourteenth among the 17 countries studied. Soskice (1990b), by contrast, granted Japan the top position as the most centralised on account of strong employer coordination. In a study of 20 countries by Layard (1990) who considers employer coordination to be the most important institutional variable in explaining superior macro-economic performance, Japan occupies a middling position.

It is clearly problematic that even authors (Layard 1990, Soskice 1990b) who focus on employer coordination differ in their centralisation ranking of Japan relative to other countries. What is meant by employer coordination? Is it something that can be scored on a three-point scale (as many authors in this field do)? Coordination is certainly a more nebulous concept than bargaining structures or bargaining levels because it is about the process of information exchange, consultation, negotiation, decision making and the exercise of sanctions over those who break any joint agreement. A moderate degree of employer coordination may be conceptualised as a process in which employers meet infrequently to exchange information and to consult with each other, but decide on the final offers separately. A high degree of coordination is one in which employers meet intensively to decide jointly on an identical bargaining offer. Operationalising the concept of coordination involves tracking both the formal and informal occasions for information exchange and decision making. Rather than rely on 'stylised facts' which tend to use formal and structural features as proxies for informal aspects, this chapter examines systematically the behavioural content of wage setting in Japan.

THE 1993/4 SHUNTO ROUND: MAIN SOCIAL ACTORS AND BARGAINING OUTCOMES

The 1993/4 Shunto process[1]

Rengo (Japanese Trade Union Confederation) has the aim of achieving an overall improvement in living standards of working people through making a three-point demand for wage increases, shorter hours and policy reform. A policy demand in 1993 included an income tax reduction of a minimum of 5,000 billion yen, considered necessary to take the economy out of the prolonged recession. Top officials of Rengo and Nikkeiren (Japan Federation of Employers' Associations) held a meeting on 5 November 1993 to agree on this demand, which was put to the government jointly on the same day. Thus, the process of discussion between management and labour on the state of the economy started early in November.

As in previous years, Rengo kicked off the 39th Shunto Round by announcing its basic policy at its Central Committee meeting on 18 November 1993. It put forward a target of 5–6 per cent wage increases (a per cent or two lower than in the previous year), or a minimum increase of 20,000 yen per month. Rengo based its guideline on its own analysis and forecast of the economy: a combination of 5 per cent wage increase, a 5,000 billion yen income tax reduction and a 5 per cent increase in public investment would lead to 2.1 per cent economic growth; an alternative scenario of 2 per cent wage increase, no tax cuts and a 2 per cent increase in public investment would lead to zero growth. In Rengo's view, wage increases were indispensable for generating effective demand in the domestic economy. This, and other policy details, were officially launched at Rengo's first Central Struggle Committee meeting on 12 January 1994. The Rengo White Paper, published at the same time, contained details of its analysis and demands.

Nikkeiren met also on 12 January 1994, to approve its Labour Problem Research Committee report. The report, among other things, pointed out that the depth of the recession made any wage increases (other than that which is necessary to grant regular seniority-based wage increases) practically impossible. If companies had any spare cash left, the report said, they should use it to prevent layoffs. It is unreasonable for Rengo to demand both wage increases and employment security in the current state of economy. If anything, the major issue for today is not wage increases but a reduction in prices (considered too high in absolute terms in Japan relative to overseas). Nikkeiren repeated its allegiance to its productivity principle formulated in 1969, which states that the average wage increase in the Japanese economy as a whole should be consistent with the real economy-wide productivity increase in the medium-term (that is, real economic growth rate minus the rate of growth of the labour force).

IMF-JC (International Metalworkers' Federation-Japan Council) worked closely with Rengo, and echoed Rengo's demand by indicating 5 per cent as its guideline at its meeting on 24 November 1993. Being a powerful coordinator of industry-level union federations in the metal-working sectors (the steel, shipbuilding, electrical machinery and automobile industries in the main), IMF-JC has had a strong bearing on the overall Shunto strategy and schedule. For 1994, it was decided at the Rengo Central Struggle Committee meeting on 20 January that 24 March should be the settlement date for the leading IMF-JC unions.

All major industry-level union federations had held meetings since December to decide on their respective 'struggle policy' (*toso hoshin*) which was more or less determined by late January. For instance, in the steel industry, Tekko Roren (Federation of Iron and Steel Workers' Unions) met during 8–10 December 1993 to agree on a demand for a wage increase of 12,500 yen per month (or 4.33 per cent) for a standard worker (35-year-old with 17 years of service), a bonus of 1,380,000 yen, shorter hours through increasing paid holidays, an increase in overtime premium, and other matters (such as retirement and shift allowances) as a package.

Mid-February saw the formal start of enterprise-level negotiations when enterprise unions submitted their demand to their respective management. Private railway unions put forward their demand for a 7.9 per cent wage increase on 14 February. This was followed by the steel unions submitting their demand for a 4.33 per cent increase on 15 February, then the automobile unions demanded 5 per cent and shipbuilding unions 4.97 per cent on 16 February. The electrical machinery unions' demand was for 5 per cent and was submitted to management on 24 February.

Throughout the period when negotiations were under way at the enterprise level, higher level organisations met to exchange information and opinions about the state of negotiations. First, at the national level, these higher level organisations have contributed to the building of a consensus. For example, Rengo, and in particular its Central Committee members (from the industry federations of steel, electrical machinery, automobile, private railways, textiles and retail distribution, electric power and telecommunications) met on 18 February and 17 March to firm up and announce its revised struggle policy. Nikkeiren and Rengo representatives had a chance to meet and exchange views when the Minister of Labour called the 201st Sanrokon (his own tripartite policy consultation forum with labour and management) on 28 February, at which the government economic forecasts were discussed. Management continued to insist on no wage increases, and Rengo decided to revise its policy at its 17 March meeting. The revised target amounted to a minimum of 3.2 per cent increase, 2 per cent required to grant regular wage increases plus 1.2 per cent for inflation. Fully aware of the tendency in recent years for such minimum guideline to be interpreted as the maximum attainable, Rengo emphasised its endorsement of the principle of self-determination by industry federations (*sanbetsu jiketsu shugi*). Rengo implicitly consented to a widening in wage settlements between industrial sectors.

The precise pattern of negotiation differed somewhat from sector to sector, particularly in the extent to which industry-level union federations became involved directly in Shunto negotiations. For example, the nine largest private railway companies and their respective enterprise unions were exceptional in holding centralised bargaining sessions (seven times in all with the involvement of officials from the industry-level union federation and the employers' association). With a strict negotiation schedule fixed at the start, a characteristic of Shunto from its inception, the private railways union federation, Shitetsu Soren, scheduled strikes to take place in two waves, first on 25 March for large companies and on 29 March for smaller companies.

In the steel sector, the industry-level union federation would have ideally wanted centralised bargaining as in private railways. But since management refused, the compromise worked out was a 'milk-round negotiation session' at which the general secretaries of the five enterprise unions and officials from Tekko Roren are present to discuss with management at each of the five companies separately. By the time the enterprise unions submitted their demand for 4.33 per cent on 15 February, the dates were fixed for these negotiation sessions: the first round on 7–8 March and the second round on 16–17 March. In the meantime, personnel managers at the five major steel companies met on a regular basis to coordinate over their one-shot take-it-or-leave-it offer (*ippatsu kaito*) (see p. 252 for details on its origin).

The steel sector negotiations were extraordinarily hard going in 1994. The five companies continued to perform badly, making a joint loss of 300 billion yen, which led to a reduction in dividend payment by the industry leader, Shin-nittetsu, and a complete deferral of payment by the other four companies. Company management stuck to their initial stance of no wage increase, in effect a 1.21 per cent increase to cover the annual increments for regular workers on the seniority pay scale. Incensed by this stubborn position, Tekko Roren took an unprecedented action, by calling an extraordinary meeting to pass a resolution denouncing management stance. Noises were made that unions might not accept the management offer and may even withdraw cooperation for future restructuring plans. Moreover, individual enterprise unions appealed directly to their company top management by petitioning the Managing Director to plea for management concession. After the second milk round negotiation session on 16–17 March, management for the first time showed a willingness to concede, but only very slightly. The one-shot offer coordinated by management at the five companies, and made on 24 March, was an increase of 1.56 per cent.

In electrical machinery, company performance was still not robust but the number of loss-making firms among the top 17 companies was projected to decline for the financial year ending March 1994. The management side in this sector insisted on 3 per cent, slightly below the 3.2 per cent needed to maintain real wages in the view of the industry-level union federation, Denki Rengo. Given the tough stance taken by management, Denki Rengo called for a 12 hour strike starting at noon on 25 March, a strike call for the first time in 14 years. In the meantime, the leading company in the automobile sector, Toyota, was also insisting on a 3 per cent increase, only to make a last minute concession by offering, on 24 March, a 3.06 per cent increase, which was accepted by the Toyota union. To avert the threatened strike, management of the major electrical machinery companies met again and gave a coordinated revised offer of 3.05 per cent. Denki Rengo made a judgement that given the relative performance of Toyota and electrical machinery companies, anything slightly less than Toyota's offer – in fact by a 0.01 per cent point – had to be accepted, and called off the strike.

Despite tough negotiations due to the recession, all bargaining units led by the IMF-JC sectors managed to settle on the scheduled date of 24 March 1994. Because of recession and the strong yen, there was hope by the labour movement in the 1994 Shunto that regulated utilities might perform the pattern-setting role instead of the IMF-JC sectors. However, the nine electric power companies settled for 3.09 per cent in the afternoon of 24 March, after the Toyota and electrical machinery settlements were known. The private railway sector avoided the strike planned for 25 March by settling for 3.94 per cent on average at the last minute. Zendentsu, the telecommunication union, and the privatised NTT settled for 3.36 per cent on 25 March, while the JR regional companies settled for 3.77 per cent during 25 and 29 March. Other major unions in the private sector followed suit. Thus, by the end of March, settlements were reached for some three-quarters of the top 290 quoted companies in the private sector which were surveyed by the Ministry of Labour.

To complete the Shunto round, we can trace the diffusion of wage settlements to the rest of the Japanese economy, in particular to smaller companies and the public sector. For the private sector, smaller affiliates and independent companies settled their wages by looking at their parent or customer companies' wage increases. By the end of March 1994, 52 per cent of firms with 5,000 or more employees settled their pay, while only 20 per cent of firms with less than 300 employees had done so; the majority of these smaller firms (62 per cent) settled in either April or May

(Rodosho 1995). The tripartite Central Minimum Wage Committee deliberated in May, and fixed the new levels by August. This constituted the end of the Shunto round for the private sector.

In the public sector, as has become customary, public corporation employees received an arbitrated settlement, while civil servants, who do not have the right to strike, were awarded salary increases without negotiation. In 1994, the management of the four national corporations (the Post Office, Printing, etc.) offered a 2.39 per cent increase on 12 April, which was rejected by the unions; the Central Labour Relations Commission stepped in to attempt mediation but failed, and the arbitration award of 3.14 per cent was announced on 29 June. The Personnel Agency notified on 2 August that the salary for national civil servants be increased by 1.18 per cent, backdated to April 1994. In the autumn, this notification was formally approved by the government and the Diet.

Bargaining outcomes

The overall settlement was 3.11 per cent, the lowest ever in the history of Shunto, and lower than the trough of 3.56 per cent in 1987. The variation of all major companies are very small, as can be seen from Table 10.1. More remarkable is the uniformity of settlements within each major sector. For example, the big five steel companies settled for an identical increase in monthly pay of 4,500 yen, equivalent to 1.56 per cent increase; this means that the wage levels are quite similar between the companies. In electrical machinery, all the top 17 companies settled for a 3.05 per cent increase. Even in the automobile industry where there was a wide variation in company performance among the 11 final assemblers, there was a gap of a mere 0.17 percentage points between the top performer, Toyota, and loss-making companies such as Nissan. One of the questions posed in this chapter is why such uniformity in settlements occurs despite a decentralised bargaining structure at the enterprise level. Information exchange at higher levels in itself would not necessarily bring about uniform settlements particularly in recession; either side of industry can theoretically agree to differ. What incentives do unions have to settle for the same wage increases? How different are the incentives on the management side? These questions will be addressed in the next two sections.

THE HISTORICAL EVOLUTION OF SHUNTO

The development of Shunto may be recounted in three broad waves: the first from 1955 to 1964 when wage settlements were strike-prone and not fully coordinated; the second period from 1965 to 1975 when the IMF-JC began to take control of the Shunto process and culminated in a clear understanding that wages could be settled to restrain inflation only if the private sector exposed to international trade led the negotiations; and the

Table 10.1 The 1994 Shunto settlements in major sectors

Sectors and companies	Settlement amount (increase in monthly pay in yen)	Annual per cent increase
Steel		
The Big Five	4,500 (for standard workers)*	1.56
Shipbuilding		
Mitsubishi Heavy Industries	9,700	3.26
Kawasaki Heavy Industries	9,651	3.20
Ishikawajima Harima	9,700	3.30
Mitsui Shipbuilding	9,260	3.14
Sumitomo Juki	9,815	3.42
Hitachi Shipbuilding	9,760	3.30
Catapillar-Mitsubishi	9,700	3.30
NKK	8,500	3.00
Electrical Machinery		
Hitachi	7,787	3.05
Matsushita	8,460	3.05
Toshiba	7,927	3.05
Fujitsu	7,662	3.05
Mitsubishi Electric	7,701	3.05
NEC	7,705	3.05
Sanyo	8,116	3.05
Sharp	7,756	3.05
Fuji Electric	7,659	3.05
Matsushita Denko	7,546	3.05
Oki Electric	7,589	3.05
Pioneer	7,880	3.05
Yasukawa Denki	8,234	3.05
Meidensha	7,538	3.05
Columbia	8,768	3.05
Fujitsu General	6,954	3.05
Iwasaki Tsushin	8,237	3.05
Automobile		
Toyota	9,200	3.06
Nissan	8,400	2.89
Honda	8,900	3.00
Mazda	8,400	3.00
Mitsubishi	8,400	3.24
Isuzu	7,700	2.99
Fuji Juko	8,000	3.08
Daihatsu	7,750	3.06
Hino	6,800	2.85
Suzuki	7,800	3.00
Yamaha	8,370	3.05

Source: Rengo (1994), pp. 30–5

Note: * Standard workers are 35-year-olds with 17 years of experience.

third period from 1976 to 1995, when coordination strengthened on both sides of industry while synchronisation of settlements without strikes became an established feature of Shunto.

1955–64

The origin of Shunto may be traced back to union leaders' wish to overcome the shortcomings of enterprise unions which were becoming a predominant form of labour organisation by the mid-1950s. In December 1954, one of the leaders, Ohta Kaoru, called for a joint struggle by industry-level federations. Eight federations (including those for synthetic chemical workers, coalminers, private railway workers, electric power workers and paper and pulp workers) joined forces to coordinate their demands in what came to be known as the Spring Offensive. By the 1955/6 round, public sector unions joined this struggle.

At the time, unions were controlled by radical leaders. This applied no less to Tekko Roren (Japan Federation of Iron and Steel Workers' Unions) which became affiliated to Sohyo. Despite a strike wave, with a 19-day strike by the top five enterprise unions in 1957 and a 49-day strike by the top two enterprise unions in 1959, steel company management did not budge from their offer of a zero per cent wage increase in their autumn wage negotiations. Following such experience, Tekko Roren decided to join the Spring Offensive struggle for the 1959/60 round. Moreover, the defeat of the Mitsui-Miike miners' strike in 1961 (with a Panglossian union claim that 'even with the company bankrupt, the mountain remains') had a moderating effect on the ideology and tactics of the steel union leadership.

In the early 1960s, the steel sector emerged as a pattern setter, and there grew a strong sense of unity among private sector union federations. Domei, a private-sector led national centre, and IMF-JC were born out of this in 1964. The need to have better access to overseas information, with the prospect of the liberalisation of the Japanese economy, also contributed to the formation of IMF-JC.

1965–75

The 1967/8 round came to be known as the IMF-JC Shunto when coordination among private-sector union federations was enhanced by Tekko Roren joining the IMF-JC in 1966. Thereafter, there emerged a rather stable pattern of settlements by steel, electrical machinery, shipbuilding and private railways, in that order. With rapid growth exceeding 10 per cent per annum in real terms, inflationary pressures were heightened in the latter half of the 1960s (see Table 10.2). Nikkeiren, fearful of wage-push inflation, insisted on its productivity principle, but it became customary to grant wage increases which exceeded the previous year's settlements.

Then the first oil shock struck in 1973, causing an inflation rate of over 20 per cent and drastic reductions in corporate profits and investments. Shunto wage settlements soared to as high as 33 per cent in the 1973/4 round, and workers continued to enjoy an increase in their real wages. However, the Japanese economy recovered quickly relative to other countries with the inflation rate coming down to a single digit figure by 1976, and wage settlements more than halved to 13 per cent on average by the next Shunto round (1974/5).

This rapid adjustment may be attributed to a concerted action preceding the 1974/5 Shunto settlement, which in many ways changed the workings and expectations of wage bargaining. First, the government did not attempt a formal incomes policy, but instead consulted intensively with top business and union leaders to impress upon them the urgency of restraining inflationary pressures. This laid a path for more intensive tripartite exchanges of information and policy consultation in subsequent years. Second, on the management side, not only Nikkeiren, but other management organisations such as Keidanren (Japan Federation of Economic Organisations) became vocal in matters concerning wage settlements. In part as a result, chairmen and presidents of companies in addition to personnel managers played a critical role in settling negotiations. Nikkeiren also took an unprecedented step in recommending a guideline for wage increases of less than 15 per cent for 1975.

Responses on the labour side were by no means uniform. However, the crisis management policy proposed by Miyata Yoshiji, the then chairman of Tekko Roren, won much support. This policy was for unions to make 'economically rational' wage demands, not demands based on an increment to the previous year's settlements as had become customary. The policy had the dual objective of restraining cost-push inflation and of preventing job losses. An implication of this was that wage increases had to be considered in tandem with management decisions such as innovation and investment.

1976–95

Having learnt the lesson from the first oil shock, responses to the second oil shock were markedly restrained. The negotiated wages in the 1979/80 Shunto rose by only 6.7 per cent, which is considerably less than the inflation rate of 7.8 per cent in 1980. Consequently, real wages fell by 1.6 per cent in 1980 for the first time in post-war history, while the economy grew by 4.5 per cent in real terms.

Throughout this period after the mid-1970s, but particularly after the 1985 Plaza Accord and the sharp appreciation of the yen, the defence of real wages, rather than its growth, became a union objective. In order to achieve this aim, unions have attempted the following two strategies. One was a greater concentration of actions within the metal industry unions. In

Table 10.2   Main economic indicators (percentages)

Year	Shunto average wage	Real GNP growth	Inflation CPI	Unemployment rate	Labour's relative share	Labour's relative share - adjusted	Number of disputes
1956	6.3	7.2	1.3	4.54	90.8	42.2	646
1957	8.6	7.6	2.5	3.85	85.4	41.2	830
1958	5.6	6.5	-0.04	4.02	84.4	42.5	903
1959	6.5	9.2	1.8	3.81	79.5	41.5	887
1960	8.7	13.1	3.8	2.79	74.7	40.2	1,063
1961	13.8	11.6	6.2	2.45	71.4	39.7	1,401
1962	10.7	8.7	6.7	2.25	74.1	42.3	1,299
1963	9.1	8.4	6.6	2.07	73.3	42.8	1,079
1964	12.4	11.3	4.6	1.87	71.7	42.8	1,234
1965	10.6	5.8	6.4	2.08	72.6	44.5	1,542
1966	10.6	10.4	4.7	2.08	69.9	43.5	1,252
1967	12.5	11.0	4.2	1.94	68.9	43.1	1,214
1968	13.6	12.2	4.9	1.77	67.0	42.3	1,546
1969	15.8	12.1	6.4	1.74	66.4	42.4	1,783
1970	18.5	10.2	7.3	1.79	67.8	44.3	2,260
1971	16.9	4.3	5.9	1.95	70.3	47.0	2,527
1972	15.3	8.4	5.7	1.97	70.0	47.3	2,498
1973	20.1	7.6	15.6	1.83	71.3	49.2	3,326
1974	32.9	-0.8	20.9	2.15	76.6	53.4	5,211
1975	13.1	2.9	10.4	2.76	78.7	55.1	3,391
1976	8.8	4.2	9.5	2.77	78.1	55.1	2,720
1977	8.8	4.8	6.9	2.91	78.5	55.3	1,712
1978	5.89	5.0	3.8	3.10	76.9	54.0	1,517
1979	6.00	5.6	4.8	2.84	76.4	54.2	1,153
1980	6.74	3.5	7.6	2.87	75.2	54.1	1,133
1981	7.68	3.4	4.0	3.04	76.1	55.1	950
1982	7.01	3.4	2.6	3.35	76.1	55.4	944
1983	4.40	2.8	1.9	3.58	75.6	55.6	893
1984	4.46	4.3	2.2	3.58	74.2	54.9	596
1985	5.03	5.2	1.9	3.52	72.8	54.2	627
1986	4.55	2.6	0.0	3.76	72.2	54.0	620
1987	3.56	4.3	0.5	3.68	71.5	53.6	474
1988	4.43	6.2	0.8	3.18	70.6	53.4	498
1989	5.17	4.8	2.9	2.87	70.5	53.9	362
1990	5.94	4.8	3.3	2.67	70.0	54.4	284
1991	5.65	4.3	2.8	2.65	70.4	55.4	310
1992	4.95	1.4	1.6	2.76	70.1	56.0	263
1993	3.89	0.1	1.2	3.25	70.7	57.1	252

Sources: Shunto average wage increase: Japan Productivity Centre (1994), p. 80.   Real GNP growth: Economic Planning Agency (1991), p. 5.   Inflation: Japan Productivity Centre (1994), p. 23.   Unemployment rate: Japan Productivity Centre (1994), p. 22.   Labour's relative share: defined as (income per employee) / (GNP per working person). Adjustment is made for the ratio of employees in the total labour force over time. Japan Productivity Centre (1994), p. 20.   Disputes: the number of strikes and lock-outs of half-day or longer. Japan Productivity Centre (1994), p. 167

particular, the four major industry federations of the IMF-JC, namely in steel, shipbuilding, automobiles and electrical machinery, adopted a strategy of settling their wages simultaneously on the same date from the 1975/6 Shunto (although the effective pattern setter remained the steel industry for another ten years when automobile and electrical machinery joined steel to form a broader pattern-setting sector). Such concerted action provoked greater coordination on the employers' side in the form of an Eight Company Round Table Meeting (Hasshakon), an informal gathering of personnel directors from two major companies from each of the four main metal sectors (see later for more details). A second union strategy to defend workers' real wages was through a macro-corporatist channel of making policy demands to the government (see Chapter 8). The *quid pro quo* for unions in exercising wage self-restraint was a greater say not only *vis-à-vis* management but also *vis-à-vis* the government. Ultimately, the overall macro-economic performance of the Japanese economy improved despite slower growth in the last two decades, because real wage increases were kept in line with economy-wide productivity increases.

Over 40 years, the Shunto process has become increasingly institutionalised. The major features which account for the successful macro-economic outcomes of Shunto are listed below. As is evident, some of the factors are intricately related to the three pillars of the Japanese system, namely lifetime employment, seniority-plus-merit pay and enterprise unionism.

First, Shunto negotiations are not over the 'rate for the job' but over the employer's total wage bill.[2] An increase in this wage bill is referred to as a 'base up' which includes what is necessary to grant annual increments in the seniority-based pay scale, and this is what is coordinated at the industry-level on both the union and management sides. It is a convenient formula for the employer because what determines the price competitiveness and profitability for him is the wage bill. The distribution of the 'base up' is also negotiated at the same time during Shunto. Moreover, because of the system of internal promotion and seniority-plus-merit pay, there is more or less an automatic linkage between the increase in union members' wages and the increase in managerial pay. Therefore, there is little scope for any significant wage drift.

Second, the synchronisation of pay settlements every year eliminates the possibility of wage leapfrogging. In Japan, spring became the timing for synchronising pay levels because new employees were recruited for lifetime employment straight from school or university when the academic year came to an end in March. Also, 1 April has become the date for making seniority and merit increments in pay. Over the four decades, synchronisation became increasingly marked particularly since the 1975/6 Shunto when the IMF-JC adopted a strategy to obtain wage offers on the same date. Over time, the synchronisation of the date for pay increases came to be accompanied by the synchronisation of settlement rates.

Third, as part of the above trend, private sector unions have come to take a greater lead in setting wage norms by settling first. In early days of Shunto in the 1950s, Shitetsusoren (General Federation of Private Railway Workers' Union) and Korokyo (Joint Council of the Public Enterprise Unions) were pattern-setters. However, a clear wedge was driven between the leading private sector settlements and public sector settlements around 1980, and by the 1990s, there was at least a one month gap between the two (Ishihata 1990, pp. 82–3). Why did the public sector fail to be a pattern setter in Japan? One reason is the aforementioned legal framework of mediation and arbitration, in which public sector workers' pay has effectively been determined without negotiation. Perhaps more important, however, is the emergence of a clear consensus between labour and management that the private sector should dominate the Shunto process. The labour movement has successfully managed the transfer of power from public to private unions by dissolving Sohyo and forming Rengo as the dominant national centre. Since wage setting in the private sector is more constrained by the employer's ability to pay than in the public sector, this trend contributed towards restraining wage-push inflation in Japan. Moreover, even within the private sector, the firm's ability to pay has become more important as a determinant in granting wage increases, as compared to other factors such as the going rate of increase (see Figure 10.2).

Fourth, within the private sector, it is the export-dependent manufacturing sector, namely the steel industry and more recently the IMF-JC metal sectors, which have taken the lead in Shunto. Unions in an exposed sector have greater incentives than those in a protected sector to be concerned with problems of international trade. If they are encompassing within an export-dependent industry and dominant within the national scene, it is likely to act in a way that avoids inflationary behaviour (Crouch 1990). The Japanese steel union federation and the IMF-JC are a case in point. When steel first emerged as a pattern setter in the early 1960s, it was indeed a leading sector of the economy in the sense of achieving high growth and profitability. However, as the industry matured and was overtaken by emerging industries such as electrical machinery, automobiles and information technology, managers and unions still looked to the steel industry for creating a consensus. This inertia in pattern setting appears to be due to a combination of the following characteristics of the steel industry. Not only is it exposed to international trade, so that wages have to be set with regard to the international competitiveness of Japanese exports. It is also a sector which supplies intermediate goods to other sectors of the economy in a stable manner, and therefore is a good guide to the state of the economy as a whole. Moreover, the steel industry in Japan is highly oligopolistic in which the Big Five, accounting for 90 per cent of the total domestic pig iron production, have shown little variations in corporate performance among themselves until recently. Such

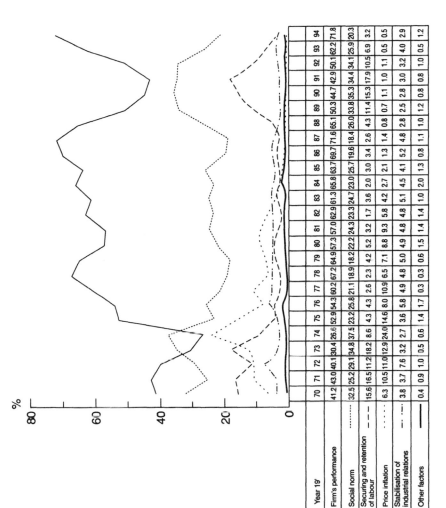

Year 19'	70	71	72	73	74	75	76	77	78	79	80	81	82	83	84	85	86	87	88	89	90	91	92	93	94
Firm's performance	41.2	43.0	40.1	30.4	26.6	52.9	54.3	60.2	67.2	64.9	57.3	57.0	62.9	61.3	65.8	63.7	69.7	71.6	65.1	50.3	44.7	42.9	50.1	62.2	71.8
Social norm	32.5	25.2	29.1	34.8	37.5	23.2	25.8	21.1	18.9	18.2	22.2	24.3	23.3	24.7	23.0	25.7	19.6	18.4	26.0	33.8	35.3	34.4	34.1	25.9	20.3
Securing and retention of labour	15.6	16.5	11.2	18.2	8.6	4.3	4.3	2.6	2.3	4.2	5.2	3.2	1.7	3.6	2.0	3.0	3.4	2.6	4.3	11.4	15.3	17.9	10.5	6.9	3.2
Price inflation	6.3	10.5	11.0	12.9	24.0	14.6	8.0	10.9	6.5	7.1	8.8	9.3	5.8	4.2	2.7	2.1	1.3	1.4	0.8	0.7	1.1	1.0	1.1	0.5	0.5
Stabilisation of industrial relations	3.8	3.7	7.6	3.2	2.7	3.6	5.8	4.9	4.8	5.0	4.9	4.8	4.8	5.1	4.5	4.1	5.2	4.8	2.8	2.5	2.8	3.0	3.2	4.0	2.9
Other factors	0.4	0.9	1.0	0.5	0.6	1.4	1.7	0.3	0.3	0.6	1.5	1.4	1.4	1.0	2.0	1.3	0.8	1.1	1.0	1.2	0.8	0.8	1.0	0.5	1.2

Figure 10.2 The most important determinant in granting wage increases (per cent of firms)

Source: Rodosho (1994), p. 10

concentration of industry made it easier for employers to coordinate their actions, especially as there was also a clear leading company, Shin-nittetsu, within the industry.

Fifth, *ippatsu kaito* – the practice of single irreversible offer pioneered by the steel employers in 1959 – spread to other sectors and contributed to the decline in the use of the strike weapon over time. On the surface, this is a mode of wage settlement in which management makes a one-shot offer to which it commits to stick whether it is acceptable to the union or not. As an indication of the diffusion of such management practice, the proportion of firms which settled after one management offer increased from only 19 per cent in 1973 (Dore *et al.* 1991, p. 22) to 54 per cent for the 1994 Shunto (Rodosho 1995, p. 82). It might be tempting to conclude from this that this is a simple reflection of the balance of power shifting in management's favour in the two decades. However, one caution before jumping to this conclusion is that large firms (employing 5,000 or more) are nearly twice as likely to settle after one management offer than small firms (employing 100–299). Particularly at large firms, much informal consultation takes place between management and union leaders before a formal offer is made. In fact, there is evidence to show that the diffusion of *ippatsu kaito* coincided with the timing of union leaders gaining greater access to confidential company information, around the first oil shock and thereafter (Inagami 1995). This has the attendant problem of lack of clarity for rank-and-file workers in the negotiation process between the time the union makes a demand and when management makes a formal offer (Sano *et al.* 1969, p. 230). However, the advantage of *ippatsu kaito* in reducing overt disputes is clear-cut. Instead of starting the wage round with a view to returning to the negotiating table several times, management makes a commitment to offering the maximum possible in its first-and-last formal offer. This has a similar effect to a situation in which a provision for a final-offer or pendulum arbitration narrows the gap between what management offers and what labour demands from the start.

Sixth, encompassing organisations are said to be able to internalise externalities (that is, free-riding on wage-push inflation in the present context) better than organisations with sectional interests (Olson 1982). In Japan, encompassingness as measured by participation in the Shunto round or the coverage of collective bargaining has not been very high. For example, roughly half of total union membership in the 1960s and three-quarters since the 1970s participated in Shunto. Given that union density has declined from 34 per cent in the mid-1970s to just below 25 per cent in the 1990s, no more than 20 to 25 per cent of total employees have their pay set directly during Shunto. As for the coverage of collective bargaining, there is official survey evidence that the proportion of *unions* which have a labour agreement with management increased from 81 per cent in 1977, 86 per cent in 1982, to 92 per cent in 1986 and 91 per cent in 1991 (Rodosho 1994, p. 23).[3] Either way, the formal coverage of bargaining has not been extensive in Japan, especially when compared to most European countries. Nor has there been a conspicuous trend towards decline in the formal coverage over time.

This formal situation should be modified in a number of ways to see if there is a functional equivalent of encompassingness in Japan. A major characteristic of Shunto is the orderly diffusion of wage norms from the private sector to the public sector, from leading pattern-setting sectors to follower sectors, from large to small firms, and from corporate headquarters to subsidiaries and affiliates. The social order roughly corresponding to all these dimensions is not so much just a ranking according to the company's ability to pay, but the ranking according to the prestige of companies.[4] Reinforcing such norm of 'equal pay increases for companies of equal prestige' are the following two mechanisms.

First, Japanese unions, as unions elsewhere, have always argued for the standardisation of wage levels and increases across the economy on the ground of fairness. In order to achieve this objective, unions in different sectors have had varying degrees of success in pursuading management to accept industry-wide bargaining.[5] For example, since 1972, the electrical machinery sector has an industry-level discussion forum (*sanbetsu roshi kaigi*) which meets around three times weekly in the spring to discuss shorter work hours, overtime premium pay, as well as wages. It is attended by personnel directors from the top six firms in the industry (Hitachi, Toshiba, Mitsubishi, Fujitsu, NEC and Matsushita); on the union side, only top officials from the industry-level federation, Denki Rengo, attend. Similarly in the car industry, an Industry-level Labour–Management Conference has been held since after 1985, when a consensus emerged on the need to discuss how the industry should restructure in response to the yen appreciation; the October meeting covers general issues while the February meeting focuses on furthering mutual understanding about wage increases. These meetings are attended by a rather large number, around 30 from Jikeiren (Japan Automobile Industry Employers' Association), and officials from Jidosha Soren (Confederation of Japan Automobile Workers' Unions). In either of these sectors, the labour side has demanded a negotiation forum, while the management side has insisted that it is no more than a discussion and consultation forum (*kondankai*). In the steel industry, Tekko Roren had also been requesting centralised bargaining with the Big Five since the 1960s, but had to compromise with the milk round (*junkai*) session since the 1980s. This is a bargaining system in which the general secretaries from the five enterprise unions and an official from Tekko Roren go around each of the five companies to negotiate over wages at the peak of the Shunto negotiations.

Next, on the management side, coordination within each key sector occurs not so much through employers' associations as through informal management groups of leading companies in each sector (as pointed out by Koshiro (1983, p. 382)). For example, the most cohesive among such intra-sectoral informal groups is the coordination among the top five steel companies, namely Shin-nittetsu, NKK, Sumitomo Kinzoku, Kobe Steel and Kawasaki Steel. Management meetings of these Big Five take place at various levels of the organisation, from the top personnel director level down to the section chief (*kacho*) level; they each meet around four to five times during the period from January just before unions publicise their demands up to the coordinated settlement date in March. The meetings are informal and behind closed doors, but there is sufficient evidence that managers do not merely exchange information but also discuss each company's wage increase proposal in the light of its corporate performance with a view to arriving at an identical wage offer (Ishida 1967, Sano *et al.* 1969, Chapter 7). Hardnosed discussions take place among the five company managers, with worse performing companies arguing for a low wage increase while better performing companies point out the danger of provoking unions and demoralising the workforce. The role of the industry leader, Shin-nittetsu, is said to be important in mediating and creating a consensus. Once a final decision on the coordinated wage offer is made, each company has an incentive to observe it; there is a clear understanding that offering a lower increase than agreed would damage worker morale, and might still just possibly elicit strike action which would disturb the existing market share in an oligopolistic market, while offering a higher increase than agreed would be self-defeating since spiralling wage increases would result in a squeeze on profits. As compared to the solidarity among the Big Five, the role of Tekko Renmei, which was formed in 1948 by merging the employers' association and the trade association, is very weak; it attempts neither to set a guideline for wage increases, nor does it have the power of sanctions over employers in the Shunto process.

Similarly, in the electrical machinery industry, employers are rather fragmented in formal terms, with multiple associations, one for electrical machinery (Denki Kogyokai) and the other for telecommunications (Tsushin Kogyo Renmei). But there is an informal gathering of personnel managers from six core companies in the Kanto region (namely Hitachi, Mitsubishi Electric, Toshiba, Fuji Denki, NEC and Fujitsu) which meets several times in the Shunto process. Denki Rengo's policy to explicitly state the minimum acceptable offer (*hadome*) below which strike action would be taken led to greater coordination among employers in this sector. As in the steel sector, the Kanto Six companies are said to engage in a frank discussion in order to arrive at a consensus, and to put their respective cards – increasingly an identical offer as in steel – on the table before they are made known to their respective unions.

Thus, in Japan, employers regulate themselves within key sectors not so much because there are employers' associations which sanction free-riders (a point emphasised by Soskice (1990a, p. 194) more in the context of Western Europe, and OECD (1994, p. 175)), but because informal yet systematic coordination exists among major companies. Two further questions arise from this finding. Why do employers wish to keep their Shunto coordinating meetings informal and non-public? And what accounts for the continued solidarity of key employers in coordinating over wage offers? An obvious answer to the first question is that making meetings formal and public would lead to union demand for formal collective bargaining at the industry-level. The answer to the second question will be explored in the next section.

LABOUR MARKETS AND PRODUCT MARKETS

Commonly, employers are said to coordinate over wages within an industry because they wish to take wages out of competition. This means that not only do employers in the same industry want to level the playing field in the labour market (so that they have an equal chance of attracting good quality employees at the time of recruitment), but also in the product market (in which labour costs are reflected in product prices). It is evident in the process of Shunto, however, that not only is there horizontal coordination among employers in the same industry, but also inter-sectoral and vertical coordination (between buyer and supplier companies). What is the rationale behind such employer coordination?

The Eight Company Round Table Meeting (Hasshakon)

A major example of inter-sectoral employer coordination is Hasshakon which has been in existence since 1976. This is an informal gathering of eight companies, two from each of the four key metal sectors, namely Shin-nittetsu and NKK in the steel sector, Toyota and Nissan in the automobile sector, Hitachi and Toshiba in the electrical machinery sector and Mitsubishi Heavy Industries and Ishikawajima Harima Heavy Industries in the shipbuilding sector. Every year, personnel directors from these eight companies meet two to three times in March to coordinate over their respective wage offers. There are also meetings of these eight companies at the departmental head (*bucho*) and section head (*kacho*) levels to iron out details. The time and place of these meetings, never mind the content of discussion, are suppposedly top secret, but the following facts are known.

First, Hasshakon was employers' response to a concerted action by the four metal industry federations. 'It seems to have been born out of the fact that when the IMF-JC side put forward a united demand and each industry federation tried to draw out management offers all at the same time, management could not respond adequately to their respective union demand if they had not grasped the content of the pattern-setting steel offer before it became public' (Miyata 1982, pp. 40–1). The formation of Hasshakon had a reinforcing effect on strong coordination, as the union side decided to form a counterpart – the Eight Enterprise Union Round Table Meeting (Hassharokon) – in spring 1977. At this forum, the general secretaries of the eight enterprise unions gather informally, usually just before the IMF-JC meetings.

At the start, the Hasshakon management aimed to arrive at an identical offer, because that had the power to convince unions that offers were fair and hence to avoid strike actions. However, even if offers were to be different among the eight companies, Hasshakon functioned as a powerful forum not only for information exchange but for checking and restraining each other's offers. The informal non-public nature of the forum gives an occasion for managers to engage in heart-to-heart discussion about affordable offers. According to Komatsu Hiroshi, a key originator of the forum and a personnel director and vice president of Shin-nittetsu until 1981:

> For instance, if offers between shipbuilding, steel and automobiles were unfortunately different, Hasshakon was a place where management sought to grasp not so much the amount of the gap in wage offers, but to understand why such offers had to be made. Otherwise, there would be turmoil within IMF-JC, and by that time the union side would normally have got wind of the exact offers we had in mind. Also, beforehand, we as steel or shipbuilding sought understanding from others that we could not possibly go along with a higher offer this time. It was quite usual for things to work in ways that would restrain others. If only your own company was doing well but many others could not keep up with you, this became a reason for restraining your offer. But badly performing companies in steel or shipbuilding could not control other companies. It was more likely to be used as an excuse by management in automobile or electrical machinery to lower their offers.
>
> (Shunto Kenkyukai 1989, p. 111)

Some observers believe that the leadership taken by the steel companies, and in particular Shin-nittetsu, the largest corporation in Japan, was crucial in uniting the management side (Miyata 1982, pp. 40–41). Its relative demise is also said to have led to less cohesion among the eight companies in recent years. But the continued existence of Hasshakon, despite the weakening of unions, may be due to the importance of steel *vis-à-vis* the other three sectors. 'There is no doubt that this forum [Hasshakon] is for the three sectors to enquire about the real intention of steel companies' (Yoshimura 1982, p. 268). In particular, automobile, electric machinery and shipbuilding companies are interested in the steel settlements because they are the major users of steel, and therefore are concerned to see that their input prices (of which the steel workers' wages constitute a significant part) are stable and predictable (Tsuda 1978, p. 13).[6]

Interviewees (for example at the employers' association level) have made a casual observation that there is a considerable downward pressure on steel wage increases because a higher-than-expected increase would be taken as a sign of easy money and lead to steel users' demand for a price reduction. However, managers at steel, electrical machinery and shipbuilding companies who are current members of Hasshakon denied at the interviews I requested that they attended the meetings with any thought of linking wage offers to steel prices. But it seems evident that at least in the past, there was a strong union pressure to link wages and wholesale prices; the IMF-JC unions used their hegemonic bargaining power to promise to deliver wage restraint only if management delivered their side of the bargain in the form of price stability (Yamada and Kobayashi 1982, p. 250).[7]

Corporate groupings in the automobile industry

Being a newer industry than the steel industry, organisations at the industry level had been in a state of flux until the early 1970s. On the management side, there are four separate organisations, namely the Japan Automobile Manufacturers Association (JAMA), Japan Auto Parts Industry Association (JAPIA), Jihanren (Japan Automobile Dealers' Association) and the Japan Automobile Employers Association (Jikeiren). Of these, Jikeiren is the organisation specialising in labour matters and is affiliated to the national body, Nikkeiren. Jikeiren was founded in 1948 in reaction to the upsurge in unionisation. But unlike in the steel industry, it was not absorbed into any of the industry associations because the interest of final assembly companies did not quite match that of parts suppliers or of dealers.

Nor is there an informal gathering of major car manufacturers, as in steel or electrical machinery. Toyota is regarded as a clear leader within the car industry, and has recently emerged as a pattern-setting firm for the entire economy, as the 1993/4 Shunto indicates. For some time, Toyota's reference group has not been within the car industry, but with a group of ten companies including Shin-nittetsu, Tore, Toyobo, Hitachi, Toshiba, Mitsubishi Heavy Industries, Ishikawajima Harima and Matsushita. In particular, Toyota and Matsushita are said to have very close links, not least because of their trading links (Matsushita supply electrical and electronic parts to Toyota), and also as the two major firms outside the Kanto region.

At the corporate level, each of the eleven assemblers has built relatively cohesive links with parts suppliers and dealers, although the degree of cohesion may differ from the tightest in the case of Toyota to looser linkages in the case, say, of Mazda or Mitsubishi Motors. If restricted to parts suppliers, an association, known generically as *kyoryokukai*, was organised for core suppliers. Each *kyoryokukai* has a committee which discusses labour matters. Although not specifically in relation to the Shunto process, this provides a forum for managers to exchange information on labour management, including working conditions and wages (Sako 1996).

On the labour side, the history of attempts at setting up a unified industry-wide union organisation had been marked with failure due to political division at the top. In 1955, Zen Jidosha, an organisation which was formed in 1948 as an industrial union, was superseded by a Nissan union-led Jidosha Roren. The more moderate enterprise unions at Toyota, Isuzu and Hino formed their own federation, Zenkoku Jidosha, in 1962. By 1965, however, the prospect of liberalising trade and capital markets led to the formation of Jidosha Rokyo, a loose association in which the competing federations participated in order to devise a labour strategy for industrial policy. Partly as a consequence of such coordination, a confederation of automobile workers' unions, Jidosha Soren (Confederation of Japan Automobile Workers' Unions), was finally inaugurated in 1972. Today, this is the largest industry-level union federation in Japan encompassing nearly 800,000 workers.

When the prospect for a unified industry-wide union organisation became evident, federations comprising the unions of the car manufacturer, and also its subsidiaries and main suppliers, were formed. Some corporate group-based union federations had existed already, for example at Honda and Mazda. But the majority of these federations were formed in the car industry in 1972 especially in order to become affiliated to Jidosha Soren. The confederation decided to accept only such corporate group-based federations as members.

Every economic downturn in 1974, 1979 and 1987 posed a threat to the security of employment within each enterprise. In response, enterprise unions came to negotiate employment security within a corporate grouping by approving temporary and permanent transfer of employees between parent and affiliate (or supplier) companies. This necessitated coordination between enterprise unions within a corporate group in order to govern the quasi-internal labour market of the group. Outside the car industry also, some industry-level union federations began to specify such corporate group-based federations as a unit of affiliation in order to organise more workplaces within the group (Shinoda 1994, pp. 361, 366). Evidence of success of this strategy is shown in an increase in union density in the car industry over the last two decades.

Coordination and adjustment over Shunto wage demands also became a major activity of corporate group-based federations of unions (Inagami 1995). Generally, corporate groupings were more commonly used as a frame of reference in wage determination the smaller the firm size (Sano *et al.* 1969, p. 106; Rodosho 1995, p. 11). This meant, however, that larger companies and enterprise unions which led a corporate group had to set their wage demand with a view to what smaller employers (some of which are non-unionised) could afford.

As an example, the Toyota enterprise union and around 80 enterprise unions at Toyota's parts suppliers are organised into All Toyota Trade Unions Federation. In the 1980s and 1990s, the Shunto settlement rates by all these enterprise unions in the Federation have differed by no more than 0.1–0.2 percentage points (Ueda 1992). Unions' interest lies in settling for the same rate (or more recently preferably for the same amount in an attempt to close wage differentials by firm size). Management also has an incentive to settle for the same rate. If a supplier had granted a wage increase above the assembler's increase, the latter would interpret this as a sign of high profitability and would be extra tough in the next round of price negotiation. At Nissan, there are regular meetings between Nissan Roren (the Nissan federation of enterprise unions) and the purchasing department of Nissan, which facilitate making a link between component suppliers' wages and component prices. Similarly, Zen Toyota Roren (All Toyota Trade Unions Federation) holds meetings with Toyota Kyohokai (the suppliers association) at the time of Shunto every year.

Thus, in this section, we have spelt out the background to why organisational encompassingness was extended to corporate groupings. The main logic lies in the way labour costs are reflected in prices of intermediate goods. Related to this is the logic of the survival of corporate groupings which require the unionised sector to take account of wage setting in the non-unionised sector.

SUMMARY AND CONCLUSIONS

This chapter examines the nature of coordination at levels higher than the enterprise in order to understand why management and labour have an incentive to establish and observe a norm set at a level compatible with the international competitiveness of the Japanese economy.

On the union side, industry- and national-level coordination has been seen as a means to overcome the shortcomings of enterprise unionism. In particular, soon after World War II when the possibility of establishing industrial unions faded, worker solidarity was the principle upon which union leaders relied to enable stronger unions to help weaker ones defend their bargaining power *vis-à-vis* management. Subsequently in the 1970s, inflation exposed the weakness of enterprise-level bargaining in defending workers' real wages. This gave an added incentive for unions to strengthen coordination at a level higher than the enterprise, by combining collective bargaining with participation in national policy making. At the same time, in order to defend employment security, enterprise unions had to increase coordination within a corporate grouping. Thus, some industry-level union federations began to specify such corporate-based union federation as a unit of affiliation. Overall, union coordination within the context of macro-corporatism and union federations organised along corporate lines have contributed to wage restraint. This has led Rengo recently to acquiesce in greater variations in wage settlements, although no union leader has come forward to argue in favour of less coordination which would allow individual enterprise unions to achieve greater wage increase where companies have the ability to pay.

Part of this reticence is due to the continuing cohesion on the management side. Originally, employer coordination most notably in the steel industry began in response to union offensive. As in any oligopolistic market, employers wish to, and have the capacity to, take wages out of competition by coordinating over their respective wage increases. In Japan, such coordination was not through formal employers' associations, although such associations exist, but through informal meetings among the main companies in each sector. It appears also that inter-sectoral coordination among employers became increasingly important in the 1970s as the interaction between wholesale input (for example steel) prices and wages was identified as a cause of inflation. The informality of coordination remains important to employers precisely because it enables them to evade union demands for industry-level bargaining. Thus, employers in Japan continue to enjoy one of the benefits of multi-employer bargaining, namely the placing of a floor under wage competition, without the drawback of being confronted by strong national or industrial unions.

This study of the wage bargaining system in Japan has also engendered the following theoretical and comparative insights. In particular, the concept of 'centralisation' or 'decentralisation' has been enriched by (i) investigating informal coordination rather than focusing on the formal level of bargaining, and (ii) giving equal weight to employer coordination and union coordination at various levels, rather than focusing on the latter. This study has shown that the dynamics of change in the history of Shunto is observable more accurately by focusing on less formal network ties, such as Hasshakon and Hassharokon. Moreover, 'centralisation' and 'decentralisation' do not lie on a simple continuum (Crouch and Traxler 1995). In particular, over time, a greater enterprise focus even in Japan (as attested by more firms saying that their performance is the most important determinant of wage increases (see Figure 10.2)) coexists with a greater level of coordination both formally (through Rengo and IMF-JC and their employer counterparts) and less formally. There has also been greater coordination within corporate groupings of enterprise unions, a peculiarly Japanese piece in the puzzle which gives a full picture of what Crouch (1993) calls 'articulation' (how different levels are joined together in mutual interaction).

Lastly, in explaining the superiority of Shunto in maintaining the performance of the overall economy, the following structural characteristics are of note. Unlike in Sweden, where trade union movements became dominated by public service and white-collar unions, the Japanese trade union movement is marked by a victory of private sector over public sector unions. There has also been a clear labour–management consensus that the export-dependent metal sector should remain the pattern setter. This fact on its own contributes much to the superior inflation–unemployment outcomes in Japan. However, the problem of adjustments between the exposed and protected sectors has manifested itself, not in the form of wage-push or imported inflation, but as a wide gap between price levels within Japan and those outside Japan. The relatively high domestic price levels in Japan undermine the purchasing power of workers' pay, and are therefore a policy concern for the trade union movement. Rengo is set to make a neo-liberal policy demand for deregulation of the protected sector in order to improve workers' living standards. For this reason, the Shunto wage bargaining process is likely to continue being closely co-ordinated with macro-corporatist policy participation by Rengo.

Acknowledgements

I would like to thank Hiroki Sato and Kaoru Iwasaki for arranging interviews with employers' associations, personnel directors of key companies, and union leaders. I am also grateful to the following for helpful comments: Steve Babson, Colin Crouch, Ronald Dore, Keith Hancock, Takeshi Inagami, Thomas Kochan, David Metcalf, Andrew Oswald, Hiroki Sato, David Soskice, Tsuyoshi Tsuru and Stefan Zagelmeyer.

NOTES

1 The main source of information for this subsection is *Shukan Rodo News*.
2 One complication to this is that the settlements in the steel industry since the early 1970s have been in terms of an increase in the monthly pay for a standard worker (35-year-old male with 17 years of work experience). Therefore, the percentage increase in this sector is not directly comparable to the percentage increase in other sectors. Within the steel industry, the older the company's workforce, the higher the necessary increase in the total wage bill.
3 The OECD estimated that the bargaining coverage rate (i.e. the proportion of total employees covered by collective bargaining) in Japan is 23 per cent (OECD 1994, p. 173). This figure appears to have been derived by multiplying the proportion of unions with agreements (0.9) by the union density (0.25). However, this completely ignores the difference in size of unions.
4 Corporate prestige comes with big size, but importantly it is also associated with an old founding date and being close to the power centre in the business world (*zaikai*); Shin-nittetsu fits the bill for top prestige in the way Toyota Motors does not, despite the fact that the latter's chairman now heads the Keidanren.
5 The basic level of collective bargaining in Japan is the enterprise. But considerable sectoral variations exist as follows. Sectors from the highest level to the lower level of bargaining are described in turn.

(a) Industry-level bargaining and agreement
Kaiin (Seamen's union) has negotiated at the industry level since 1920. Today, however, the union has only 50,000 members, down from 200,000 at one time. The employers' side is fragmented, and the union negotiates separately with Gaiko Romu Kyokai (overseas), Naiko Senshu Dantai (domestic), Zennaiko and Oogata Car Ferry Romu Kyokai.
(b) Industry-level bargaining and enterprise-level agreement
(i) Shitetsu Soren (General Federation of Private Railway Workers' Unions) has 180,000 members, and negotiates with Min-ei Tetsudo Kyokai (Private

Railways Association) which is an employers' association of the nine largest companies, employing 5,500 workers all together. Also, the union negotiates with the six bus companies jointly, and with each of the nine regional federations. This form of negotiation is called group bargaining (*shudan kosho*), but the actual collective agreement is signed with each of the companies. There is no such thing as an industry-level framework agreeement.

(ii) The textile section of Zensen Domei (Japanese Federation of Textile Industry Workers' Unions) bargains collectively with each of the following employers' associations, consisting of ten spinning companies (employing 30,000 workers), seven synthetic fibre companies (40,000 workers), nine woollen spinning companies (10,000 workers) and six woollen dyeing companies (a few thousand workers). Collective agreements are signed with individual companies, however.

(c) Industry-level coordination and enterprise-level agreement

Industry-level federations such as Denki Rengo (National Federation of Electrical Machinery Workers' Unions, 800,000 members), Zosen Juki Roren (National Federation of Shipbuilding and Heavy Machinery Workers' Unions, 130,000 members), Denryoku Soren (Federation of Electric Power Workers' Unions, 240,000 members) and Tekko Roren (Japanese Federation of Iron and Steel Workers' Unions, 210,000 members), have the power to decide at the industry level the settlement guidelines and the minimum acceptable offer below which a strike may be called, and have the right to judge when a strike is desirable, that is whether or not individual company offers are worthy of accepting or rejecting. The exact form which industry-level coordination takes differs from industry to industry.

6 In calendar year 1993, out of 60.2 million tonnes of shipment of steel materials within Japan, around 17 per cent was to the three sectors (electrical machinery, automobiles and shipbuilding) (Ministry of International Trade and Industry (1994) *Statistics on Japanese Industries*). Just over half (57 per cent) of the weight of a typical car is accounted for by steel (*Financial Times* 26 April 1995).

7 According to Chiba Toshio, a one time deputy general secretary of the Federation of Iron and Steel Workers Unions:

> We took this stance (of pressurizing both the government and business) not so much due to the situation in the steel industry, but more from a macro viewpoint for the sake of the stability of the whole Japanese economy. Management also took a similar stance at least immediately after the first oil shock when the situation was most serious. When the problem of revising steel prices emerged due to the sharp increases in energy prices, the steel industry followed the Inayama philosophy of endurance. Even with the quadrupling of oil prices, the steel prices were held constant for two years. That invited a lot of dissatisfaction from parts of the industry. There was also a criticism that if cost increases were not passed onto prices to maintain an appropriate profit, things would be out of hand later on. But Mr. Inayama, the president of Shin-nittetsu at the time, rejected it out right and stuck to a stance of endurance. We, on the union side, supported his position whole-heartedly.
>
> (Yamada and Kobayashi 1982, p. 250)

Brown, William (1986) 'Facing up to incomes policy', in Peter Nolan and Suzanne Payne (eds) *Rethinking Socialist Economics*, Cambridge: Polity.
Bruno, M. and Sachs, J. (1985) *Economics of Worldwide Stagflation*, Oxford: Basil Blackwell.

Calmfors, L. and Driffil, J. (1988) 'Bargaining structure, corporatism and macro-economic performance', *Economic Policy*, vol. 6, pp. 13–61.
Crouch, Colin (1985) 'Conditions for trade union wage restraint', in N. Lindberg and C. Maier (eds) *The Politics of Inflation and Economic Stagflation*, Washington DC: The Brookings Institution.
—— (1990) 'Trade unions in the exposed sector: their influence on neo-corporatist behaviour' in Renato Brunetta and Carlo Dell'Aringa (eds) *Labour Relations and Economic Performance*, Basingstoke: Macmillan.
—— (1993) *Industrial Relations and European State Traditions*, Oxford: Oxford University Press.
Crouch, Colin and Traxler, Franz (eds) (1995) *Organized Industrial Relations in Europe: What Future?*, Aldershot: Avebury.
Dore, R. P. (1987) 'Building an incomes policy to last', in *Taking Japan Seriously*, London: Athelone Press.
Dore, R., Inagami, T. and Sako, M. (1991) *Japan's Annual Economic Assessment*, London: Campaign for Work.
Dore, Ronald, Boyer, Robert and Mars, Zoe (eds) (1994) *The Return of Incomes Policy*, London: Pinter Publishers.
Economic Planning Agency (1991) *Keizai Yoran* (*Summary of Economic Statistics*), Tokyo: Okurasho Insatsukyoku.
Hazama, Hiroshi (1981) *Nihon no Shiyosha Dantai to Roshi Kankei* (*Employers' Associations and Industrial Relations in Japan*), Tokyo: Nihon rodo kyokai.
Inagami, Takeshi (1995) *Seijuku Shakai no nakano Kigyobetsu Kumiai* (*Enterprise Unions in a Mature Society*), Tokyo: Japan Institute of Labour.
Inagami, T., Whittaker, H., Ohmi, N., Shinoda, T., Shimodaira, Y. and Tsujinaka, Y. (1994) *Neo-Koporatizumu no Kokusai Hikaku* (*International Comparative Research on Neo-corporatism*), Tokyo: Japan Institute of Labour.
Ishida, Hideo (1967) 'Keieisha no dantai kosho strategi' ('Management's strategy toward collective bargaining') *Keio Business Forum*, vol. 5, pp. 60–79.
Ishihata, Nobuo (1990) *Nihon no Rodo Kumiai* (*Trade Unions in Japan*), Tokyo: Japan Institute of Labour.
Japan Productivity Centre (1994) *Katsuyo Rodo Tokei* (*Practical Handbook of Productivity and Labour Statistics*), Tokyo: Japan Productivity Centre for Socio-Economic Development.
Katz, Harry (1993) 'The decentralisation of collective bargaining: a literature review and comparative analysis', *Industrial and Labour Relations Review*, 47(1), pp. 3–22.
Koike, Kazuo (1962) *Nihon no Chingin Kosho: Sangyobetsu Reberu ni Okeru Chingin Kettei Kiko* (*Wage Bargaining in Japan: The Structure of Industry-level Wage Determination*), Tokyo: University of Tokyo Press.
Koshiro, K. (1983) 'Development of collective bargaining in post-war Japan', in T. Shirai (ed.) *Contemporary Industrial Relations in Japan*, Madison: University of Wisconsin Press.
Layard, R. (1990) 'Wage bargaining and incomes policy: possible lessons for Eastern Europe', Centre for Economic Performance, London School of Economics Discussion Paper No. 2.
Leonard, J.S. (1988) 'Wage Structure and Dynamics in the Electronics Industry', *Industrial Relations*, 28(2), pp. 251–75.
Milner, S. and Metcalf, D. (1994) 'Spanish pay setting institutions and performance outcomes', Centre for Economics Performance, London School of Economics, Discussion Paper No. 198.
Ministry of International Trade and Industry (1994) *Statistics on Japanese Industries*, Tokyo: MITI.

Miyata, Yoshiji (1982) *Kumiai Zakkubaran (My Frank Views on Unions)*, Tokyo: Toyo Keizai Shinposha.

OECD (1994) *OECD Employment Outlook*, Paris: OECD.

Ohmi, Naoto (1994) 'Gendai Nihon no macro-corporatism' (Macro-corporatism in contemporary Japan), in Inagami *et al.*

Olson, Mancur (1982) *The Rise and Decline of Nations: Economic Growth, Stagflation and Social Rigidities*, New Haven: Yale University Press.

Pierce, Richard (1994) *Is Unemployment Still Lower if Employers and Unions Coordinate Wage Bargaining? An updated study of unemployment across the OECD, 1988–1993*, unpublished MSc Report, London School of Economics.

Rengo (1994) *Rengo Seisaku Shiryo (Data for Rengo's Policy)*, Tokyo: Rengo.

Rodosho (Ministry of Labour, Japan) (1994) *Rodo Kyoyaku to no Jittai (The State of Labour Agreements and Other Matters)*, Tokyo: Rodo Gyosei Kenkysho.

—— (1995) *Shiryo Chinage no Jittai (Survey on Wage Increases)*, Tokyo: Ministry of Labour.

Rodosho (annual) *Shiryo Rodo Undoshi (History of the Labour Movement)*, Tokyo: Ministry of Labour, Labour Policy Bureau.

Sako, Mari (1996) 'Supplier associations in the Japanese automobile industry: collective action for technology diffusion', *Cambridge Journal of Economics* vol. 20, no. 6.

Sano, Yoko, Koike, Kazuo and Ishida, Hideo (1969) *Chingin Kosho no Kodo Kagaku (A Behavioural Science of Wage Negotiation)*, Tokyo: Toyo Keizai Shinpo Sha.

Shimada, Haruo (1983) 'Wage determination and information sharing: an alternative approach to incomes policy?' *Journal of Industrial Relations*, 25(2), pp. 177–200.

Shinoda, Toru (1994) 'Ima mata corporatism no jidai nanoka' ('Is this once again an era of corporatism?'), in T. Inagami *et al.*

Shunto Kenkyukai (ed.) (1989) *Shunto Kawarunoka (Transformation of Shunto?)*, Tokyo: Eidel Kenkyusho.

Sisson, Keith (1987) *The Management of Collective Bargaining: An International Comparison*, Oxford: Basil Blackwell.

Soskice, David (1990a) 'Reinterpreting corporatism and explaining unemployment: co-ordinated and non-coordinated market economies' in Brunetta, R. and Dell'Aringa, C. (eds) *Labour Relations and Economic Performance*, London: Macmillan, pp. 170–211.

—— (1990b) 'Wage determination: the changing role of institutions in advanced industrialized countries', *Oxford Review of Economic Policy*, 6(4), pp. 36–61.

Takanashi, A. *et al.* (1989) *Shunto Wage Offensive: Historical Overview and Prospects*, Tokyo: Japan Institute of Labour.

Tsuda, S. (1978) 'JC no soba keiseiryoku o saguru' ('Investigating JC's capacity to create a norm') *Gekkan Rodo Mondai*, October, pp. 4–13.

Tsuru, Tsuyoshi (1993) 'Shunto: the spillover effect and the wage-setting institution in Japan', International Institute for Labour Studies Discussion Paper, DP/51/1992.

Ueda, Hiroshi (1992) 'Jidosha buhin meeka ni okeru frekishibiriti no kakuritsu to roshi kankei' ('Flexible manufacturing system and labour relations in the auto parts suppliers'), *Kikan Keizai Kenkyu (Osaka City University Journal)*, 15(3), pp. 51–71.

Windmueller, J. P. and Gladstone, A. (eds) (1984) *Employers' Associations and Industrial Relations : A Comparative Study*, Oxford: Clarendon Press.

Yamada, S. and Kobayashi, K. (1982) *Seisaku to Undo (Policy and Movements)*, Tokyo: Kyoikusha.

Yoshimura, Yosuke (1982) *Daikigyo Roshi no Kenkamatsuri (Ritualistic Quarrels Between Labour and Management at Large Companies)*, Tokyo: Japan Institute of Labour.

11 Business diversification strategy and employment relations

The case of the Japanese chemical textile industry

Michio Nitta

The purpose of this chapter is to examine the impact of business diversification strategy in Japanese firms on employment relations by looking at the experience of the chemical textile industry. The companies in the industry have reached an advanced stage of maturity and have therefore been actively diversifying into other lines of business.[1]

Business diversification is particularly important in understanding the relationships between business strategy and employment relations. On the one hand, it is a necessary condition for firms to provide 'employment security' for the member of their 'internal labour markets' in the dynamically changing market economy. On the other hand, it may become a catalyst for changes in the traditional structure of 'internal labour markets' characterised by the 'homogenisation principle' by the introduction of a more heterogeneous workforce.

Before examining data on the chemical textile industry, we need to establish a clearer and more realistic vision of employment relations in large Japanese corporations than that offered by the stereotypical 'three pillar' model.

THE JAPANESE-TYPE 'INTERNAL LABOUR MARKET'

It has often been pointed out that the most basic feature of the employment relations of larger Japanese firms is the practice of giving priority to tapping the in-house human resources to fill core jobs rather than bringing in outside talent from the general labour market.

Nobody will doubt that one of the most important tasks for successful management is to secure competent people to fill core managerial positions or to perform jobs requiring special professional and technological expertise, or skills necessary on the shop-floor. Of course, not all positions in business corporations require a high level of competence. There are some jobs that are relatively easy, and it is not very difficult to find new recruits for such jobs from the general labour market. However, recruiting talented and skilled people from outside often proves not only difficult, if not totally impossible, but also costly. In cases where a firm gives its employees what the human capital theory calls 'firm-specific training' (Becker 1975), there is an incentive for management to minimise the rate of turnover in its workforce.

Moreover, when the accumulation and the sharing of information within a firm become important, and when a certain type of teamwork becomes crucial, the firm may find the practice of internal recruitment all the more appropriate.

To be sure, this practice of internal recruitment has its own disadvantages. It may imply a lost opportunity for a firm to employ outside talent. When a company tries to develop a new line of business outside the scope of its traditional operations, it needs people with new ideas. It is often difficult to find such talent in-house, because employees with many years of service may have grown too accustomed to the existing operations to think of something entirely different.

None the less, it is undeniable that with the growth of large firms, such an internal recruitment practice has become important. One of the advantages inherent in large businesses is the magnitude and continuity of their information accumulation, as well as their capacity for innovation based on this information. This is why an increasing number of larger corporations in most countries, with varying institutional characteristics and strengths, have come to adopt employment practices which make much of the 'internal labour market'. This is particularly true for jobs of white-collar personnel, such as managers and professionals, but it is also becoming the case with many jobs of production workers (Koike 1988).

In the light of this, it is difficult to say with certainty that the employment system, based on the practice of recruiting of capable personnel from within the firm itself, constitutes a characteristic feature of the Japanese employment systems distinct from those found in other countries. What is important in an international comparison of employment practices is to identify the type of internal labour market-oriented employment systems at work in one country and then to compare it with the one at work in another. An accumulation of comparative studies is not large enough to enable us to make a typological analysis on an empirical basis. However, the findings of pertinent studies already available seem to allow it to be said, hypothetically, that the Japanese-type employment system founded on the internal labour market, is characterised by two basic factors: one being the principle of homogeneous treatment of employees (Inagami 1986) and the other being the adoption of the 'lifetime employment' practice as a core industrial relations strategy (Nitta 1988). I will now elaborate on each of these factors.

For the first factor, the following three aspects can be observed.

1. The homogenisation principle in personnel management by status. Also known as a 'single status' system, this principle or system is based on the denial of stratified grouping of the workforce within a company (White and Trevor 1985). In theory, many enterprises have abolished this system of express stratification between the blue- and white-collar groups, which was prevalent in the pre-World War II days.

In reality, however, one can identify two distinct groups of employees within a firm, the blue-collar group, which mainly undertakes jobs on the shop-floor and has relatively fewer chances of promotions to middle and senior management posts, and the white-collar group, which starts with clerical, lower managerial, and professional posts and has a greater likelihood of being promoted to middle and senior management posts. It has been argued, however, that conceptually, and as a matter of institutional policy, such a difference in careers results from job assignments based on each employee's 'ability' and performance evaluation. This is continuously conducted in accordance with a uniformly applicable in-house evaluation standard, which ensures employees are not treated differently as a result of their backgrounds or qualifications. In fact, there are people who, following a blue-collar career, assume middle or senior management posts. In terms of wages, fringe benefits or employment security, the difference between the two groups is small.

2. The homogenisation principle in the management of personnel by types of jobs. This principle aims to minimise the differences in rewards accorded to workers doing different types of jobs. Generally speaking, the wage paid to a worker is determined partly by length of service and partly by that worker's 'ability' evaluation score. As a matter of practice, younger workers are often assigned to lower-graded jobs and workers with longer service take jobs of a higher grade with better conditions. It seems reasonable, therefore, to assume that there is some correlation between the 'ability' of a worker and the type of job assigned. As a result, there is some correlation between the wage received and the type of job performed.

3. The homogenisation principle in the management of individual careers. This principle, particularly evident for the white-collar group, is not meant to favour specific groups of employees (for example those who have gained MBAs at American business schools) in the formation of careers. Every effort is made to avoid the formation of a so-called elite group, and future elite candidates are assigned to low-ranking jobs to start with and are promoted slowly, enabling them to experience a wide range of jobs.

In the process of career formation, a certain degree of specialisation develops in some job areas. However, in principle, a career is not limited to narrowly specified areas. Employees are expected to perform any job to which they are assigned and to perform it well.

In recent years the dual career ladder system, which comprises a traditional managerial career ladder and a newly introduced specialist career ladder, has become popular. The more restricting duty place system, which classifies employees into national staff status and local staff status, has spread among retail chain stores and other firms in the service sector. Thus, there are signs of growing diversification in career management. However, this trend is still limited to partial changes largely because of a reluctance on the part of employees to adopt new careers. The homogenisation principle has not been drastically changed in this respect.

With regard to the second point, 'lifetime employment' as an industrial relations strategy, this is discussed at a greater length in an earlier paper (Nitta 1988) and so I shall only briefly touch on it here. As a strategy of labour-management relations, the lifetime employment strategy serves as a key stabiliser in solving or managing potential and actual conflicts between workers and management.

There are three aspects to this strategy: (1) in order to avoid discharges as much as possible, both management and labour should make lifetime employment one of the most important objectives and use various employment adjustment measures, such as flexible working hours and transfers across the boundaries of workshops, departments and plants; (2) in return for the assurance of employment, employees and their labour unions should take a cooperative stance toward rationalisation measures; and (3) management should commit itself to a fair distribution of the fruits of productivity gains in rewarding such cooperation.

Together, the principle of homogeneous treatment and the lifetime employment practice form the two key elements of the employment system of large Japanese corporations founded upon the Japanese-type internal labour markets and have formed a strong basis of employee integration. Paradoxical as it may sound given that the homogenisation principle connotes some sense of egalitarianism, these two elements have also helped make personnel management based on ability evaluation a success, because they stimulate a large segment of employees, including blue-collar workers, to compete hard with each other in improving their abilities.

If the Japanese employment system with its dependence on the internal labour market is conceptualised as outlined above, the question that needs to be addressed here is: What impact will business diversification have on the system's key elements?

BUSINESS DIVERSIFICATION IN THE CHEMICAL TEXTILE INDUSTRY

The Japanese chemical textile industry is a typical maturing industry. In the latter half of the 1950s, and as part of the rapid growth of petrochemical industries, chemical textile companies began to change their rayon-centred production structure into one based mainly on such synthetic textiles as nylon, polyester and acrylic fibre. The subsequent

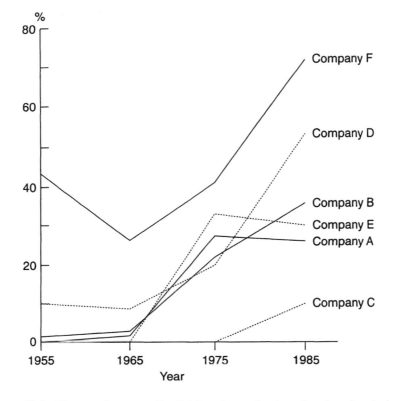

Figure 11.1 Shares of non-textile divisions in total sales of major chemical textile manufacturers, 1955 85

Source: Various *Annual Reports* of the companies concerned

levelling off of demand for apparel goods and the growing competition from newly developing textile producing countries combined to push the industry into a maturing phase relatively early. As evident from Table 11.1, the industry's employment capacity peaked early, during the 1960s, and after the first energy crisis of 1973 it experienced a sharp curtailment of employment along with excess production capacities being shut down.

In the face of these changes in the market environment, the leading chemical textile companies began to diversify their business structure in the latter half of the 1960s. Since the latter half of the 1970s, in partic- ular, the percentage of the sales in the non-textile divisions in comparison to their total sales increased still further, with some companies even begin- ning to see this percentage rise to, or go beyond, 50 per cent (Figure 11.1). Business fields targeted for diversification varied from one company to the next, but new fields of activities which gained importance quantita- tively included various chemicals and plastics and the products made from these. Given this general trend, it is not far off the mark to say that many chemical textile companies have endeavoured to transform themselves into general chemical manufacturers. However, the transformation process has gone far beyond that. Business diversification by chemical textile firms has extended into a large variety of sectors including pharmaceutical, electronic materials, construction materials, housing and real estate and the leisure and hotel industries. Indeed, it is one of the most diversification-oriented industries in Japan.

DIVERSIFICATION WITH EMPLOYEES RETAINED

Following the diversification of business operations, the distribution of a company's workforce among its divisions has changed. Table 11.2 shows the changes in the composition of union members by division at one of the five leading companies. The table eloquently reveals that from 1964 until 1984 the percentage of union members belonging to the company's textile division steadily declined, while the percentages of those in the petrochemical and other divisions increased.

Table 11.1   Employees in the chemical textile manufacturing industry by division, 1955–85

	1955	1960	1965	1970	1975	1980	1985
Rayon manufacturing division		53,782	30,913	15,842	10,495	7,341	
	61,419·						6,054
Acetate manufacturing division		2,152	2,661	2,175			
					52,138	33,823	
Synthetic fibre manufacturing division		4,676	20,338	48,623	53,609			25,392
Total	66,095	76,272	82,197	71,626	62,633	41,164	31,446

Sources: MITI *Kogyo Tokeihyo* (Census of Manufacturers) various years

Table 11.2   Composition of employees in Company F by division, 1964–84 (per cent)

	1964	1974	1984
Textile division	47.8	43.8	37.7
Petrochemical division	10.5	19.2	22.6
Chemical products division	20.7	11.9	11.8
Other products division	1.5	5.8	6.9
Offices	19.4	19.4	20.9
Total (rounded)	100.0	100.0	100.0

Source: Annual Report for the 1985 Convention of the F Labour Union

In order to make possible such a significant change in the composition of the workforce among divisions, massive reassignments were undertaken. Generally speaking, the transfer of workers that accompanies business diversification has two aspects to it. First, reducing the number of employees working at older, declining divisions is considered an indispensable prerequisite for restructuring, and a substantial portion of these workers are bound to be reassigned. Second, due to the necessity for personnel capable of taking charge of the new business operations, a certain number of employees would be recruited for these jobs from the existing divisions.

Of these two aspects, the former has attracted attention in the discussion on the lifetime employment practice. In the chemical textile industry, as in other industries, there are many cases where worker transfers have been carried out with the express intent of honouring the management's commitment to assuring lifetime employment. And this has certainly played a significant role in coping with the employment effect of business restructuring.

Take, for instance, a textile factory with 250 employees which was closed down in the aftermath of the 1973 energy crisis. Fifty per cent of the employees were reassigned to another factory located in the same industrial complex, another 15 per cent were transferred to facilities in other areas, and 18 per cent were loaned out to companies which had close business ties with the firm in order to assure them the maximum employment security possible. Some employees found it difficult to accept transfers because of their age or family circumstances, and the company took the extraordinary measure of transferring younger employees working in other factories within the same complex in order to create vacant posts for the older employees from the factory that had closed. Even so, 17 per cent of the employees chose to leave or retire by receiving severance allowances with premiums.

When this plant was shut down, business conditions in the industry were so unfavourable that even one of the major chemical textile firms was forced to carry out a massive staff reduction by persuading more than 1,500 of its employees to accept voluntary severance. An employment crisis as serious as this was extraordinary; it was basically caused by sudden and violent changes in the outside economic environment. Despite this, the company in no way changed its basic policy of offering employees made redundant as a result of business restructuring, chances of being transferred to different shops or factories within the company.

Turning to the issue of reassignment, no hard data are available that directly reveal the procedure by which chemical textile firms recruit personnel necessary for taking charge of new businesses. However, our interview with union officials and personnel managers at these firms have revealed that the core members staffing the new operations are recruited from within the company as a matter of principle, supplemented by the hiring of young and inexperienced new workers. In some exceptional cases, outside experts are scouted to staff new business-related posts which require a high degree of expertise, but their number has been very limited.

Let me take the case of one chemical textile company which has made successful advances into the construction materials and the housing sector. Despite the great differences that separated the old and the new operations both in terms of technologies involved and the nature of product markets, the core personnel for these new divisions were recruited from within the company and were trained on the job.

Data indirectly showing the practice of internal recruitment are presented in Table 11.3. More specifically, the table compares the percentage of employees on loan from four large chemical textile firms to their subsidiaries and affiliated firms within their respective groups with the total workforce of these subsidiaries and affiliates. As explained below, many firms diversifying into new lines of business often follow the practice of establishing a subsidiary or affiliated firm and entrusting it with the operation of the new business. Viewing this fact alongside what the table shows, that is, the fact that employees on loan from large chemical textile companies comprise between 20 and 50 per cent of the total workforce of the subsidiaries and affiliated firms under their wing, it seems safe to conclude that the practice of recruiting core personnel for new businesses from within the firm is actually taking place.

In summary, the leading Japanese chemical textile firms have basically followed a human resource strategy of undertaking business diversification with employees retained in keeping with the practice of lifetime employment.

LABOUR UNIONS' POSITION WITH REGARD TO DIVERSIFICATION

All the labour unions representing the employees of the five leading chemical textile companies interviewed are taking a cooperative stance toward business diversification. They go even further, occasionally expressing their opinions at the official meetings of labour–management consultation and unofficial meetings with top management that management should develop and promote dynamic strategies. The unions believe that such strategic moves are essential for sustained growth of the firms, and thus for safeguarding the employment of their members.

The labour unions refrain from proposing specific alternative business strategies: not only do they admit that they have limited knowledge and capabilities to make sound judgements on business strategies and operations, they also see the responsibility for the companies' operations as ultimately resting with management. But when it comes to questions of employment security, they can become very vocal. For example, they often demand that management, when deciding on locations for new operations,

Table 11.3 Employees of major chemical textile companies loaned out to their subsidiaries and affiliates as percentages of the workforces of the receiving firms, 1986

A Company Group	approx 20%
B Company Group	approx 35%
E Company Group	approx 30%
F Company Group	approx 50%

Sources: The data have been obtained from each of the enterprise-based unions concerned

give priority to sites suffering from a decline in job opportunities due to business diversification and restructuring.

In order to deal effectively with the key question of investment, the unions diligently gather information on various issues related to business strategies and day-to-day operations from their members, including white-collar employees without management status, and from some non-member managers as well. In this respect, the labour unions supplement management by performing the function of an in-house communication network.

A LIMITED ADVANCE TOWARD MORE HETEROGENEOUS EMPLOYMENT SYSTEMS

Theoretically, as a firm pushes ahead with business diversification and as its requirements of human resources grow more heterogeneous, it may find the principle of homogenisation objectionable. This tendency has not yet set in as far as the leading chemical textile companies are concerned. Nor is there evidence of a widening disparity in wage across divisions and job classifications in recent years. On the contrary, the disparity seems to have decreased as a result of a switch from the job evaluation-based system, which was widely introduced in the 1960s by large Japanese corporations, to the in-house qualification-based system, which provides individual employees with extra benefits for a wider range of skills and higher abilities (Ishida 1985). In a sense, business diversification thus far seems to have had the effect of narrowing, rather than widening, the wage differentials among divisions and job classifications, most likely because management is finding it imperative to narrow these so as to facilitate smooth employee transfers across divisions and departments.

This is not to say that no problems arise from business diversification or that it has effected no changes. Take the example of a leading chemical textile firm which went into the real estate business selling houses and condominiums. It found it necessary to change the working hours of its staff (because sales people in this area have to work at night or on weekends and holidays to suit the convenience of their customers) and to introduce a stronger monetary incentive to encourage sales activities. But even in this case, only minor adjustments were introduced, such as

Table 11.4 Annual wage hikes at major chemical textile companies, 1965–85 (per cent)

	Company					
	A	B	C	D	E	F
1965	9.5	10.5	9.6	10.7	9.7	9.8
1966	11.0	11.7	–	12.4	11.1	11.3
1967	13.1	14.0	17.1	15.5	13.7	13.8
1968	14.6	15.6	18.8	17.1	15.0	15.1
1969	16.2	16.9	19.1	18.1	16.8	16.7
1970	17.7	18.6	19.6	19.7	18.8	19.5
1971	15.5	17.1	17.4	18.2	17.3	17.5
1972	14.5	14.8	16.0	16.3	15.9	15.6
1973	20.5	20.5	22.1	21.7	22.1	21.6
1974	31.2	31.3	31.2	32.9	31.9	31.6
1975	14.8	14.8	7.4	14.8	14.8	14.8
1976	7.5	7.5	8.5	7.5	7.5	7.5
1977	8.2	8.2	8.64	8.0	8.0	8.2
1978	4.25	4.25	5.98	4.25	4.25	4.25
1979	5.2	5.2	7.24	5.2	5.2	5.2
1980	6.5	6.5	7.58	6.5	6.5	6.5
1981	7.7	7.7	8.18	7.7	7.7	7.7
1982	7.125	7.025	7.56	7.125	7.125	7.105
1983	4.194	4.170	4.26	4.197	4.195	4.185
1984	4.40	4.40	4.56	4.42	4.42	4.40
1985	5.10	5.10	5.29	5.12	5.12	5.10

Source: Chemical Textile Section of the Zensendomei (Japanese Federation of Textiles, Garment, Chemical, Distributive and Allied Industry Workers' Unions) (1985)

compensation for the longer working hours of sales people and a special incentive as part of the annual bonus. The main principle of homogeneous treatment of employees was still kept intact.

That the principle of homogenisation stands firm against the backdrop of business diversification is demonstrated by Table 11.4, which records the annual wage rises agreed upon at spring wage negotiations between each of the six leading chemical textile firms and their unions. The wage rises offered by the six firms have remained more or less in concert with each other since the 1970s, when they began to take steps towards business diversification in earnest (Table 11.1). This means that despite the growing disparities in the degree of diversification among those firms, and despite the significant differences in their textile producing divisions' shares in their annual sales, the differences in the rates of wage rises and, therefore, in average wages among them have not changed. Had they shifted towards more heterogeneous employment systems concurrently with the promotion of the diversification strategy, they would have had great difficulty in keeping the parity in their wage increases.

One of the reasons why the principle of homogenisation remains unchanged can be found in the manner of diversification itself. Even though the chemical textile industry is well advanced in business diversification compared with other industries, many of the new businesses into which these firms have diversified are in the manufacturing sectors with strong technical links to their original lines of business, such as chemical products. Therefore, their demand for labour has not become heterogenised to the extent that the magnitude of their business diversification would suggest.[2]

Also important are the various methods which have been called into play to cope with the heterogenisation of the companies' labour demand without drastically changing the employment systems based on the principle of homogenisation. One such method is the practice of assigning relatively young, inexperienced, but potentially capable workers to new divisions. For example, a firm which aggressively built a large-scale operation in housing threw a large number of new recruits fresh from universities into the new business. Under the wage system, in which the length of service still carries significant weight, this practice helps keep labour costs for the new divisions low until the young employees grow older. However, another method of far greater importance is the extensive use of subsidiaries and affiliated firms, otherwise known as the method of 'organisational diversification'.

'ORGANISATIONAL DIVERSIFICATION' AS A SUBSTITUTE FOR HETEROGENEOUS EMPLOYMENT SYSTEMS

Organisational diversification (OD) is much used by leading chemical textile firms. The OD percentage, shown in Table 11.5, is calculated by dividing the number of employees of subsidiary and affiliated firms of a chemical textile company by the number of employees of the parent firm. As of 1987, this ratio either stood high or even exceeded 100 per cent for Companies A, B and D, while it was between 30 and 60 per cent for Companies C, E and F.

Table 11.6 reports the change in the percentage of employees of Company B loaned out to other firms. Although a full time-series of the statistics is unavailable, the data points to a striking trend toward organisational division. The percentage of employees loaned out by Company B more than doubled from 14.1 per cent in 1970 to 28.6 per cent in 1985. Especially remarkable is the increase after 1975. Although not all the employees on loan to other firms were at subsidiaries or affiliates of Company B, our interviews with union officials at the company have confirmed that most were actually working at subsidiary or affiliated firms.

It must also be pointed out that not all the subsidiary or affiliated firms have been established primarily for the sake of facilitating business diversification. Some of the chemical textile firms have traditionally given their

Table 11.5   Employees of major chemical textile company groups, 1982 and 1987

	1982			1987		
	Parent company employees (A)	Employees of subsidiaries (B)	OD % (B)/(A)	Parent company employees (A)	Employees of subsidiaries (B)	OD % (B)/(A)
A Co Group	7,227	7,491	103.7	6,447	7,228	112.1
B Co Group	13,895	8,393	60.4	11,835	10,369	87.6
C Co Group	1,757	757	43.1	1,838	618	33.6
D Co Group	3,542	5,162	145.7	4,110	3,773	91.8
E Co Group	6,289	3,433	54.6	5,842	2,893	49.5
F Co Group	16,095	8,337	51.8	15,641	9,576	61.2

Sources: Toyo Keizai Shimpo-sha (1982, 1987)

Notes: 1. Employees of subsidiaries and affiliates firms are inclusive of those on loan from the parent companies and other companies. 2. OD % = (Number of employees of subsidiaries and affiliated firms) / (Number of employees of the parent company) × 100. 3. Due to unavailability of data for some affiliated firms, the figures for D Company Group are underestimated. 4. Company F absorbed one of its affiliated firms during the period under consideration. The OD% for F Company Group in 1982 would be 79.6% if the employees of the absorbed company in 1982 were excluded from the employment of Company F.

Table 11.6   Changes in the ratio of Company B's employees loaned out to other firms, 1970–85 (per cent)

	1970	1975	1980	1985
Male and female employees	14.1	16.7	23.0	28.6
Male employees	16.8	18.6	23.7	30.2

Source: Obtained from the B Labour Union

sales and raw materials supply divisions organisationally independent statuses. There are also cases in which stock holding is used as a means of strengthening business ties with firms in the downstream sectors (for example, weaving, apparel). There are also instances where newly diversified business operations are kept within the parent company.

It is undeniable, none the less, that there are a significant number of subsidiary and affiliated firms which are established or used as a means of business diversification. In fact, organisational diversification through those firms is used quite often, especially when a company needs to transform some of its functional divisions: its engineering or research and development division might branch off as a separate business entity. Alternatively, a firm might launch into a wide array of highly heterogeneous businesses only remotely connected to chemical textile manufacturing, such as foods, interior decorating, housing and real estate, medical equipment and electronics. Establishing joint ventures with other domestic or foreign firms is another channel of organisational diversification that is gaining in importance.

The motives behind organisational diversification resulting from business diversification are not uniform. Some firms may choose to diversify for accounting considerations for the parent companies, while others may do so as a means of shock treatment to rectify the existing corporate culture. However, the desire to evade the problems of having to meddle with the principle of homogenisation in employment practice and to keep this principle untouched is, as discussed above, another very important motive.[3]

It is difficult to ascertain the relative importance of this factor quantitatively. However, in the course of my interviews, I have come across several cases in which companies have actually opted to set up separate firms primarily in order to avoid making special adjustments to the employment practice, such as introducing an incentive wage system and flexible working hours for sales people. It should be pointed out, moreover, that the level of remuneration for those directly employed by subsidiary and affiliated firms is generally lower than that for the employees of the parent companies. In so far as the comparative per capita labour cost of the member companies is concerned, the adoption of the organisational diversification method makes the corporate group-wide employment system more heterogeneous.

TOWARD A UNIFIED GROUP-WIDE EMPLOYMENT SYSTEM?

The question still remains as to whether it is desirable or possible to pursue this strategy of organisational diversification to its limit. If it is necessary at all to keep some level of organisational linkage[4] among member firms of a corporate group, some form of organisational order, composed of an employment system, for instance, will be required. Labour unions are naturally keen on establishing such an order.

For example, Labour Union B, which organises the employees of Company B, recently established the Federation of Labour Unions at the Company Group B, together with three other unions representing the employees of three major subsidiaries of Company B. The newly formed federation's principal aim is to set up uniform working conditions applicable to all the employees of the companies belonging to the B Company group. Pursuing this goal, the federation formed a unified bargaining team to negotiate basic wages and annual bonuses. The four member unions of the federation also changed their membership subscriptions to the industrial organisation, Zensendomei (the Japanese Federation of Textile, Garment, Chemical, Distributive and Allied Industry Workers' Unions), replacing their individual subscriptions by a single, collective subscription in the name of the newly formed federation. This change was intended to strengthen the authority and the function of the group-wide organisation.

There had been a more loosely tied, less powerful group-wide council of unions encompassing the four unions above and fourteen other smaller unions representing the employees of the more minor subsidiaries and affiliates under the wing of Company B. The newly formed Federation B plans to invite these other unions to join it. Such moves to strengthen ties among unions on a corporate group-wide basis is not limited to the unions of the B Company group.

On the other hand, should this kind of effort have an eroding effect on the vital function that the organisational diversification method performs in providing an escape valve for the parent company's increasingly heterogeneous demand for labour, contradictions are bound to surface between the corporate business strategy and labour's insistence upon organisational order. It will be interesting to watch closely how labour and management will deal with this dilemma.

One point of particular interest in this regard is that there are considerable differences among the organisational strategies adopted by different firms. For example, while Company F is clearly a front runner in business diversification among large chemical textile firms (see Figure 11.1), its degree of organisational diversification, as shown in Table 11.5, is 60 per cent, much lower than the figures for Companies A and B (90 and over 100 per cent respectively). At the same time, as is evident from Table 11.3, the percentage of employees loaned out by Company F when compared with the combined workforce of its subsidiaries and affiliated firms stands at 50 per cent, much higher than the ratios for other firms (20–35 per cent). These comparisons indicate that Company F has relied less on the organisational diversification strategy than its competitors.

Thus firms generally have considerable room for choice in reformulating their human resources strategy to suit business diversification, and future developments will show us which approach works better.

CONCLUSION

As illustrated above, employment systems of major chemical textile companies have not deviated very far from the traditional Japanese employment systems built on the Japanese-type internal labour market, although some expedients have been tried to deal with the increasingly heterogeneous demand for labour. Some indications can even be found of a reverse trend at work toward strengthening the principle of homogenisation and thus toward promoting diversification while retaining existing employees.

On the other hand, organisational diversification is being executed as a substitute for making the employment system heterogeneous. One of the likely new questions of interest will be that of whether a unified group-wide employment is desirable or not.

Despite much talk about the radical shifts in or even the collapse of the traditional employment practices in Japan after the collapse of the 'bubble economy', the basic strategies for Japanese firms to adapt employment systems to a changing environment have not drastically changed. They try to consolidate the 'core' employee group, while organising various subsidiaries, using more contract-based workers. To better understand the logic behind the behaviour of the Japanese firms, the study of the impact of business diversification in the chemical textile industry presented in this chapter provides a useful case study.

NOTES

1 For a general discussion on the characteristics of business diversification in Japan, see Yoshihara *et al.* (1981).
2 This observation is in agreement with the findings of Yoshihara *et al.* (1981).
3 For a general discussion on the relationship between organisational diversification and the employment practices of large Japanese firms, see Nagano (1988). Kagono (1988) develops an interesting hypothesis that 'organisational diversification' is used by large business corporations as a means of an organisational strategy to encourage a 'paradigm shift'.
4 For a discussion on the concept of organisational linkage between firms, see Imai (1982).

REFERENCES

Becker, Gary S. (1975) *Human Capital*, 2nd edn, New York: Columbia University Press.
Imai, Ken'ichi (1982) 'Naibu soshiki to sangyo soshiki' ('Internal organization and industrial organization'), in K. Imai, H. Itami and K. Koike (eds) *Naibu Soshiki no Keizaigaku (Economics of Internal Organization)*, Tokyo: Toyo Keizai Shinposha.
Inagami, Takeshi (1986) 'Changing Japanese-style Employment Practices', *Japan Labour Bulletin*, 25(10), pp. 5–8.
Ishida, Mitsuo (1985) 'Chingin taikei to roshi kankei' ('Wage systems and industrial relations'), *Nihon Rodo Kyokai Zasshi* (Monthly Journal of the Japanese Institute of Labour), no. 315 (August), pp. 3–14 and no. 316 (September), pp. 39–49.
Kagono, Tadao (1988) *Kigyo no Paradaimu Henkaku (Paradigm Shift Within Firms)*, Tokyo: Kodansha.
Koike, Kazuo (1988) *Understanding Industrial Relations in Modern Japan*, London: Macmillan.
Nagano, Hitoshi (1988) *Kigyo Gurupu-nai Jinzai Ido no Kenkyu (A Study on Manpower Transfer Within a Corporate Group)*, Tokyo: Taga Shuppan.
Nitta, Michio (1988) 'Structural changes and enterprise-based unionism in Japan', *The Proceedings of the 30th Anniversary Symposium: Searching for a New System of Industrial Relations*, Japanese Institute of Labour, 1988.
White, Michael and Trevor, Malcolm (1985) *Under Japanese Management*, London: Heinemann.
Yoshihara, Hideki, Akimitsu, Sakuma, Hiroyuki, Imai and Tadao, Kagono (1981), *Nihon Kigyo no Takakuka Senryaku (Diversification Strategies of Japanese Firms)*, Tokyo: Nihon Keizai Shinbunsha.

12 Worker participation
Collective bargaining and joint consultation

Keisuke Nakamura

This chapter discusses worker participation in management at corporate, establishment and shop-floor level, especially at large firms in the private sector. Worker participation in management here means that workers have a say in managerial decision making individually or collectively through their representatives, and that they regulate it or in some cases play a role in helping to execute the decisions. Although there are various forms of worker participation in management such as worker director schemes, profit-sharing schemes, joint consultation, collective bargaining, quality circles and so on, the following issues are analysed using a three-tiered model (Kochan *et al.* 1986):

(1) participation in strategic decision making at a top tier through joint consultation;
(2) negotiation on staffing and transfer at a functional tier through collective bargaining and/or joint consultation; and
(3) job-centred individual participation at a workplace level tier.

First of all, the practices of the above-mentioned worker participation are described using a body of case studies and questionnaire surveys. In each section, the characteristics of the practices are pointed out. Then some theoretical explanations are systematically developed in order to understand worker participation in management in Japan.

PARTICIPATION IN STRATEGIC DECISION MAKING

Table 12.1 shows the ratio of private large-sized firms which discuss with their workforce business issues at joint consultation committees. According to the table, around 70 per cent of the respondents hold such discussions.[1]

How much say workers have in each issue, formally or in a written agreement, is shown in Table 12.2. A first glance reveals that the extent of their influence varies among firms and that in general it is limited, at least formally.[2] It varies also with the issue and the firm size. As for larger firms with 5,000 workers or more, 30 to 40 per cent of them not only explain about business issues (with the exception of the introduction of new equipment) but also listen to workers' opinions. Moreover, around 20 per cent of these particular firms try to reach consensus between labour

Table 12.1 Firms which discuss business issues with workers

Business issues	Percentage of firms
Basic business policy	76.1
Business performance	76.6
Accounting	67.4
Changes in organisational structure	76.4
Production plan	70.6
Investment plan	68.3
Policy on rationalisation	75.2
Introduction of new equipment	62.3

Source: Japan Productivity Centre (1981)

Note: The sample (432 in total) is taken from firms with 500 employees or more; 409 of them are unionised.

and management about those issues. However, workers in smaller-sized firms of 1,000 or more but less than 5,000, are not so influential. Three-quarters of firms explain business issues to their workforce but only half discuss the introduction of new equipment. Compared with those business issues, the introduction of new equipment is the issue on which workers feel most strongly. Nearly half of the firms with 5,000 workers or more try to reach consensus between labour and management on this issue, and the equivalent figure for the firms with less than 5,000 workers is just over 20 per cent.

In summary, worker participation in strategic decision making through joint consultation in private large-sized firms is quite widespread, although there is no legal basis. Almost all of these firms are unionised, and therefore it is correct to say that enterprise-based unions usually communicate with management about business issues in private large-sized firms. The extent of workers' influence in some firms, however, seems to be rather limited, while in others workers' opinion is respected and a consensus tried to be reached. In spite of the observed limitation mentioned above, it should be noted that there is a gap between 'formal' or 'written' rules, and actual practices.

The Japan Productivity Centre (1990) describes the practices of joint consultation in fifteen leading firms in various industries. At fourteen of them a wide range of business issues are discussed between unions and management at joint consultation committees. No firms have written agreements which stipulate that the firm must agree on any of these issues with the union, but a close look at the practices at ten firms shows a different picture.

At three firms, Ajinomoto, Fujitsu and Honda, the collective agreements say that management should report and explain business issues to the union, but in reality information is exchanged between labour and management. In addition, the unions make suggestions concerning

Table 12.2 Establishments which discuss business issues at joint consultation committees, by the extent of workers' influence (per cent)

Business issues	Size of firm	Dealt with by JCCs	Of which			
			Report and explain to workers (%)	Listen to workers' opinions (%)	Consult with workers (%)	Need consent of workers (%)
Basic	5,000–	100.0	69.1	12.1	16.1	2.7
business policy	1,000–4,999	100.0	76.7	11.6	6.6	5.1
Basic	5,000–	100.0	61.7	12.1	21.3	5.0
plan on production and sales	1,000–4,999	100.0	77.5	9.9	7.1	5.5
Changes	5,000–	100.0	58.2	12.3	25.8	3.8
in organisational structure	1,000–4,999	100.0	75.0	9.2	11.8	4.0
Intro-	5,000–	100.0	42.8	12.4	38.0	6.9
duction of new equipment	1,000–4,999	100.0	55.7	21.4	21.6	1.3

Source: Ministry of Labour (1994)

Note: To consult with workers means that both labour and management exchange their opinions to reach consensus; failing that, the final decision is made by management.

business policies based on the opinions of the shop-floor, and occasionally they ask management to revise its policies. For that purpose, the unions have a special department or committee which analyses and monitors business policies. According to the union officers, management takes these suggestions seriously and makes every effort to implement them. With regard to Ajinomoto and Fujitsu, Inagami and Kawakita (1988) also describe the unions' serious involvement in strategic decision making. At the remaining seven firms, including Kyowa Hakko and Matsushita, the collective agreements do not specify the extent of the workers' influence at the top tier and only require that union and management talk or exchange opinions about business issues. But in reality, the unions are involved in strategic decision making just as seriously as in the above three cases. At Kyowa Hakko, the union offers its members business analysis training (Shiraki 1983). Matsushita is renowned for having the most advanced worker participation system. Koike (1985) describes in detail how a branch of the Matsushita union gathers complaints and requests regarding business issues from the rank and file in order to put forward proposals. Regardless of formal written agreements, many unions in private large-sized firms actively participate in strategic decision making.

Although these studies depict and analyse the practices, they are rather static and do not analyse the dynamics of worker participation fully.

The dynamics of worker participation at a top tier can be observed when firms face drastic change and are forced to restructure. By the end of the 1970s many Japanese firms suffered as a consequence of the severe recession and were obliged to make massive cuts in the workforce. Inagami *et al.* (1980) treat the case of a firm manufacturing communications equipment, where serious labour disputes occurred after a plan was introduced to reduce the workforce by 1,000 to 1,500. Some unions which had previously been opposed to management changed their policies to being more cooperative and more participative, in the face of a business crisis. Yamamoto (1983) takes up such a case in a steel firm and Kamiya (1983) treats one in a heavy electric firm. The similar case of an electric manufacturer is discussed by Mitsuoka (1985). Even when relations between labour and management were cooperative, problems still occurred, and Nitta (1985) analyses the strength of the union voice in strategic decision making on the plant closure of a steel firm. These case studies illustrate the following characteristics equally well.

First of all, unions became actively involved in restructuring firms, discussing plans with management. They examined the proposals made by management carefully at all levels, including the shop-floor, while others made their own suggestions.

Second, one of the union's basic policies is for the survival and growth of its firm, which is an objective shared by management. The unions finally agreed on the restructuring plans proposed by management, except for the employment adjustment plan.

Third, this policy is supported by many of the union members. Even in a case where a strike broke out, its continuation was vetoed by more than three-quarters of union members.

Finally, while management positively accepts union participation at a strategic level and makes every effort to revise restructuring plans to incorporate union's demands, it never concedes to the most crucial matter, such as workforce retrenchment or plant closing plans. As a matter of course, unions resist such plans at the outset, but are finally persuaded to accept them.

The crisis at the end of the 1970s has furthered worker participation at the top tier level.

According to Sato and Umezawa (1982), 65.2 per cent of the 682 unions which responded to their questionnaire survey replied that labour and management discussed basic business policy, business performance, and the production and sales record and plan more often than before the crisis (30.5 per cent replied 'no change'). Sixty-six per cent said that management gave more information about business issues (30.2 per cent replied 'no change'), and 70.8 per cent said that the union participated more actively than before (23.1 per cent replied 'no change').

Worker participation in strategic decision making has increased considerably in practice since the end of the 1970s. But it should be noted that some unions have no participation policy or are not allowed to participate, even in private large-sized firms, as indicated in Table 12.1. According to Inagami (1995), 56.5 per cent of 1,050 unions responding to their questionnaire survey replied that the union has an effective say in management strategy, while 40.1 per cent disagreed.

NEGOTIATION ON STAFFING AND TRANSFER AT A FUNCTIONAL LEVEL

Table 12.3 shows to what extent workers have a say over transfer in private large-sized firms. As to transfer within the firm, 70 to 80 per cent of enterprise unions have a say in the planning process as well as in the selection of individuals. Unions are more involved with transfer between establishments than transfer within establishments. As far as written agreements are concerned there are two types of union, active and passive.

An active union discusses the transfer through collective bargaining, negotiates a consensus or takes part in joint consultation. Twenty to 30 per cent of unions seem to be of this type. A passive union receives only a report and explanation about the issue, around 40 per cent of unions can be classified into this passive type.

In order to discover the precise nature of the unions' opinions on transfer, case studies are surveyed. Koike *et al.* (1976) conducted pioneering research in this field. The following are their findings concerning temporary transfer between sections of the plant and between plants. The union is given a week's notice of the number to be transferred, their names, the workshops they are to be transferred to, and the reasons. The custom is that management only enforces the transfer after receiving the union's permission. The selection of individual transferees is the supervisor's responsibility; in some cases the union is consulted by the supervisor but it may also become engaged in a grievance procedure.

Transfer is usually carried out to adjust an imbalance of the workforce among sections, plants or establishments. Therefore, in order that unions have an effective say over transfer, they need to have one on the staffing level. Koike (1977) discusses the practices of a steel plant and four chemical plants. In these studies, the change in staffing level is discussed by the union and management. Management must explain the reason for the transfer in order to get the union's permission. This procedure is stipulated in the agreement in three of the four chemical plants, and remains an unwritten rule in the steel plant. After reaching consensus on the staffing level, the subject of transfers is brought up. In the steel plant, the union is involved in neither the planning process nor in the selection process. Selection is the supervisor's responsibility, but the outcome is conveyed to the union which in turn checks the intention of the selected

Table 12.3 Unions with voice over the planning of transfer and the selection of transferees (per cent)

Types of transfer	Total num- ber	Collective bargaining	Joint consultation					No say
			Need consent	Consult	Report and explain	Others	Others	
Temporary transfer within establishment								
Planning	246	0.8	5.7	20.3	37.8	2.0	2.8	30.5
Selection	245	0.4	6.1	13.1	38.4	2.0	4.9	35.1
Temporary transfer between establishments								
Planning	244	2.9	10.7	27.9	33.6	1.2	3.3	20.5
Selection	244	0.4	12.7	15.2	38.2	1.6	4.9	26.2
Transfer within establishment								
Planning	264	0.8	4.9	18.2	39.8	0.8	4.2	31.4
Selection	265	0.0	9.1	10.2	46.0	1.1	5.7	27.9
Transfer between establishments								
Planning	263	2.7	12.2	20.9	36.9	1.1	3.8	22.4
Selection	264	0.8	15.2	13.6	42.0	1.5	4.5	22.3

Source: JTUC Research Institute for the Advancement of Living Standards (1991)

Note: The total number of unions differs among types of transfer because 'has not transferred yet' and 'no answer' have been excluded.

persons. In the four chemical plants, though the unions are given prior notice, it is the supervisor who selects individuals to be transferred.

Since these pioneering studies, there have been several detailed investigations of labour and management relations concerning transfer and staffing. Inagami (1983), Hata and Totsuka (1985), Koshiro and Nagano (1985), Koyama (1985) and Kamii (1991, 1994) clarify the practices in the automobile industry. The studies, which investigated three car manufacturers in all, make the following points clear.

First of all, unions are involved in the preparation of the monthly production plan which has a bearing on staffing levels. The degree of the union's involvement, however, differs among cases. In two of the three companies studied, the unions are consulted through joint consultation committees at top and plant level. But in the one remaining case of a major leading company, the union receives only a report and explanation about the monthly production plan, after which it puts forward some requests.

Second, as to temporary transfer between sections, the extent of the unions' influence varies. In the two cases mentioned above, labour and management discuss such issues as necessity of transfer, the period of transfer and the number to be transferred, as well as the location of transfer. In the final case the union is informed about the transfer by management and checks the transfer plan on a case-by-case basis.

Third, selection of temporary transferees is the supervisor's responsibility. In one of the two cases above, the union sometimes has a say in the selection rules; in the other the union is given prior notice about the selection and union officers meet the candidates to ask their views. In the final case, there is a rotation system to prevent the same workers from being transferred repeatedly.

Fourth, the unions are more involved with permanent transfers. In all three cases, various issues concerning transfer are discussed between labour and management at joint consultation committees. Working conditions, including wage levels, are also raised so that they are secured at least at the same level as before. Rules governing the selection differ among cases. In the first case the union proposes its own selection criterion and must get management agreement; in the second case management has to get the union's final approval. In the third case the union is not involved. Finally, in none of these cases do the unions reject the issue of transfer.

Detailed case studies have also been carried out in the steel industry; Nitta (1981), Ishida (1986, 1989) and Yamamoto (1983) are three such case studies. They make the following observations.

Unions have an active and minute say in determining staffing levels, particularly by preventing cutbacks through prior consultation. In the early stages the workers' views are noted by the unions who then inform management. Every attempt is made to accommodate the complaints and demands of the workers. With regard to temporary and permanent transfers, the unions are equally involved through prior consultation. They make every effort to communicate to management the demands of those workers being transferred and to have management take them into account. The selection criterion is another matter on which the unions have a say. Ultimately though, the unions do not oppose the reduction of staffing levels, including transfers, and the plans proposed by management are implemented in all cases. 'The union did not oppose any reduction to the staffing level in principle itself, but put forward proposals which would make production easier' (Nitta 1981: p. 222). 'There are no opinions against the proposal of curtailment of staffing level itself' (Ishida 1986: p. 167) and 'the union approves in principle any proposals that are admittedly necessary to restructure the firm' (Yamamoto 1983: p. 296). This is also the case with transfers. While working conditions are secured at least at the same level as before, 'the union considers the transfer absolutely necessary' (Nitta 1981: p. 172), and 'From the beginning the union is agreeable to the proposal of flexible transfer' (Ishida 1989: p. 24). 'It was difficult for the union to oppose the transfer of excess workers to high temperature workshops' (for example furnaces) (Yamamoto 1983: p. 295).

There are other case studies in the textile industry (Suwa and Sato 1980) and the newspaper industry (Kuwahara 1983), where similar features and practices can be found.

To summarise, unions make a committed and vital contribution to the question of temporary and permanent staffing levels as far as the case studies are concerned. In many cases the unions are involved in determining the selection criterion but selection itself is left to the supervisors. Unions with less influence can also be found in a few case studies, as is indicated in Table 12.3. Even when unions have an active say, they do not oppose the practice of transfer and reduction of staffing levels. Rather, they recognise the necessity and try to mitigate the effects as much as possible. Conversely, management willingly accepts union involvement in order to secure flexibility of transfer and staffing levels. To this end, the union's cooperation is required.

JOB-CENTRED INDIVIDUAL PARTICIPATION

Job-centred individual participation means here that 'without monetary incentives or compulsion by managers individual workers or voluntary groups of them consciously pursue improved work performance and quality, better working methods, adequate equipment and measures for safety and sanitation, and elimination of defects, in order to obtain intrinsic job satisfaction' (Ujihara 1979: p. 184). This type of participation is found in quality circles. Juran (1967), who attended a national convention of quality circles in Japan in 1966, noted with surprise that they reflected a radically different perspective from the Tayloristic principle. Quality circles are problem-solving groups formed by workers to discuss ways in which work methods, product quality, equipment, and so on, can be improved. They arose from a proposal by JUSE (Japanese Union of Scientists and Engineers) at the beginning of the 1960s (Ishikawa 1984, Kogure 1988) and spread rapidly, especially after the oil crisis (Takezawa 1978, 1979, NIEVR 1986).

According to the Ministry of Labour (1994), 69.6 per cent of the establishments of the firms with 5,000 workers or more have small group activities including quality circles, and the equivalent figure for establishments of firms with 1,000 workers or more and less than 5,000 is 60.8 per cent. The Ministry also surveys the workers' response to these small group activities. In firms with 5,000 workers or more which have small group activities, 86.4 per cent participate in them frequently or sometimes. The equivalent figure for firms with 1,000 workers or more and less than 5,000, is 89.8 per cent. As shown in Table 12.4, while some workers evaluate small group activities in a positive way, others regard them rather

Table 12.4 Workers' views on small group activities (multiple answers)
(per cent of workers)

Types of response	Size of firm	
	5,000–	*1,000–4,999*
They brighten the atmosphere of the workplace	38.0	47.5
They make daily operations easier	48.6	51.9
They improve worker's ability	31.2	42.6
They make the work worthwhile	16.9	20.5
They are not voluntary but compulsory, which makes me depressed	31.4	35.3
They are carried out after work which is burdensome	22.5	12.7
The reward for the performance is not enough	3.2	24.4
Proposals are seldom picked up	6.1	13.3
Others	5.7	3.7

Source: Ministry of Labour (1994)

negatively. It is worth noting here that although there is a variety of responses to small group activities within the firms the majority accept them positively.

Quality circles are a form of employee participation. Workers meet formally at regular intervals to discuss and suggest possible improvements to their working methods, etc. Today, in many workplaces workers assume greater responsibility for production control. Koike and Inoki (1987), based on detailed case studies in cement, food and chemical, beer brewing, battery manufacturing and machinery industries, illustrate that workers are carrying out 'unusual operations' in dealing with changes and abnormalities. Changes include the introduction of new products, new product mixes, shifts in production methods and production runs, and changes in the composition of the workforce. Being able to deal with these changes successfully is now an essential skill. Abnormalities include product defects, and to deal with this workers require additional skills to help identify them, to diagnose causes, and to carry out the necessary corrective action. Koike *et al.* (1987) find similar practices in a large automobile components plant and a large industrial machinery plant.

In a detailed case study of a first-tier component manufacturer in the automobile industry, Nakamura and Hashimoto (1992) find that experienced workers participate in process design with production engineers off line, and that they undertake quality control and progress control tasks while production is running smoothly. They collect data on product quality, diagnose causes quickly when irregularities are found and take corrective action. They also carefully check both the production plan and the production flow to decide which parts should be put into line next. Nakamura *et al.* (1994) study work organisation in a final assembly line of VCRs in a huge electric firm and discover the same pattern. Moreover, it illustrates that workers are trained to be able to undertake such production control tasks through structured career development and off-the-job training.

The fact that workers in large firms usually are engaged in production control tasks indicates that they enjoy job-centred participation at the workshop level. There are some critical views against these findings (see for example Berggren 1992, Dohse *et al.* 1985), but the above-mentioned studies are based on close observation which took account of workers' career development and seem to have discerned practices at the workshop level accurately.

WORKER PARTICIPATION AS A SYSTEM

At each level of the three tiers, Japanese workers participate in management in large firms and exercise substantial influence through their unions or individually. However, as is pointed out repeatedly, even in large firms some workers do not or cannot enjoy worker participation. In the following some theoretical explanations are developed in order to understand the system of worker participation in Japan, and the logic underlying the system.

To begin with, the 'white-collarised union model' (Koike 1983) is examined. Based on observation at the shop-floor level, and also on the 'exit or voice model' (Hirschman 1970), Koike (1983) develops his hypothesis as follows.

Those workers who now carry out 'unusual operations' possess 'intellectual skills', which have been acquired systematically through on-the-job and off-the-job training. Their skills can be referred to as 'high and late ceiling type' and are much more firm-specific than in other internal labour market settings. In this sense blue-collar workers in large Japanese firms have become white-collarised. Job rotation and job allocation within the workplaces which is determined by supervisors is important in terms of the formation of such intellectual skills. It does not mean, however, that they implement job rotation and transfer within the workplace in an arbitrary way. Rather, they give careful consideration to the expectations of their group members (see also Koike 1977). This is partly because supervisors are promoted from within the rank and file and therefore most likely to represent the worker's views. Job rotation and transfer within the workplace is carried out as part of custom and practice.

Beyond the workplace, however, supervisors do not have much say. But workers with more firm-specific intellectual skills naturally wish to have an active say in their employment status. Dismissals, promotions and transfers outside their normal workplaces are areas where workers want to have a voice, because they affect their careers and thus their compensation greatly. These are issues for which unions traditionally assume responsibility and it is for this reason that unions actively participate in the issue of staffing levels, both temporary and permanent, at a functional level.

Moreover, in a more deeply internalised labour market setting, exit costs workers too much and in order to avoid it, it becomes essential for them to have a say in management decisions. Because their careers are firmly built in the firm, whether it prospers or declines strongly affects their employment status. At the same time, workers with intellectual skills are sufficiently capable of exercising voice in management decisions. The result is union participation in strategic decision making at a top-tier level.

'White-collarised union' results in union participation in management at a functional as well as top-tier level. Because white-collarisation involves job-centred participation at a workplace level, it then leads to participation at the other two levels, according to this hypothesis. Unions have, however, alternatives other than participation in strategic decision making, even under a deeper internalised labour market setting. It is not for all of the workers, but for those who have acquired firm-specific intellectual skills with long length of service, that exit choice costs too much. They may be given employment security contingent on an agreement on layoff based on 'seniority rule'. The 'white-collarised union' model does not explain why Japanese enterprise unions do not take this alternative. In order to explain their decision, 'lifetime employment strategy' (Nitta 1988) should be taken into account. According to Nitta, labour and management share the following 'lifetime employment strategy'. Both give top priority to employment security of all employees regardless of trade, age and length of service, as far as industrial relations issues are concerned. Even when a reduction in the workforce is unavoidable, firms dispatch and transfer workers to related or even non-related firms and resort to requests for voluntary retirement with additional severance pay as the last measure in order to avoid outright discharge. Unions employ a 'lifetime employment strategy' as its policy, and thus it is difficult for them to choose the alternative of layoff based on seniority. The result is union participation in strategic decision making to secure employment for its members.

The combination of the 'white-collarised union model' and 'lifetime employment strategy' seems to succeed theoretically in explaining worker participation at all tiers. But why does management accept the unions' demand for participation at the top tier?

In this respect, Nishiyama (1975, 1980) offers a unique but authoritative hypothesis. He raises the question: Who governs the large-sized limited companies in Japan and what is the basis of its governance? An empirical study of the structure of stockholders and creditors of listed companies concludes that there are no particular groups in any of the companies which are capable of exercising the controlling power to appoint or dismiss the chief executive officers. Based on his findings,

Nishiyama concludes that controlling power is basically held by chief executive officers in large-sized limited companies and that the basis of their power is status or possession rather than ownership. Chief executive officers are promoted from among the employees and appointed by former chief executive officers. They are free of any interference from creditors and stockholders when they run their firms smoothly. Their objective in managing a firm is its survival. The pursuit of profits is not their objective but the means of its growth and maintenance.

If one accepts the line of argument proposed by Nishiyama, union participation in strategic decision making is more likely to be accepted by management. Chief executive officers can listen to any groups when making strategic decisions, and it is not surprising that they choose to listen to the employees' organisation which they themselves formerly belonged to, if the employees should ask them to. Moreover, they share the same objectives. Both consider survival and growth of the firm as important, which increases the likelihood of chief executive officers accepting union participation at the strategic level.

Combining both the deeply internalised labour market model and changes in corporate governance structure in a sophisticated way, Aoki (1984, 1988) develops the 'cooperative games' theory, which also explains union participation at the top tier. In his model, executive officers act as arbitrators between investors and the employee group in deciding how to make and distribute the organisational quasi-rent which is produced from cooperative behaviour of stockholders and employee groups. The organisational quasi-rent is assumed to be distributed among dividend layout, wage increase and investment. What is important in Aoki's model is that how to make and distribute organisational quasi-rent is internally most efficiently decided at the same time by the actors. In other words, 'it is not internally efficient that only the pay level is co-determined by collective bargaining and that strategic management decisions are made unilaterally by share price-maximising management posterior to wage bargaining . . .' (Aoki 1988: p. 157). According to his model, union participation at the top tier is a natural result of pursuit of internal efficiency by the actors.

Aoki's cooperative games theory gives a theoretical answer as to why unions are eager to participate in strategic decision making and why management accepts their demands. As is pointed out repeatedly, however, there are some cases where unions either do not participate in strategic decision making or are not allowed to. It is unclear how Aoki's theory explains these cases.

These are the theoretical explanations for worker participation in management in large Japanese firms. Deeper internalisation of the labour market, lifetime employment strategy and changes in corporate governance structure are the keys to understanding worker participation as a system. They also explain why there is no serious difference between labour and management in their basic objectives as well as why both co-operate in running the internal labour market flexibly. These three keys do not automatically produce worker participation in management at the three levels, and there are some cases without worker participation at any level. This means worker participation in management depends as much on union leadership as it does on management attitude. In this sense, the prevalence of worker participation in management, especially at the strategic level, is a result of both labour and management's efforts to resolve the difficulties and develop mutual trust.

NOTES

1   Data on joint consultation committees is also available in the Survey on Labour–Management Communication which was carried out by the Ministry of Labour in 1972, 1977, 1984, 1989 and 1994. The survey was sent to establishments and considerably underestimates the extent of worker participation in strategic decision making in large firms. This is because large firms usually have several establishments other than the headquarters establishment, without responsibility for strategic business policies. The survey merely gives the number of establishments with worker participation in strategic decision making as a proportion of all establishments whether they have strategic responsibility or not. This is why the Japan Productivity Centre (1981) is used even though the information is not current.
2   The figures in Table 12.2 are percentages of those establishments where workers have varying degrees of influence towards business issues through joint consultation. It is the headquarters establishment that is responsible for basic business issues, and only at the headquarters would workers be able to voice their views on these issues. Since there is necessarily only one headquarters establishment per enterprise, the figures in the table, although at the establishment level, seem to approximate those at the enterprise level.

REFERENCES

Aoki, M. (1984) *Gendai no Kigyo (The Modern Firm)*, Tokyo: Iwanami Shoten.
—— (1988) *Information, Incentives and Bargaining in the Japanese Economy*, Cambridge: Cambridge University Press.
Berggren, C. (1992) *Alternatives to Lean Production*, New York: ILR Press.
Dohse, K., Juergens, U. and Malsh, T. (1985) 'From "Fordism" to "Toyotism"? the social organisation of the labour process in the Japanese automobile industry', *Politics and Society*, 14(2), pp. 115–46.
Hata, T. and Totsuka, H. (1985) 'Zen A jidosha rodo kumiai no shokuba katsudo hoshin' ('Union policy on shopfloor activity of a trade union'), *Shakai Kagaku Kenkyu*, 36(5), pp. 136–55.
Hirschman, A.O. (1970) *Exit, Voice and Loyalty: Responses to Decline in Firms, Organizations, and States*, Cambridge, MA: Harvard University Press.
Inagami, T. (1983) 'Pai no zodai to rodo kumiai no taio – jidosha A sha' ('Enlarging the pie and union's response: the case of an automobile firm'), in Japan Institute of Labour (ed.) *80 Nendai no Roshi Kankei (Industrial Relations in 1980s)*, Tokyo: Japan Institute of Labour.
—— (ed.) (1995) *Seijuku Shakai no naka no Kigyobetsu Kumiai (Enterprise-based Unions in a Mature Society)*, Tokyo: Japan Institute of Labour.

Inagami, T. and Kawakita, T. (ed.) (1988) *Yunion Aidentiti (Union Identity)*, Tokyo: Japan Institute of Labour.

Inagami, T., Kamiya, T. and Fukui, M. (1980) 'B sha (Tsushinki) no jirei kenkyu, (A case of B firm (communications equipment manufacturer)'), in Japan Institute of Labour and Institute of Vocational Research *Koyo Chosei no Jisshi ni saishite no Roshi Kyogi nado no Jittai ni kansuru Chosa* (*Research of Joint Consultation over Employment Adjustment*), Tokyo: Institute of Vocational Research.

Ishida, M. (1986) 'Nihon tekkogyo no roshi kankei – B seitetsusho no jirei chosa' ('Industrial relations in Japanese steel industry – a case study of B steel works'), *Shakai Kagaku Kenkyu*, 38(2), pp. 135–78.

—— (1989) 'Nihon tekkogyo no roshi kankei (2) – B seitetsusho no jirei chosa' ('Industrial relations in Japanese steel industry (2) – a case study of B steel works'), *Hyoron Shakai Kagaku*, no. 38, pp. 1–45.

Ishikawa, K. (1984) *Nihonteki Hinshitsu Kanri (Japanese Type Quality Control)*, 2nd edn, Tokyo: Nikkagiren Shuppansha.

Japan Productivity Centre (1981) *Shin Kankyo ka no Roshi Kyogisei (Joint Consultation Scheme under New Environment)*, Tokyo: Japan Productivity Centre.

—— (1990) *Roshi Kyogisei no Jujitsu wo Motomete – Kigyo, Sangyo, Chiiki no Genjo to Seika (Toward Enrichment of Joint Consultation Scheme – the Present Condition and the Result of Enterprise-Based, Industry-Wide, and Regional Joint Consultation Scheme)*, Tokyo: Japan Productivity Centre.

JTUC Research Institute for the Advancement of Living Standards (1991) *Kigyonai Koyo Shoshisaku no Keisei Katei ni okeru Roshi Kankei no Arikata ni kansuru Chosa Kenkyu Hokokusho (Research of Industrial Relations on the Formation of Employment Practices)*, Tokyo: JTUC Research Institute for the Advancement of Living Standards.

Juran, J.M. (1967) 'The QC circle phenomenon', *Industrial Quality Control*, 23(7), 329–336.

Kamii, Y. (1991) 'Furekishibiriti to rodo kumiai kisei – A sha wo chushinni' ('Flexibility and Union Regulation – Focusing on A Firm'), in Totsuka, H. and Hyodo, T. (eds) *Roshi Kankei no Tenkan to Sentaku – Nihon no Jidosha Sangyo (Transformation and Choice of Industrial Relations – A Case of Japanese Automobile Industry)*, Tokyo: Nihon Hyoronsha.

—— (1994) *Rodo Kumiai no Shokuba Kisei – Nihon Jidosha Sangyo no Jirei Kenkyu* (Union Regulation at Shopfloor Level – Case Study on Japanese Automobile Industry), Tokyo: Tokyo Daigaku Shuppankai.

Kamiya, T. (1983) 'Keiei kiki ni okeru roshi kankei no tenkan – katoki no shomondai' ('Transformation of industrial relations under business crisis – issues in the period of transition'), in Japan Institute of Labour (eds) *80 nendai no Roshi Kankei (Industrial Relations in 1980s)*, Tokyo: Japan Institute of Labour.

Kochan, T.A., Katz, H.C. and McKersie, R.B. (1986) *The Transformation of American Industrial Relations*, New York: Basic Books.

Kogure, M. (1988) *Nihon no TQC (TQC in Japan)*, Tokyo: Nikkagiren Shuppansha.

Koike, K. (1977) *Shokuba no Rodo Kumiai to Sanka – Roshi Kankei no Nichibei Hikaku' (Union at Shop-floor Level and Participation – International Comparison of Industrial Relations between Japan and U.S.A.)*, Tokyo: Toyo Keizai Shinposha.

—— (1983) 'Howaito karaka kumiai moderu' ('White collarized union model'), in Japan Institute of Labour (eds) *80 nendai no Roshi Kankei (Industrial Relations in 1980s)*, Tokyo: Japan Institute of Labour.

Koike, K. (1985) 'Denki sangyo A – howaito kara no zodai to keiei sanka' ('A case of a company in electric industry – an increase of white collar workers and participation in management'), in M. Sumiya (ed.) *Gijutsu Kakushin to Roshi Kankei (Technological Innovation and Industrial Relations)*, Tokyo: Japan Institute of Labour.

Koike, K. and Inoki, T. (eds) (1987) *Jinzai Keisei no Kokusai Hikaku – Nihon to Tonan Ajia (Skill Formation in Japan and Southeast Asia)*, Tokyo: Toyo Keizai Shinposha.

Koike, K., Muramatsu, K. and Yamamoto, I. (1976) 'Kojo no nakano ido to rodo kumiai' ('Transfer within the plants and union'), *Chosa to Shiryo*, no. 58.

Koike, K., Muramatsu, K. and Hisamoto, N. (1987) *Chiteki Jukuren no Keisei – Aichi ken no Kigyo (Formation of Intellectual Skills: in the Firms in Aichi Prefecture)*, Aichi: Aichiken Rodobu.

Koshiro, K. and Nagano, H. (1985) 'Jidosha sangyo – Jidosha meka to buhin meka no jirei' ('Automobile industry – cases of final assembler and parts manufacturers'), in Sumiya, M. (ed.) *Gijutsu Kakushin to Roshi Kankei (Technological Innovation and Industrial Relations)*, Tokyo: Japan Institute of Labour.

Koyama Y. (ed.) (1985) *Kyodai Kigyo Taisei to Rodosha – Toyota Seisan Hoshiki no Kenkyu (Gigantic Enterprise and Workers – Study of the Toyota Production System)*, Tokyo: Ochanomizu Shobo.

Kuwahara, Y. (1983) 'Shinbun sangyo' ('Newspaper industry'), in Japan Institute of Labour (ed.) *80 nendai no Roshi Kankei (Industrial Relations in 1980s)*, Tokyo: Japan Institute of Labour.

Ministry of Labour (1994) *Roshi Komyunikeihon Chosa (Survey on Labour Management Communication)*, Tokyo: Ministry of Labour.

Mitsuoka, H. (1985) 'Shokuba gorika to rodo kumiai' ('Rationalization at the shopfloor level and union'), *Komazawa Daigaku Keizaigaku Ronshu*, 17(1), pp. 1–52.

Nakamura, K. and Hashimoto, S. (1992) *Seisan Bungyo Kozo to Rodo Shijo no Kaisosei – Jidosha Sangyo Hen (Subcontracting System and Segmented Labour Market in Japanese Automobile Industry)*, Tokyo: Japan Institute of Labour.

Nakamura, K., Demes, H. and Nagano, H. (1994) *Sagyo Soshiki no Nichidoku Hikaku – VTR Seisan Shokuba no Jirei (1) (Work Organization in Japan and Germany – A Research Report of VCR Production (1))*, Tokyo: Deutsches Institut fuer Japan-studien.

NIEVR (National Institute of Employment and Vocational Research) (1986) *Nihon ni okeru Shoshudan Katsudo no Jittai to sono Tenkai Joken ni kansuru Kenkyu Hokokusho (Research of Small Group Activities and the Backgrounds of their Diffusion)*, Tokyo: NIEVR.

Nishiyama, T. (1975) *Gendai Kigyo no Shihai Kozo: Kabushiki Kaisha Seido no Hokai (Corporate Governance Structure of Modern Firms: the Collapse of the Limited Company System)*, Tokyo: Yuhikaku.

—— (1980) *Shihai Kozo Ron: Nihon Shihon Shugi no Hokai (Corporate Governance Structure: Collapse of Capitalism)*, Tokyo: Bunshindo.

Nitta, M. (1981) 'Tekkogyo ni okeru roshi kyogi no seido to jittai (1) (2)' ('The system and the practices of joint consultation in steel industry (1) (2)'), *Shakai Kagaku Kenkyu*, 32(5), pp. 151–225; 32(6), pp. 87–193.

—— (1985) 'Tekkogyo ni okeru rodo kumiai no keiei sanka – kojo kyushi wo meguru roshi kyogi no jirei bunseki' ('Union voice in strategic decision making – a case study of plant closing negotiation'), *Musashi Daigaku Ronshu*, 33(2)–(3).

—— (1988) 'Kozo henka to roshi kankei senryaku' ('Structural change and industrial relations strategy') *Nihon Rodo Kyokai Zasshi*, no. 342, pp. 50–9.

Sato, H. and Umezawa, T. (1982) *80 Nendai no Rodo Kumiai Katsudo ni kansuru Jittai Chosa* (*Survey on Trade Union Activities in the 1980s*), Tokyo: Japan Institute of Labour.

Shiraki, M. (1983) 'Kumiai no sanka eno shiko to shokuba – Kagaku C sha' ('Union's propensity for participation and the shopfloor – a case of C chemical firm'), in Japan Institute of Labour (ed.) *80 Nendai no Roshi Kankei* (*Industrial Relations in 1980s*), Tokyo: Japan Institute of Labour.

Suwa, Y. and Sato, H. (1980) 'A sha (seni) no jirei' ('A case of a textile firm'), in Japan Institute of Labour and Institute of Vocational Research *Koyo Chosei no Jisshi ni saishite no Roshi Kyogi nado no Jittai ni kansuru Chosa* (*Research of the Joint Consultation on the Employment Adjustment*), Tokyo: Institute of Vocational Research.

Takezawa, S. *et al.* (1978) 'Denki sangyo ni okeru rodo seikatsu no shitsuteki kaizen no doko' ('Developments in quality of working life in the electric machinery industry'), *Nihon Rodo Kyokai Zasshi*, no. 236, pp. 67–82.

—— (1979) 'Jidosha sangyo ni okeru rodo seikatsu no shitsuteki kaizen no doko' ('Developments in quality of working life in the automobile industry'), *Nihon Rodo Kyokai Zasshi*, no. 240, pp. 53–69.

Ujihara, S. (1979) 'Dantai kosho to roshi kyogi' ('Collective bargaining and joint consultation'), in M. Sumiya (ed.) *Gendai Nihon Rodo Mondai* (*Labour Problems in Contemporary Japan*), Tokyo: Tokyo Daigaku Shuppankai.

Yamamoto, I. (1983) 'Keiei sanka to rodo kumiai no hatsugen – chusho seitetsu B rodo kumiai' ('Participation in management and union voice – B enterprise-based union in a medium-sized steel firm'), in Japan Institute of Labour (ed.) *80 Nendai no Roshi Kankei* (*Industrial Relations in 1980s*), Tokyo: Japan Institute of Labour.

13 New unionism
Beyond enterprise unionism?

Hiroyuki Fujimura

INTRODUCTION

Trade unions in Japan have been losing power not only in society at large but also in firms for two main reasons. One is the decline in union density which is down to 24 per cent in 1995. The other main reason is the opposing alignment of the parties with which the unions are linked. The Social Democratic Party of Japan, supported by former Sohyo-affiliated unions, is a member of the ruling coalition, while the New Frontier Party, with which the former Domei-affiliated unions are associated, is a non-government party. This means that trade unions have difficulties in integrating their political efforts to secure legislative changes to improve socio-political systems.

As political problems are treated in Chapter 8, this chapter concentrates on the issues concerning the new union movement among enterprise unions in Japan. First, the conceptual framework for analysing 'new unionism' in Japan is discussed. As the decline in trade union density after the first oil shock in 1973 was a turning point for the Japanese trade union movement, special attention is paid to the pattern and the reasons for the decline. The chapter then turns to the nature of the new union movement, and in particular the Union Identity movement. Lastly, relative success of these union efforts to thwart union decline though such a movement will be evaluated.

CONCEPTUAL FRAMEWORK OF NEW UNIONISM IN JAPAN

After World War II, Japanese trade unions began organising at enterprises. When General MacArthur and the Labour Division of the Supreme Command of the Allied Powers (SCAP) started encouraging the organisation of trade unions as part of their policy to democratise Japanese society, Japanese workers formed their unions at their enterprises. Although some of the trade unions kept their craft-based or occupation-based forms, it seemed natural for Japanese employees at the time that all those working at a firm should be organised in one union regardless of their occupation.

Enterprise-based unions have been regarded as one of the basic pre-modern elements of Japanese society for a long time. Many Japanese scholars were eager to analyse the Japanese society by applying criteria developed in the West.[1] They took European society as a model which Japan should emulate, and criticised every custom and practice in Japan which did not coincide with that model. Enterprise unions came under such criticism. They maintained that trade unions should have been organised on the basis of industry or occupation, and that Japanese trade unions should be reorganised into industrial unions. Not even the excellent book, *British Factory – Japanese Factory* by Dore (1973) which argued that British industrial relations might converge towards the Japanese patterns, influenced their view that enterprise unions constitute a pre-modern element in Japanese society. They kept stubbornly to their opinion until a considerable number of western scholars started giving a high opinion of the Japanese economy in the 1980s.

In contrast to other developed countries, the Japanese economy succeeded in retaining its high performance level after the two oil shocks in the 1970s. Consequently, the investigation of reasons why the Japanese economy continued to grow relatively rapidly while maintaining low unemployment became an important research theme in the West. Some scholars pointed out the role of the government in the economy (Kim *et al.* 1995), and others emphasised the main bank system as the major reason for Japan's economic success (Aoki and Patrick 1994). Much attention was also paid to the stability of the industrial relations system (Dertouzos *et al.* 1989). In particular, it was observed that good communication was established between labour and management at the firm level through joint consultation committees. Consequently, it is easy for management to solve specific problems in the firm by consulting with unions because they are organised at the firm. Enterprise unions are willing to work together with management in order to solve problems. This in turn enables Japanese firms to improve their productivity and to gain competitiveness in the world markets.

Enterprise unions, however, exhibit several critical weaknesses. Twenty years ago, Shirai (1983) indicated that there were seven such weaknesses: (1) enterprise unions dispersed union resources for the overall labour movement because of their highly decentralised structure; (2) they impeded the possible development of a united labour movement; (3) they were unwilling to organise certain categories of workers, including the unemployed; (4) they lacked the will to make an effort to protect the interests of retired workers who had long been union members; (5) they suffered from administrative and financial inefficiencies; (6) they were susceptible to employer interference and pressure; and (7) they suffered from relatively weak bargaining power *vis-à-vis* employers, including the government. Japanese trade unions have been exercising considerable effort to overcome these weaknesses without changing their enterprise-based form. Thus far, they have not been successful in remedying all of their shortcomings. However, it is worth taking note of a movement which started in the late 1970s and which had opened a path to overcoming some of the problems of enterprise unions. That movement is known as the Union Identity (UI) movement.

The UI movement is characterised by the primary attention enterprise unions have paid to the inner issue of better communication between union leaders and union members. Unions then extended their activities to issues outside their organisation. In particular, their main interest has been in the area of organising non-regular employees in their firms and workers in subsidiary and subcontracting companies. They also started taking care of members' well-being outside their workplace. For example, unions prepared various programmes which enriched their members' private lives.

Katz (1993) indicates that collective bargaining is becoming more decentralised in some developed countries. Decentralisation of the labour movement in these countries would damage the position of trade unions because of the same sort of problems which are faced by Japanese enterprise unions. Some Japanese unions have been conducting the UI movement in order to overcome some of the weaknesses of the decentralised union structure. The UI movement may be regarded as the beginning of new unionism in Japan. Before the UI movement, most enterprise unions used their financial and human resources to improve the working conditions of their members only. But the UI movement changed this way of thinking. Union leaders now consider it important to look after unorganised workers in order to sustain the trade union movement in Japan. The philosophy behind new unionism in Japan is that enterprise unions should try to improve the working conditions of all workers by retaining the enterprise-based structure and by extending their activities outside their members.

The decline in union density after the first oil shock and the apathy of union members forced Japanese enterprise unions to change their way of managing their organisation. The following section begins by analysing the patterns of, and reasons for, union decline.

TRADE UNION DENSITY

Union density decline

Table 13.1 shows the change of union density after World War II. The fifty years since 1945 can be divided into four periods. The first period, from 1945 to 1949, is characterised by a burst of trade-union organising activity. In 1949 the union participation rate reached its historical peak of 56 per cent. As already mentioned, General MacArthur and the labour division of the Supreme Command of the Allied Powers (SCAP)

Table 13.1 Union membership and participation rate

Year	Membership (in 1,000s)	Organisation rate (%)	Year	Membership (in 1,000s)	Organisation rate (%)
1945	381	3.2	1970	11,605	35.4
1946	4,926	41.5	1971	11,798	34.8
1947	5,692	45.3	1972	11,889	34.3
1948	6,677	53.0	1973	12,098	33.1
1949	6,655	55.8	1974	12,462	33.9
1950	5,774	46.2	1975	12,590	34.4
1951	5,687	42.6	1976	12,509	33.7
1952	5,720	40.3	1977	12,437	33.2
1953	5,927	36.3	1978	12,383	32.6
1954	6,076	35.5	1979	12,309	31.6
1955	6,286	35.6	1980	12,369	30.8
1956	6,463	33.5	1981	12,471	30.8
1957	6,763	33.6	1982	12,526	30.5
1958	6,984	32.7	1983	12,520	29.7
1959	7,211	32.1	1984	12,464	29.1
1960	7,662	32.2	1985	12,418	28.9
1961	8,360	34.5	1986	12,343	28.2
1962	8,971	34.7	1987	12,272	27.6
1963	9,357	34.7	1988	12,227	26.8
1964	9,800	35.0	1989	12,227	25.9
1965	10,147	34.8	1990	12,265	25.2
1966	10,404	34.2	1991	12,397	24.5
1967	10,566	34.1	1992	12,541	24.4
1968	10,863	34.4	1993	12,663	24.2
1969	11,249	35.2	1994	12,699	24.1
			1995	12,614	23.8

Sources: Ministry of Labour (various years), Management and Co-ordination Agency (various years)

encouraged the organisation of trade unions as part of the democratisation of Japanese society. SCAP policy towards the unions became more restrictive, however, because of the Cold War. This was the starting point of the second period. From 1950 to 1960, the union participation rate decreased by 24 points to 32 per cent in 1959.

The third period is one of remarkably stable union participation. Between 1961 and 1975 the union organisation rate remained around 34 per cent. In this period the highest ratio was 35.4 per cent in 1970, and the lowest was 33.1 per cent in 1973. This period coincided with a high economic growth era in Japan.

In 1976 the fourth period started, being the second period of decline. After the first oil shock the Japanese economy fell into a deep recession, and the union participation rate started to go down. The decline continued until, today, less than one in four employees participates in a trade union. What is it about the oil shock which is responsible for the decline?

Reasons for union density decline

Structural shifts in the composition of employment

Metcalf (1989) identifies five 'ingredients', the interaction of which is the key to the decline in union membership and density: (1) macro-economic factors, (2) the composition of employment, (3) government legislation, (4) employer responses in the form of union recognition and derecognition, and (5) union behaviour. When the fall in union density was noticed as a serious problem, researchers first concentrated on the second factor, that is the structural change of employment. They argued that the proportion of employees in tertiary industry was growing, and since employees in that sector generally had a lower propensity to unionise, union density was bound to fall. Other changes in employment composition were also pointed out, such as shifts towards white-collar jobs and higher proportions of female and part-time workers. An increase of new 'titular' and 'specialist' posts was considered too, because these posts often had managerial titles that led workers to resign from their union, as Japanese law prohibits membership of individuals who 'represent the interest of the employer'.

The structural changes of employment are not enough to explain the density decline because in some industrialised countries, such as Sweden and Germany, trade unions succeeded in raising the union participation rate, even though proportions in tertiary industry became larger. Ito and Takeda (1990) estimated the contribution of changes of industrial structure to the union density decline. Their estimation shows that the structural changes could explain 24 per cent of the density decline between 1975 and 1979, 31 per cent between 1979 and 1982, and 28 per cent between 1982 and 1989. They concluded that structural changes were not the dominant explanation of the decrease of union participation rate, and changes within industries had to be examined.[2]

Changes within industry

Table 13.2 shows union density changes by industry from 1970 to 1994. We can divide these industries into two groups; one where density is declining, and the other where it is stable. The former group consists of manufacturing, finance and insurance, transport and communication, services and government. Construction and wholesale and retail trade industries belong to the stable group.

The year in which density begins to fall differs from one industry to another. In manufacturing and government it was 1978, after the first oil shock. Finance and insurance, transport and communication and service industries, on the other hand, only began losing their union density after the second oil shock in 1979. The first oil shock hit the manufacturing industry and prompted a reduction in the proportion of regular employees

Table 13.2 Union density by industry (per cent)

Year	Construc-tion	Manufac-turing	Whole-sale and retail trade	Finance and insurance	Trans-port and commun-ication	Services	Govern-ment
1970	24.9	38.7	8.5	68.3	65.0	23.9	71.4
1971	20.6	38.6	9.5	61.7	64.2	23.6	73.3
1972	18.7	38.6	10.0	61.0	66.5	22.5	69.2
1973	18.5	37.5	9.3	57.2	63.2	22.6	75.9
1974	19.4	39.0	9.8	58.0	65.6	22.9	69.3
1975	18.3	41.1	10.1	59.7	65.3	23.4	68.6
1976	18.3	39.5	9.6	59.3	63.7	22.4	79.9
1977	17.2	39.1	9.2	60.5	65.3	22.5	82.8
1978	16.9	37.6	9.5	63.3	64.4	22.5	74.2
1979	16.8	36.0	9.6	60.8	61.0	21.5	73.1
1980	16.5	35.3	9.4	56.1	62.3	21.0	74.6
1981	17.2	34.9	9.5	54.4	65.5	21.0	75.8
1982	18.2	35.5	9.7	51.6	61.8	20.3	73.8
1983	18.6	35.8	9.5	49.5	59.6	18.8	73.8
1984	19.6	34.4	9.3	48.5	59.9	18.0	78.4
1985	19.7	33.7	9.3	49.3	57.9	18.2	76.4
1986	17.9	34.0	8.9	49.5	56.8	17.6	75.2
1987	18.2	34.2	8.8	49.7	56.5	16.7	72.4
1988	17.4	32.6	8.8	50.0	57.4	16.3	71.9
1989	17.5	30.9	9.0	49.9	50.1	15.5	76.9
1990	17.1	30.1	9.0	49.7	48.3	14.8	74.9
1991	17.3	29.9	8.8	47.6	56.1	14.1	72.6
1992	18.1	29.6	9.0	48.8	46.7	13.7	72.1
1993	19.4	29.9	10.2	48.4	43.8	14.9	62.9
1994	18.9	29.8	10.3	47.2	44.6	14.7	62.5

Sources: Ministry of Labour (various years), Management and Co-ordination Agency (various years)

in order to recover market competitiveness. It also hit government revenue, resulting in a huge deficit which led the Government to pursue a policy of reducing public sector employees. The other three industries in the declining group maintained relatively good performances just after the first oil shock, but they were forced to change their employment policy in the recession which followed the second oil shock.

Construction and wholesale and retail trade show relatively stable participation rates. Wholesale and retail trade industry has a high proportion of female and part-time workers, and this proportion has been getting higher. It is true that the level of its union density is low at around 9 per cent, but the stability of the participation rate is worthy of notice. It is partly due to the efforts of Zensen Domei (the Japanese Federation of Textile, Garment, Chemical, Commercial, Food and Allied Industries Workers' Union) to organise chainstore workers. As Freeman and Rebick

(1989) indicate, in the 1970s and 1980s Zensen structured its union leadership to concentrate on organising drives and succeeded in increasing membership despite declining textile employment.

In construction, Zenken Soren (the Japanese Federation of Construction Workers' Union), the biggest craft union in Japan, with a membership of 678,000 in 1995, showed great effectiveness in organising construction workers, especially carpenters and plasterers. Zenken Soren consists of affiliated unions which are usually organised at the prefectural level, and about one-third of the members are self-employed. As Zenken Soren offers an insurance scheme for medical care, both employees and the self-employed are organised in the same union. This practice is very effective in maintaining membership and seems to contribute to the stable union density in construction.

Union density by firm size

Changes of union density by firm size can also give clues to the reasons for the union participation decline. Table 13.3 shows changes in union density by firm size during ten years. We can observe that the union organisation rates fell in each firm size. Large firms still have a high union density, but the proportion of organised workers is decreasing year by year. It is the medium-sized firm that experienced the steepest decline of density from 1985 to 1994 of 6.7 points. The proportion of unionised employees in small firms was very low to start with, but the 0.8 point decline – from 2.5 per cent in 1985 to 1.7 per cent in 1994 – is significant given that 49 per cent of all workers are in these small firms.

Table 13.4 shows the elasticity of union membership to total employees by firm size. Between 1975 and 1980, large firms with 1,000 or more employees had the most serious problem of losing members. Though the number of employees increased by 0.4 per cent, membership decreased by 6.9 per cent, which resulted in an elasticity of –17.83. While large firms recovered their membership between 1980 and 1985, after 1985 the number of employees increased more rapidly than union members in part due to the proliferation of management posts in large firms. The medium-sized firms enjoyed the highest growth rate of employees, though the number of union members did not increase with the same speed. On the contrary, one per cent of employee growth was followed by only less than 0.1 per cent increase in union membership. Small firms show a drastic decline of union membership. Except for the period of 1975–1980, their union membership was decreasing quickly.

Failure to organise new establishments

Structural shifts in employment can explain only a part of union density decline. Neither an increasing proportion of female and part-time workers

Table 13.3   Union density by firm size (per cent)

Year	Total	Firm size (number of employees)		
		1–99	*100–999*	*Over 1,000*
1985	24.4	2.5	28.3	64.5
1986	23.9	2.4	27.3	65.6
1987	24.0	2.3	27.4	68.0
1988	23.5	2.2	26.8	66.1
1989	22.5	2.1	25.7	62.0
1990	21.9	2.0	24.0	61.0
1991	21.4	1.8	23.3	58.7
1992	21.8	1.8	22.5	57.2
1993	21.3	1.8	22.0	58.2
1994	21.2	1.7	21.6	59.8

Sources: Ministry of Labour (various years), Management and Co-ordination Agency (various years)

Table 13.4   Elasticity of union membership by firm size

Period	30–99			100–999		
	Change in no. of employees (%)	*Change in union membership (%)*	*Elasticity*	*Change in no. of employees (%)*	*Change in union membership (%)*	*Elasticity*
1975–80	20.2	2.3	0.11	12.1	0.2	0.02
1980–85	7.3	–2.8	–0.38	16.2	2.2	0.14
1985–90	14.2	–8.0	–0.56	19.9	1.4	0.07
1990–94	7.5	7.0	–0.93	12.3	1.1	0.09

Period	1,000 and over			Total		
	Change in no. of employees (%)	*Change in union membership (%)*	*Elasticity*	*Change in no. of employees (%)*	*Change in union membership (%)*	*Elasticity*
1975–80	0.4	–6.9	–17.83	11.2	–3.4	–0.32
1980–85	9.1	9.6	1.05	8.0	6.8	0.86
1985–90	11.6	5.6	0.49	15.0	3.2	0.21
1990–94	8.0	5.7	0.72	8.6	5.0	0.58

Sources: Ministry of Labour (various years), Management and Co-ordination Agency (various years)

Notes: The figures of 1975–80 and 1980–85 are cited from Ito and Takeda (1990). Other figures are calculated by the author.

nor proliferation of management posts are dominant reasons for the fall of the union participation rate. It has also been verified that union density was going down both in most of the industries and in each size of firms. A different explanation must be discussed.

Freeman and Rebick (1989) conclude that failure to organise workers in newly established firms is the most important reason for the decline.[3] Tsuru and Rebitzer (1995) are of the same opinion as Freemen and Rebick concerning the importance of organising workers in new firms.[4] So why have Japanese trade unions failed to create unions in newly established firms? There are three factors involved; employers' opposition, employees' interest, and union behaviour.

Employers' opposition

It is nominally easy for employees in Japan to establish a trade union. Japanese labour law requires neither majority support for certification nor the recognition of exclusive bargaining rights with a duty to offer fair representation to all. In theory unions can be established irrespective of management, but in practice management has an important role in union formation. When some active employees have reached consensus and decided to establish a union, union organisers, usually sent by the industry-level federation of enterprise unions, visit managers to explain the advantages of having a union, such as obtaining more information about working conditions in other firms, the possibility of finding new business partners, and so on. It is important that they convince managers, because many employees do not want to join unions which the employer opposes.

Many employers have a negative image of a union. One employer said to a union organiser that he did not want employees to establish a *kumiai* (trade union), but he wouldn't mind if they organised a *yunion*. *Kumiai*, for him, suggests the traditional left-wing union, always against management policy, and always a problem to management. Union organisers first have to remove such misunderstandings of trade unions. Once employers understand the meaning and importance of unions, most of them become supportive, and organisers can conduct their activity easily.

As Tsuru and Rebitzer (1995) indicate, employers' opposition to organising a union is not such a serious problem in Japan. But there are many small and medium-sized firms which have employee representative bodies, with functions very similar to those of unions', which employers are reluctant to see transformed into registered unions. And, incidentally, if we count these as quasi-unions, the union participation rate would be much higher. This phenomena is discussed in Chapter 14.

Failure to attract non-union workers

Non-unionised workers may want to establish or join trade unions if they could expect to improve their conditions. Tsuru and Rebitzer (1995) analyse their survey data on the sources of interest in unions.[5] The lack of interest can be explained by the attitudes of members of existing unions, which are frequently ambivalent. The majority of firms have a union shop agreement. Union membership within some period of time after being hired is compulsory and automatic. Even if members think they get very little benefit from their unions, and want to quit in order to save membership fees, they are not allowed to do so. Many union members lose their interest in unions, and look on the membership fees they pay every month as something like a tax. This raises the question of the inherent character of enterprise unionism.

Some of the enterprise union leaders were deeply aware of the apathy of union members and took the situation very seriously. In their view, without reform of union activities, enterprise unions would totally lose their influence over industrial relations. The Union Identity movement started as a way of recovering the attractiveness of unions to their members.

UNION IDENTITY MOVEMENT

What is UI?

The Union Identity (UI) movement started in the late 1970s, when the trade union density in Japan began declining after the first oil shock. Even though the majority of enterprise unions had union shop provisions, the deep recession forced management to reduce employment. At that moment, trade union leaders recognised two crises of the union movement: first, the decline in union density would decrease the influence of trade unions in society, and second, existing union members were becoming sceptical about the value of trade unions. Although the former crisis was as serious as the latter, leaders of enterprise unions mainly tried to solve the second problem. The first problem was to be dealt with at higher levels of the union organisation.

Until the first half of the 1970s, people believed that Japanese workers, especially in large firms, secure in the lifetime employment system, would be rarely dismissed until retirement age. But the first oil shock and the following recession revealed that even a large company could not but dismiss its employees in order to survive. Union members expected that the trade union should have protected their employment, but they were made to realise that the union could only negotiate conditions for voluntary retirement schemes. Besides, union members, especially younger members, lost interest in union activities. Attendance at union meetings dropped off. Recognition of these problems was the starting point of the Union Identity movement.

Background of the UI movement

Three changes around unions

After the first oil shock, three major changes became conspicuous in Japanese firms. The first concerned management strategy. During the high economic growth era, most Japanese companies took expansion of product markets as a matter of course. In 1960s and the first half of 1970s, the more they offered products to the market, the more people bought them. However, the first oil shock forced the Japanese people to recognise the fact that growth always comes to an end. The slow down of market growth was accompanied by the diversification of consumer preference. Such economic pressures and more flexible technologies led firms to restructure the workplace. Management came to rely more on part-time workers, and tried to keep the number of regular employees as small as possible. Large firms, which had subsidiary companies and subcontractors, started group-wide personnel management in order to be able to shuttle employees around rather than dismissing them.

The second change was an increase in the proportion of white-collar workers, who were usually highly educated people. Until the middle of the 1970s, it was not so difficult for union leaders to bring the requests of their members together. Almost everybody was interested in wage increases and better working conditions. But white-collar union members were not satisfied only with improvement of working conditions. They required unions to have a voice in personnel management policies, such as transfer from one section to another, performance evaluation, job assignment, and so on. This change meant that union leaders had difficulty treating all members alike. They had to deal with a much wider variety of members' needs.

The third change was the maturing of industrial relations at the enterprise level. After big labour struggles in the 1950s and the first half of the 1960s, management and trade unions tried to develop good relations. Instead of collective bargaining, they developed joint consultation systems, which enabled management and unions to discuss even delicate problems. They gained in mutual confidence, and began sharing confidential management information. In some companies the chairman of the trade union is informed of top secret data which only a few top managers can access. Since such information is confidential, union leaders cannot explain to their members the process of negotiation with management in detail. The rank and file have little idea of what their leaders succeeded in gaining from management, and what they lost. The negotiation process is unclear, so that union members come to distrust their leaders and lose interest in union activities.

Some evidence of declining members' interest

There are several investigations of union members' perceptions of union activities on the firm level. Sato and Fujimura (1991) report on the kind of problems identified by union leaders at the plant level. They partici- pated in a questionnaire survey conducted by Gendai Soken (the Research Group of Modern Society, financed by industrial federations of enterprise unions) in 1990. They mailed questionnaires to 2,391 unions at the plant level, and obtained responses from 1,150. Table 13.5 summarises answers to the question, 'Does your union have any of the following problems?' Respondents were asked to choose all the problems which apply out of 17 statements which were listed in the question. This table shows the top ten items.

The most serious problem is to recruit both full-time and to a lesser extent part-time union officers. Today the social status of union officers in Japan is not as high as it was until the 1970s when trade unions offered one form of promotion in firms for those who did not have occasion to finish higher education. If a person was talented and good at leadership, he could become a union leader regardless of educational background, and come to participate in the decision-making process in the firm through collective bargaining and joint consultation. An ambitious production worker could expect to reach higher status through the trade union move- ment. It is still true that any union member has the opportunity of becoming chairman of the union, but most members do not consider it a good form of promotion.

The second biggest problem is that more and more union members show little interest in union activities. This is mainly because their inter- ests are diversifying and union leaders cannot cater for them. When trade unions organise events like concerts which are far from members' inter- ests, participation falls off. Requirements of members are diversified by generation and section, so that it is really hard for union leaders to organise activities which satisfy all of the members.

As Sato and Fujimura (1991) indicate, most unions take these problems seriously and many of them have started trying to find remedies. Fifty- four per cent of unions claimed to have taken counter-action, and 18 per cent said they were preparing to do so. Only 2 per cent of unions see no need to take action. Awareness of increasing apathy as a problem is the starting point for recovering trade union power within the firm.

Programmes and results of the UI movement

Four programmes of UI

The activity characterised as the Union Identity Movement falls under four heads: renewal of trade union symbols; total welfare policy; active participation in the firm's decision-making process; and organising non-regular employees. Renewal of trade union symbols involves, for example, (a) change of union name (for example, XYZ Adventure Club), (b) change of union flag design and colour (for example not using red, but blue), (c) new logos, (d) using plain words instead of traditional, difficult ones, and (d) redesign of union newspaper (for example using more illustrations and photos).

Table 13.6 shows the high percentage of unions which have renewed union symbols. These data were collected through a questionnaire survey by a research team led by Professor Inagami. In 1993 this team mailed questionnaires to the secretaries of 2,415 enterprise unions; 1,050 unions returned questionnaires, giving a 47 per cent response rate. Nearly half of the unions replying belonged to the manufacturing industry and three quarters were in firms with more than 1,000 employees.

The most popular activity was the redesign of the union newspaper, an important tool for communication between union leaders and members.

Table 13.5   Problems faced by trade unions (multiple responses allowed) (per cent)

Hard to recruit full-time union officers	79.2
Increasing apathy of members	78.0
Increasing diversity of members' requests	62.8
Decreasing participation in union events	50.7
Hard to find part-time officers	48.3
Increasing difference in the interests of older and younger workers	43.0
Decreasing number of participants in shop-floor meetings	40.3
Increasing difference in the interests of different workshops	24.3
Decreasing membership because of increase of non-regular employees	21.8
Hard to unify members' opinion because of diversified business operation	15.9

Source: Sato and Fujimura (1991)

Table 13.6   Renewal of union symbols (per cent)

		When did you make changes?	
	Yes	*Within the last 10 years*	*Within the last 2–3 years*
Changing union name	25.1	14.4	72.0
Changing design of union flag and colour	39.0	17.4	76.8
New logo	36.9	21.4	66.9
Using plain words instead of traditional ones	29.0	12.2	84.5
Redesign of union newspaper	83.1	17.2	74.2

Source: Inagami (1995)

Until the beginning of the UI movement most union newspapers were unattractive; all text, no illustrations and photos, and rarely read even though they contained useful information. With a more attractive layout and many illustrations and photos, union papers are now very appealing, and more frequently read.

Table 13.6 also indicates when unions made these reforms. One remarkable point is that about three-quarters of unions undertook such reforms very recently, although some started at the end of the 1970s and the beginning of the 1980s.

The second programme of UI movement is the so-called 'total welfare policy'. Before the beginning of UI, most trade unions concentrated on improving conditions within firms. They concentrated on getting more wages, shorter working hours and a better working environment. It is true that trade unions sometimes organised events in which members' families were welcome to participate, but they did not have clear policies for members' lifestyle outside the firm. In the UI movement union leaders have recognised the importance of developing such activities. As one union's slogan puts it: 'We take care of members and their families 24 hours a day'. Many unions have developed these total welfare programmes, and offer various kinds of programmes.

One of the most popular programmes is a Life Plan Seminar for middle-aged members. The seminar provides members with a good opportunity to make plans for their future lives, especially after retirement. Many Japanese business people have a serious problem after they retire, especially evident in losing orientation in life. Before retirement, they always had a lot of things to do, both in their workplaces and with their families. After retirement, however, they have all the time to themselves. The problem is that they do not know how to spend their time, first, because they did nothing but work before retirement, and second, because their children are already grown up and do not need to be taken care of by their parents. Participants in the seminar are invited to think about what they would do after retirement, and how they would use their time. Although this problem may be unfamiliar to westerners, Japanese union members are very grateful that their unions organise this seminar.

Beside the seminar, trade unions also provide, if needed, legal consultation and services for their members. For example, in case of inheriting their parents' fortune, a member can ask a lawyer to solve legal problems. It is not usual in Japan for anyone to have daily contact with a lawyer. As trade unions usually have contacts with lawyers, union leaders can introduce a lawyer to those members in need of legal advice. If union members would see their unions as the last resort for solving private problems, those unions would succeed in recovering their attractiveness to their members.

The third objective is to participate more actively in the firm's decision-making processes. Cooperation with management is necessary in order to realise the total welfare programmes, because work is still an important part of members' life. In the Inagami survey, 56.5 per cent of unions acknowledged that they had a say in management policies. In order to make a timely participation in decision making, it is necessary for union leaders to gather information concerning management. The Inagami survey also reports that 64.0 per cent of unions have informal regular meetings with management, and that 57.7 per cent of unions obtain confidential information about management policy.

If management wants to introduce some new systems, it is common in Japan to form a joint consultation committee between management and labour to discuss the new system in detail before coming to an agreement. For example, when management plans to change the wage system, an offer is made to the union to form a joint committee which would clarify anticipated problems of the new system. Such a committee would consist of about ten persons, with equal numbers representing management and labour. Management cannot, and in fact generally does not, introduce the proposed new system unless the trade union representatives agree to it, because management is well aware that the union's cooperation is necessary to implement the new system. In this way, trade unions can influence the content of a proposed new system through discussion (see Chapter 12 for more details).

The fourth programme of the UI movement is to organise non-unionised employees. Trade unions usually limit their membership to regular, full-time employees. As long as management continues recruiting regular employees, union shop provisions guarantee their membership. After the first oil shock, however, management has been shifting employment to part-time workers who are mostly excluded from unions. Also, the proportion of managerial workers has been getting higher, and those who work in small subsidiaries within the group are not organised in any unions. Some trade unions started organising such workers in order to retain their influence over management.

According to the Inagami survey, 10.6 per cent of unions tried to organise part-time workers, and 12.1 per cent of unions started organising titular managers who did not represent the interest of the employer. In the 1996 Shunto (Spring Offensive), Denki Rengo (All Japan Federation of Electric Machine Workers' Union) requested its management to agree to their activity to organise middle managers, many of whom suffered from corporate restructuring during the recent recession. Management consented to the activity. Although the number of unions which have started expanding their organising activity is still small, it is nevertheless noteworthy that some enterprise unions look after the interests of non-union employees.

Results of the UI movement

It is hard to estimate at this moment whether the UI movement has succeeded or not; the movement is still in progress. But some results of

the questionnaire survey by the Inagami team indicate that the UI movement has not been able to stop the spread of apathy. Union leaders were
asked whether union members became more interested in union activities in the last ten years. Only 16 per cent said 'yes'; 37 per cent said that
members were less interested, and 47 per cent reported 'no change'. They
were also asked whether participation in events and meetings organised
by unions had increased. The answers were the same: 'yes' 13 per cent,
'no' 37 per cent, and 'no change' 49 per cent. The research team prepared
one more question, 'Do you think that in these ten years your union has
succeeded in stopping the decline in member interest? Thirteen per cent
of responses were positive, and 65 per cent were negative.

These figures seem to project a pessimistic future for the union movement in Japan. But it should be noted that one-seventh of the unions
acknowledge a positive direction in their activities. If Japanese enterprise
unions had not carried out the UI movement, the situation would have
been worse. But due to the short history of the UI movement, it is difficult to assess whether the experience and the practices of those enterprise
unions which are at the forefront of the UI movement would spread to
other unions.

THE FUTURE OF ENTERPRISE UNIONS IN JAPAN

The UI movement shows a possibility of remedying three out of the seven
weaknesses of enterprise unions which Shirai (1983) indicated twenty
years ago. Through the UI movement, some enterprise unions have started
organising both part-time employees in their firms and workers in
subsidiary companies, as well as retired workers who had been union
members for many years. These unions have also improved their administrative and financial structure, and the use of their resources is more
efficient than before. The other two and a half faults might be solved by
Rengo. Rengo has the potential to amass and mobilise resources of enterprise unions, and thus further develop the labour movement in Japan. In
theory, Rengo could also exercise its capacity to exert a strong influence
on government policy making. But thus far, due to political instability,
Rengo does not have such a strong position *vis-à-vis* the government. The
extent to which the UI movement and Rengo can really overcome the
weaknesses of enterprise unions is still unclear. But it should be noted
that some enterprise unions have been spreading their activities into new
areas such as organising non-regular workers, thus contributing to the
strengthening of the trade union movement in Japan.

One and a half of Shirai's seven weaknesses of enterprise unions remain
unsolved, however. They concern the weak voice of unions *vis-à-vis*
management. Shirai indicated that unions were susceptible to employer
interference and that their bargaining power was relatively weak. A decentralised trade union structure inevitably leads to a weakness in union

bargaining power. At first sight, it appears unrealistic to expect this problem to be solved without changes in the union structure. But in reality, some enterprise unions show a relatively strong position against management through their discussion in joint consultation committees. It is sometimes difficult for outside observers to evaluate in what ways trade unions have a say in changing management policy, because the discussion in consultation committees is kept confidential. However, interviews with union leaders conducted by the author show that some unions have a voice in decision making by checking to make sure that management policies are in the interest of the union members. In this way, advanced enterprise unions have been overcoming to some extent the problem of weak bargaining power inherent in the enterprise union structure.

This checking power of enterprise unions relates to a problem of corporate governance in Japanese companies. Unlike in US firms, neither shareholders nor outside directors have a strong voice in Japanese firms. The function of checking management policies was carried out by main banks until the late 1970s, but since the mid-1980s it has gradually become ineffective. Consequently, chief executive officers in Japanese companies have a very strong unchecked power to make decisions. The lack of a countervailing power poses a serious problem of corporate governance in the event of managerial misconduct. Enterprise unions might be the last resort for checking top management policy making. If enterprise unions succeed in playing this role of monitoring managerial decision making, they would bring about new unionism in Japanese society.

NOTES

1   There are a lot of books and articles in Japanese concerning this problem. A very well-known book in English by Chie Nakane (1970) belongs to this genre.
2   Freeman and Rebick (1989) estimated the influences of these changes on union density. Their conclusions are as follows: (a) less than a quarter of the 1975–86 decline in density is attributable to the changing sectoral mix, (b) at most 0.4 points of the within-industry decline is due to the growth of temporary employment, which lowered female union membership, and (c) perhaps 1.1 percentage points in the decline of male union density in existing unionised firms between 1981 and 1986 could be due to ageing and the proliferation of management posts. They demonstrated that the structural shifts could explain only a part of the density fall.
3   They simulate what would have happened to density from 1975 to 1985 if the rate of net depreciation had remained at its 1965–75 level while the rate of new organisation followed its historic path. Their estimation shows that 3.7 points out of the 5.7 1974–86 drop in union density are explained by failure to organise new workers, while the calculation for manufacturing indicates that all of the five point drop from 1974 to 1986 was due to the same determinant.
4   They use their own data obtained through an interview survey of 1,104 employees aged 18–59 who lived within 30 km of central Tokyo in 1992. They find that a man in a firm founded between 1970 and 1974 has a 14 percentage point lower probability of being a union member than a man in a firm founded

prior to 1970. They also estimate that women in a firm founded between 1970 and 1974 are only one or two percentage points more likely to be union members than their counterparts in older firms. Failure to organise workers in newly established firms has a greater influence on the union participation rate of male employees than that of female workers.

5 They indicate the following points:

(a) Male workers in the private sector support unions to the extent that they are dissatisfied with wages and benefits. This, in turn, implies that the failure of unions to win wage increases for their male members will significantly limit interest in unions among men.
(b) Unions have an important role in improving lines of communication between employees and management, but indirect evidence suggests that this is a benefit not much valued by Japanese workers, so that the weak union effect on wages and benefits has even more importance.
(c) The difficulties Japanese unions have in organising new establishments are more plausibly traced to a failure to interest workers in forming unions than to the determination of the employer to resist new unions.

REFERENCES

Aoki, Masahiko and Patrick, Hugh (1994) *The Japanese Main Bank System*, Oxford: Clarendon Press.
Chaison, G.N. (1990) 'A note on the severity of the decline in union organizing activity', *Industrial and Labour Relations Review*, 43(4), pp. 366–73.
Dertouzos, Michael L., Lester, Richard K. and Solow, Robert M. (eds) (1989) *Made in America*, Cambridge MA: MIT Press.
Disney, R. (1990) 'Explanation of the decline in trade union density in Britain: an appraisal', *British Journal of Industrial Relations*, 28(2), pp. 165–77.
Dore, R. (1973) *British Factory – Japanese Factory*, Berkeley: University of California Press.
Freeman, R.B. and Pelletiert, J. (1990) 'The impact of industrial relations legislation on British union density', *British Journal of Industrial Relations*, 28(2), pp. 141–64.
Freeman, R.B. and Rebick, M.E. (1989) 'Crumbling pillar? Declining union density in Japan', *Journal of the Japanese and International Economies*, 3(4), pp. 578–605.
Fujimura, H. (1993) 'Rodo kumiai josei yakuin no kokusai hikaku' ('An international comparison of women union officers'), in Shakai Seisaku Gakkai (ed.) *Gendai no Josei Rodo to Shakai Seisaku*, Tokyo: Ochanomizu Shobo.
Inagami, T. (ed.) (1995) *Seijuku Shakai no naka no Kigyobetsu Kumiai* (*Enterprise Unions in Matured Society*), Tokyo: Japan Institute of Labour.
Ito, M. and Takeda, Y. (1990) 'Rodo kumiai soshikiritsu no suii to sono henka yoin' ('Change in union participation rate and reasons for the change'), *Rodo Tokei Chosa Geppo*, 42(6), pp. 6–14.
Katz, H.C. (1993) 'The decentralization of collective bargaining: a literature review and comparative analysis'. *Industrial and Labour Relations Review*, 47(1), pp. 3–22.
Kim, Hyung-ki, Muramatsu, Michio, Pempel, T.J. and Yamamura, Kozo (eds) (1995) *The Japanese Civil Service and Economic Development: Catalysts of Change*, Oxford: Clarendon Press.
Kuruvilla, S., Gallagher, D.G., Fiorito, J., and Wakabayashi, M. (1990) 'Union participation in Japan: do western theories apply?', *Industrial and Labour Relations Review*, 43(4), pp. 374–89.

Management and Co-ordination Agency, Statistics Bureau (1995) *Rodoryoku Chosa Nenpo* (*Labour Force Survey*), Tokyo: Japan Statistical Association.

Metcalf, D. (1989) 'Employment subsidies and redundancies', in R. Blundell and I. Walker (eds) *Unemployment, Search and Labour Supply*, Cambridge: Cambridge University Press, pp. 103–20.

Ministry of Labour (1995) *Rodo Kumiai Kiso Chosa Hokoku* (*Basic Survey on Labour Unions*), Tokyo: Okurasho Insatsukyoku.

Nakane, Chie (1970) *The Japanese Society*, Berkeley: University of California Press.

Sato, H. and Fujimura, H. (1991) *Ekuserento Yunion* (*Excellent Unions*), Tokyo: Daiichi Shorin.

Shirai, Taishiro (1983) 'A theory of enterprise unionism', in T. Shirai (ed.) *Contemporary Industrial Relations in Japan*, Wisconsin: University of Wisconsin Press.

Tsuru, T. and Rebitzer, J.B. (1995) 'The limits of enterprise unionism: prospects for continuing union decline in Japan', *British Journal of Industrial Relations*, 33(3), pp. 459–92.

14 Labour–management relations in small and medium-sized enterprises

Collective voice mechanisms for workers in non-unionised companies

Hiroki Sato

INTRODUCTION

Employment systems and labour–management relations in small and medium-sized companies have fewer features which are present in large companies. In particular, long-term employment and enterprise unions, which are often said to be the major characteristics of industrial relations in Japan, exist mainly in large companies. First, long-term employment, as indicated by the length of service, applies less to workers in small and medium companies than to those in larger companies. The Basic Survey of Wage Structure in 1991 for all industries by the Ministry of Labour reveals differences in the average length of service according to company size. Namely, while the length is 13.7 years (15.9 years for male workers alone) at firms with 1,000 or more employees, the figures are 10.3 years (12 years for male workers) at firms with 100–999 employees, and 9.4 years (10.4 years for male works) at firms with 10 to 99 employees[1] (Rodosho 1991).

Next, another feature of Japanese industrial relations, namely enterprise unions, is less present in smaller firms. In fact, union density is extremely low among small and medium-sized enterprises. Although unions are rarely present at smaller enterprises, it is known that in many cases there is a collective voice mechanism for labour, other than a trade union. Based on his case study of smaller companies, Koike (1977) reported that there was an employee organisation in three out of seven companies he studied. Koike also found that the employee organisation negotiated working conditions including wages with management, and therefore regarded such an organisation as a virtual enterprise union (Koike 1981). Moreover, the Survey on Labour–Management Communication compiled by the Ministry of Labour (Rodosho 1972) showed that labour–management consultation systems were well diffused even in non-unionised smaller companies. Koike concluded from this that there were employee organisations in non-unionised companies which were functioning as a mechanism for workers to express their collective voice. In other words, collective labour–management relations appear to exist even in non-unionised smaller companies.

In Japan, unlike in Germany, there is no legal obligation for firms to establish permanent employee representation bodies or labour–management consultation systems. However, various laws, such as the Labour Standards Law, obligates management at firms without a union which represents the majority of workers to sign an agreement with those who represent the majority of employees or to consult with them over such issues as overtime and weekend working and the alteration of work rules. By law, there are four modes of voice which can be exercised by employee representatives in this majority employee representation system, namely a labour–management agreement, discussion, consultation and the nomination of members for various committees such as for health and safety. Moreover, since the mid-1970s, many more laws have been introduced which require the majority employee representation system. As a result the majority employee representation system covers most parts of employee relations in Japan today. Employee representatives may be chosen every time an issue arises, and need not form a permanent representation body. However, it is possible that this legally backed system of consulting a majority of employees might have promoted the adoption of voice-type employee organisations or labour–management consultation systems at non-union firms.

This chapter discusses the actual state and functions of employee organisations as well as labour–management consultation systems in non-unionised small companies, comparing them with functions of trade unions. But before doing so, the next section describes the significance of the small firm sector in the Japanese economy in terms of employment and the diffusion of enterprise unions in smaller companies.

EMPLOYMENT AND UNIONISATION AT SMALL AND MEDIUM-SIZED ENTERPRISES

Employment at smaller companies

Small and medium-sized enterprises provide considerable employment opportunities, though the exact share of employment at small firms is difficult to estimate. In Japan, small and medium-sized enterprises are defined in the Basic Law concerning Small and Medium-sized Enterprises, according to two quantitative standards: the amount of paid-in capital and the number of employees. The precise definition using these two quantitative standards differs from industry to industry (see Table 14.1). Even with this definition, it is impossible to accurately estimate the numbers of small and medium-sized enterprises and their employees because of a statistical limitation. For example, the Establishment Census, compiled by the Management and Coordination Agency, surveys establishments and their employees but does not survey enterprises and their employees. According to the Establishment Census in 1994 the number of small and

Table 14.1 Definition of small and medium-sized enterprises according to the
Basic Law concerning small and medium-sized enterprises

Industry type	Small and medium-sized enterprises	Small enterprises
Manufacturing etc.	With 300 or fewer employees or with 100 million yen or less capital	With 20 or fewer employees
Wholesale	With 100 or fewer employees or with 3 million yen or less capital	With 5 or fewer employees
Retail	With 50 or fewer employees or with 10 million yen or less capital	With 5 or fewer employees
Services	With 50 or fewer employees or with 10 million yen or less capital	With 5 or fewer employees

medium-sized private establishments in all industries, excluding agriculture and forestry, totalled 6.47 million (99 per cent of the total) with about 41.42 million employees (76.5 per cent of the total). While the latter figure includes all those in the labour force (including self-employed and family workers), it does not show how many of them are employees. In the meantime, the Employment Status Survey in 1992 compiled by the Management and Coordination Agency gives the number of employees by enterprise size. According to this survey of all industries in the private sector, excluding agriculture and forestry, employees in enterprises with less than 300 workers accounted for 67.2 per cent of the total. (The share of employees in companies with less than 30 workers was 36.5 per cent.) Although neither survey adopts the same definition as in the Japanese Basic Law concerning Small and Medium-sized Enterprises, it can be said that approximately 70 per cent of employees in Japan work at smaller companies. Thus, the small firm sector is providing very considerable employment opportunities in the Japanese labour market.

Unionisation rate

In almost all cases, Japanese trade unions are organised at a company or an establishment, and labour–management relations are generally conducted within the company or the establishment.[2] Unions thus organised within a company or an establishment are usually called enterprise unions. The percentage of unorganised workers does not give a simple clue to the share of companies or establishments without a union. The latter is of particular interest in Japan precisely because the basic unit of union organisation is the enterprise. The percentage of organised workers may differ widely from the percentage of unionised enterprises. This is because even if the proportion of union members declines within a company, labour–management relations, which normally presuppose a union, are often maintained as long as a union exists in the company. This situation is supported partly by the Japanese Constitution and the Trade

Union Law which guarantee the right of collective bargaining, as well as the rights to organise and to strike, regardless of the proportion of individuals who are organised at a company.

Usually, the percentage of organised workers is calculated as the ratio of union members in the Basic Survey on Labour Unions compiled by the Ministry of Labour to the number of employees in the Labour Force Survey compiled by the Management and Coordination Agency. This commonly used indicator of unionisation gives a different impression from an alternative indicator, namely the unionisation rate on an organisation basis. The first column in Table 14.2 gives the proportion of unionised establishments which can be obtained by dividing the number of unionised establishments by the total number of establishments, both available in the Survey on Labour–Management Communication (Rodosho 1989). It should be noted that the unionisation rates in the first column of the table are not at the corporate level but at the establishment level.

Table 14.2 shows the following. First, when the unionisation rates for establishments of different sizes are compared, almost all establishments of companies with 1,000 or more employees are unionised, while the figure is nearly 70 per cent for companies with 300–999 employees. Labour–management relations, which presupposes a union, are maintained in establishments of companies with 300 or more employees.

Table 14.2 Estimated unionisation rates by company size in the private sector (per cent)

The proportion of establishments with unions		The proportion of employees who are union members		
Company size*	1989	1987	1992	Company size*
5,000 or more	97.6 ⎫			
	⎬ 90.1	64.6	58.0	1,000 or more
1,000–4,999	81.1 ⎭			
		39.4 ⎫	33.1 ⎫	500–999
500–999	67.4	⎬ 33.4	⎬ 28.9	
		27.0 ⎭	23.7 ⎭	300–499
100–299	31.8	18.7	15.3	100–299
		6.3	4.8	30–99
50–99	24.0			
		0.4	0.3	29 or less

Sources: Rodosho (1987, 1989, 1992), Soumucho Toukeikyoku (1987, 1992)

Notes: 1. Unionisation rates for establishments were calculated based on the *Survey on Labour–Management Communication* (Ministry of Labour 1989, Table 5 on p. 5). The figures include establishments with more than one union. 2. Rates of organised workers were calculated based on the number of union members in *Basic Survey on Labour Unions* and the number of employed workers in *Report on Employment Status Survey*. The latter report was used since it provides finer divisions for company size than the Labour Force Survey. * Company size = number of employees.

Second, the smaller the company size, the lower the unionisation rate becomes whether it applies to establishments or workers. At the establishment level, the rate is particularly low for companies with less than 300 employees.

Third, although establishment and individual-level unionisation rates cannot be compared directly because classifications are different for the two levels, the unionisation rate is higher at the establishment level than at the individual level for each company-size category. For instance, at companies with 300–999 employees the percentages of organised workers were 33.4 per cent in 1987 and 28.9 per cent in 1992, while the unionisation rate for establishments was 67.4 per cent in 1989. When a focus is placed on establishment-basis rates, nearly a third of establishments of companies with 100–299 employees and about a quarter of establishments of companies with 50–99 employees were unionised. These figures are considerably higher than the unionisation rates of workers. The latter significantly understates the presence of unions in smaller enterprises.

Fourth, unionisation rates for establishments differ greatly between companies with 300 or more employees and those with less than 300 employees, with the latter being lower. Over time the rate has declined more at establishments of smaller companies with 100–299 employees than at large companies.

LABOUR–MANAGEMENT CONSULTATION SYSTEMS AND EMPLOYEE ORGANISATIONS IN NON-UNIONISED ENTERPRISES

This section analyses the diffusion of labour–management consultation systems and their relationship with employee organisations at smaller enterprises which tend not to be unionised.

Diffusion of labour–management consultation systems

The Survey on Labour–Management Communication by the Ministry of Labour provides the data concerning the diffusion of labour–management consultation systems. In the survey, a labour–management consultation system is defined as a permanent organ for labour and management to discuss issues such as corporate management, production, working conditions and welfare provisions. The survey has been conducted five times including once in 1994. However, the data concerning the presence or absence of labour–management consultation systems by company size and whether they exist at union or non-union establishments are available only for three years – 1972, 1977 and 1984. Table 14.3 shows the percentages of establishments of companies employing 100–299 workers with labour–management consultation systems, separately for those with unions and those without. According to the table, labour–management consultation existed at nearly 40 per cent of non-union establishments of companies with 100–299 employees.

How widespread are labour–management consultation systems among even smaller companies? Although the 1989 survey on labour–management communication included establishments of companies with 50–99 employees for the first time, the report does not provide the results by company size nor the extent of overlap between the presence of consultation and unions (Rodosho 1989). This information gap is filled by a 1991 survey by the In-Company Communication Study Group which found that 28.6 per cent of non-union companies with 50–99 employees had introduced labour–management consultation systems (which is defined similarly to that in the Ministry of Labour's Survey on Labour–Management Communication).[3] According to these data, labour–management consultation systems exist in about one-third of non-unionised companies with 50–299 employees.

Diffusion of employee organisations

Employee organisations are generally known for their social, cultural and recreational activities as well as for mutual aid functions. However, some of them have a 'voice' *vis-à-vis* corporate management concerning working conditions or management practices, in addition to cultivating mutual friendship among fellow workers. Table 14.4 shows the diffusion of employee organisations, some with a voice function. Unions exist at 27.7 per cent of the companies with 50–299 employees, while employee organisations exist at 51.7 per cent of these companies. At smaller companies with 50–99 employees the diffusion rate of employee organisations is higher at nearly 60 per cent, while their unionisation rate is relatively lower.

Table 14.5 suggests that nearly one-third of employee organisations function as a voice institution providing employees with an opportunity to discuss working conditions with management. Voice-type employee organisations are defined as organisations which discuss working conditions such as wages, hours and the work environment with management. As for companies with 50–299 employees, the unionisation rate is 27.7 per cent and the diffusion rate of voice-type employee organisations is 15.7 per cent. When companies in this size bracket are considered, therefore, employee organisations should be taken into account, in addition to trade unions, because it is likely that the former also provide a mechanism for collective voice. The diffusion rate of voice-type employee organisations and the unionisation rate add up to 43.4 per cent. Assuming that voice-type employee organisations are functioning similarly to trade unions, it can be said that labour voice institutions are present in more than 40 per cent of companies with 50–299 employees.

Table 14.3 Diffusion rate of labour–management consultation systems among establishments with 100–299 employees (per cent)

	1972	1977	1984
Unionised establishments	70.9	69.8	77.4
Non-unionised establishments	31.2	38.0	36.8

Sources: Rodosho (1972, 1977, 1984)

Note: The data for 1984 are based on Part 3 of the report by In-company Communication Study Group (1991).

Table 14.4 Organisation rates of trade unions and employee organisations by company size (per cent)

	Trade unions	Employee organisations (voice type only)
Total sample (375 companies)	27.7	51.7 (15.7)
Manufacturing industries With 100–299 employees (92 companies)	41.8	42.9 (21.4)
With 50–99 employees (105 companies)	23.8	59.0 (21.9)
Non-manufacturing industries With 100–299 employees (92 companies)	31.5	46.7 (9.8)
With 50–99 employees (74 companies)	9.5	58.1 (9.1)

Source: In-Company Communication Study Group (1991)

Notes: 1. The trade unions column shows the proportion of establishments with one or more unions, regardless of the presence of an employee organisation. 2. The employee organisations column shows the proportion of establishments with an employee organisation but without a trade union. Out of 104 unionised companies, an employee organisation existed in 45 companies which are not included in the rate for employee organisations. 3. The presence of an employee organisation was surveyed by asking the question: 'Is there any employee organisation for various purposes including for social activities?' Voice-type employee organisations are those which discuss working conditions, such as wages, hours and working environment, with management.

The relationship between labour–management consultation systems and employee organisations

In what ways are labour–management consultation systems and employee organisations related to each other? Labour–management consultation systems exist at most unionised companies, generally functioning as a means of communication between labour and management. As stated above, labour–management consultation systems have been diffused to a considerable extent even among companies which are not unionised. Then who are the labour representatives for a labour–management consultation system in a company where there is an employee organisation but no union? A detailed discussion on this issue will shed light on the relationship between the labour–management consultation system and an employee organisation.

The Ministry of Labour surveys on labour–management communication, except for the one in 1984, studied the nature of employee representatives in the labour–management consultation system (Rodosho 1972, 1977, 1989, 1994). The 1994 survey report unfortunately does not reveal how the nature of employee representation differs according to company size or to the presence or absence of unions. But it reports that employee representatives are determined by mutual voting at 78.1 per cent of the firms, and appointed by an employer at 25.8 per cent of non-unionised companies. The 1977 survey included statistics by company size and according to the presence or absence of a union; employee representatives were determined by mutual voting at 63.9 per cent of non-unionised companies with 100–299 employees, appointed by an employer at 17.6 per cent of companies, and by other means at 18.6 per cent. In other words, employee representatives are elected among employees for more than half of labour–management consultation systems in non-unionised companies. However, these figures alone are not sufficient to clarify the relationship between employee representatives and an employee organisation. Table 14.5 shows the diffusion rate of labour–management consultation systems according to types of collective voice mechanisms, such as trade unions and employee organisations, and employee representatives for labour–management consultation systems. The results are summarised as follows.

First, the diffusion rate of labour–management consultation systems is extremely high among unionised companies at 90 per cent. Employees are represented by an enterprise union, and the union represents employees when they consult with management.

Second, labour–management consultation systems have been introduced into just over a third of non-unionised companies with an employee organisation. Moreover, approximately 60 per cent of companies with a voice-type employee organisation have labour–management consultation systems which function similarly to those at unionised companies.

Third, regardless of the nature of employee organisations, voice-type or social-gathering-type, they provide representatives for employees wherever a labour–management consultation system is in place in the majority (60 to 70 per cent) of instances.

Finally, according to the survey by the In-Company Communication Study Group (1991), either a union, a voice-type employee organisation or a labour–management consultation system exists in more than half of companies with 50–299 employees.

Table 14.5 Presence of labour–management consultation systems and employee representatives among companies with 50–299 employees (per cent)

	Presence of labour–management consultation systems			Employee representatives for labour–management consultation systems			
	Yes	No	No reply	Trade union	Employee organ-isation	Other	Unknown
Establishment with union	90.4	8.7	1.0	95.7	2.1	0.0	2.1
Establishment with employee organisation	35.4	62.0	2.6	0.0	64.7	30.9	4.4
(Voice type)	(59.3)	(40.7)	(0.0)	(0.0)	(68.6)	(31.4)	(–)
(Social gathering type)	(24.8)	(71.4)	(3.8)	(0.0)	(60.6)	(30.3)	(9.1)
Establishments without union or employee organisation	10.8	89.2	0.0	0.0	0.0	75.0	25.0

Source: In-Company Communication Study Group (1991)

FUNCTIONS OF THE LABOUR–MANAGEMENT CONSULTATION SYSTEM AND EMPLOYEE ORGANISATION IN NON-UNIONISED COMPANIES

Functions of the labour–management consultation system

According to the re-classified data based on the Survey on Labour–Management Communication (1984), functions of labour–management consultation systems in unionised and non-unionised companies are compared for companies with 100–299 employees. Although a comparison was attempted for companies with 50–99 employees, it was impossible due to a lack of comparable data. The following analysis is based on Part 3 of the report by the In-Company Communication Study Group (1991).

First, the frequency of holding joint labour–management meetings is investigated. Excluding expert committee meetings, 15.3 meetings, on average, are held every year among unionised companies, and 14 meetings among non-unionised companies. The difference in frequency is slight between the two cases, in which more than one meeting is held per month. This means that labour–management communication is maintained through frequently-held joint labour–management meetings even at companies which are not unionised.

Next, the contents of labour–management consultation and the influence of employee voice are discussed. Actual agenda items for labour–management meetings are given in the first column of Table 14.6.

It is obvious that fewer items are discussed at non-unionised companies. But employees can voice their views on a considerably wide range of issues through joint labour–management meetings even at non-unionised companies: basic managerial policy is on the agenda in 55.7 per cent of such companies; transfer and secondment at 52.4 per cent; working hours and holidays at 80.3 per cent; and wages and bonuses at 66 per cent of such companies.

Table 14.6 also shows the extent of consultation for each item, which suggests the degree of influence of the employees' voice. The survey asked about four levels of consultation from the viewpoint of management: explanation and reporting without consulting opinions; consulting employees' opinions after giving an explanation; discussion aimed at gaining an agreement with the final decision to be made by management; and discussion which must lead to an agreement between labour and management. Evidently, worker voice becomes stronger as one moves from the first to the fourth levels. The survey asked establishments how each agenda item was treated in practice. Column (2) of Table 14.6 lists the proportion of firms for which the agenda items fall in the latter two levels. Compared with unionised companies the extent of consultation is generally limited among non-unionised companies, particularly concerning working conditions such as wages and bonuses. Nevertheless, wages and bonuses are treated as an item to be discussed or to be agreed among 45.7 per cent of non-union companies.

As stated in the above, the scope and the extent of consultation are limited in labour–management consultation systems among non-unionised companies with 100–299 employees, compared with those among unionised companies. However, it is also true that labour–management consultation systems often serve as a mechanism for collective employee voice in non-unionised companies. Wages and bonuses are placed on the agenda for meetings in 66 per cent of non-unionised companies with labour–management consultation systems. In addition, about 30 per cent of labour–management consultation systems among non-unionised companies treat wages and bonuses as an item for discussion or agreement. According to column (3) of Table 14.6, non-union employees are also given voice opportunities to exert their influence through the labour–management consultation system in areas in which unions commonly have a say: about 60 per cent of such non-union companies consult over hours and holidays, about 30 per cent on wages and bonuses, and about 20 per cent on basic corporate plans such as production and sales.

Functions of employee organisations

An employee organisation functions as a means for employees to express their collective voice in non-unionised companies, although as mentioned above not all of them have a voice concerning managerial policies or

Table 14.6 Agenda and extent of consultation for labour–management consultation institutions (companies with 100–299 employees) (per cent)

	(1) Placed on agenda			(2) Extent of consultation if placed on agenda (discussion + co-decision)			(3) Discussed or co-decided	
	(a) U*	(b) NU**	(c) (a)–(b)	(d) U	(e) NU	(f) (d)–(e)	(g) U	(h) NU
Basic managerial policies	65.0	55.7	9.3	15.4	16.3	–0.9	10.0	9.1
Basic plans for production, sales, etc.	66.6	63.0	3.6	22.3	33.0	–10.7	14.9	20.8
Changes in corporate structure	64.8	53.2	11.6	30.0	23.7	6.3	19.4	12.6
Rationalisation of operation by adopting new technology, etc	59.3	63.7	–4.4	30.5	38.3	–7.8	18.1	24.4
Standards for recruitment and assignment	59.9	45.4	14.5	26.1	34.0	–7.9	15.6	15.4
Job transfer and secondment	75.3	52.4	22.9	55.0	48.2	6.8	41.4	25.3
Layoff, work-force reduction, dismissal	77.5	47.5	30.0	91.9	79.2	12.7	71.2	37.6
Changes in working modes	87.4	70.7	16.7	82.7	65.6	17.1	72.3	46.4
Working hours and holidays	92.9	80.3	12.6	90.5	72.4	18.1	84.1	58.1
Health and safety at work	86.3	81.0	5.3	66.7	68.6	–1.9	57.6	55.6
Mandatory retirement system	84.1	60.9	23.2	95.7	58.9	36.8	80.5	35.9
Wages and bonuses	89.1	66.0	23.1	95.6	45.7	49.9	85.2	30.2
Criteria for retirement allowances and pensions	83.1	56.1	27.0	91.9	53.2	38.7	76.4	29.8
Education and training plans	66.2	58.7	7.5	30.7	53.7	–23.0	20.3	31.5
Welfare provisions	88.8	100.0	–11.2	62.7	73.3	–10.6	55.7	73.3
Cultural or sports activities	61.7	93.8	–32.1	52.5	69.4	–16.9	32.4	65.1

Source: Reclassification of Part III of In-Company Communication Study Group (1991)

Notes: 1. Figures for (1) and (3) are percentages of companies with labour–management consultation. Figures for (2) are percentages of companies which placed the items on the agenda. 2. The Rodosho (1984) classified agenda items into four categories: (a) those for which management informs employees; (b) those over which management consult with employees; (c) those which are discussed between management and labour, but management decides in the event of a disagreement; and (d) those which are co-divided by labour and management. Figures for (2) and (3) take the last two categories into account. 3. Raw data were acquired from the Rodosho (1984). * U = Unionised; ** NU = Non-unionised.

working conditions. According to the survey by the In-Company Communication Study Group (1991), voice-type employee organisations, which were defined as those which discussed working conditions with management, accounted for 30.4 per cent of the total employee organisations. Therefore, the majority of employee organisations were more like social clubs, limiting the scope of activities to organising cultural and recreational events or mutual aid. This sub-section will focus on voice-type organisations and compare their functions with those of trade unions.

Prior to discussing their functions, the structure and scope of such organisations are analysed.[4] Voice-type employee organisations as a rule (91.5 per cent of them) expect participation of all eligible employees at the firm. Constituent members of an employee organisation differ widely: all levels of employees up to executives are members in 28.8 per cent of employee organisations; middle management is included in the membership in 44.1 per cent, and supervisors in 11.9 per cent of employee organisations. General employees are only members at 15.3 per cent of the organisations. In other words, as many as a quarter of voice-type employee organisations involve executives as their members, though it seems that executives are included as honorary members in quite a few organisations, and were not participating in day-to-day activities. Under these circumstances, therefore, executives are actually acting as officers of employee organisations in only a very small number of cases (3.4 per cent). As for voice-type organisations, middle management are included as their constituent members and, in addition, they serve as officers in about a half of the organisations. In reality, however, quite a few small companies with 50–299 employees are run by an owner-manager, and middle managers are allowed very limited power within them. It is in effect similar to the practice in large companies in which section managers and supervisors are members of an enterprise union.

While most employee organisations (79.7 per cent) are assisted financially by the company for their activities, only a few (1.7 per cent) are totally financed by the company. The organisations which are run with membership dues alone account for 20.3 per cent while those mostly financed by membership dues account for 35.6 per cent.

Next, the nature of labour–management communication which involves voice-type employee organisation is discussed in the In-Company Survey. The frequency of discussion with management was lower than at unionised companies in 1989. While 15.4 per cent of enterprise unions met with management three times or less per annum, 35.6 per cent of voice-type employee organisations did so. Of the latter 35.6 per cent held ten or more discussion meetings a year, while 50.9 per cent of unions met with the same frequency.

Voice-type employee organisations are characterised by their practice of discussing working conditions with management. Table 14.7 gives the contents of such discussion meetings, revealing that opportunities for

Table 14.7 Contents of discussion between management and trade unions or voice-type employee organisations (all applicable items chosen) (per cent)

	Trade unions	Voice-type employee organisations
Wage increase	96.2	44.1
Bonuses	86.5	28.8
Retirement allowance	58.7	10.2
Wage system/personnel system	68.3	32.2
Working hours and holidays	94.2	78.0
Job reassignment	35.6	18.6
Education and training	23.1	25.4
Working environment health and safety	72.1	62.7
Welfare facilities	58.7	42.4
Long-term management plan	24.0	8.5
Annual management plan	41.3	33.9
Other	2.9	1.7
Unknown	1.9	3.4

Source: In-company Communication Study Group (1991)

Note: The survey did not ask about the extent of consultation.

handling these items are lower compared with those of unions, except in the case of education and training. For instance, more than half of the voice-type employee organisations do not discuss wage increases with management. Though voice-type employee organisations are defined as those which discuss working conditions with management, some of them do not place wage increases on the agenda, while working hours are discussed by 78 per cent of the organisations including an agreement on overtime, based on article 35 of the Labour Standards Law. Although employee organisations which do not deal with wage increases may not be regarded as voice-type organisations, at least 30 per cent of them have a voice concerning not only basic working conditions but also management and personnel systems which influence working conditions.

Functions of voice-type employee organisations are evaluated by management (see Table 14.8). As the table shows, they have various functions other than to organise social activities: conveying employee's grievances and demands to management; collecting employee's opinions and demands; conveying management information including management policies to employees; and making proposals to management concerning corporate policies and other matters. The table also gives a comparison of the functions of employee organisations with those of enterprise unions, and suggests that only slight differences exist between them. Thus there is evidence that corporate management requests voice-type employee organisation as fulfilling a function similar to that of an enterprise union to facilitate labour–management communication. The main difference lies

Table 14.8 Evaluation of functions of trade unions and employee organisations in facilitating in-company communication (all applicable items chosen) (per cent)

	Evaluation of trade unions			Evaluation of employee organisations	
	Total	*With enterprise-union*	*With voice-type employee organisation*	*Total*	*With voice-type employee organisation*
Hearing complaints and demands concerning working conditions	54.1	93.3	37.3	54.9	72.9
Hearing employees' opinions concerning management policies and plans	26.4	46.2	16.9	28.3	39.0
Notifying management policies and plans to employees	37.3	59.6	28.8	41.3	61.0
Promoting mutual friendship among employees	44.0	60.6	33.9	82.4	94.9
Collecting employees' various opinions and demands	49.3	77.9	35.6	52.0	55.9
Not helpful in particular	20.8	2.8	30.5	4.8	3.4
No reply	6.1	1.0	13.6	0.8	0.0

Source: In-Company Communication Study Group (1991)

Note: 'Total' includes all survey respondent companies, regardless of whether or not they have unions or employee organisations.

in the fact that voice-type employee organisations function only to a limited extent in collecting employees' opinions and conveying their demands to management, compared with trade unions.

To summarise, a considerable number of voice-type employee organisations have a voice not only for basic working conditions but also for corporate management practices. Although this is an evaluation made by the management side, voice-type employee organisations perform various functions in terms of labour–management communication, conveying employees' demands, collecting their opinions, and notifying corporate information to employees. This suggests that most employee organisations in non-unionised companies function well as a collective voice mechanism for labour.

PRESENCE OF COLLECTIVE VOICE SYSTEMS AND TREND IN UNIONISATION

It has been shown in this chapter that a collective voice system exists and is fulfilling a certain set of functions at a considerable number of non-union companies. The last issue to be addressed here is in what ways a system of collective voice affects the unionisation of a company. Does it enhance or undermine unionisation?

Among non-unionised companies, a voice-type employee organisation (or a labour–management consultation system) may weaken management's awareness of the need to accept unions in order to achieve smooth labour–management communication or industrial democracy. On the other hand, if the labour side perceives that either a labour–management consultation system or a voice-type employee organisation eventually provides labour with opportunities for collective voice, they may not find it necessary to unionise their company. It is generally known that an employee organisation requires less membership dues than a union does, which also discourages employees from organising a union (Tokyo Metropolitan Labor Research Institute 1990). In his survey of individual workers in 1993, Hisamoto analysed the views of workers in companies with a voice-type employee organisation (Hisamoto 1993). The study revealed that the share of workers who wanted a union was smaller in companies with a voice-type employee organisation than companies with a social-gathering-type employee organisation. Further, he found that a considerably large proportion of workers in the former were strongly opposed to unionising the company. Given such attitudes on the part of labour and management, it is likely that the presence of a voice-type employee organisation or the introduction of a labour–management consultation system in a non-unionised company will undermine workers' will to organise a union. While they exert an adverse effect on unionisation, however, it is a separate issue whether they also affect adversely the diffusion of industrial democracy among small and medium-sized companies.

NOTES

1 Furthermore, the share of employees with more than 20 years of service is considerably larger at 31 per cent (38.7 per cent for male workers) at large firms (with 1,000 or more employees), than at smaller companies – 17.5 per cent (22.9 per cent for male workers) at firms with 100–999 employees and 13.5 per cent (17.6 per cent for male workers) at firms with 10–99 employees. Although the duration of workers' service has always been generally shorter in small than in large companies, the average length of service for small firms has also become longer. According to the Ministry of Labour's Basic Survey of Wage Structure, the average length of service among companies with 100–999 employees was 5.4 years in 1965, 6.3 years in 1970, 7.9 years in 1975, 9.8 years in 1980, 10.6 years in 1985 and 11.2 years in 1990. A similar trend has been observed for companies with 1,000 or more employees and those with 10–99 employees as well.
2 According to the 1994 Basic Survey on Labour Unions by the Ministry of Labour, enterprise unions account for 94.2 per cent of all unions; 91.1 per cent of all union members belong to enterprise unions. Although some regionally-based general unions (called *godo rodo kumiai*) are organised in the sector of smaller companies, in which workers can participate on an individual basis, their share is very small among all the unions. The 1994 survey on labour affairs in smaller companies by the National Small and Medium-sized Enterprise Association (1994) revealed that the percentage of companies with some members of such general unions accounted for 0.9 per cent of the total. (Companies with an enterprise union accounted for 8.4 per cent of the total.)
3 The In-Company Communication Study Group (1991), of which Sato was a member, conducted in January 1990 a postal survey of companies with 50–299 employees and obtained valid responses from 375 companies (an effective response rate of 18.8 per cent).
4 According to a survey by the Tokyo Metropolitan Labour Research Institute (1990) conducted by Sato, voice-type employee organisations were formed at the initiative of the 'company president' in 42.3 per cent of the cases, 'top manager other than company president' (21.2 per cent), 'senior employees' (18.3 per cent), 'general employees' (18.3 per cent), 'supervisors' (13.5 per cent), and 'others' (3.8 per cent). A smaller proportion (28.8 per cent) of employee organisations of the social gathering type were founded at the initiative of the company president. Thus, a rather large share of voice-type employee organisations was formed at management's initiative.

REFERENCES

Hisamoto, Norio (1993) 'Kumiai hitsuyo kan to sono yoin' ('Necessity of a labor union and relevant factors') in Toshiaki Tachibanaki and Soken Rengo (eds) *Rodokumiai no Keizaigaku: Kitai to Genjitsu* (*Economics of Trade Unions: Expectation and Reality*), Tokyo: Toyo Keizai Shinposha.
In-Company Communication Study Group (1991) *Chusho Kigyo ni Okeru Kigyonai Komyunikeishon no Jittai* (*Actual State of In-Company Communication in Small and Medium-sized Companies*), Tokyo: Labour Affairs Research Centre.
Kaufman, B.E. and Kleiner, M.M. (eds) (1992) *Employee Representation: Alternatives and Future Directions*, Madison: IRRA Series.
Koike, Kazuo (1977) *Shokuba no Rodokumiai to Sanka: Roshikankei no Nichibei Hikaku* (*Labor Unions at Workplace and Participation: Comparison of Labor–Management Relations between the US and Japan*), Tokyo: Toyo Keizai Shinposha.

—— (1981) *Chusho Kigyo no Jukuren-Jinzai Keisei no Shikumi* (*Skills at Small and Medium-sized Companies: Mechanisms of Human Resources Development*), Tokyo: Dobunkan.

National Small and Medium-sized Enterprise Association (1994) *Chusho Kigyo Rodo Jijyo Jittai Choso Hokokusho* (*Survey on Labour Affairs in Small and Medium-sized Companies*), Tokyo: National Small and Medium-sized Enterprise Association.

Rodosho (Ministry of Labour) (ed.) (1972, 1977, 1984, 1989 and 1994) *Roushi Komyunikeishon Chosa* (*Survey on Labour–Management Communication*), Tokyo: Okurasho Insatsu Kyoku.

—— (1987, 1992) *Roudou Kumiai Kiso Chosa* (*Basic Survey on Labour Union*), Tokyo: Okurasho Insatsu Kyoku.

—— (1991) *Chingin Kozo Kihon Chosa* (*Basic Survey on Wage Structure*), Tokyo: Okurasho Insatsu Kyoku.

Soumucho Toukeikyoku (Statistical Bureau, Management and Coordination Agency) (ed.) (1987, 1992) *Shugyo Kozo Kihon Chosa* (*Report on Employment Status Survey*), Tokyo: Okurasho Insatsu Kyoku.

Tokyo Metropolitan Labour Research Institute (1990) *Chusho Kigyo ni Okeru Jugyoin Soshiki no Yakuwari* (*Roles of Employee Organisations in Small and Medium-sized Companies*), Tokyo: Tokyo Metropolitan Labour Research Institute.

Appendix

INFORMATION ON INDUSTRIAL RELATIONS IN JAPAN

This appendix provides a brief introduction to the main sources of information on labour statistics, the industrial relations situation and research trends in Japan. The total accumulated sources of information, with varying degrees of ease of access, are vast. This brief guide covers sources in Japanese and English. While Japanese-language sources far outweigh English-language sources, the latter are becoming increasingly available as indicated below. It is hoped that this guide will assist readers in identifying the relevant sources.

OFFICIAL LABOUR STATISTICS

There are a large number of sources on labour statistics in Japan. In order to obtain an overview of what is available, the most informative starting point is 'Rodo Tokei o Yomu' ('A Guide to Reading Labour Statistics'), a special feature in *Nihon Rodo Kenkyu Zasshi* (*The Monthly Journal of the Japan Institute of Labour*, Issue No. 419, January 1995). The article takes up 34 statistical sources on labour and provides an explanation of each. The main official surveys, many of which are referred to by contributors to this book, are as follows. Those which are in Japanese but with an English translation of the statistical tables are marked with a plus (+) sign.

> + *Chingin Kozo Kihon Tokei Chosa* (*Basic Survey of Wage Structure*)
> *Chingin Hikiageto no Jittai ni kansuru Chosa* (*Survey on Wage Increases*)
> *Koyo Doko Chosa* (*Survey on Employment Trend*)
> *Koyo Kanri Chosa* (*Survey of Employment Management*)
> *Maitsuki Kinro Tokei Chosa* (*Monthly Labour Survey*)
> *Rodo Kumiai Kihon Chosa* (*Basic Survey on Trade Unions*)
> *Rodo Kyoyakuto Jittai Chosa* (*Survey of Collective Agreements*)
> *Rodo Sogi Tokei Chosa* (*Survey on Labour Disputes Statistics*)
> + *Rodoryoku Chosa* (*Labour Force Survey*)

Roshi Komyunikeishon Chosa (*Survey on Labour–Management Communication*)
+ *Shugyo Kozo Kihon Chosa* (*Employment Status Survey*)

Compilations of various statistical sources are also available. The following two publications are particularly useful:

(a) *Rodo Tokei Nenpo* (*Yearbook of Labour Statistics*), edited every year by the Ministry of Labour and published by the Institute of Labour Administration. This publication compiles a selection of official labour statistics. Explanations and tables are given in both Japanese and English.

(b) *Katsuyo Rodo Tokei* (*Practical Handbook of Productivity and Labour Statistics*), edited by the Labour Statistics Committee of the Japan Productivity Centre for Socio-Economic Development, and published by the Industrial Relations Department of the same Centre. This is not only a selection of various official labour statistics. It also provides data which are processed to be meaningful for trade unionists, managers, and other users. Internationally comparative data are also included. Every other year, an English edition, titled *Practical Handbook of Productivity and Labour*, is published.

These two publications appear once a year. The most up-to-date statistics between the annual publications are accessible through a summary report in *Rodo Tokei Chosa Geppo* (*Monthly Labour Statistics and Research Bulletin*) edited by the Policy and Research Department of Ministry of Labour and published by the Institute of Labour Administration. Statistical tables in this publication are labelled in both Japanese and English.

LATEST TRENDS ON LABOUR

Every year Ministry of Labour makes an analysis of the trend in labour markets and publishes it as *Rodo Hakusho* (*White Paper on Labour*) (published by the Japan Institute of Labour). Every year, aside from the usual analysis of trends over time, *Hakusho* selects a specific topic for analysis. The special topic featured in the 1995 edition, for example, was 'Coping with structural changes in labour market through job creation'. *Hakusho* also contains a collection of the main labour statistics at the end of the volume. A shorter summary of *Hakusho* is published in English under the title of *White Paper on Labour* by the Japan Institute of Labour.

In order to follow the latest trends in industrial relations, the following monthly or weekly publications are useful.

Japan Labour Bulletin (published by the Japan Institute of Labour)
This is an English-language monthly newsletter, with short pieces on the latest situations, such as on labour markets, management of human

resources, industrial relations, labour policy and labour statistics. Further, each issue contains one article on a specific topic, written by Japanese academics and researchers. The articles in the Bulletins have been compiled into a booklet and are thus far published in three volumes under the title of *Highlights in Japanese Industrial Relations: A Selection of Articles from the Japan Labour Bulletin* (Vol. 1 was published in 1983, Vol. 2 in 1988 and Vol. 3 in 1993).

Rosei Jiho (*Labour Policy Information*, published by the Institute of Labour Administration)
This is a weekly journal published by a private institute. It carries the most up-to-date briefings on government statistics, articles introducing personnel management systems of various companies, reports on councils and study meetings sponsored by the government, information on labour policy trends and summaries of surveys conducted by private research institutes. It also publishes results of surveys carried out by those research institutes specialising in personnel management or working conditions.

Shuukan Rodo News (*Weekly Labour News*, published by the Japan Institute of Labour)
This newspaper mainly covers the topics of trade unions and industrial relations. It reports on the results of official surveys on labour and trends in labour policy. The back numbers of this newspaper are available in bound editions, titled *Shukan Rodo News Shukusatsuban* (from Vol. 1 October 1959), published by the Japan Institute of Labour.

INFORMATION ON RESEARCH TRENDS

The major Japanese academic journals on industrial relations are as follows.

Nihon Rodo Kenkyu Zasshi (*Monthly Journal of The Japan Institute of Labour*, published by the Japan Institute of Labour)
This is an interdisciplinary refereed journal, with articles covering various issues on labour economics, labour law, personnel management, industrial sociology and occupational psychology.

Ohara Shakai Mondai Kenkyusho Zasshi (*Ohara Institute for Social Research Journal*, edited by Ohara Institute for Social Research Hosei University and published by Hosei University Publication Bureau)
This refereed journal is published by a research institute attached to a university, but it is not an in-house journal and accepts contributions from researchers from outside the institute. Many of the articles published are studies on labour history and industrial relations.

Kikan Rodo-Ho (*Quarterly Journal of Labour Law*, published by Sogo Rodo Kenkyujo (Consolidated Labour Institute))
This is a specialised periodical on labour law, issued by a publisher specialising in labour, with contributions mainly from labour lawyers.

The *Monthly Journal of the Japan Institute of Labour* and the *Ohara Institute for Social Research Journal* contain, at the end of each issue, a useful list of recent books, articles and reports in the broad area of labour and industrial relations. The coverage of topics is slightly different in each, but both list reports which are not publicly available as well as published materials. In addition to these, articles on labour which have appeared in various academic journals and commercial magazines are contained with classification by item. The *Ohara Institute for Social Research Journal* is particularly good on covering the labour history literature. The items contained in the lists are available for reference in the library of the institutes concerned.

ENGLISH LANGUAGE INFORMATION ON LABOUR

English-language academic journals on labour and industrial relations (for example *Industrial Relations Journal*, *British Journal of Industrial Relations*, *Industrial Relations*, *Industrial and Labour Relations Review*, *International Labour Review*) frequently carry articles on industrial relations in Japan. But there are also, within Japan, English-language academic research papers and articles in in-house university journals which do not have a wide circulation. Thanks to the initiatives taken by the Japan Institute of Labour, a bibliography of English-language books, reports, articles and papers published in Japan is being made available on-line to overseas researchers. The on-line service may be accessed at http.//www.mol.go.jp/jil/. The Institute has also prepared an English-language video tape to introduce the industrial relations situation in Japan.

USEFUL ADDRESSES IN JAPAN

(* indicates the existence of a public library)

* *Nihon Rodo Kenkyu Kiko* (The Japan Institute of Labour)

Publications Section:
Shinjuku Monolith Bldg, 2-3-1 Nishi Shinjuku, Shinjuku-ku, Tokyo, Japan
Tel.: 03-5321-3074
Fax: 03-5321-3015

Library:
4-8-23 Kamishakujii, Nerima-ku, Tokyo, Japan
Tel.: 03-5991-5032
Fax: 03-3594-1110

Ohara Shakai Mondai Kenkyujo (Ohara Institute for Social Research)

Hosei University
4342 Aihara-cho, Machida City, 194-02 Tokyo, Japan
Tel.: 0427-83-2307
Fax: 0427-83-2311

Romu Gyosei Kenkyujo (The Institute of Labour Administration)

1-4-2 Higashi Azabu, Minato-ku, Tokyo, Japan
Tel.: 03-3584-1231
Fax: 03-3584-0126

Seifu Kankobutsu Saabisu Sentaa (Sales Office of the Government Publications Office)

1-2-1 Kasumigaseki, Chiyoda-ku, Tokyo, Japan
Tel.: 03-3504-3885
Fax: 03-3304-3889

Access to Japanese-language on-line search and ordering of government publications: http://www.gov-book.or.jp/ and an English-language home page at http://www.gioss.or.jp

Shakai-Keizai Seisansei Honbu (Japan Productivity Center for Socio-Economic Development)

3-1-1 Shibuya, Shibuya-ku, Tokyo, Japan
Tel.: 03-3409-1123
Fax: 03-3409-1007

The Information Centre for Social Science Research on Japan

Institute of Social Science, University of Tokyo
7-3-1 Hongo, Bunkyo-ku, Tokyo, Japan
Tel.: 03-3812-2111
Fax: 03-3816-6864
http://www.iss.u-tokyo.ac.jp/

Index

Occupational Safety and Hygiene Law
54, 59
OECD 4, 28–9, 34, 36, 117, 151–5, 254
off-the-job training 92, 138–40, 143,
176–7, 289
Ohira, Masayoshi 218
Ohmi, Naoto 236
Ohta, Kaorv 246
oil crises 2, 3, 44–5, 54, 79, 81, 94,
200–2, 247, 252, 296–301, 305–6, 310
Olson, Mancur 237, 252
on-the-job training 114, 138–40, 143,
147, 171, 174, 177
Oogusa, Y. 179
Ootake, F. 179
organisational diversification 275–8
organisational quasi-rent 291
overstay (foreign workers) 172–3
overtime 32–3, 36–7, 136, 316

part-time workers 10, 32–3, 67, 131–2,
140–1, 144–8, 179–80, 306, 310–11
path dependence 22
Patrick, Hugh 19, 297
pay *see* wages
Pempel, T.J. 17, 187, 188
pensions 13, 151, 153–61 *passim*, 166
performance-related: pay 13–14, 57;
promotion 107
Phelps, E.S. 137
Philips curve 47–8
Plaza Accord (1985) 32, 247
policy participation, Rengo and 187–211
political characteristics of trade unions
187–90
political parties: national centres and
190–4; Rengo and 205–8; union
dependence 189–90
Practical Skills Training System 174,
176–7, 178, 181
Preparatory Committee for
Unification 198
privatisation 17; public sector and 11,
215–23
product diversification 10
product markets (Shunto process)
255–9
productivity 8, 27, 48, 164, 189, 210,
221; Shunto 241, 246, 249; spinning
industry 40–1
Progressive Unification Candidates
208
promotion 5, 229–30; discrimination

131–8; management (issues) 104–16;
nenko principle 6–7, 11–14
Provisional Commission for
Administrative Reform 218–25
passim
Public Employment Offices 66
public pensions 156–61
public sector, privatisation and 215–33

quality circles 16, 287, 288

railways (privatisation) 11, 215–32
Raisian, J. 27
Rebick, M.E. 301–2, 304
Rebitzer, J.B. 304–5
recession 3–4, 12, 180, 299, 305; and
corporate strategy 79, 83–5, 94; and
labour law 56, 63; labour market
trends 32, 36, 39, 44, 48; Shunto and
237, 240, 243–4
Red Purge 192
redundancies 11, 57, 271
regular workers (in total workforce)
46
relocation of staff 32–3, 136
Rengo 13, 16–18, 20, 311; and policy
participation 187–211; privatisation
and 217, 224, 231–2; Shunto and
240–4, 245, 250, 259–61
Rengo Sogo Seikatsu Kaihatsu
Kenkyujo 121–2, 124
Rengo Soken 21
'representation gap' 21
research trends (information sources)
334–5
residence status 169, 170
retention rates 117–18
retirement 309; age 8, 9, 13, 28, 48,
50, 118–20, 161–4, 166; pensions 13,
151, 153–61, 166
Rodosho Seisaku Chosabu (Ministry
of Labour, Policy and Research
Department) 115–16, 118–19
Rosenbaum, J. 105, 106
Round Table Discussion Meeting of
Industrial Labour Problems 203
Rowe, M.P. 72

Sachs, J. 239
Sako, Mari 11, 257
Sano, Yoko 252, 254, 258
Sato, Hiroki 113–15, 122, 124–5,
180–1, 283, 287, 307, 308
secondment 115, 118–19, 120, 127

Printed in the United Kingdom
by Lightning Source UK Ltd.
122478UK00002B/205/A